WHY TH...
DOESN'T WORK

and what we should do about it

F. Yates.

Also published by Robinson

The Nature of Unhappiness

WHY THERAPY DOESN'T WORK

and what we should do about it

DAVID SMAIL

ROBINSON
London

Constable Publishers
3 The Lanchesters
162 Fulham Palace Road
London W6 9ER
www.constablerobinson.com

Illusion and Reality first published in the UK
by J. M. Dent & Sons Ltd 1984
Copyright © D. J. Smail 1984

Taking Care first published in the UK
by J. M. Dent & Sons Ltd 1987
Copyright © David Smail 2001

This combined edition published by Robinson, an imprint of
Constable & Robinson Ltd 2001
Copyright © David Smail 2001

A copy of the British Library Cataloguing-in-Publication Data for
this title is available from the British Library

ISBN 1-84119-349-6

Printed and bound in the EU

Contents

Foreword

The publication under one cover of *Illusion & Reality* and *Taking Care* gives me the opportunity to review the role of psychotherapy as it has developed since the original appearance of the first of these in 1984.

Let me say straight away that I see no reason at all to modify the view that follows from these two books, i.e. that psychotherapy does not work. Some elaboration is necessary, however, if this statement is not to create unnecessary antagonisms and offend the sensibilities both of well-intentioned practitioners of therapy and of recipients of their services who have benefited from them. There is also a risk of appearing to fall into a personal paradox: more or less my whole professional life has been spent in the practice of clinical psychology, which in several of its aspects is barely distinguishable from psychotherapy.

To say that psychotherapy can never be beneficial would be like saying that human relationships have no effect, and that would be patently absurd. But to say that psychotherapy may be beneficial is not the same as saying that it 'works', for one needs to understand *what about* the process of therapy may be beneficial before one can move confidently to a *technical* statement about its 'working'. I may, after all, benefit in all sorts of ways from a visit to my GP, but that does not imply that 'medicine works'.

One needs to distinguish at the outset between psychotherapy as an activity, or, as for example Paul Gordon terms it, a 'calling',[1] and psychotherapy as a business.

For one person to offer help to another, even for money, does not in my view amount to the professional practice of an

established technical procedure so long as it is recognised that
what is involved is a *personal* relationship between two (or, of
course, possibly more) people. The recipient of such a service
may or may not find it beneficial, and if he or she does indeed
feel in some way 'better' as the result of it, the improvement
need be attributed to nothing more than the personal influence
of therapist on client. Though, from a psychologist's viewpoint,
it is certainly of interest to find out what exactly has been
helpful, there is no particular onus on anybody to do so:
nothing has been claimed of a technical nature beyond the
therapist' s (implied) promise to try to help the client.

Where, however, a practitioner sets him- or herself up,
however implicitly, on a *professional* basis as the purveyor of a
curative technique, a claim is indeed being made that the therapist is in possession of transmissible knowledge which is not
merely personal, but could be applied by (more or less) anyone
with the right training and credentials. It is in *this* sense that
psychotherapy does not work.

And it is in this sense also, of course, that the vast majority of
psychotherapy and counselling is practised. Psychotherapy is a
business, indeed has become an industry, which almost invariably seeks to justify its practice through appeals to established
knowledge, procedures of training and accreditation, and so on.

There are very few practitioners of psychotherapy who
eschew the professional model. Perhaps their most eloquent
spokesman is Peter Lomas,[2] whose books have over the past
twenty years insisted on the *personal* nature of the therapeutic
relationship, but his voice and those of others like him (see, for
example, House and Totton[3]) form a tiny minority among the
vast chorus of professionals and would-be professionals who
seek to patent and restrict to themselves the practice of one of
the myriad 'brand-name' therapies that exist.

At the very foundations of the whole field of psychotherapy
lies an insistence on a form of rationality which simply will not
be gainsaid. That is to say, almost everyone who practises,

writes or researches in the area starts out with a set of assumptions that seem impermeable to the lessons of experience as well as to any kind of critique. Furthermore, these assumptions seem also to lie at the root of the expectations of nearly all actual and potential clients of therapy. Even though they may not be explicitly stated these assumptions imply that psychological distress must be the outcome of a quasi-medical condition afflicting individuals from within, and psychotherapy *must* have the characteristics of a quasi-medical technique of cure.

In effect this means that the individual in need of therapy will be seen as harbouring psychological or emotional 'problems' which, if not exactly of his or her own making, represent a kind of personal affliction, an abnormality which places him or her outside the usual run of healthy humanity. In view of this, it is felt, there *must* be techniques which can be brought to bear on the individual to excise from his or her personal psychological make-up those elements that are causing difficulty. If, furthermore, it can be shown that someone has been helped with personal distress by supposedly 'psychotherapeutic' intervention, it *must* be the case that the process whereby this is achieved can be isolated, analysed and if necessary repeated and communicated to other would-be practitioners.

Given these assumptions, it seems only reasonable that, as is the case, professional psychotherapists should struggle to set up rigorous training courses and systems of accreditation, registers that restrict practice to those 'properly qualified', and so on. Clients' interests, surely, demand as much. Similarly, research in psychotherapy becomes narrowly focused on isolating the 'active ingredients' that bring about client change, and the practice of therapy in the public sphere – the British National Health Service, for example – is constrained to demonstrate its 'evidence-base'.

So strong is the hold of these assumptions that their grip has been weakened hardly at all by decades of actual experience, not only of their not having borne fruit, but of their having been in most essential respects contra-indicated. Ever since the mid-twentieth century volumes and volumes of research have pointed to the ineffectiveness of psychotherapy as a *technique* and to the importance instead of the personal characteristics of those involved and their interrelationship. The vast body of this research is ignored and the avenues it could have suggested – for example the possibility that, for some people, some *individuals* make better therapists than others – have remained almost entirely unexplored.

The nature of scientific research is such that there will always be a handful of studies which, against the general trend, seem to offer support for any hypothesis you care to consider. This is certainly the case with the professional 'therapy works' camp. Set in an ocean of research which points to the relative ineffectiveness of therapeutic techniques are two or three studies (mainly aggregates of other people's work) which offer some comfort to the professionals. These are the studies that are regularly trotted out as 'definitive'. The reader who wishes to gain some insight into this state of affairs could do no better than peruse *Controversies in Psychotherapy and Counselling* (Sage Publications, 1999), a volume edited in the best of faith by Colin Feltham, but which demonstrates despite itself the scholastic rigidity into which the theory and practice of professional therapy has fallen. There seems, in fact, no longer to be any real debate: the *necessity* of psychotherapy as a technical cure for individual psychological ills has become too important to deny.

It is not as if there is not and has not been a perfectly respectable literature arguing the ineffectiveness of psychotherapy as technical cure,[4] rather it is the case that this literature has simply been dismissed or ignored. No doubt this is in part the result of a mechanistic rationality that is deeply embedded in our culture – we can scarcely imagine that causes and cures of emotional distress could operate in any other way than that envisaged in the 'ruling paradigm'. But in addition to this are other powerful reasons why we cling to the myths of psychotherapy.

Although we all – and especially theorists and practitioners of the social sciences – like to think of ourselves as *essentially* reasonable people, we are in fact governed far more by *interest* than by reason: a fact which we disguise from ourselves as much as from others. All of us – clients almost as much as professional therapists – have a large stake in the model of psychotherapy and counselling that holds sway. To countenance any alternative hypothesis (for example of the kind I advance in *Taking Care*) concerning the causes and cures of distress would not only threaten the livelihood of the professionals, it would also, beyond striking a note of cultural discord, involve us in a very radical re-evaluation of our social organization. We will not, I think, give up the notion that 'psychotherapy works' until it has been squeezed dry of its very last drop of plausibility. And because psychotherapy and the phenomena it encompasses are so fundamentally vague and difficult to pin down, it is questionable whether that moment will ever arrive. We are, I fear, destined still to travel a long road of further 'professionalisation' of therapy before we become as a society more ready to consider the kind of political alternatives that seem to me more likely to bear fruit.

The critique I offer here is not intended as a moralistic one. That we are influenced far more by our interests than by a reasonable examination of the evidence is not so much a matter for censure or disapproval as a psychological observation. I do not believe that we can choose *not* to be influenced by our interests and so it seems unreasonable to me to blame people for acting in accordance with them. Those therapists and counsellors who assume that I am accusing them of charlatanism are therefore mistaken. It is no less important for us to acknowledge and accept our being influenced by our interests than it is for us to investigate and understand any other form of human motivation (it is incongruous that, for example, we seem happy enough to be thought to be harbouring the most morally dubious 'unconscious' impulses, but become outraged at any suggestion that our actions could be shaped by interest).

But there is no doubt that the rampant pursuit of self-interest, however unaware of it we may be (and it is all the more dangerous for being blind), can lead to some very unfortunate circumstances when it is carried out in the name of 'science'. In her book *Manufacturing Victims* (Constable, 1999) Tana Dineen documents patiently the way the 'psychology industry' has developed, particularly in North America. The picture she reveals of an unrestrained marketing of flimsy, half-baked psychological nostrums – one whose outline is clearly visible in Britain too – gives us ample reason for pausing to consider how we should interpret psychological and emotional distress and what might be the most appropriate framework for tackling its causes. For when psychotherapy becomes nothing other than a business it becomes prey to the same kind of financial pressures and 'growth imperatives' as any other business. More and more of ordinary life becomes subjected to the professionals' attention as psychological pathology, and what should have been a cautious scientific exploration becomes a collection of wild consumerist claims and fantasies.

Psychotherapy as a calling has, in my view, a perfectly respectable role to play as a personal arrangement between two (or more) people who understand thoroughly the nature of their undertaking and expect of it no technical wonders. As a 'cure' for psychological distress this role is necessarily limited as it requires of both parties – therapists as well as clients – certain personal resources which are not in plentiful supply in current society,[5] and in any case the most that can be hoped for may be more a matter of (up to a point) personal enlightenment rather than anything approaching 'cure'.

By maintaining that psychotherapy is not the answer to the psychological ills that our society inflicts upon us I am by no means saying that there are no answers, just that we have to look elsewhere for them. There is, I hope, more than a hint in these pages of where that is. In any case, the question of what makes it possible for people to 'get better' (and for us to avoid inflicting the damage in the first place) is one I pursue further in the companion volume to this, *The Nature of Unhappiness*.

Notes

1. Paul Gordon, *Face to Face. Therapy as Ethics*. Constable, 1999.
2. Peter Lomas's most recent book is *Doing Good? Psychotherapy out of its Depth*, Oxford University Press, 1999.
3. Richard House & Nick Totton (eds), *Implausible Professions*, PCCS Books, 1997.
4. Apart from a huge number of relatively inaccessible research papers, one thinks immediately, for example, of Thomas Szasz's characteristically distinguished contribution *The Myth of Psychotherapy* (Oxford University Press, 1978). More recent volumes include William M. Epstein, *The Illusion of Psychotherapy* (Transaction Publishers, 1995) and Donald A. Eisner, *The Death of Psychotherapy* (Praeger, 2000). There is no shortage either of consumers of psychotherapy having been critical of their experience: see, for example, Ann France, *Consuming Psychotherapy* (Free Association Books, 1988) and more recently Anna Sands, *Falling for Therapy* (Macmillan, 2000).
5. I have developed this view of what can and cannot be achieved in psychotherapy in a number of recent articles and talks. See for example my chapter 'A century of psychotherapy' in Lucy King (ed.) *Committed Uncertainty in Psychotherapy. Essays in Honour of Peter Lomas*, Whurr Publishers, 1999. I have posted a number of unpublished talks to my website at www.djsmail.com.

Illusion & Reality

The Meaning of Anxiety

Preface to Previous Edition

Illusion & Reality is the first of a series of (so far) four books which attempt to place the experience of psychological distress within the social environment which gives rise to it. The other three are *Taking Care*, *The Origins of Unhappiness* and *How to Survive Without Psychotherapy* (the latter two published by Robinson in one volume, *The Nature of Unhappiness*). With hindsight (and in reassuring confirmation of the psychological theory they elaborate!) it is possible to see how each of these books is shaped by the context in which it was written.

Being the first, *Illusion & Reality* examines the predicament of the individual person from the perspective of the person him/herself (the later works travel progressively further out into the social environment in order to pinpoint the origins of distress). Above all else it is about the individual's subjective view of the world and the injuries done to his or her subjectivity by the world into which (as the existentialists would say) s/he is thrown.

Being conceived and written in the early 1980s, it is also, I now see, about the predicament of people (i.e. all of us) who were caught up in the disintegration of 'old' certainties (the 'post-war consensus') which were in any case largely illusory (hence, in part, the title) and at the mercy of brutal market forces which were about to sweep them up and toss them into a torrent of change and insecurity. Although I would change very little in my analysis of subjectivity, I think perhaps I do accord it a little too much independent power. What the later 1980s and the 1990s have made starkly apparent is just how vulnerable we are to social forces operating far beyond our personal spheres of influence, and though some of the more obvious threats seem to have changed (the nuclear threat, for example, seems to have receded) the subjective person is, if anything, even more embattled against apparently irresistible, largely economic, pressures than was the case fifteen years ago.

But if our subjective voice is weaker, it is all the more important that we should be able to recognize its cry, and the kinds of pointers to the significance of subjective experience and its expression, the clinical examples of which I made use, are I think as relevant now as they were then.

Anxiety is a sign, an indication of a sometimes terrifying disillusionment in which safe myths about the conditions of our existence become peeled away to reveal an altogether less reassuring form of knowledge about the world. The point of this book, though its outlook may at times seem rather bleak, is, however, precisely one of reassurance: that the unnerving knowledge we may possess of a hard and painful reality represents in fact a true insight into the way things are and not a form of craziness.

If anything, illusory ideals of living envelop our subjectivity even more oppressively than they did at the time this book was written. The triumphant progress of 'marketing' – the colossal investment of intelligence, ingenuity and technical sophistication which perfects the arts by which we are seduced into consumerist culture – has put significant sections of a whole generation out of touch with the social and biological bases of reality. I have accordingly been struck in very recent times by the number of young people I encounter (people for whom the late 1970s to the mid-1990s constituted the formative years of their lives) who have not just, so to speak, fallen for the advertising, but have invested their lives, energies, ambitions – have indeed *put their faith* – in a glossy, fashionable world of apparent social ease and affluence which they have helped to create and come to inhabit, but in which they are at the same time assailed by a profound insecurity about who they are and how they figure in relation to others.

These are not people who function poorly or, as the psychiatrists like to say 'inadequately', in the modern world – indeed they are often socially, educationally and vocationally very successful – but they suffer from what is to me a new form of anxiety (new, anyway, in its pervasiveness). Deeply troubling though not disabling, the discomfort and unhappiness of their actual experience of themselves contrasts strangely with the apparently ideal existence they have managed to achieve. Fulfilled ambition and a kind of biological unease exist side-by-side; realized ideals bring no gratification but only a sense of being cut loose from embodied reality – far from being buoyed up by success the body may even seem to collapse under an invisible strain, giving rise, for example, to pains in the back or the bowels.

These are, so it seems, young people who have received too little instruction in what it is to be human, how to recognize and take account of what their own bodies tell them about their relations with the world. As a result, they are not able to interpret the promptings of their own subjectivity. For them, 'reality' has become the production of a 'postmodern' apparatus of media-generated images with which no embodied relatedness is possible. But the body, even if rendered irrelevant to the fashionable universe of discourse still has to be lived in.

Central to this 'new' form of anxiety is the sense that achievement is empty of satisfaction – what the person is supposed to want, and so acquires, he or she simply does not desire. A life conditioned by marketed ideals of 'success' can become so detached from subjective bodily *desire* that the person simply finds it impossible to say what he or she wants, and 'pleasing oneself', even (or rather especially) in such basic wants as food or sex, can become something which has to be assiduously learned from scratch. Such anxiety is reduced through coming to experience, refine and elaborate the *desire* which links body to world. As always, however, the cost of becoming free from marketed illusions is the possibility of expo- sure to real pain, i.e. pain which is instantly identifiable as stemming from the injuries inflicted on embodied individuals by a far from perfect social environment. In other words, 'disillusionment' is a precondition for true experience.

The 'official' institutions through which people may seek to under- stand the experience of anxiety have, sadly, gained in neither sophistica- tion nor validity since this book was first published in 1984. Psychiatry has if anything retrenched to its traditional position of biological explanation and physical treatment, with a touch of social Darwinism thrown in. No doubt such retrenchment is in response at least partly to financial starva- tion and pressures to contain the politically defined 'seriously mentally ill' who might otherwise become too conspicuous a blot on the landscape created by 'care in the community'. The deregulation of the market in health care has let loose a flood of' 'alternative' approaches to therapy and counselling which are remarkable only for the illusoriness of their promises and the childlike wishfulness of their 'theories'. With counsellors on hand, apparently, to soothe away the ravages of reality in almost any eventuality, the authentic voice of the subjective person has become muffled to the point of extinction.

There is a tragic irony in the fact that the vast majority of people who come to consult clinical psychologists like me tend to be those who find it most difficult to abandon their personal conviction in the truth of their subjective experience. Not that this is an intellectual process that they themselves would recognize; it is an emotional one. The inability to abandon a fundamentally true insight into the nature of the social world in favour of a convenient illusion is reflected in psychological pain – though 'psychological' here is too abstract and insubstantial a word for something which is so firmly embodied. Emotional distress, far from being an indication that something is wrong with the person, is far more likely to point to something wrong with his/her world. As much as anything, this book is about the possibility of understanding the 'language' of pain.

Perhaps all distinguishable eras of social development are characterized by their regnant ideological illusions. It sometimes seems to me that maybe 'psychology' is one of the principal illusions of the twentieth century. The raw materials of emotional distress are much more bodies and worlds than they are psychologies. Distress arises from the subjection of the embodied person to social forces over which s/he has very little control. 'Psychology', such as it is, arises out of the person's struggle to understand and conceptualize the nature of his/her experience. It is a matter of meaning. But changing the experience of distress cannot, either logically or practically, be achieved purely by trying to operate on the meanings to which the body–world interaction gives rise. Yet this is precisely the mistake psychology, in particular of course therapeutic psychology, has made. It is as if we can eradicate the experience of distress by changing the way we think or talk about it. Pure magic.

This book spells out the beginnings of an alternative understanding. Even so it is undoubtedly not without its own illusions. One that I can discern quite easily after the passage of thirteen years is my misplaced deference to Freudian theory and my too sweeping condemnation of behaviourism. Psychoanalysis (as Richard Webster's comprehensive refutation of Freud demonstrates*) derailed us right at the beginning of the century from developing with anything approaching scientific validity a view of the way people suffer emotional distress not because of who they are but because of what is done to them. Behaviourism – in, admittedly, a hopelessly inadequate and ludicrously over-simplified manner – at least made some kind of effort to put us back on the rails. In any event, the only possible ground upon which our illusions can be stripped away, upon which we can start the essential process of disillusionment, is that of our subjective experience. For it is here and only here that reality reveals itself to us.

David Smail
Nottingham, March 1997

CHAPTER ONE

The Myth of Normality

This book is written in the hope that it may help remove some of the mystery which surrounds psychological distress, not just from an abstract point of view, but in terms which make concrete sense to people who are frightened or anxious about aspects of their lives which they experience as abnormal. My choice of the terms 'abstract' and 'concrete', rather than 'theoretical' and 'practical', is deliberate, because it seems to me that it is precisely through a *theoretical* framework that the nature of psychological distress can best be confronted, and to some extent alleviated. For reasons which I shall discuss in a later chapter, it seems to me that an adequate theory – i.e., an explicit set of ideas or concepts – is exactly what most people have no access to when trying to get to grips with 'symptoms' of their psychological malaise, and this is why such 'symptoms' seem, often, so mysterious: while one may concede that there are 'experts' who *do* understand them, one cannot, it seems, understand them oneself, and, without recourse to these experts, cannot expect to.

I have been careful not to raise my sights higher than expressing a hope that this book may contribute to a 'demystification' of psychological distress, and that is because I certainly do not believe that it could 'cure' such distress in individual readers. Although the popular culture, as well as many 'experts', makes an equation between psychological 'symptoms' and illness, with the implication that individuals play host to such symptoms in the way they might to symptoms of, say, appendicitis (with similar possibilities for 'cure') it seems clear to me that human misery, of which psychological distress forms a significant part, does not crop up, as it were, *within* individual people, but arises out of the interaction of people with each other and from the nature of the world we have created. Until we change the way we act towards each other, and the social institutions we have constructed, we shall not get much relief from the symptoms of anxiety, depression and despair which beset all of us at some times in our lives, and some of us nearly all the time. The 'experts' will not change the world – they will simply make a satisfactory living helping people to adjust to it; the world will only change when ordinary people realise what is making them unhappy, and do something about it. To arrive at such a realisation, they will first, I believe, have to develop proper conceptual grasp of the roots of their distress.

'Changing the world' is, of course, largely a political enterprise, and political issues are by no means irrelevant to psychological and psychiatric disorder. This is not, however, to be a sweeping political tract: people experience misery and despair within the immediate context of their own lives and relationships, and it is within this arena that they have to get to grips with them. I wish to suggest not so much that people must change the world (though that would be nice!) as that they must change *their* worlds, and that to do that they must first develop their *own* grasp of what is happening in that limited, personal world in which they pursue their existence.

This is not, then, to be a 'self-help' book in the sense of 'what to do about your anxiety' or 'how to overcome your fears and be a more successful person', etc. There are many such books, and many of them, indeed, contain elements of fairly sound practical advice. They are nearly all, however, books whose aim is to *adjust* the reader to a world which is taken as *given*, as simply real and there and to be reckoned with, but not altered. This is, at least tacitly, to see 'symptoms' as arising *within* individuals in exactly the way that I believe to be false, and it is therefore an enterprise which must be doomed to failure in any fundamental respect.

In my work as a psychotherapist, I find many patients who have turned at one time or another to self-help books (of the kind that this is not) in the hope of finding some quick, relatively painless solution to their difficulties. Some patients, undoubtedly, have been significantly helped by such books, one or two to a quite profound extent, but on the whole most seem to find them curiously unsatisfying, however sensible the advice they contain appears to be. Partly, no doubt, this is because, to be effective, psychological help is best given in the context of a living human relationship. But also, I suspect, the relative lack of impact of such books lies in their failure to offer a theoretical account of the nature and origins of psychological distress which is both accurate *and* makes sense to 'ordinary' people.

Again, in my work with patients, I have found that it is through unravelling with them some of the *conceptual* mysteries surrounding their 'symptoms' – the ideas, that is, that they have about them – that enough progress is made for them to get down to tackling their difficulties and dilemmas in ways which make a practical difference to their lives. This, usually, is not to 'cure' their 'symptoms', but to bring them face-to-face with circumstances in their lives which are painfill and distressing, and which they can ignore only at the cost of 'neurotic' suffering. Often, admittedly, this is to replace one kind of suffering with another, and whether or not this seems a good idea depends on one's values. To me, it seems more constructive, and essentially more hopeful, to recognise that real difficulties, real evils and real pain arise in the world around us through our conduct towards one another, than to resort, albeit unawares, to self-deceiving strategies which, for example, allow 'illness' to provide the explanation, and indeed the form, of our misery.

It is, then, in the hope that some of what I have learned through my work with people in distress may prove of use to others that this book is written. It will cure nobody's predicament, but I hope it may help some to confront theirs with greater understanding and courage than might otherwise have been the case.

It has never been my feeling that the 'patients' who have consulted me over the years are 'abnormal' in any particularly meaningful sense, though it is often the case that they have been defined as such by others (family, friends, doctors, psychiatrists and other professional colleagues) or by themselves. It seems likely to me that it is the extent rather than the kind of unhappiness which drives someone to seek professional help, and it seems therefore logical to conclude that there must be many, probably a majority of people who have not yet been driven that far but who are almost equally unhappy. The problems of 'patients', that is, point to a malaise which is likely to be general among 'normal' people in our society rather than specific to a particular, relatively small group of people who are thought to have succumbed to some kind of personal inadequacy.

There is in my view absolutely no convincing evidence that the kinds of difficulties complained of by the vast majority of people who consult psychiatrists, psychologists and psychotherapists are the result of any kind of 'illness', mental or otherwise, and yet this is the explanation most widely subscribed to in our society. If I am right – and I am certainly not alone in taking such a view – then what is needed is a more satisfactory account of how such difficulties arise, and one which is available to, as well as understandable by, 'ordinary' people, i.e. people other than the 'experts' whose job it is to develop an understanding of such matters. In fact, there are many such experts who have, I believe, developed accounts of psychological distress which are far more illuminating and useful than those current in our general culture, and from this point of view there is very little new in what I shall be saying. However, it does seem to me time that the experts stopped simply talking to each other and started trying to make their ideas and concepts available to those 'ordinary' people who are in the best position to make constructive use of them, or, failing that, at least deserve the chance to pass judgment on how useful such ideas and concepts might be.

Let me start my own attempt at this enterprise, then, with some observations which may seem fairly obvious, but which, I believe, on the whole we fail to take seriously. These observations centre round the tacit belief to which most of us subscribe that the majority of people are by and large pretty well adjusted, contented, and lead conventionally well-ordered lives.

In contrast to this happy state of affairs – indeed, partly because of the belief that it is so – it seems to me that most people keep the way they feel about themselves as a deep and shameful secret. Much of our waking life is spent in a desperate struggle to persuade others that we are not what we fear ourselves to be, or what they may discover us to be if they see through our pretences. Most people, most of the time, have a profound and unhappy awareness of the contrast between what they are and what they *ought* to be. Even at a relatively superficial (but extremely pervasive) level, for example, many people feel weak and silly when they ought to be strong and confident, ugly and insignificant when they should be attractive and striking. As a consequence of this we spend enormous amounts of time and energy in guarding against others' getting a glimpse of our 'true', shameful selves by constructing what we feel will be acceptable public versions of ourselves, but which we know to be a hollow sham (unless, that is, we come after a while to believe in our own posturing, fall for our own 'image').

The aim that society sets us is to *be* something: to be recognised in at least some sphere, and if only by our immediate family and acquaintances, as successful or admirable or in some way to be reckoned with. What you *do* matters not half as much as the aggrandisement which doing it brings you. The very word 'successful' – perhaps most properly applied to actions – is now more usually applied to people; there are a few people who are happy if their activities are attended by success, but many more whose idea of happiness is to be *seen* as a 'successful person' no matter how dubious the route by which they achieve it.

Behind many 'symptoms' of anxiety lies an injury to the person's self-esteem, a despairing, inarticulate awareness that he or she has not lived up to the standards of adequacy which we are all complicit in setting. The most obvious ideal, of course, is that, as well as successful, you should be strong, confident, attractive and powerful; the world is your oyster, and if you fail to find a comfortable place in it, there must be something the matter with you.

However banal it may seem, nothing holds up to us the nature of our aspirations better than television advertisements. In the early days of the medium, perhaps it was possible to see television advertisements as little more than naive and transparent, but sometimes quite amusing, lies, but now, though we may think we take them with a pinch of salt, they confront us almost remorselessly with the ideals we cannot live up to: the happy, loving family eating their cornflakes against views of waving wheatfields, eagerly waiting for the joys of the day to unfold; slim, beautiful women whose smooth and unblemished limbs slide effortlessly into blue denim skins, later to catch the strong and approving gaze of confident young men who will cherish them with just the right amount of lust; unwrinkled middle-aged couples, with lovely children, whose new washing machine unites them in a love burning only just less brightly than on their wedding night; mature, square-jawed men whose credit cards place the world of travel and technology instantly within their knowing grasp; beer-drinking workers who know how to be men in a man's world; wielders of power tools who cast contemptuous eyes over their neighbours' botched jobs; people who know the ropes and fit into the world, handle others with easy assurance, get what they want without ruffling any feathers, live their lives in material ease, basking in the admiration and affection of those around them, but being tough if they have to be.

Perhaps not everyone has quite lost sight of how far in fact the ideals to which television advertising gives a caricatured, but nevertheless accurate, outer form are really impossible to achieve in the world we actually live, but there are very many people who are cast into despair because of their failure to live up to them. Although we should be successful, confident, in control, even-tempered, honest, honourable, likeable, bold, etc., etc., our actual experience of ourselves, as far as we can bear to look at it, is quite otherwise, and to get a really clear view of the motives and intentions of our actions is almost inevitably to be assailed with anxiety because we are so unlike what we are supposed to be.

At another level, the ideal world is represented as well as upheld by its institutions. As people, we succeed or fail to the extent to which we manage to live up to the standards set for us by the educational, political, legal, cultural and social establishment. It is from such institutions, and their representatives, that we gain our ideas about what is right, true, and real, as well as about what kinds of personal characteristics are admirable. We accord the representatives of our institutions with all the qualities we know ourselves to lack: the experts are expert, the educated clever and knowledgeable, politicians have our interests at heart, scientists are wise, doctors know how to cure disease, lawyers are motivated by a concern for justice. The rich, successful and aristocratic, the 'personalities' and household names, the celebrities and stars live lives somehow bigger and more significant than our own; their births, marriages and deaths are to be celebrated or mourned on a par with (sometimes even more than) those within our own families. These, it seems, are ideal people representing an ideal world, people whose outward characteristics we may strive to imitate even if we can never really hope to attain their status, people who have broken free of our own doubts and uncertainties, anxiety and shame. The secrets of power, wisdom and knowledge are available to only some members of our society, and are enshrined in institutions to which only things like a knighthood, a Ph.D. or 'stardom' gain access, though we may share in this kind of ultimate reality by identifying ourselves with its values. Most of us seem to have lost sight of the fact that our institutions are created by people like ourselves – are, indeed, our own creations – but instead experience them as unalterably, objectively real, part of the world which it would just not make sense to question. You might, it is true, see your teacher or your doctor as fallible, but you are less likely to challenge the standards represented by education or medicine as institutions: the *values* embedded in our institutions, that is, we tend to see as fixed, unquestionable and obviously correct.

Looking at the world around them, few people can escape getting a fairly clear impression of what it is to 'fit in' to our society, what it is to be normal, competent and stable. Even if we cannot all achieve the *ideals* of confidence, attractiveness, power and success, at least we can expect to be *normal*. For example, if you are a man, this might mean being able to perform your job satisfactorily and reasonably successfully, at the same time getting on all right with your fellow workers, providing at least adequately for your family, enjoying a satisfactory social life, being a good sexual partner, being able to stand up effectively to unfair opposition, and so on. If you are a woman, you may find that as well as having to fulfil some of the above expectations in relation to your job and should also be able to run a home properly, bear and bring up children rewardingly, look attractive, get on with your in-laws, enjoy the company of other mothers (especially if you are not working), be sexually responsive, and so on. The *norms* for how we should be are all around us, everywhere, all the time: we learn them from our parents and at school, see them apparently exemplified by our friends and neighbours, imbibe them from the television, have them, as I have said, enshrined in our institutions. Though fame and stardom and brilliant success may clearly not be achievable, anyone ought to be able to cope with the basic requirements presented by life.

If you *cannot* cope with these basic requirements, you are likely to conclude that there is something the matter with you – you are not *normal*. Unless you have a lot of courage and a strong belief in yourself, you are not likely to conclude that it is the norms themselves which are wrong. If you do conclude that you are not normal, you are likely to feel anxiety and shame, and you are likely to want to keep the extent of your abnormality a fairly closely guarded secret. It is of course likely that you are not the only one to be nursing a secret fear that you do not come up to the standards set by our society, but because other people too keep their shame to themselves, it becomes impossible to share the experience of 'inadequacy', and it looks as though just about everyone is normal except you.

In fact, it is my contention that the ideal world in which we profess belief is riddled with myth, and that the secret world of anxiety and pain in which we actually live our lives is the real one which we truly share. *Why* this should be so it is not my present aim to attempt to clarify, because this would take us beyond the individual's immediate experience; what I want to establish first is that the kind of experience we are so ready to call abnormal is in fact almost universal, for only in coming to gain an *accurate* grasp of our predicament will we be able to see beyond it to the possibility of changing it.

Any inquiry into the nature of and reasons for a person's psychological distress must progress through a number of levels of varying complexity. At the most superficial level is the statement of the 'problem'. Frequently, one can see quite clearly in this the contrast between how people feel and how they think they *ought* to feel; there is also often a contrast between how people appear (in fact as quite 'normal') and how they are afraid they appear (as 'abnormal' or even 'crazy'). In presenting the following brief examples of 'problems', all I want to do is suggest that the kinds of things that people who have come to me as patients complain of are not signs of 'abnormality' or 'illness', but are in many cases typical of feelings we all share to a greater or lesser extent at various times in our lives. They do, however, present us with a challenge to our understanding. I have chosen 'cases' of kinds which occur very frequently in most therapists' experience, and though I have kept them utterly realistic, I have for obvious reasons not described any individually recognisable person (though I hope many readers may be able to recognise *themselves* at least indirectly among these descriptions). Although, in some instances, a kind of explanation for the difficulties and feelings described may be to varying degrees apparent, it is not at this stage my intention to focus on explanation, but merely to establish the breadth and generality of manifestations of the experience of psychological pain.

Frank is a handsome, friendly, well-dressed man just turned forty. He was the bright boy in his family — the only one who went to grammar school. He went to university, and eventually became an accountant. He is ambitious and successful. But most mornings he awakens sick with dread at what the day might bring. At first he could not understand why he should feel so 'ill', but it now seems that at least part of the problem is that he's tortured by the fear that friends and colleagues, and even his wife, will 'realise' what a phoney he is, that all his qualifications and success have somehow, as he feels it, been achieved under false pretences. If people knew, for example, how hard he had had to work for his exams, they would realise that he is not very clever at all. His promotion at work only came about because of the sudden death of one of his competitors for the job, who was in fact (in his view) by far the most able. Every day, he feels, he is likely to make some fatally stupid error at work that will expose him for the fraud he really is. Now their children are a bit older, his wife is taking a course in business studies and may well end up doing a responsible job more competently than him, and then she too will see through his façade and lose interest in him. Quite often, he feels so unmanned by this that his sexual performance is affected, which makes him feel all the more weak and inadequate.

Arthur is a turner in an engineering shop. He has always been shy and sensitive, and never had many friends. He was not much good at football at school, though that was all his father was interested in his being. He has one or two interests which his workmates find unusual – he likes antiques, and reads books on ancient history. The men at work talk most of the time about cars, sex and football, and cannot understand why Arthur has not got a girlfriend. He worries about being thought homosexual, and sometimes suspects that people are talking about him behind his back. He feels awkward and stupid and blushes a great deal. He longs in secret for a girlfriend, but feels that, unlike his workmates, he has not got the dash and know-how to get one, and if a girl does show any interest in him he shies away in the fear that she would expose him as sexually incompetent. At twenty-five, he still lives at his parents' home, spending most of his time in his room listening to records and reading. He is a pleasant, good-looking, quietly spoken young man, and none of those around him realise how painful he finds his life.

At eighteen, Susan went to live with a man only a few years older. She had known him for a couple of years, and was attracted by his exuberance and apparent mastery of life; she liked his sense of humour, and nothing seemed to get him down. She loved him, as she put it, wholeheartedly, and denoted herself to his needs. She got pregnant, but though she wanted the baby, had an abortion because her boyfriend said he would leave her if she did not. A year later he left her to pursue an affair with a married woman. Although they had had a lot of rows, and he had hit her on several occasions, once actually breaking one of her fingers, she missed him desperately and could not imagine making a relationship with anyone else. Though she does not look it, Susan is obsessed with the feeling that she is too fat. She tries to starve herself, but spoils it all by going on sudden binges of eating cream cakes, and then has to make herself sick to get rid of them. She feels that she is in some way revolting, and deserves nobody's love.

Joan is at a loss to understand why she cannot go shopping on her own without becoming so dizzy, sick and breathless that she is afraid of fainting, even dying, on the street. At first she thought she must have some unusual, and possibly even fatal, illness but now she realises that

*the feeling which overcomes her is of fear – intense, crippling panic. But
she can think of no reason for her fear – there seems to be nothing in her
life so out of the ordinary that it could account for such extreme feelings.
She has two healthy little children, a hard-working husband who has
already made enough for them to buy their own house, and her mother,
who was always a great support, lives not far away. She was very
ashamed of her 'symptoms' at first, and went to great lengths to disguise
them – she would make excuses not to have to go out on her own, or
would try to arrange it so that her husband, or a neighbour with whom
she was on fairly friendly terms, would come with her. But finally it
began to haunt her so much that, secretly, she had to go and confess it all
to her doctor.*

*Mary lives in what is by most standards a very large house in a very
smart suburb, and is married to a very well-off, successful and good-
looking businessman. She has two daughters who go to private boarding
schools, a car of her own, and plenty of help with the house. And yet
she wakes up every morning long before it is time to get up, feeling an
overwhelming sense of unease and a kind of hopeless, dead futility. Her
day is a nightmare of unreality and pointlessness. She stands in her
beautifully equipped kitchen trying to plan the menu for a dinner party,
but stares out of the window at a garden from which, though the sun is
shining brightly, all the colour seems to have been drained. With tears
rolling down her face, she goes back to bed and lies staring at the ceiling.
For seven years she has been receiving treatment for her 'depression', is
on permanent medication and has had electric shock treatment, but all
more or less to no avail. To her friends and acquaintances, however, she
seems poised and assured, intelligent and charming.*

*The Masons seem to their friends, families, colleagues and neigh-
bours a particularly happy and united family. Husband and wife both
have quite responsible and rewarding jobs, and their two children are
outgoing and friendly, and successful at school. And yet, for ten years,
Mrs Mason has been in love with another man, though their affair had
been very short-lived. Her children and their father had been very close,
and she had wished to give them, and him, no pain, so she stayed with
them, and her lover eventually married someone else and went to live in*

another part of the country. But she spends her life with a constant awareness of loneliness, of missing something of which, in any case, she got only a very brief glimpse. She suspects that her husband also feels lonely, but probably without knowing why.

Apart from feeling despairing, broken and angry, what Mrs Robertson finds most difficult is trying to make sense of how, completely out of the blue, her husband could leave her and their three teenage children to go off with a woman fifteen years younger than himself. She sees no future for herself and thinks a lot about suicide, but knows that the children need her. Her two sons took their father's departure fairly well, but her daughter has become difficult to handle.

About eighteen months after the birth of her second baby, Sheila started to develop a kind of panicky fear that she might accidentally be endangering her own and other people's children. She spent a lot of time checking that she had not left knives where they could be reached, that she had not somehow injured the baby when bathing him, that she had not dropped something into prams which she passed in the street, possibly smothering their occupants. After a while the checking began to dominate her life, though she concealed it quite skilfully. It also extended to other things – she might have left windows open, doors unlocked, the telephone off the hook.

Brian, a fairly senior civil servant whose job requires him to travel quite frequently between large British cities, suddenly developed an embarrassing fear of trains – particularly those which have to travel through tunnels of some length, and his worst fear was of getting trapped on a train which had come to a halt in a tunnel. At first he would sit through the ordeal of train journeys with his jaw clenched, white and damp with dread, but then it got too much and he had to start making excuses about not being able for one reason or another to make the journeys his job demanded. Eventually that would no longer wash, and so, shamefaced, he went to his doctor.

Walter was so good at football at school that he was given a trial for a first division club, which was enthusiastic about his prospects. But, in his late teens, he found reasons for giving up his sporting ambitions and became an apprentice joiner instead. The trouble was that Walter felt

*(unreasonably, according to those who have examined him medically)
that his penis was unusually small, and the ordeal of communal
changing rooms became impossible for him to bear, even though nobody
had ever said anything.*

*For as long as she can remember, Brenda bore the brunt of her
father's rage. Sometimes when sober, and nearly always when drunk,
he would shout at her and hit her without provocation. Her mother got
much the same treatment, but dealt with the whole situation by keeping
out of the way as much as possible and meekly doing her husband's
bidding. So when, at the age of sixteen, Brenda met Tom, it was for her
like a gift from heaven – he was so kind and understanding, relaxed and
easy-going. So she ran off with him when she was seventeen and
married him when she was eighteen. Their friends think they make a
lovely couple, but Brenda is in despair because she has lost all her sexual
feelings: she cannot bear Tom to touch her, though a nicer, kinder, more
tolerant husband she could not wish to have.*

People who have experienced 'symptoms' of the kinds
described above often characterise them as having occurred out
of the blue, and have no idea about what, if anything, may have
made them vulnerable to them. As this book progresses I shall
consider why it is that states such as these seem, often, so
mysterious and unpredictable, but the point to bear in mind for
the moment is that, whether or not these people had an
understanding of what led up to their condition, all of them felt
out of step in some way with those around them, whose lives
seemed almost tauntingly normal, stable and happy in
comparison with the pain, shame and often secret despair they
themselves felt. They seemed to themselves, in other words,
outside the norms of our society. It rarely occurred to any of
them that, to others, they appeared perfectly normal themselves
– if anything it would have seemed to them that, in some form
or other, their differentness from other people would be
observable at a glance.

Not only did most of these people feel abnormal, misfits in an otherwise smoothly functioning world, but many experienced themselves as having 'broken down' – or at least as 'having a breakdown' or being in danger of having one. Again, I shall discuss in a later chapter the kinds of explanation for 'breakdowns' which our society offers, but, until they had become drawn into the 'official' apparatus which exists for helping those in distress of the kinds mentioned above, these people were by and large bereft of any plausible explanation for their misery apart from a feeling that they were in some way inadequate or at fault. It did not, for example, occur to them that their experience was the natural outcome of a particular state of affairs – the reasonable upshot of their life history, so to speak – nor on the whole were they encouraged in such a belief when they were eventually driven to consult the experts. Still less did it occur to them that their state might be one commonly experienced by others: that is, not only natural, but frequent. For a variety of reasons, people are extremely reticent about revealing their worries and vulnerabilities to others, which, as I have already suggested, reinforces a view of the social world, subscribed to wittingly or unwittingly by most of us, which is in fact much more a myth than an accurate picture of reality. Even more seriously, people are not simply careful to keep quiet about their private fears – they are often unable even to see for themselves what they are. It is as if we have no proper system of ideas nor a proper language with which to understand and describe our feelings, but must rely on 'symptoms' to give them some kind of communicable form.

I do not believe that there can be anybody who has reached beyond the tenderest years without experiencing acute psychological pain over his or her feelings of inadequacy in relation to others, anxiety about his or her performance of socially expected functions and tasks, depression or despair at some kind of failure or loss. There can be very few people who have not at some time experienced so-called 'symptoms' of anxiety, whether it be exaggerated fears about their appearance (their physical adequacy), lapses in sexual performance, fears of insects or animals, or heights, of meeting others or being made in some way conspicuous in groups of people, of being exposed to ridicule by the opposite sex (or by their own sex – there are many men who find it impossible to urinate in even the threatened presence of others in public lavatories, many women for whom communal fitting rooms in clothes shops are a torture).

There are, however, quite a lot of people who *claim* to live lives unruffled by such shames and embarrassments, who make a show of adequacy which is to the envy of their friends and to the chagrin of those who, admitting at least to themselves their vulnerability, compare themselves as the result even more unfavourably with their fellow human beings. What may start out as a need to ward off anxiety by convincing others of one's own adequacy may end up as an ability to deceive onself that one is totally invulnerable. Such invulnerability is, however, often bought at the cost of those around one who have to suffer the effects of the insensitivity and egotism that such self-deception needs to maintain itself: for example, the hard, tough man who inflexibly pursues his success and refuses to countenance emotional doubt or weakness in himself may well, if married, have a wife almost screamingly desperate to have herself acknowledged as a person with feelings, but who may have to settle for the role of a silly, weak, inadequate woman who needs his stern and unbending 'protection'.

The chief way of protecting yourself from the basic anxieties which are almost universal in our culture is to develop a pose, or an 'image' behind which you can hide your 'true self'. Such poses are often to be met with: the joker, the hard man, the plain speaker, the martyr, the seducer or seductress, the simple girl, the big bearded teddybear, the dizzy blonde, the battleaxe – the reader will be able to think of many more examples. Most of us develop such images up to a point – indeed it would be hard to get by in the world without one – but difficulties are likely to ensue if people fall for their own images to the extent that their 'true self' disappears. This may be what happens with some people who come to be labelled 'psychotic', but it is probably most easily observable in the case of some so-called 'celebrities' who find themselves almost willy nilly having to live up to the expectations that they themselves have created in bringing themselves to public attention. The 'normal', mythical world in which most of us believe is heavily populated by such unreal figures. I find it interesting that several psychiatrists and psychologists have written about the contrast between the false image and the true self as if the development of the former is an abnormal phenomenon; whatever might have been the case at the time of their writing, it seems to me now that the development of a false image has become the rule rather than the exception. I shall consider this possibility further when looking, in Chapter 3, at the subject of shyness.

Despite our readiness to consider them at, as it were, a distance (for example in literature and popular entertainment), our cultural mythology has it that negative experiences such as psychological anguish, self-doubt, anger and hatred towards others (particularly family members), helplessness and inade-quacy – the kinds of feelings in which 'symptoms' tend to be embedded – are not things which trouble 'normal' people over much. And yet the true nature of society is such that it is virtu-ally impossible to get far through life without feeling any or all of these things. But because of our institutional myths, we find when we do feel them that there are very few means at our disposal whereby we might take them seriously. Instead, we are confronted only with standards of how we *ought* to be: our parents should love and protect us and we should love and respect them, we should succeed at school and at work while cooperating amicably with others, we should be sexually 'normal', have happy marriages, love our children, increase and enjoy our material possessions, earn the respect of those with whom we come into contact, and in general conform to what is expected of us in the context of our particular place in society. We are born, it seems, into an absolutely real and unalterable world which cannot be expected to bend as we come up against it, so that we must therefore adapt to it. You may, of course, grow up in a council flat or a stately home, a middle-class suburb or a slum, but whatever your experience you are not likely to see the world as something you can alter.

After a time, you may well become aware that the particular world you occupy departs in some respects from the ideals and values of the wider society, or that you personally do not match up to what seems to be valued: if you are stupid you ought to be clever, if you are poor you ought to be richer, if you are ugly you ought to be beautiful, if you are (at a certain age) single you ought to be married, if you are shy you should be confident, if fat you should be thinner, if skinny you should be plumper, and so on and on. If you fail, as you are bound to do, in these or any other respects, you will find whole armies of professionals ready to iron out the bumps: psychiatrists, psychologists, social workers, educators, religious advisers, cosmetic surgeons, beauticians, accountants, family therapists – the list can be extended indefinitely. In the vast majority of cases the professionals share a common aim – to fit you better into society, not to alter our social institutions so that they will make more comfortable room for you. In other words, when you fail you will find almost no one ready to take your failure seriously, and no conceptual structure, no language, in which to consider it – you will just be exhorted to try even harder to succeed. With a little help from your professional advisers, you will have to bend and distort your already battered image to comply more closely with what is acceptable.

But, of course, however much we do not like to acknowledge the fact, the very essence of our social organisation and cultural ideals demands that there must be a very large proportion of failures. For some people to succeed, others must fail; for one person to be clever, another must be stupid; for a girl to be beautiful, others must be plain. All the time, unremittingly, people are forced to compare themselves with others in terms of what they *are*, that is, in terms of what valuation society places upon them. For every good-looking, assured, rich and powerful man there will be thousands who view him with envy and shame, and struggle the harder to conceal their own implied inadequacy, disguising their hatred when necessary with an outward show of admiration which may even turn eventually to slavish deference. For every tanned, taut-skinned, smooth and lissom girl there will be thousands who look in the mirror at their white, soft, gently bulging bodies with disgust and only just concealed despair.

Our values are not such that they could be positively achieved by everybody, or even by most people: they are bound to generate failure and distress more than comfort and happiness.

Most people, metaphorically, walk round under the baleful gaze of a relentless judge – the 'generalised other' who measures you with a cold eye and, almost inevitably, finds you wanting. No wonder so many people find themselves, for example, cowering in their homes, sick with dread if they have to venture out into the world beyond their own four walls (and worse, by succumbing to their fear, relegating themselves to a new class of failures – the 'agoraphobics'). And yet, I wonder whether people such as these really are failures, or whether between us we have managed to create a society in which cruelty has got out of hand. It may perhaps be that the person whose anxious dread has shattered the mythical reality in which we are taught to believe has caught on to a truth which the rest of us are desperate not to acknowledge, and for which there are almost no words to provide an understanding.

CHAPTER TWO

The Reality of Threat

The deepest preoccupations and concerns of 'human nature' or at least, the ways in which they are expressed and experienced – vary with the times and circumstances in which human beings find themselves. For all that we should like to believe otherwise, human beings are not machines whose nature has been fixed once and for all; the 'truth' about people is not static.

My own view of what those preoccupations and concerns are is, then, shaped by the social conditions in which we find ourselves; as times change, so will the preoccupations and concerns. And this is just as well, for if people were to continue to experience themselves as they seem mostly to do now, the future would look very bleak indeed (as it is, only a fool would say that it is rosy).

It is certainly not easy to penetrate behind the mythical world in an attempt to find out why our investment in it is so heavy and so extensive: on the whole, it allows itself to be talked about, so to speak, only in its own terms and in its own myth-creating language. There are very few circumstances available to us in which we can, in good faith, investigate with others the meaning of our experience, the sources of our secret despair. Whether it be with oneself or others, honesty is threatening, and in any case few people are capable of achieving it even if they want to. Honesty breaks through the screen of myth, giving glimpses of a truer world which may be almost unbearably frightening to live in.

This, perhaps, is why psychotherapy as an institution has become a prominent feature of our age. Although, like our other institutions, psychotherapy is used most frequently to strengthen rather than weaken the grip of myth, it does at its best at least afford the possibility of working towards honest communication: it is one of the few arenas in which people can pursue the truth about themselves and their lives without the threat of blame or disapproval, and without risk of hurting or offending the person to whom they are revealing themselves.

It is, then, through my experience of talking to people in psychotherapy that I have caught my own glimpses of what seem to be some of the features of our predicament, of some aspects of the real world behind the myth.

It is perhaps no accident that, as a species, we base our relations with each other on the threat of annihilation, for the preoccupation shown by nations with the nuclear destruction of other nations does no more than give an outer, one might almost say symbolic, form to the threat of annihilation with which most individuals live in their day-to-day lives. This latter is not, to be sure, so much a physical threat as a psychological one – a fate worse than death which, often enough, makes suicide seem preferable.

In order satisfactorily to function, we depend, throughout our lives, on the presence of others who will accord us validity, identity and reality. You cannot *be* anything if you are not *recognised* as something; in this way your being becomes dependent on the regard of somebody else. You may be confirmed, or you may be disconfirmed, and if the latter is the case, often enough and pervasively enough, you simply cease to exist as a person.

John was an orphan, and had been brought up by an aunt and uncle, only the former of whom had shown him any real warmth. He was shy, and made few friends, though he was an extremely gifted boy who excelled at all sports as well as being academically competent at school. When in his early twenties, he was one day walking along a path in the middle of a small park when he suddenly became terrified that he would float off the face of the earth. He knew, of course, the factual impossibility of this, but

nevertheless from that day on became incapable of leaving his home
without intolerable feelings of panic. He was unable to go out at all for
some years unless accompanied by his wife, and then only with great
discomfort.

In fact, John had had very little experience of confirmation
by others, and if, literally as well as metaphorically, he strayed
far enough from the gaze of those who had regard for him, the
reality of his existence ebbed away, so that he was left floating in
empty space.

Even those who move confidently in a relatively secure
network of confirming relationships cannot be unfamiliar with
the experience of disconfirmation: it must happen to everyone
at various points in their lives. Think, for example, of the times
when you have openly and innocently exposed your feelings to
somebody important to you, only to be met by an icy rebuff
which totally misperceives your intentions: for a moment you
are enveloped in a sick, acid, freezing loneliness which seems to
drain the very blood from your veins. This is the pain worse
than all others, and, if experienced in more than occasional
small doses, the fate worse than death.

Because we are so dependent on *being* something, and
because that must in turn depend on the recognition and
confirmation of others, it becomes enormously important to
feel *loved*. Love seems to be the prototype confirmation,
tangible proof of the acceptance and recognition of what you
are, the ultimate approval. I am not sure that this is, so to speak,
an eternal verity, but it does seem to me that this is what most
people mean by and experience as love in the present age. With
a constant supply of love you can go confidently from strength
to strength; if the supply is threatened or interrupted, or otherwise in question, you are overcome with anxiety, panic and
dread; without it, you cease to exist as a real person, but may
live a false, defended life in which pain is never far from the
surface.

This means that love is not simply a positive experience, something that may be relied on in some circumstances (for example in families) and welcomed as a nice surprise in others (for example courtship), something which makes the world a nice, brighter place. It makes of love, in fact, a most terrible weapon which can be used to confirm or annihilate, to blackmail or torture as well as to cherish and nurture. The threat with which we live is the threat of not being loved.

Richard has been dealt a number of unusually unkind blows by fate in the course of his life. Most of these he deals with courageously and energetically, but sometimes his confidence collapses and he gives way to states of anxious panic which he experiences as physical illness. He remembers how, as a child, he used to fear that, every time he left the house, his parents would fetch another little boy from the attic whom they loved much more than him.

Anne felt her mother's hatred so much that she used as a child to comfort herself with the fantasy that perhaps she was an orphan whose parents would really have loved her (at the time of course, she would not have been able to put it in quite these words). Her unusual ability to see her early experience so clearly is perhaps what enables her now to take a remarkably brave and constructive grip on her life, even if she pursues her aims in great fear and trembling.

It is not surprising that most forms of psychotherapy concentrate at some point on early childhood experience, for it is of course in relation to one's parents (or substitute parents) that one first gains an idea of what one is, and of whether that 'self' is or is not lovable. People's fundamental feelings about their self-worth take shape throughout childhood as they become aware of what they are worth to those closest to them (usually, of course, parents).

Our mythical culture takes it more or less for granted that parents love their children (those who betray the myth too grossly – and usually get the social services into trouble as well –

invoke our most extreme self-righteous horror), but as a generality this seems to be far from the case, unless, that is, one can
see love as coming in some very strange disguises. It is of course
true that many parents feel intensely bound up with their children, but too often affection is conditional on the child's
conforming to parental needs and expectations, and its withdrawal can at any moment project the child into the cold isolation which threatens to nullify its existence.

Many parents are so in need themselves of the kind of
nurturing confirmation they know they should give to their
children that the latter simply become competitors, and some
parents are certainly unprepared for the demands children will
make on them, find their offspring exhausting and draining, and
are unable to meet their needs. This is bound to be the case at
some times with all parents, and yet many become extremely
guilty and anxious at discovering how irritable and destructive
they are capable of feeling towards their children. Others simply
give vent to their irritation.

*Kathleen is a lonely woman, longing for the warmth and support of the
people she left behind in Ireland (though her large family was not
particularly affectionate). Her husband is a self-employed builder who
works most weekends and evenings and can no longer bear to listen to her
complaints of homesickness. She has no real friends on the estate where
they live, finding the people cold and spiteful. She gets her main comfort
from drinking, which is beginning to get a grip on her. One evening after
she was supposed to be in bed, Kathleen's three-year-old daughter came
down the stairs asking for a glass of milk. Kathleen, interrupted in her
lonely relationship with a pint of cheap sherry, found herself beside herself
with rage, screaming hysterically at her daughter, and hurling a bottle of
milk to smash against the wall not far from the girl's head. She was so
frightened and ashamed by this episode, which she dared not confess to her
husband, that she forced herself to confide in her doctor.*

For many people, children quickly become allies or enemies

in the unhappy battles they are waging with their husbands or wives. Countless fathers, for example, find themselves eased out of the family circle (often into the potting shed, the garage, or the pub) while their children became instructed by their mother in what beasts men are (male children brought up in this regime often develop into fastidious, anxious men who have a kind of disgust for all things masculine, which of course makes their own lives very difficult to lead; female children from such a background often have an instinctive loathing and contempt for men which they themselves find hard to understand). Because so many men in our culture are heavily defended against any kind of emotional sensitivity (betraying, perhaps, a tacit knowledge of the dreadful risks to which their need for love exposes them), their wives often feel neglected, misunderstood, lonely and anxious, and their daughters fail to learn what really goes on underneath the male façade, so that they later relate to men on models they have perforce had to construct from fantasy. Such men are often particularly intensely threatened by love in all its aspects, and fend it off with, at best, distance and indifference and, at worst, brutality: their daughters may become anxious, submissive and profoundly lacking in confidence, their sons defensive and uncertain.

Many parents are made intensely anxious by any sign that their children are developing in ways which do not conform to their expectations and (usually implicit and unexamined) values. A child may find itself hated simply because it looks like a relative who is disliked or found threatening by either or both of its parents. Coercion, ranging from the periodic withdrawal of affection to full-blown assault and battery, is a ubiquitous feature of parent-child relations, and children quickly learn to distort themselves to fit expectations if they are not to be thrown, as it were, into outer darkness. Particularly in middle-class families, positive parental expectations can place enormous stress upon their children – they must be clever, do well at school, harbour no unrefined thoughts or feelings, become doctors or lawyers, etc.: again, the manipulative use of love is the weapon which works towards the desired result.

In families with several children, the latter often come to occupy well-defined roles, any departure from which on their part is met with instant disconfirmation and rejection. There are many girls, for example, who come to occupy the 'Cinderella' role: the less pretty daughter with the heart of gold who becomes the family drudge, the one who always helps the others, takes responsibility, keeps her expectation of personal success and happiness low (and ends up with a bleak life of service to others). If, in the family, she makes any attempt to establish a more satisfying place for herself, she is made to feel that her golden heart has turned to stone, that she is becoming corrupted by selfishness and getting above herself; in later life her internalisation of these values means that she is unable to please herself without feeling overwhelming anxiety and guilt.

The control of children through the withdrawal of love happens in the subtlest of ways, and is usually denied by the parents at any explicit level – their own anxiety does not permit them to see what they are doing. Many children are brought up in an emotional world which is structured by magic: control is exercised by hints and hidden threats, in which punishment is somehow transmitted by non-human powers, and any attempt at rebellion is likely to be met with a kind of blast of superstitious dread.

Jane, an only child, spent her entire childhood being overwhelmed by her parents' assurances of their love for her, and they were zealous in attending to her every want. Anger and hatred were not allowed in her household. Her mother spent a lot of time consulting horoscopes and spiritualist manuals, and the family's life was ruled by the never quite expressed necessity for warding off the powers of evil. One of Jane's memories, which she could make no sense of, is of taking a Christmas present from her mother upstairs and, secretly, jumping on it. In her early adult life she became troubled by obsessional fears that she could harm people by wishing them ill, which she found herself doing compulsively. What worried her most was that her evil wishes were always directed at those whom she loved most, like her mother for instance.

Parents can do the most appalling things to their children out of their concern for them.

After a row with her father when she was fifteen, May stormed out of the house and walked round the park for, for her, an unusually long time. When she got back after dark, her father, beside himself with anger and anxiety, dragged her down to the doctor demanding that he examine her to see if her virginity was still intact.

People, on the whole, are not aware of the extent to which they have been blackmailed, coerced, distorted and subdued by the many uses to which 'love' and its withdrawal can be put. For most individuals, their experience is simply their experience, and certainly as children they had no way of knowing that things might have been different. Even people whose childhood has been one long history of neglect and rejection (a much more frequent feature of our world than we like to think) often speak respectfully of their parents and see themselves as having had a reasonably normal and even happy childhood. At first, the link between their lack of confidence and feelings of worthlessness on the one hand and their childhood experience on the other is hard for them to see. We tend to take it for granted that what we experienced from our parents as children is what is meant by parental love.

It is difficult for anybody who takes the trouble to inquire into the backgrounds of people in distress not to become angry with parents. There is no doubt that family life is frequently a scene of horrific violence – more often subtle and psychological than overt and physical – and it seems unforgivable that morally responsible adults could inflict the kinds of things they do on their innocent offspring. And yet, of course, the victims become themselves parents, and in all probability perpetrate similar violence on their own children. We tend to blame only those we have not taken the trouble to understand. I can sympathise with Mrs X who tells me how she hit her daughter – can even encourage her not to feel too bad about it – because I also know that she is coping with an unemployed and alcoholic husband and an overcrowded council flat with noisy and aggressive neighbours. It is therefore foolish of me to feel righteous anger when she tells me how her father used regularly and for no apparent reason to belt her until she bled even up to the age of seventeen, when she ran away to get married. Such relationships are not due simply to the wickedness of individuals, but take place in a cultural setting which makes our (mythical) ideals hard to achieve.

However, our experience as individuals starts at a given point, and a purely sociological analysis leaves us personally untouched as we struggle to understand what has happened to us and how we are to deal with it. The relations between parents and children, the corrupted love which threatens annihilation, indeed sets up a vicious circle in which the apportionment of blame is irrelevant, but as people we can approach the problem personally only from our particular vantage point. For most individuals, their first experience of the 'other', the remorseless judge who may bestow or withdraw confirmation, is personified in their parents.

There are of course those who conclude that the 'nuclear family' is an inevitable source of oppression and exploitation, and that human relations would be better learned in other kinds of nursery. Although I am sure that what happens in families is by no means unrelated to the culture beyond them (in ways some of which we shall consider later), this does not seem to me an argument for their abolition. That love is abused is no reason for dismantling its most effective cradle. It is the very powerfulness of love which makes it so dangerous, and it seems to me preferable to try to understand the ways in which it is misused rather than to get rid of it altogether.

The greatest misuse to which we put love, I believe, is to make it the conditional ground on which people can *be* rather than the unconditional ground from which they can *do*: we love people as objects rather than subjects. Love has become a certain kind of approval, the bestowal of confirmation or disconfirmation on people who meet or fail to meet certain objective criteria. As others have pointed out, children quickly get an idea of themselves as having certain kinds of 'selves' which are describable in terms of either approving or disapproving labels. John *is* clever, or brave, or naughty or strong; Jane *is* pretty, or wilful, or silly, or delicate. With the partial exception of physical labels, which have implications to be considered in a later chapter, these words are misapplied. Only actions can be clever or stupid, brave or cowardly, good or bad, etc. What I do stupidly today I might do cleverly tomorrow, but I shall find it more difficult if I have already accepted the label 'stupid' – I may well find, indeed, that it is more important to live up to the label than to risk disconfirmation by stepping out of role. We have to earn the love of those who are important to us by becoming the objects they wish us to be.

Sometimes it may lie within a child's possibilities to become what its parents want it to be, and it may conform, most often not without strain, but sometimes glowing with satisfaction and confidence at the confirming approval this brings: in this case the child ends up with a validated 'sense of self', a clear, self-conscious picture of the kind of person he or she has become, frequently not untainted by a kind of self-congratulatory bumptiousness which is unlikely to be punctured just because people take exception to it.

Many children, however, are in some or many important respects unable to fulfil the expectations of their parents, and carry round with them, so to speak, raw, painful areas of disconfirmation which leave them exposed to sudden attacks of self-doubt and uncertainty, sudden ebbings of self-confidence which may well be experienced as 'symptoms' of anxiety or depression.

Annette remembers vividly a day when, at the age of about six or so, she was playing a solitary skipping game in the back yard, and accompanying it with a song she had learned at school, the words of which she has since realised are mildly obscene. Suddenly her mother stormed out of the back door, hit her hard across the face, and ordered her to bed. In retrospect, Annette can see why her mother reacted as she did, though at the time she gave her daughter no explanation. One of Annette's 'symptoms' is to fear that people will think her stupid or bad if she talks or acts spontaneously in public, and consequently she is mildly 'agoraphobic'.

It would of course be foolish to suggest that one such incident as this could determine the future course of someone's experience. The significance of the memory lies rather in pointing to what might have been (indeed, in view of other evidence which there is little need to spell out here, probably was) a pervasive state of affairs in this person's childhood.

Because they are disconfirmed as people (objects), it is natural for children to conclude that they are in some way flawed 'selves', they do not come up to scratch in certain essential respects: they are, quite simply, in some ways unlovable. The child does not as a rule criticise its parents' conception of it; understandably, the parental view is accepted by the child as the one which accurately mediates reality. If the child is unloved, it must be because it is unlovable. Even as adults with quite clearly elaborated concepts of right and wrong and good and bad, and who are able to see – in others – what does and does not constitute adequate child-rearing practice, there are many people who cannot actually experience their own quite often horrendous treatment as children as having been anything but their 'own fault'. If their parents treated them badly it must have been because, despite their best efforts, they could not overcome their children's unlovableness suffficiently to love them. Under the surface feelings of anxiety or panic, then, there is often a self-loathing which seems the appropriate response to what the person has learned about him- or herself from an apparently objective parental assessment. Often, people are reluctant to expose themselves to any experience which might suggest that they are worth more than they think they are, as if it becomes more comfortable to live in the role assigned to you than to risk an even worse fate by rebelling against it. I can think, for example, of many women whose (in particular) fathers conveyed, whatever they actually felt, little more than hatred towards them, who move from one degrading and pain-filled relationship with men to another, with very little hope and a great deal of despair, and yet who even consciously reject more promising-looking relationships on the grounds that they 'don't deserve' them.

Love is the stamp of approval on an objective 'self', but rarely is the approval total, and life may at any moment throw up circumstances which expose those raw and unconfirmed aspects of ourselves which we shamefully hide from the public gaze. Since we have no articulate understanding of our condition, we experience such moments as the incomprehensible onslaught of anxiety: a symptomatic attack which appears 'out of the blue'. We go through life like commodities on a conveyor belt, being probed by some electronic eye for flaws, with the rubber stamp 'reject' ever poised to fall upon us should such a flaw be found.

The Other thus becomes a terrible threat as well as a potential saviour: we depend for our self-confidence and well-being on the endorsement of the other and yet we are just as likely to be annihilated by him or her.

The parent as Other is, as it were, its first and most powerful instance, but clearly almost anyone else can occupy its place in the individual's experience. As you go through life you are assessed, docketed and judged according to an ever-widening range of criteria – at home, at school, at work, at leisure, by family and friends, teachers and colleagues: you fall almost continuously under an evaluating, objectifying gaze. It can surely be no accident that anxiety is so often experienced by people when they are, literally, exposed to the gaze of others. So-called 'agoraphobia' is rarely experienced by people as a fear of open spaces – indeed, many 'agoraphobics' feel quite comfortable walking alone on deserted roads or in the open countryside, in fog or in the dark. It is in crowded places – shops and buses, busy streets, restaurants, parties and other social gatherings, where the real panic usually strikes. Most people who experience this kind of anxiety, which can be excruciatingly painful and frightening, readily make the connexion between fear and social exposure when they are offered it, but not so many make it for themselves: at first, often, the 'symptoms' are seen as inexplicable, indicative perhaps of some kind of physical illness. While people may be able to say that they are afraid of making a public spectacle of themselves in some way, for example by passing out on a bus or vomiting in a restaurant, the concept of simply fearing the gaze of the Other is not one which makes immediate sense to the average Anglo-Saxon mind. If you are afraid, it is thought, it must be of something specific, if you are worrying, you must be worrying about a 'problem' – it does not seem reasonable to suggest that fear can be a state of being. This is perhaps how some people are able to deceive themselves about the meaning of their sensations – it cannot be fear, they argue, because there is nothing immediately present which could reasonably give rise to fear; the sensations must therefore be signs of illness.

Usually, of course, vulnerability to the generalised gaze of the Other – to strangers in a supermarket, even to faceless windows in a street – is not in itself a total 'explanation'. The person's confidence, belief in him- or herself as a satisfactory object, has been initially sapped in some other context, usually parental, often, secondarily, marital. But the way the dread of annihilation takes us, the panicky feeling of strangeness and the ebbing away of one's familiar existence (sometimes called 'depersonalisation' by psychiatrists) is indicative of something much wider than our personal weaknesses and failures: it is the negative aspect of a way of life to which we all subscribe, the price we pay for objectifying each other under our mutual gaze. Under that gaze we freeze and tremble, flush and stammer because we know full well, and utterly realistically, what it can do to us: it can annihilate us.

The dependence on the other for confirmation renders every relationship in which the other features (that is, as things are, just about every relationship) fraught with awful danger. 'Loving' relationships become secret, undercurrent battlegrounds, in which we stalk each other warily sniffling the atmosphere for indications of rejection. To allow yourself to be loved by another is to put yourself totally in his or her power, to hand him or her the means of your destruction, because, by and large, we love one another only as objects (it may not be without significance that a leading school of depth psychology sees love as an aspect of 'object relations', indeed, is known as the 'object relations school').

Though objectifying confirmation and disconfirmation is a ubiquitous feature of our social organisation, nowhere is the dangerousness of the risks we run in 'loving' more evident than in the relations of men with women and women with men. Perhaps it is the very 'otherness' of the opposite sex which makes the acceptance and confirmation of one of its members so initially warming and rewarding – for example in the (relatively rare) experience of 'falling in love'. However, the fact that, even when it does occur in its most florid form, this state of relationship never seems to last all that long suggests that for people to live and move and have their being in each other places a strain on their capacities to meet each other's needs which only almost superhuman generosity on each individual's part can overcome. Sooner or later the lover's needs take precedence over those of the beloved, and that is the point at which they will discover whether a continued relationship – as, as it were, consenting adults who can accept a measure of their own aloneness – is possible. The greater the dependence of one partner on another, the greater the likelihood that he or she will end up feeling bitterly rejected.

It is certainly no accident that so many people who are overcome by 'symptoms' of anxiety acute enough for them to seek professional help are relatively young women with small children, cut off from close contact with their own families, and dependent for the survival of their identity on husbands who have changed from being attentive lovers to near-strangers who come home late, tired from work, and unwilling to talk about anything. No longer confirmed under the loving gaze of any 'significant other', trapped in a form of drudgery which is these days no longer socially valued, such women find themselves additionally drained by the demands of their own children who call upon resources for love and attention which seem rapidly to be running dry. Even in spite of the current raised consciousness of feminist principles (which seem not to have penetrated far beyond the orbit of those relatively liberated and independent women who have least need of them) our cultural mythology has it that this kind of situation is utterly 'normal' and desirable, so that women who find themselves in it have, so to speak, no critical purchase upon it: if they feel unhappy, anxious and unreal, it must be because they are either 'ill' or 'inadequate', and if they detect in themselves feelings of destructive violence towards their children (a not uncommon 'symptom' consequent upon their depleted ability to meet their children's needs) their alarm and guilt may quickly drive them to their doctor. Since sexuality is so responsive to the relational context in which it is set, it is very often also the case that women in such circumstances find themselves less eager than they once were to make love to their uncommunicative husbands, and frequently they experience this as a puzzling and alarming development.

It is easy to cast men in the role of villain in these circumstances. But they have their problems too. Focused on breadwinning, unaware that many of their needs for confirmation may be being met to some extent through their relations with people at work, they are confused and irritated by their wives' demands on them (cannot see the nature of their underlying needs), and become hurt and angry to find that the validating sexual warmth which satisfied their most fundamental need for confirmation (as well as their lust, which is all that their wives by now can see) is no longer half so readily available. Eventually, nursing their pain behind a wall of feigned (or self-deceiving) indifference, they retire into the back room with their personal computers, or into a shed in the back yard with their rabbits or their CB radios. This, certainly, may not be the world as presented to us by the colour supplements, but it is much more real.

In the arena of male–female relations there are many variations on this theme, but the major components are usually not dissimilar to those sketched out above. The reasons for this state of affairs are no doubt complex and manifold, stretching through individuals' personal histories out into the culture beyond and the socially determined roles which men and women are expected to adopt. No doubt to a significant extent it is a man's world, and perhaps for the most part men are better placed to survive some of its more painful demands, but for one sex simply to blame the other would be to miss one central and very important point, and to decrease the chances of men and women understanding each other. The point is that to depend on the Other – in this case the sexual partner – for confirmation of one's being is bound to lead to disconfirming annihilation, because such a demand can only be met through a self-denying generosity and sacrifice on the other's part which is beyond the competence of ordinary mortals. Once the dependency is created, the confirmation supplied and then withdrawn, the loved and loving other becomes the hated and annihilating other, and men and women find themselves opposing each other with bristling hostility and contempt. Our very 'selves' have become objectified commodities in an emotional market-place, and, having lost the freedom of our subjectivity, we are at the mercy of those others who may choose us or reject us, purchase or replace us, install us at the warmth of their hearth, or leave us on the shelves.

One does not have to be a psychotherapist to see everywhere evidence of the pain that men and women inflict on each other and themselves. For example, having failed once to extort the necessary confirmation from their partner, or having received it for only a relatively fleeting period, people may of course embark, through a series of either actual or fantasised affairs, on a search for it elsewhere (this seems to be the particular, if by no means the sole province of the middle-aged). The initial reassuring warmth of a new sexual liaison is something that can be endlessly repeated but rarely emotionally consummated. For women with children whose freedom of action is more limited, many sad hours may be spent in daydreams of a rescuing knight. One only has to glance at the popular literature designed for women and young girls to see how far our culture still offers them salvation as the handmaidens of men, where all they have to do to earn undying faithfulness is love and serve. For men, the passionate submission of a series of otherwise aloof, sultry and sexy (though emotionally undemanding) young women is supposed to be what will charge their batteries sufficiently for them to conquer the world. Trite as these myths are, one detects them over and over again in the fantasies which fuel people's hopes, and sometimes guide their actions, while they drive each other to despair. There are also, of course, those whose experience of parental attitudes and strife has determined them, albeit unawares, never to enter the fray themselves, so that their sexuality becomes attached to safer 'objects', and they find themselves, like electronic machines, being 'turned on' by a wide range of stimuli which need not necessarily have anything much to do with other people at all.

The all-pervasive threat of annihilation means that we have to armour ourselves against the dangers of relationship, cultivate an indifference towards tenderness so that we are anaesthetised to the pain its withdrawal can inflict. Our fear of loving and being loved is apparent at every level of our social existence, from the personal to the institutional. Karen Horney, a psychoanalyst of great distinction whose major work was carried out towards the end of the first half of this century, pointed out that a fundamental strategy of 'neurosis' is to seek security rather than satisfaction. Thirty or so years later, this now seems to be almost everyone's central preoccupation, and, indeed, forms the major rationale even for international relations. Our concern is not to betray our vulnerability, not to become 'exposed' (perhaps this is why, at the national level, 'spies' are singled out for particular vituperation and especially savage punishment, and why, at the level of popular culture, espionage seems so fascinating). It certainly seems hardly questionable that the 'denial of tenderness' is a predominantly male phenomenon, and it is undoubtedly the case that many men who seek professional help with 'symptoms' of anxiety which seem to be getting out of hand are in fact paying the price for developing such a rigidly tough posture towards the world that the defence starts to crack and their relationships with those important to them start to disintegrate in a way which exposes their tender foundations. Frequently also, men find that they simply cannot keep up with the demands for toughness that their role seems to make of them: they feel weak, effeminate, silly and useless. But defensiveness is not a purely male prerogative, and we shall be considering later other ways in which we try to ward off the worst threats to which we are exposed by our objectified existence, as well as some of the costs we incur thereby in terms of crippling our capacity for creative, subjective existence and less destructive relationships.

One cannot comfortably go through life with a continuous awareness of the threat of annihilation under which one lives. Just as one cannot, without succumbing to despair, hold in one's mind for long the extent of the largely unseen apparatus we have painstakingly built for the destruction of our planet, so one cannot live with a continuous conscious examination of the ways in which we threaten each other psychologically: we conduct our lives within our defences, largely unconscious that they exist, and taking for granted the ways we relate (or fail to relate) to each other as features of an unalterable reality. Like well-defended space craft, we find the painful and destructive rays we direct at each other bouncing off our hardened shells as we cruise aimlessly through a life-space structured as much by market forces and technical 'progress' as by any human purpose of our own. Every so often a shot penetrates, and, because he or she has failed to develop the requisite armour, a person disintegrates like a dot on a space-invaders screen. Because defensiveness has become the norm, the medium in which we live, we notice its presence no more than a fish notices the water it swims in, but pretend rather to be guided by the mythical values we see as 'objectively' established around us. We have no language with which to comment upon our true predicament, but experience it inarticulately through our 'symptoms' and our dread.

CHAPTER THREE

Shyness and the Self as Object

It is almost impossible, in our culture, not to be self-conscious that is, aware of oneself as being under the gaze of others, of being evaluated by them and vulnerable to rejection by them. We do not define *ourselves* as people, but are defined by those with whom we come into contact, and it is our awareness of their opinion of us which furnishes our consciousness of self.

Very early on – most probably from our parents – we start to get an idea of ourselves as being this, that or the other 'kind' of person, we discover (so it seems) that we have 'selves' which are describable in certain more or less definite terms. We cannot, as things are, escape the definitions which are imposed upon us, nor find a way to make ourselves immune to the ever-present threat of having a negative, rejecting judgment passed upon us. The person who professes not to care what others think of him, but rather to rest content in his confidence in his own worth, is simply deceiving himself: as long as one claims to *be* anything, the claim must in the final analysis depend on the endorsement of others if it is to be valid.

The processes whereby we, as it were, negotiate what kind of objectification will eventually be imposed upon us are, however, extremely complex and subtle, and, because they are not in themselves objective, are largely opaque to our inspection: if challenged, we would probably deny that we were engaged in such processes at all. Yet it is obvious from even the most everyday interactions between people that everyone has very sophisticated ways of coping with others, ways which imply some kind of awareness (even if it would be impossible to the intricate and finely balanced subjective world in which we conduct our relations with each other, register and react to the impressions we give and receive, administer and respond to offers of love or threats of annihilation. Because of the enormous delicacy involved in our dealings with each other in these respects, and because of the extreme dangers inherent in them, we do not normally comment upon what we are up to: language, it seems, is far too crude to be allowed, as it were, to clothe our transactions in the coarse obviousness of words. Words objectify and make concrete what we seem to prefer to keep as a screened, fluid sensitivity which does not have to answer for its insights and actions, keep to its promises, or meet the crass demands of logical analysis. And yet we rely on this unexamined and mercurial faculty to tell us the truth about what is going on between us far more than on the verbal accounts we give each other and ourselves as 'explanations' and excuses. Indeed, were we to rely on our *explicit* psychological theories – whether lay or professional – for the conduct of our social life, we should find it virtually impossible to maintain any semblance of order or predictability in our dealings with each other, and would spend much of the time laboriously trying to work out what was happening with the aid of a totally inadequate vocabulary.

The psychotherapist, certainly, would get nowhere without a heavy reliance on the accuracy of his or her intuitive understanding of patients, since very often what patients are prepared to say about themselves is very far indeed from being the case. And it is only because the therapist knows (trusts) that the patient *shares* the categories of understanding yielded by intuition that he or she is able to appeal to the patient's good faith (i.e. abandonment in the safety of the therapeutic relationship of the possibilities for deception offered by language) so that the truth may be acknowledged.

There is nothing special in these respects about psychotherapists and their patients. The immediate knowledge of interpersonal 'truth' afforded by intuitive sensitivity and the possibilities for obscuring it inherent in language are universal phenomena.

It is not that the heavy hand of 'scientific psychology' has not attempted to grasp this faculty and render it amenable to objective inspection. Through ponderous analyses of eye-contact, gesture, facial expression and other 'objective', 'behavioural' indices, psychologists have hoped to be able to make 'predictable' and 'controllable' the last vestiges of our subjectivity. But even in so far as this project appears to succeed (so that, for example, salesmen, 'communicators' and the socially withdrawn may be able to be trained in the secrets of 'body language') it simply renders even more recondite and invisible the springs of our subjectivity as we learn that we can no longer trust the 'behavioural cues' which formerly gave us a glimpse of our intentions. It is, therefore, a mistake to suppose that the hidden 'I' which enacts our conduct can ever be made available to objective analysis or 'scientific' description, and the attempt so to make it only widens further the arena in which we can deceive ourselves and each other.

In terms of the considerations raised in earlier chapters, intuitive sensitivity is the faculty whereby we cope with the 'real' world of dangerous and threatening relationships, and language the faculty which mediates the mythical, 'objective' world which we would all much prefer to believe in. Depending on the heaviness of a person's stake in the mythical world, it is entirely possible for him or her to disclaim any trust in or respect for the knowledge which intuitive sensitivity makes available – to disconfirm it, that is, in either the self, or others, or both.

Both as a society and as individuals, it seems to me, our insistence on preserving our myths at all costs and defending ourselves from the painful realities of our social lives and their inherent threat of annihilation, means that we have become increasingly concerned to deny the evidence, if not of our own senses (though, perhaps, that is what it comes down to), then at least of our own sensitivity. (The very fact that I am driven to use such a clumsily unsatisfactory term as 'intuitive sensitivity' shows how impoverished is our conceptual apparatus for the understanding of this faculty.) Most people simply deny what at another level they know to be the case, or suffer agonies of indecision over whether to trust their experience or not. Interestingly, there is a minority of people who seem to find it impossible *not* to trust the experience which their intuitive sensitivity gives them, even though they would much rather abandon it: they would rather not have the pain of knowing the truth, but cannot seem to find the secret of escape from it which others have so easily developed.

A patient asked me recently whether I thought his wife really did love him. How can one answer such a question? However complete the behavioural catalogue one could build up on what she did and did not do for him, one could never be certain that his description was accurate or that she was not simply a good dissembler. His question, in fact, was asked out of utter despair, indicating really that he could no longer trust himself to judge his own experience: nobody can know (in the sense of objective certainty) what he wanted me to tell him, they can only trust what they sense – there is no other court of appeal in the final analysis. It is of course the false promise of objectivity to give us 'proofs' of our world which rest on an authority (for example that of 'Science') more trustworthy than our own frail powers of perception and reason; indeed, objectivity warns us with all the solemnity which can be mustered by its collective institutions of the dire perils we run if we are so foolhardy as to trust our own judgment. Small wonder, then, that in the case of my patient (who was in fact struggling with the dawning awareness that his wife did *not* really love him) reliance on his own experience seemed an impossibly risky undertaking, so that he sought the 'objectivity' of my view. He might as reasonably have asked me if the desk between us was really there (indeed, more reasonably, since at least the desk, unlike his wife, formed part of my experience as well as his). There are occasions, beloved of philosophers, when it might make sense to check with another whether one's experience (even of so well established an object as a desk) is shared, but even this is no objective guarantee of its validity – that judgment remains ultimately and irrevocably personal and subjective.

This is not to say that intuitive sensitivity is infallible – perhaps in part because of the degree to which it has been spurned and ignored in our culture and consequently is as a faculty poorly understood and weakly developed from a conceptual standpoint, it is quite easily put in the service of self-deception. Even so, it is, in the last resort, all we have to go on.

The main escape route offered by our culture from the uncertainties which our sensitivity reveals to us is, then, via objectivity. The more we can turn ourselves into objects (preferably machines) the less attention we need pay to the painful subtleties of our interaction with each other, and the more we can abandon our own experience in favour of a set of socially determined myths which clearly delineate our place in the world and the ways in which we may relate to each other.

Our, as it were, 'official' psychology tells us that we consist of 'selves' which are in turn collections of more or less fixed definable attributes, describable in terms of their relative value along a number of identifiable dimensions. One of psychology's central concerns is thus to establish what characteristics people 'have' (i.e., possess as fixed qualities) and to 'measure' their relative strength or weakness. In this way, it is felt, psychology can be 'scientific', that is, can describe features of human 'personality' and endow them with dimensions which can be measured as if they were objects in physical space. By taking this approach, it is hoped that psychology – in this instance the psychology of personality – might achieve the same sort of success as that achieved by the natural sciences like physics and chemistry in the mastery of inanimate matter, but in this case in put it into words) of the difficulties and dangers to self-esteem involved in our relations with each other. Even a simple greeting between neighbours, or a chance conversation in a bus queue, can convey enormous amounts of information about what each participant thinks of the other, and about how they would like to be thought of. The skill and subtlety which people display in relating to each other even in such unimportant encounters as these suggests that everyone is a psychologist, both in the sense of having a highly developed practical ability to deal with other people and in the sense of having an implicit theory about the reasons why people conduct themselves as they do: even if we cannot say how we do it, we show by and large great ingenuity in negotiating the relational dangers of everyday life. In order successfully to carry out these interpersonal operations, so to speak, we must rely on the most subtle and fleeting of 'cues', placing our bets on the kind of 'subjective' evidence which no self-respecting professional psychologist would touch with a barge pole. Indeed, it is almost impossible to say how one reaches the intuitions one does about other people – how, for example, one knows the difference between a true and a fake smile, catches the flash of anxiety in somebody's eye, becomes aware of a current of sexual interest between two total strangers who have only just met.

This kind of sensitivity, infinitely finer and more accurate than any of the crudely obvious insights offered by the 'body language' analysts, is, I believe, present in just about everybody, though people vary greatly in the extent to which they are willing to place their trust in it. It gives us access to a world we all share, just as our physical senses (because, presumably, of the similarity in physical structure between our bodies) give us access to a natural world about which we have built up a huge and complex (scientific) shared understanding. This is a theme which will be developed in greater detail towards the end of this book.

The world to which our intuitive sensitivity gives us access is the mastery (in particular the 'prediction and control') of human 'behaviour'. Because, so the reasoning goes, natural science is among other things 'objective', and relies heavily on numerical measurement, so psychology must adopt the same standards if it is to gain scientific respectability.

Both science as a whole, and psychology in particular, are of course integral parts of our culture, and as such it is important to remember that they meet the needs we feel and tackle the tasks we set them. However much some of them might like to be, and however much they are seen as such by many people, scientists and psychologists are not creators of our culture, discoverers of ultimate truths which then shape our view of the world, but rather interpreters and refiners of our most fundamental concepts and understandings (and myths). Thus 'offficial' psychology's most heavy investment seems to be in the kind of 'objectification' of human beings which I argue leads often to the exacerbation of some kinds of psychological distress, but does strengthen defences against the recognition of our real and fundamental vulnerability. The psychologist, with his tests and techniques (often grandiosely called 'measuring instruments'), his power to label and categorise, becomes the very personification of the cold gaze of the Other. For the psychologist the mysteries of human nature have in principle been solved, the general scheme of things is established, and it becomes only a question of how to fit the individual most accurately into his or her allotted slot; no longer is there any need to face the agonizing uncertainties which arise out of human beings' relations with each other as they struggle to evolve a social order and a satisfactory conception of human nature (it is precisely this *evolutionary* nature of psychological phenomena, which by definition can have no final end point, which psychology fails to take account of).

The ways in which we bring about our own objectification are thrown into sharp relief through an examination of the psychological test catalogue of Britain's leading publisher of psychological 'measuring instruments'. Such tests are developed by psychologists, commercially published, and made available for purchase only to suitably qualified 'experts' – clearly, if people are to be restricted to their role as objects they must not be allowed to have access to the means whereby their dimensions can be measured; this is an interesting, if tacit, admission by psychologists that the objects of their study are not really objects at all, for if they were there would be little danger of their tampering with their own dimensions in such a way as to make their measurement inaccurate, and consequently little need to keep the means of measurement a closely guarded secret from them. There are in the catalogue many tests which focus on intelligence and other cognitive 'skills' related to memory, perceptual ability, and so on. These 'skills' are thus 'scientifically' established as possessed by people in finite, measurable amounts, and people may be ordered and categorised relative to each other according to the degree to which they possess them. This obviously has very practical consequences in terms of assigning people to particular strata in educational and vocational settings, much as physical objects could be sorted and graded according, for example, to their size and weight. Should people possess qualities which are not stably measurable in the way insisted upon by psychologists, or which are of no interest to, or have simply been overlooked by them, these will of course remain unappreciated and untapped. As well as intelligence and cognitive 'skills', there are many 'dimensions' of 'personality' which have become the focus of psychological testing. A cursory glance at the catalogue shows that you may, for example, be categorised according to the degree to which you are: submissive, hostile, emotional, masculine/feminine, self-sufficient, introverted/extraverted, sociable, anxious, aggressive, creative, controlling, affectionate, cooperative, stable, competitive, confident, mature, healthy, conforming, conscientious, neurotic, independent, depressed, evasive, exuberant, realistic, conservative. To name but a few.

But what possible sense can it make to endow a person with, for example, the characteristic 'affectionate'? People are not affectionate, though their *conduct* might be. Of a *person* one would have to ask *when* is he or she affectionate? With whom? In what circumstances? Under what conditions? Where? In what respects? And the same is true of pretty well all the attributes by means of which this approach attempts to objectify people. Hidden behind this approach is the production-line mentality of our culture, the unquestioned assumption that human beings are to be packaged and graded and valued in the same way as the other, inanimate goods which we learn to covet. Very prominently, the competitiveness of our social organisation is evident as a shaping influence on the ways in which we characterise ourselves – what you are is scarcely conceivable except in terms of how you compare with others. There is virtually no room here for the subjectivity of the person, although, of course, our subjectivity is at work behind the scenes in constructing this kind of picture of our world, and in this example is, as it were, temporarily invested in the psychologists whom we appoint to choose for us how we shall be described as objects.

It is no accident that a central concern of social psychology is with 'self-presentation' and 'impression management'. Social psychologists recognise, accurately enough, that you are what you manage to persuade others to take you as: you cannot validly claim to *be* something which the 'significant others' around you repudiate. What one *is* thus becomes a matter of social transaction, and this in turn inevitably breeds a technology of manipulation and deceit in which the plausibility of the front you manage to present becomes all-important. This brand of social psychology reports faithfully enough on the way things are, and does its best (through 'social skills training', etc.) to make life easier for some of those who have difficulty in coming to terms with some of the more brutal aspects of social existence. What it does *not* concern itself with is the philosophical and moral validity of this view of 'being' – above all it does not question (as, for example, has been done in existentialist philosophy) whether it is in itself legitimate to see human beings as 'being' anything. As long as we take for granted an objectifying culture and its materialistic and mechanistic principles, we quite naturally arrive at a 'reality' in which the essence of human relations lies in manipulation, exploitation, deception and competition. If, however, we took account of our subjectivity (which remains submerged and inarticulate in an objectifying culture) we might have to recognise that, though a person may *do* things in ways which can be described as having this or that effect or value, he or she cannot reasonably be described as 'being' anything in particular. In other words, it may not in fact make much sense to talk about people as *having* 'selves' – in the sense of objectively determinable or describable collections of characteristics – at all. This is not to say that people may not conduct themselves in relatively consistent ways which may be anticipated with some confidence across different times and places, but, understandable though it may be, to slip from this way of seeing their *activity* to describing them as such-and-such a kind of *person* is to rob them of their subjectivity and to deny them the possibility of self-initiated change.

A society in which what really counts more than anything else is what kind of an object one is, is almost inevitably going to end up paying particular attention to people as bodies. After all, objectivity values above all measurable physical dimensions, and even if we feel some slight discomfort about the plausibility of measuring 'personality', one thing that a person's body definitely does lend itself to is weighing and measuring; the body has the advantage of actually being an object in the physical world. Small wonder, then, that our culture is obsessed with physical appearance, and that some of the most acute and painful vulnerabilities that people experience are in connexion with their shape or size.

In recent years, of course, the feminist movement in particular has drawn angry attention to the ways in which women are exploited and abused as physical objects, and it is probably true that more women than men suffer tortures of shame and embarrassment, guilt and self-disgust over their bodies. Massive industries both fuel and feed on this sensitivity. Beauty is a possession which can be owned, or (more particularly) a commodity which can be bought. But it is not only women who suffer in this way, although they are more likely to feel unhappy about their bodies as a whole (that they are simply 'horrible' or 'disgusting' *in toto*); men frequently feel shame about particular parts of their body (noses, hair, genitals, hands, feet, etc.) or about their height (too short, too tall).

However much you may hide your ignoble thoughts or dissemble your baser feelings, your body can be instantly transfixed by the gaze of the Other, may become an all-enveloping emblem of shame from which there is no escape – or almost none. There is no chance of hiding your bulging stomach from your lover's eyes, and you await his judgement as a prisoner awaits the sentence from the bench. No judgement can be more cruel, no sentence harder to bear, than one about which the person can *do* nothing – even the prisoner can expiate his crime.

Phyllis's husband – considered in most respects a kind, conscientious man – told her in a fit of spleen occasioned by her sexual unresponsiveness that he sometimes wished she looked like the girls on the Pirelli calendar at work – their breasts didn't look like fried eggs.

Women – possibly because they are less enthusiastic objectifiers than men – seem less unthinkingly cruel in what they say to men, and, paradoxically perhaps (or simply because they are more used to it), seem quite often to receive such insults more stoically than most men would.

Geraldine talks quite cheerfully about her husband's opinion that her 'arse is like a jelly in a paper bag', and with only a flicker of pain in her eyes. She is in fact obsessed with her physical appearance, and has consulted cosmetic surgeons on more than one occasion, but sees this as her personal concern and is unaware of the potential judgement of the Other on which it rests.

Not only may one be objectified by others into a particular bodily form, but as a paid-up member of the objectifying culture, may oneself use one's body as the objective peg on to which to hang a host of psychological difficulties: there are for example many women who would in any case by most current standards be accepted as looking unusually attractive but who themselves insist that their bodies are in some way substandard or 'horrible'. It is as if this, at least, would be a tangible difficulty, somehow easier to contemplate than the psychological complexities which in truth lie behind their anxiety. Even more paradoxically, unacceptable physical appearance may become a kind of protective shield behind which a person can shelter from the risk of engagement with the world. For example, obese people who try but fail to slim may sometimes be using what they see as their ugliness as an excuse for a dreaded lack of success in life or love: they can tell themselves that they are unsuccessful because they are fat, not because they are inept or unlovable, but to become slim in actuality would expose them to the risk of real failure. Thus although being, as it were, trapped in a body which does not come up to scratch in the eyes of the Other can be one of the most painful humiliations our culture can inflict on people, the defensive aims of objectivity may still be served, even to these people's advantage, by enabling them to use their physical shame to evade responsibility for what they do.

In the absence of a socially accepted and agreed sphere for the operation of subjectivity (which might render physical appearance irrelevant to issues of personal worth), people who find themselves trapped in negatively valued, objectified bodies have three main options. The first is simply to suffer the imposed labelling – ugliness, skinniness, fatness, etc. – possibly turning it to advantage in the way outlined in the previous paragraph. Such a stance is almost bound to be associated with enormous insecurity and rock-bottom self-esteem. The second is to make use of those services in our society which offer to put the problem right in its own terms, for example through body-building, cosmetic surgery, slimming courses, make-up, and so on. This course is by no means always easy, quite apart from the lack of reliability of many of the procedures involved, as it may conflict with other psychological needs: for example, obesity is often the result of comforting one's basic insecurity through eating, and in this case it becomes very difficult to slim and at the same time lose thereby the solace of food, so that insecurity, anxiety, shame and guilt (at periodically giving way to greed) all become compounded in one unhappy existence (in which, for example, binge eating followed by self-induced vomiting may play a prominent part, as may a kind of pervasive guilty secrecy and deceitfulness which extends into areas of life apparently quite unconnected with food).

Because of her parents' – particularly her father's – brutality towards her, June was taken into care at the age of seven. At sixteen, she is a sweetly pretty, somewhat overweight girl who goes out of her way to charm those she meets with a kind of gentle pliability (towards women) and a mild sexual invitingness (towards men). And yet her inarticulate conception of herself is as rotten through and through. She overeats secretly and makes herself vomit, and the staff of the home she lives in have periodically to clear her room of hidden, half-eaten tins of putre-fying food. She hoards dirty underwear in corners of cupboards and drawers until it becomes almost rancid, and she lies systematically about any aspect of her conduct (which in fact involves nearly all of it) which she thinks could put her in a bad light. Despite sometimes desperate efforts to make people love her, she is convinced that nobody could, so that sooner or later she rejects people who have grown fond of her before they get the chance to reject her. There is little in her life other than

*pain, veiled self-indulgence, secrecy, deceit and guilt. Her body she
regards with loathing.*

Because their anxieties stem often from an unhappy but
unexamined subjectivity, people who seek or permit the physical modification of their body through surgery (sometimes
pursuing this aim with tremendous single-mindedness) may
find once their efforts have been successful that the alteration to
their objectified self leaves them no better off than before.

The third course open to those who find themselves imprisoned in a body they have come to hate is to demonstrate their
indifference to it by attempting to overcome matter with spirit.
In some ways this comes close to acknowledging the importance of subjectivity, but nevertheless still makes the mistake of
overvaluing the body as an objectified symbol of self: the
triumph consists not in acting upon the world *through* the body
as an instrument of will, but in destroying or subjugating the
body as a means of proving independence from it.

*After a miserable childhood, a disastrous marriage and a series of
unhappy love affairs, Grace, who used to be a lively, attractive woman,
and in many ways the social focus of her family and a wide circle of
friends, suddenly became extremely 'phobic' (afraid under almost any
circumstances to leave her home), withdrawn, and reticent about her feelings. It became a matter of honour with her not to disclose her unhappiness to anyone – even to her children to whom she was otherwise very
close. She also found herself unable to eat proper cooked meals, and for
years lived off tea and biscuits and the occasional sandwich. Naturally,
she lost a great deal of weight, and became, physically, a shadow of her
former self. To her great distress, she also found that at times, especially
following some kind of emotional friction with someone important to
her, she would experience a compulsion to lacerate her body (usually
parts of her limbs not exposed to public view) with a piece of broken glass
which she kept especially for this purpose. She began to accept only after
a long time in psychotherapy that her experiences and activities – which*

before she had found frightening and alien – could be made sense of as an attempt to establish the independence of her spirit and her will from bodily needs and the need for affection from others. It is of course by no means certain that this is a correct interpretation, but it certainly helped, for both Grace and her therapist, to clarify an otherwise extremely puzzling set of circumstances.

There are many people who display a kind of self-denying asceticism towards their bodily needs, as if any self-indulgence would swamp them with a kind of obliterating objectivity from which there would be no escape: they are aware that the objectified body is a trap, and yet are trapped in their very hostility towards it, cut off from any way of conceptualising their subjectivity other than as a battle against the flesh, and quite unable to enjoy themselves. Several psychologists and psychiatrists have suggested that this kind of fundamental attitude may be what lies behind the puzzling phenomenon named officially 'anorexia nervosa'. Perhaps one of the most illuminating accounts of this condition is, however, not that of an 'expert', but has been written by someone who herself suffered very acutely from it.*

The fact that (particularly female) beauty is regarded as a *possession* in our culture, means that those who do not meet the quite narrow standards established for it, or 'lose' it through the normal processes of ageing, etc., experience a great deal of shame and pain which might be avoided if (as I shall argue in a later chapter could usefully be encouraged) its fundamentally subjective character were more widely acknowledged. It may, in other words, be much more the case that beauty is truly in the eye of the beholder, a phenomenon of personal relationship, rather than an attribute to be measured by the impersonal gaze of the Other.

The insistence of our culture on turning people into

*See Sheila MacLeod, *The Art of Starvation*, Virago Press, 1981.

objectified selves, collections of measurable characteristics centred in bodies valued almost solely for their appearance, means that some form of *self-consciousness* is virtually inescapable. A child may just manage to exist for a few years in an unself-conscious absorption with a world to which it relates through its more or less unreflecting activity, but it cannot survive for long without becoming aware of the importance of others' opinions of it as an object, and so it must learn to dissemble its feelings, attend to its appearance, conform to official standards of education and attainment, manipulate its image so that its status relative to others can be maximised. This requires a constant monitoring of how the self appears to others, an unremitting concern with 'impression management' and a developing expertise in understanding and handling the conceptual apparatus and values of objectivity – the ingestion and acceptance, that is, of the standards of our mythifying culture. 'What does the Other think of me?' becomes the single most important question which can be asked.

Success at the game of impression management entails an almost wilful overlooking of the experience of social life rendered by the kind of intuitive sensitivity discussed towards the beginning of this chapter. Although, certainly, one could not operate fluently in the world without *tacitly* making use of such sensitivity, it is perfectly possible *explicitly* to disavow or disown it. Everyone in one sense knows that the emperor is naked (just as, for example, everyone knows that possession of a Rolls Royce and a beautiful wife is totally irrelevant to an individual's personal worth) but it is expedient to deny what one sees and to profess one's faith in the prevailing values – and if you play your cards right you might end up with the Rolls Royce and the wife, and, most important of all, the admiration from the Other which goes with them. If, on the other hand, you insist on your knowledge of the emperor's nakedness, you may not find the ready assent from others which could confidently be expected only if you assume their good faith toward their own experience; in fact, their strenuous denial that they share your experience may leave you in such isolation that ultimately not only they but you yourself begin to question your sanity.

It is, I think, precisely the stance one takes towards experience rendered by intuitive sensitivity which determines the kind of self-consciousness one will develop (bearing in mind that, as things are, self-consciousness is inescapable).

Those people who are considered psychologically 'healthy' in our society are on the whole those who have a confident appreciation of themselves as satisfactory objects; they have learned, that is, successfully to manage the impression they give to others, and to extort from them a validation of how they wish to appear. They have also learned that to preserve the relative comfort offered by this mode of existence they must disregard or deny what their intuition tells them about its falsity (persuade themselves that the emperor is not really naked); they have describable 'selves' which can, in the best objective tradition, be broken down into a series of positively valued traits or attributes. The truth, of course, is that human existence is uncertain and vulnerable, complex and delicate, and human relationships shot through with pain and threat as well as joy and comfort. The evidence for this truth is available to all but the wilfully blind. The advantage of wilful blindness (of allegiance, that is, to the coarsened values of objectivity) is that it obviates the necessity for the kind of gentle, sensitive, risky, tentative, dangerous transactions required for the conduct of civilised, caring relationships; it replaces the agonising difficulties raised by questions to do with the morality of our conduct towards one another with the simplified values of the market economy. It is thus in the interests of the socially 'successful' to treat people as things or commodities, and to disregard those aspects of their own experience which suggest that to do so is a distortion of the truth.

There are, however, also those who are unable to escape the

evidence of their intuitive sensitivity, even although, often, they can well appreciate the expediency of doing so. Many people who find themselves unable to disregard the insights they gain into the motives and feelings of those around them see their sensitivity as a kind of affliction. I remember one patient who talked for a long time about her 'weakness' until I realised that what she meant was an unusually accurate sensitivity to the real feelings of the members of her family, and in particular to the petty dishonesties and tactical subterfuges to which they resorted in their dealings with each other. Her father in particular had spent most of his time during her childhood in trying to bully her out of her perceptions (even to the extent of threatening physical torture if she did not deny what she knew to be true). She felt confused and guilty about her empathetic ability to understand others, seeing herself as if cursed with the possession of a kind of original sin which made her unworthy of their company. And yet she could not abandon her sensitivity, despite the fact that most of the rest of the population seemed to find it easy to do so.

The affliction of intuitive sensitivity is experienced most often in the form of shyness – the form, that is, of self-consciousness negatively valued in our culture. Not all kinds of shyness stem from this origin, but it does seem to be the case that many of those who experience shyness to an excruciating degree are at the same time people who are very acutely aware of the emotional currents passing between themselves and others. Very shy people often have a kind of raw, flinching sensitivity to others, so that they approach them like cats testing the bounds of their territory. The shy person's consciousness of self is nothing like that of the confident impression manager: the shy person is aware only of a painfully inadequate, useless, negatively valued self, or even of a complete lack of self ('I've got no personality'). In this respect, perhaps, shy people are close to the recognition of a truth which their more confident fellows have more successfully repressed, i.e. that in fact selves of the kind of which they so painfully feel the lack are mythical inventions of an objectifying culture. But they are not on the whole able to articulate this truth nor to gain any comfort from it; instead, they are to be found standing in corners, aching with a sense of their own futility and uninterestingness to others, searching despairingly and vainly for the words that will introduce them to others as worthy of attention and acknowledgment, enviously wondering at the apparent smoothness and ease with which others seem to fill out their existence as forces to be reckoned with and confidently conduct their relations with each other. At the same time, the shy person may secretly harbour a kind of arrogant contempt for the shallowness and boringness of the easy socialiser he or she so bitterly envies, finding solace in the view that when social contacts do materialise in his or her world, they have at least got real depth and significance. But the all too familiar experience is for two shy people, at a party for example, to end up together in a corner, each embarrassed at the obviousness to the others around them of their pathetically settling for safety in mutual support, each secretly disgusted that they could not appeal to someone less like themselves. It is hard to escape the objective culture, and thus not to experience shyness as a crippling affliction. Wherever he or she goes, the shy person feels positively magnified under the gaze of the Other, the inadequacies of self exposed even to the most fleeting glance and most casual encounter, and yet quite unable to abandon his or her intuitive sensitivity to social relations in order to join in the game of impression management.

Although unable successfully to manipulate their appearance as objects, and although the values implicit in their sensitivity have much more to do with subjectivity than objectivity, shy people's experience of themselves is often as almost completely objectified: only others, it seems, can act freely and control their own fate, only others can have opinions or attitudes or feelings which could make an impact on someone's life. For shy people the Other is everywhere, and it never occurs to them that they could be Other for others, that anyone could care what *they* thought about things. They are paralysed, others are free.

That some people seem so easily to be able to disregard their own experience in favour of an objectifying mythology while others are tormented by their inability to do anything other than take their experience seriously presents us with a mystery for which there seems to be no satisfactory explanation, particularly in view of the fact that, as I have suggested, intuitive sensitivity is often maintained despite a wish that it should not be, and in the face of constant discouragement from others that it should be. The kind of shyness which is experienced as so distressing that it drives a person to seek professional help for it seems often to stem from a particular set of circumstances (though this need by no means always be the case). The most familiar pattern is where people found themselves alone as sensitive children in relatively insensitive families, receiving no particular support from anybody for their somewhat inward (but probably psychologically quite accurate) view of things. Never confirmed as an objective self in the same way as those around them (indeed, quite often strenuously disconfirmed as such) they end up with a strong sense of personal worthlessness but an equally strong conviction that their personal experience yields insights about people and their relations with each other which cannot be discounted. Nearly all those who complain in later life of experiencing anxiety so great that it disrupts their lives describe themselves as having been shy as children. It is thus generally felt in our culture that shyness is a negative characteristic, to be discouraged where possible in children, and treated if necessary in adults.

However, it seems to me that this is so only because of the coarsely insentitive values of objectivity to which most of us bear allegiance. Because, perhaps, of their greater awareness of the complexity, delicacy and danger inherent in our relations with each other, shy people often (though again, of course, not always) treat others more kindly and gently, more empathetically and conscientiously than their more confident fellows, and may show greater psychological honesty and perceptiveness than is possible if one is to be successful in the brashly competitive world of objectivity. Shy people are not always wrong to fear the hostility and ridicule of others, since, though painfully and against their will, they may represent a living challenge to objective values, a threat to the continued maintenance of myth. It is perhaps particularly in young male society that the shy person runs the greatest risk of teasing and humiliation, because it is precisely here that objectifying insensitivity is maintained with greatest tenacity. Broadly speaking, young men tend more than anyone else to repudiate their tenderness and vulnerability, and a shy person in their midst threatens to draw their attention to sensitivities they would rather ignore. For a shy young man there can be almost no experience more excruciating than suffering daily the hostile banter of his fellows in a workshop, office or factory, and the degree of isolation and self-doubt that can be generated in such situations, in the absence of solid confirmation or support, can be almost if not quite unhingeing.

Whether virtue or vice, social disease or (as I have tended to argue here) potential spiritual strength, shyness is certainly not comfortable, and does not make for a rewarding life. The obvious answer to this is of course to seek methods of 'treating' shyness in order either to mitigate its more painful effects or to transform it into the kind of confidence which the shy person longs for and envies so much in others. This answer is, however, only obvious if the basic values of our culture remain unquestioned. If, indeed, one were to imagine a world populated entirely by the kinds of people we tend in general to regard as most successful and 'adjusted' – for example by the kinds of 'stars' and 'personalities' whose lives are thought so worthy of our attention by gossip columnists and television producers one might quickly find oneself longing for the presence of a little pained sensitivity and inarticulate, tongue-tying feeling in those around us, for without it we should stand in danger of being overwhelmed by the artificial and the fake. Only sensitivity to our own experience can drag us back from self-deception.

There is nothing objectively 'wrong' with shy people, it is simply that they are misplaced in a culture which cannot afford to endorse their experience. It would seem in the long run more valuable to question the standards of the culture than to attempt to change the people.

One does of course come across a fortunate, but extremely small minority of people who manage to conduct themselves sensitively and spontaneously in the world without recourse to fake objectified selves and without suffering the tortures of shyness; people, that is, who are confident in their subjectivity, guided by their own experience (their intuitive sensitivity), and yet able to relate warmly and openly to others without feeling threatened and without having to take refuge in some specialised creed or dogma to protect them from the Other's objectifying gaze. But the very rarity of such people must lead us to question the healthiness of our social and psychological climate in which the vast majority can survive only by succumbing to the prevailing mythifying standards or by aligning themselves with an opposition to those standards which convinces itself of its worth through adherence to, for example, freakish religious dogmas or a kind of uniform, organised anarchy (itself often orchestrated and exploited by the very forces it purports to challenge).

Most people, then, have given subjectivity up as a bad job.

The prevalence and force of objectivity creates conditions which make it very hard for people to exist as individual subjects, relatively easy for them to experience themselves and others as objects. We have dissociated ourselves from our subjectivity (which, however, we cannot totally eradicate, and which runs riot behind the scenes, creating the myths which we take as the objective standards which must rule our lives) and can therefore only experience life passively, as objects. As people, therefore, we are morally paralysed and powerless rather than being responsible for our own conduct, we see our 'behaviour' as at the mercy of blind natural laws, the existence of which we may establish through the objective methods given us by 'science', but which we cannot conceive as being created by ourselves. Indeed, it has always been one of the more euphoric claims of those bewitched by the determinist and mechanist dogmas of 'modern science' that morality itself is defunct as a conception necessary to the understanding of man's 'behaviour', and is relevant only to the blurred and murky intellectual scene which preceded the scientific enlightenment. The fallacy of such reasoning is, I should have thought, blindingly obvious (since our subjectivity is so clearly at work in the rejection of our subjectivity!) but its influence nevertheless pervades our lives at every turn.

Having the status of object, certainly, may promise (as it happens, I think, falsely) to release us from some of the terrors attendant on subjectivity – for example, from some forms of psychological pain, loneliness and responsibility, fragility and the threat of fundamental failure, the necessity for individual courage and decisiveness. Objective status also delivers, when it is working well, a certain kind of passive material comfort, an apparent freedom from effort in our daily lives and in the conduct of our relations with each other. The lot of the table tennis ball may not be an entirely happy one, but it is spared the tensions experienced by the players, the painful necessity for training and practice, the threat of humiliating defeat at all times it is neutral with respect to the 'rules' which actually govern its behaviour (which are of course enacted by the players) and could, if endowed with a modicum of reflective consciousness, comfort itself with the thought that there is in any case nothing it could do to improve its situation. By placing ourselves in a universe in which *we* are subject to the interplay of laws objectively established as independent of us, we create conditions for ourselves very similar to those of the table tennis ball – batted to

and fro, often painfully perhaps, but at least without having to
take the responsibility for it.

This, indeed, is how many people seem to experience their
lives – so used to responding passively to the force of circumstances that when called upon for some kind of stance, some
kind of directing, subjective moral initiative of their own, they
are left limp and confused, searching helplessly for a directive
from somewhere else, for the requisite objective solution to
release them from their dilemma. This is particularly evident,
for example, in the sphere of child upbringing. Since we have
forgotten that children are subjective, and therefore moral
beings, we expect them to develop like objects manufactured in
stages or, nurtured only by the provision of material necessities,
like plants or vegetables which can be relied upon to produce
the desired characteristics at the appropriate time. As far as
giving *direction* to their children is concerned, many people
seem to feel that this is none of their business, and can only be
done by reference to the appropriate experts and authorities,
since how people *ought* to be is, like everything else, a matter to
be established and programmed objectively. Thus grown men
and women will expect their children to achieve that same
estate without any moral guidance or example from them –
satisfactory upbringing in this sense will, it is expected, be
achieved through the school, the experts, the television, material indulgence, etc., no matter what the extent of parental
neglect of or indifference to their children's spiritual development, and independently of whatever kind of example of how
people are (and should be) the parents themselves knowingly or
unknowingly set.

It is perhaps a sign of the very times I am criticising that I am
likely to be misunderstood as suggesting here that children
should be more severely disciplined and strictly trained in the
conventional moralities than they are. But in using the word
'moral' I do not mean to be moralistic, but to point rather to the
necessity for taking a deliberate stance (as opposed to occupying

one unwittingly and accidentally) towards questions of how we should conduct ourselves with each other, of taking an interest in and being concerned with the way a person develops, recognising and trying to meet their spiritual and emotional needs, making room for them to develop their special interests and abilities, advocating those standards which seem truly in the person's best interests and have been confirmed in the parents' own experience, and so on. For the objectified individual, all such questions (and they are, of course, certainly not unproblematic!) are fraught with threat and difficulty, so that the easiest choice in bringing up children is either to oppress them or indulge them and leave the process of 'socialisation' to those (mythically) better trained to deal with them. The end result, naturally enough, is a generation of hostile or bemused adolescents who have even less conception of themselves as subjective people, as moral beings, than the parents who presided so helplessly and non-committally over their development.

To *stand for* something, whether in child-rearing or any other sphere, is of course to risk error; it is also to challenge one's status as object and to become conspicuous under the gaze of the Other, to give away one's position and to invite rejection. But it is also the only way through which social evolution can take a truly moral direction; it is the inescapable consequence of recognising and taking seriously the fact that it is we who make the world, not 'it' or 'them'.

In the prevailing conditions it is of course quite likely that anyone who does take a stance will stand out as eccentric in some way, or will certainly feel in danger of so doing; in any case he or she is likely to find it a lonely experience.

Annette (p. 36) is one of those people who have been unable to abandon their own experience. She observes others with an acute intuitive sensitivity which she communicates with great warmth and humour, and her descriptions of what passes between herself and those she is close to strike me often as highly perceptive. She can at times be movingly passionate about what she sees as valuable or suspect about the way people treat each other, and takes, for example, a deep interest in her own and others' children, so that she might find herself reflecting for hours at a time on the significance for her of a relatively fleeting (and by others unnoticed) event. Though she had a less than average education and comes from what most would consider a rather deprived background, there would clearly, were she given the chance, be few intellectual tasks beyond her. But despite all this she experiences herself as a kind of ludicrous simpleton, feeling that people regard her as a mildly contemptible oddity, impractical and unable to deal sensibly and stably with the ordinary demands of life. Partly, certainly, she is blind to the degree to which people do in fact appreciate her, but partly also she is an isolated moral force in a sea of objects who see her propensity for taking stands as mere foolhardiness.

Our culture seems to have much to offer those who opt for an objective existence: libraries and popular bookshops, for example, are full of advice on what objective rules to follow to bring about a wide range of desired end results, from becoming slim and beautiful to achieving sexual joy, phenomenal powers of memory, ability as a creative writer, successful motherhood, and so on. You simply practise the 'skills' which the experts have managed to distil from their objective knowledge of things. But there is very little on offer *at the same level of availability* to those who seek help in enlarging their understanding of what their own experience tells them to be the case, in elaborating and enriching the stand they feel bound to take indeed, they might well find themselves admonished for their temerity and advised to leave any such dangerously subjective enterprise to those better qualified to understand such things. Thus whoever takes a stand does so in fear and trembling, and no doubt their risk of error is greater because of their isolation from any confirming culture which acknowledges the value of subjectivity. Moral support is in short supply.

Drained of subjectivity, we are deprived of all those

potentialities which are associated with it – instead of acting we can only react, we can consume but not create, follow but not initiate, conform but not determine. Objectivity devalues and ultimately nullifies the abstract, the spiritual and the moral, replacing them with a coarse materialism which brutally asserts its own justification as simply self-evident. Nothing which is not concrete and measurable is held to exist – ideas, meanings, emotions, wishes, intentions, are dismissed as pre-behaviourist, 'mentalistic' clap-trap. Thus the person finds him- or herself as a mechanism in a machine world, confused, helpless and morally paralysed because out of touch with any means of influencing that world, frightened and bewildered when personal experience suggests that the myths of objectivity do not in fact confer the blessings expected ofthem, but still unable to harness that semi-articulate experience to any effective form of intervention as the world becomes more and more dehumanised.

Security and passive stimulation through consumption have become our primary preoccupations. To escape the annihilating possibility of an entirely negative objectification and to enjoy the material 'benefits' of a mechanised existence constitute, respectively, our greatest anxiety and our foremost aim. The operation of these concerns is clearly to be seen even in what ought otherwise to be our most delicate and tender transactions: for example, sexual love becomes in part a battle to hide and protect one's most vulnerable, tender sensitivities from the partner at the same time as extorting from him or her the maximum of physical stimulation. Not seeing that tenderness and sexuality are inextricably related, and that denial of the former leads to impoverishment of the latter, the objectified 'lover' is seized by a craving for stimulation which becomes the more desperate in proportion to the emotional anaesthesia which underlies it – an anaesthesia which is likely to be misidentified as arising from, perhaps, a lack of 'expertise', or an unduly prudish attitude to what, it is thought, ought to be the limitless opportunities of sexual licence, in which pornography, mechanical aids, 'sex therapy' and so on all have their proper part to play. Only someone prepared to abandon his or her subjective experience in favour of an objectifying, mechanizing mythology would find him- or herself supporting this kind of sexual philosophy; the solemn reverence in which sex therapy is held by professional psychologists and psychiatrists, as well as the enormous economic success of the sex-aid and pornography 'industries', suggest that such abandonment of experience is on no small scale.

Many people who seek help for sexual 'problems' view themselves in this way – with, that is, a kind of bemused objectivity which utterly fails to place their sexuality in the context of a relationship (although 'relationship' is a word all too glibly used to characterise the unexamined situation in which two nervous or hostile strangers find themselves in bed together). Sex has become a mechanised commodity (in which failure of the sexual 'equipment' is seen precisely as mechanical breakdown), and the pursuit of sexual satisfaction a feverish campaign which, because it misperceives the nature of intimacy, is doomed to empty frustration. Sex is, indeed, our sad substitute for intimacy: the last shred of comfort which can be extracted by some of those (frequently women) most damaged and objectified by our depersonalising culture is through their being physically arousing to another.

Apart from a somewhat coldly critical concern that she should conform to conventional standards of behaviour, Margaret's mother had been largely indifferent to her as a child, leaving the practical aspects of her upbringing to an older sister, who herself had taken on the job none too willingly. Her stepfather, on the other hand, was viciously punitive towards her, and was particularly suspicious and censorious about possible sexual misdemeanours, even before she had reached puberty. Margaret's primary conception of herself is as an obstacle, a nuisance, a bad object, there only to inconvenience the lives of others. She is shy,

*slightly awkward and ungainly in her movements, and has an underfed,
pinched air about her. Her clothes haue a distinctly second-hand look,
suited more to a maiden aunt than a girl of nineteen. She has no friends
of either sex. Surprisingly, in view of a rather incongruous primness and
conventionality about her manner, she confesses with anguish that she
considers herself morally beyond the pale, as she is virtually addicted to a
disco club in town, following attendance at which she almost invariably
finds herself having sex with someone on the building site which adjoins
it. The boys or men are never the same, and they never take her home or
ask her out. Following these episodes she always feels shame and disgust
with herself, and vows never to go back. A lot of things in her experience
of her past life seem to contribute to this almost compulsive pattern, but
not the least important factor is that these brief, sad and in many ways
degrading sexual encounters provide the only warmth in her existence:
even she can stimulate someone else's body to some kind of interest in
her, and be wanted for a moment. It is important to note that Margaret
feels no sexual satisfaction or excitement in these 'relationships', and
indeed in this respect feels positively anaesthetised.*

Freud did us no great service, perhaps, in suggesting that the
origin of intimacy and tenderness is to be found in sexuality, but
this view still holds sway despite the arguments which have
been levelled against it, forcefully and cogently, by several influential psychologists and psychiatrists since Freud's time.* Only
the adult who has overlooked what it was like to be exposed to
the full blast of what H. S. Sullivan called the 'lust dynamism'
could mistake the child's need for and expression of tenderness
as 'really' sexual, and Freud's views have always stretched the
credulity of those who have paid serious attention to their own
and others' experience of sexuality as it makes itself known in
puberty. This is not, of course, to say that non-sexual love and
tenderness do not entail their own powerful and potentially

*See, for example, I. D. Suttie, *The Origins of Love and Hate*, Penguin
Books, 1960; H. S. Sullivan, *The Interpersonal Theory of Psychiatry*, Tavistock
Publications, 1953; E. Fromm, *The Art of Loving*, Allen & Unwin, 1957.

destructive forces, nor that hatred and jealousy form no part of the child's experience. The appeal of Freud's view can in part be understood in the opportunities it presents for objectifying the otherwise subjective, and in some respects abstract concept (faculty, experience) of love. Though only indirectly a concern of Freud's, the possibilities for measurement and reduction to physical properties offered by the identification of love with sex were too good to be missed, and an uncomfortably subjective phenomenon was turned into a manageably objective one. Freud thus played into the hands of a concern for objectification already rampant in our culture, the subsequent achievements of which are readily to be seen all around us. These include the belief (which of course engenders the appropriate 'behaviour') that a 'good' sex life will provide the foundation of happiness and satisfactory relationships, as well as the confused response to the discovery that this does not actually happen. In fact, sex out of the context of an intimate and loving relationship is not usually found to be particularly satisfying at all, but because of the power of the myth of the primary importance of sex, experience of this is attended most often by an increasingly desperate attempt to extort validity for the mythical proposition. In this way an anaesthetised sexuality has to be increasingly stimulated and heated up if it is to be preserved at all in its mythified role as the foundation of our psychological structure and the origin of our possibilities of relationship.

The fact that we must relate to each other as objects, the continuous presence of the Other's gaze which threatens almost literally to turn us to stone, mean that real intimacy is indeed almost impossible to achieve. Intimacy would involve an effort to explore each other's subjectivity, to listen charitably and experience empathetically, to shun labels and categories, to be alert to uniqueness, to allow the possibility of evolution in the psychological and relational spheres, to acknowledge uncertainty and creativity while trying to articulate and examine in good faith the stance we take to each other and the world.

Instead, the characteristic and familiar way we relate to one another in our objectified interpersonal space is to bristle with suspicion and hostility as we seek to evade and impose our labels on each other. We listen to each other only with ears cocked critically for objective fallacies in argument, itching to anchor the struggle for meaning in some concretely measurable error. Most conversations between two people are double mono-logues in which each party seeks to establish for him- or herself a kind of massively impregnable solidity of 'being'. We project our safely established objective evaluations over each other, anxiously attempting to expunge every trace of ambiguity or uncertainty, only satisfied when we have pinned down and categorised each other like so many dead butterflies, suitably varnished with the viscous language we have developed to prevent the last possibility of change.

CHAPTER FOUR

The Domination of Words

Without the use of language we should not be able to represent either to each other or to ourselves our views of reality and truth. It is only through using words that we can agree about the nature of the world and describe our experience, make objective what we sense and feel, give concrete form to dimly perceived meanings, build concepts which we may test against the experience of others, extend our processes of thought and memory so that we can criticise and elaborate them to a degree of complexity which would otherwise be quite impossible. We live in a medium of words.

In giving concrete, objective form to our experience, words take on a kind of hard finality which makes them difficult to resist as the determiners of truth. *Sharing* the meanings of words constitutes an important step towards objectifying the things they refer to – clearly, nothing could be considered objectively established if individuals could not be brought to agree about its nature. In this way language implies almost by necessity an objective world, since, if its members are to be able to communicate sensibly, the community which speaks a given language *must* share the meanings embodied in it. This object in my hand is a pencil, and about that one would expect every competent speaker of English to agree: it is 'true' that it is a pencil, a 'real' object in the world, about the existence and nature of which it is easy to suppose there can be no dispute. Naming something goes a long way towards defining it objectively, and we can quite easily forget that the name is in fact no more than a conventional sign for a whole complex of meanings, experiences, expectations, etc. Through language the unknown is made known, the inarticulate articulated. Simply to describe something is to remove from it a degree of anxiety-arousing mystery. Patients told their diagnosis may feel relieved even though they have not the slightest idea what the diagnosis signifies. Popular science programmes on the television thrive merely through giving names and incomprehensible descriptions to phenomena utterly mysterious to the viewer. ('This', says the presenter, 'is a molecule' – and the camera zooms in on a structure of wire and plastic balls, leaving the average viewer not already acquainted with molecules presumably satisfied but surely none the wiser.)

Of course, it is obvious on reflection that words are in a sense arbitrary, that, even when their meanings are universally shared, they carry no reality in themselves, no guarantee of objective truth (where 'objective' here implies a truth beyond what people simply agree about). A pencil could equally well be called something else, and in any case lays claim to our attention only because we have endowed it with a particular function: it cannot be considered apart from the human purposes we have created it for. Even a pencil is not exactly a 'thing in itself'. But though this is fairly obvious, I think that in the ordinary course of our daily lives we forget that words are things which, fundamentally, are attached to our experience for reasons which suit us. Even logical truths (like 2+2=4) are presumably of interest only to human minds. But rather than seeing words as our own creation, we become mesmerised by them and by the concepts which we have created with them, and we find it hard to shake off the idea that they relate to an absolute and *impersonal* reality. We tend to forget that words are the result of our imperfect struggle to articulate our experience (and thereby to *create* an elaborate linguistic network of metaphor for our experience), and see them instead as the representatives of a reality which *imposes itself upon* us objectively.

In many matters of general agreement – as, for example, what constitutes a pencil – doubts and difficulties about truth and reality can for present purposes be left to philosophers. In other areas, however, this is not the case. For example, there are many areas of discourse in which the ordinary person takes on trust the 'fact' that names are meaningful in the same way that 'pencil' seems to be meaningful. This is particularly the case where names carry the endorsement of experts – especially 'scientific' experts. Few people not acquainted with psychiatric controversy, for example, would question that there is a 'mental disease' called 'schizophrenia'. Yet many people who are so acquainted argue that the concept of 'mental disease' is a myth (which may perhaps be another way of saying that, on closer acquaintance with the phenomena involved, it is not the case that, for example, 'schizophrenia' refers to anything about which agreement is possible in the way that 'pencil' does). I believe that much of the language we use to describe our psychological distress and the social context in which it occurs is mythical in this sense. Our everyday language, thus, supports the mythical view of the world discussed in Chapter One, and many of the verbal concepts we use are those imposed upon us by our cultural bias towards objectivity.

It might be objected here that if, as I have suggested, words are attached to experience arbitrarily, then *any* verbal formulation of experience is mythical. But by 'arbitrary' what I mean to suggest is that words in themselves have no *necessary* reality or guarantee of accuracy, even though they appear to single something out in experience to make it real. I do not mean to say that words become attached to our experience haphazardly or at random. *How* we attach words to experience will reflect the purposes for which we wish to use them: for example, either to try to describe our experience as accurately as possible, or, on the other hand, to force it into pre-set moulds.

These points will perhaps seem obvious to anyone who has given any thought to such matters, but it may nevertheless be worth reminding those (both lay and professional) who too readily take it on trust that the nature of the world as described by prestigious and socially accredited people (doctors, scientists, academics, psychologists) must be accurate, that such is by no means necessarily the case. Indeed, there seems to me to be a real danger that, at the everyday level of social living, we may become unaware of there being any reality beyond language: what can be *said*, if it is uttered with enough authority, or by someone with a sufficiently convincing 'image', simply becomes part of the received truth and does not have to be questioned or judged. Evaluation and judgment are subjective faculties which pay attention to the content of an utterance and decide whether or not to accept it. Passive acquiescence, on the other hand, is manipulated by 'authorised' sources of objectivity, in which the content of the utterance is unimportant compared to the 'credibility' of the utterer (hence, presumably, the obsessive concern of the news media with 'images' and 'personalities' as against the actual substance of what people say). We have, in other words, given up our ability to judge the nature of the world, to believe or disbelieve in any active sense, but rather wait in a slightly bemused way for our opinions to be revealed to us by those accredited to do so. 'Belief', indeed, is a concept anathema to objectivity, because it is rooted in the subjective person rather than in the 'verifiable', concrete structures of the world; so, in our objectifying language, the *activity* of believing is turned into the *possession* of 'credibility'. That the Other has credibility removes from you the trouble of believing or disbelieving. Words are the medium through which we become turned into passively consuming objects; they cut us off from access to our own judgement and experience because they impose upon us a ready-made world which we must accept as true because it is objective.

If this state of affairs is to be counteracted, it becomes vital to reassert the distinction between experience and language. This is not necessarily an easy distinction to make, since experience and language are so clearly interrelated, and indeed without language the distinction could not be made at all, nor could experience be described. It is also possible to argue that language *determines* the form of our experience, so that the two could not be considered as in any sense distinct. It is certainly true that one could not *think*, in the sense in which that term is usually taken, nor reflect upon experience, without the use of words. It is also true, however, that words are *not* necessary for the execution of highly complex and purposeful activity which must depend for its success to a great extent on the organised living-out of experience (there are many different ways of trying to say this, none of them very satisfactory: for example, one might say that we live out our experience in an organised manner, or that we act in an experienced manner, or that we have ways of organising our experience which are not verbal). Anybody who doubts the phenomenon I am trying to refer to need only watch a cat catching a mouse.

These issues do not allow simple answers, and are, clearly, philosophically and psychologically very complex. However, quite apart from the academic arguments involved, my own experience of, in particular, collaborating with patients in the investigation of their difficulties and dilemmas convinces me that it is important to focus on the distinction between experience and language, and that doing so reveals two very clear functions of language which are not immediately apparent to naive reflection. The first, already touched upon, is that language has come to be used in our society as, so to speak, the blunt instrument of objectivity; the second is that, in this age at least, the primary function of language has become that of misrepresenting the truth.

The world is given to us in our experience. Indeed, as infants, we experience the world in advance of any ability to describe it, and we make our most fundamental evaluations of and distinctions between our experiences long before we have acquired language (it has always seemed to me entirely wrong to assume that babies are somehow not very clever: the intellectual demands on a new-born infant must be enormous, and its ability to deal with them prodigious).

The use of language gives us two possibilities in relation to our experience: we can describe it (to others, or, more essentially, to ourselves) either in good faith or in bad faith. We can, that is, either use the linguistic tools that become available to us to represent as accurately as possible the nature of the world we find in our experience, or we can attempt to force our experience into the ready-made (objective) structures which are culturally embedded in our language. To take the first course is to remain true to our intuitive sensitivity, to take the second is to run the risk of succumbing to the prevailing mythology.

Language presents us with the opportunity for constructing realities alternative to that given more immediately in our experience. The opportunities open to animals to misrepresent the nature of the projects they engage in are not great, though they are certainly not absent. A dog admonished as it starts to enact a clear intention to steal the Sunday joint may feign a kind of indifference to the meat, perhaps by diverting its stealthy approach to some more innocent aim; gestures of submission nullify what was but a moment before a cat's blatantly aggressive conduct. But on the whole such attempts at dissembling are transparent and easily understood, and there is little chance of an animal being able to lie effectively in the sense, for example, of pursuing a project while appearing not to (unless its entire existence is an embodied deception, as through the medium of camouflage). But human beings may much more easily pursue a particular line of conduct while using the possibilities given by language to claim that their intentions are quite otherwise.

Ben's mother told him one day: 'You have two ways of smiling – one when you're happy, and one when you've been naughty.' The following day she walked into the kitchen when Ben (aged three) was taking some forbidden sweets from a cupboard. He turned towards her, smiling, and said: I'm smiling because I'm happy.'

Quite apart from the chances it gives us for lying and dissem-

bling, the magic of language enables a palliative gloss to be
placed over painful experience, and the power of words is such
that, once a person has become linguistically accomplished, an
alternative construction of experience can be as compelling as
the experience itself. Since the means whereby we represent
experience to ourselves are linguistic (i.e., we can only think
about experience through the use of words) we become in
some senses the victims of our own articulateness; it can come
to seem that what we tell ourselves is all there is to tell, that
reality is what we tell ourselves about it. And further, language
already contains culturally constructed palliatives for painful or
puzzling experience – the child may find it hard to question its
mother's authoritative view that, for example, its rage or frustration is 'tiredness', which is but a small step from accepting,
say, the doctor's view that terror-stricken confusion is 'schizophrenia'. Our ability to reflect upon our experience is only as
good as the linguistic tools available to us to do so – the less
articulate person may have an awareness that 'something is not
quite right', but will not be able to make that awareness
concrete without having his or her consciousness 'raised'
through the provision of finer and more sensitive (linguistic)
concepts. (This is one of the ways in which the more educated
exercise dominion over the lesser.) For everyday purposes, it
seems that reality *is* the best description I am able to give myself
of it.

One need only reflect on one's own experience to be
convinced of the power language has to construct alternative
versions of events – think, for example, of an occasion when
something happened between you and somebody else which
constituted at the time a painful blow to your pride or an
enraging threat to your peace of mind. The chances are that in
the course of the hours following this event you reconstructed it
'in your mind' several times (i.e. told yourself several alternative
explanatory versions of it) until you settled on a version which
seemed best to account for the facts. The chances are, too, that

the version which best accounted for the facts was also one which left least injury to your self-esteem.

The relativity of 'truth' is nowhere more evident than in the accounts married couples give of issues of contention between them. It is a familiar experience for 'marital therapists' to find that, as they make their assessment during the initial stages of therapy, they are so impressed by the wife's account of her husband's brutality and insensitivity – so coherent, heart-felt and well integrated is her story – that they can scarcely contain their indignation. When the husband is interviewed, however, *his* account of the same events shifts them into a new perspective, in which his pained reasonableness, his desperate frustration at his wife's capriciousness, can only testify, so it seems, to the truth of what he is saying. One does not, of course, conclude that either partner is lying – both stories are in one perfectly good sense 'true', but both are indeed stories – accounts that each party has elaborated to him- or herself until they accord most comfortably with the reality each has constructed. Where one's self-esteem is implicated, it is extremely hard to stand in a relation of good faith to one's own experience.

One of the myths most firmly embedded in our popular culture is that the individual has a special claim to accuracy when accounting for his or her own conduct – that I can see better than you what my projects and motives are. Thus it is not on the whole considered inappropriate, when seeking an explanation for someone's conduct, to ask him why he did it – indeed, there are many situations in which it is considered not only proper but essential to extract such an account, as if its extraction provided the shortest and most accurate route to the truth. This is not to say, however, that, for example, the indignant parent or the suspicious policeman does not recognise that the person subject to inquiry might lie about his motives, but it does suggest that there is an expectation that the truth is available to him if he chooses to tell it.

However, anybody used to talking to small children who have not yet achieved a practised ability to give plausible accounts of their actions will have been struck frequently by the nature of their inability to render any such account. The question 'why did you do it?', however insistently posed, is likely to be met by a kind of blank puzzlement which only those blunted by insensitivity or blinded by theoretical prejudice are likely to interpret as just a stubborn refusal to produce the truth. It seems clear that small children act unself-consciously and unreflectively in the sense that they do not attach words to what they are doing, and depend for their ability to learn how to give such verbal accounts on linguistically more mature people *telling* them why they act as they do. After a time they begin to be able to tell *themselves* what others have told them, but not necessarily with any greater accuracy.

Jeremy was a ten-year-old in the care of the Local Authority. He had spent the first two hours of one particular morning barricaded in his room, systematically destroying every object in it, including the windows. Eventually he was extracted by the staff and subjected to a searching inquiry by three child care officers as to what was disturbing him. Anxiously concerned, gently and without any threat, they asked him in every way they knew how why he had done it, what was worrying him. They racked their brains to present him with possible alternative explanations, but always with a request for his affirmation or denial. In other words, they were absolutely convinced that he knew the explanation for his conduct, and that he could in principle put that knowledge into words. However, it seemed clear from his expression of pain, confusion and bewilderment that Jeremy had not the slightest idea why he had acted as he had. What he desperately needed (and did not get) was someone to tell him why, so that he himself could acquire a verbal purchase on his anguish. (Telling someone the reasons for his or her actions, or the nature of his or her feelings, is one of the most difficult and easily abused responsibilities of loving.)

Honest reflection on one's experience would, I should have thought, strongly suggest that the situation with adults is little different from that with children. The explanations we offer for our actions are no more than accounts which may or may not be accurate, but which have no special claim to truth simply because they are given by the person whose conduct is in question. This becomes most clear in those situations where our professed intentions are at odds with our fundamental desires. The man who has promised himself and others to give up smoking might, at the end of a desperate day without cigarettes, tell himself that he is going to take the dog for a walk. As it happens, he walks the dog past an off-licence where he 'decides' to buy a can of beer for himself and a bar of chocolate for his children. As he makes these purchases, he impulsively buys a packet of cigarettes, telling himself that if he has a packet in the house it will calm his agitation even though he will leave them untouched. Half an hour after arriving back home he 'decides' that just one cigarette will relieve the withdrawal symptoms sufficiently to enable him to get through the following day without smoking. His massive dishonesty would of course be apparent to anybody who watched him, and quite possibly his wife knew from his first expression of altruistic interest in the dog what his true intention was.

Most of the time, perhaps, our conduct is sufficiently free of conflict for us to be able to provide a relatively accurate commentary upon it, and this can easily lend plausibility to the belief that the commentary (which is likely to be replete with terms such as 'decision', 'intention', etc.) somehow precedes and even causes the conduct. It may only be at moments of despair, when conflict has driven us into a position which we had sworn to ourselves never to occupy, that we catch a glimpse of the disjunction between actions and words. In fact, I think, we are in no better position than anyone else to say why we do what we do. We, as they, must 'read off' the reasons for our actions, the intentions saturating our conduct, from the activity itself, and since we may often have a greater stake than they in the valuation placed upon our conduct, our interpretation of it may have a much weaker claim to truth than theirs.

That people's own accounts of their actions have any particularly privileged claim to accuracy has long been rejected by most psychologists, and it is now quite well established through carefully conducted experiments that people can perform complex intellectual tasks, or skilfully execute highly sophisticated intentional activity, without having any conscious awareness of how they do it (i.e., without being able to put it into words), although they might be quite ready to give more or less plausible accounts which they themselves feel convinced are true.★ It is also, of course, one of Freud's greatest claims to fame that he showed how people could be utterly unaware of the determinants of their actions, and he argued quite explicitly that the motives which lurk in our 'unconscious minds' lurk there not least because we manage not to attach to them words which accurately describe them.

However, in our everyday dealings with each other we tend to have an unquestioning faith that, unless people choose to lie, the verbal explanations they give of their actions and motives are the most reliable indications we have of what they actually are up to. Even our most revered institutions, as, for example, the legal system, depend often on this assumption – although witnesses may be called to cast doubt on defendants' veracity, it is frequently assumed that the latter could give a true explanation of their actions if they chose to, unless, perhaps, they were 'suffering from' 'insanity'. It is thus a widespread assumption throughout our culture that a person's activity is the result of a process of deliberation in which, before embarking upon any particular course, he or she draws upon a kind of cerebral

★A particularly interesting, though technical, account of much of this experimental work is given in R. E. Nisbett and T. D. Wilson, 'Telling more than we can know: verbal reports on mental processes', *Psychological Review*, 1977, vol. 84, pp. 231–59.

commentary in order to 'decide' what to do. No doubt we are misled in this by virtue of the fact that the only way we have of communicating in any kind of analytic detail about our conduct is through words – even sports coaches or teachers of music are forced to rely heavily on words in order to make available to reflection the utterly inarticulate performances of their pupils. It is thus easily, if naively, concluded that, say, an accomplished batsman is guiding his actions with a similar, though internal, kind of commentary, when in fact, of course, everything happens far too quickly to allow of any such possibility; he can only criticise his performance verbally *after* the event.

As a general rule, then, we assume that if a person gives us an account of his actions which he sincerely believes to be the case (i.e., he is not lying) this is the best guide we have as to the true state of affairs. It is the prevalence of this myth which makes possible the phenomenon of self-deception. That people are capable of 'kidding themselves' is of course something widely acknowledged in our culture, though I suspect that this possibility is considered only in relatively rare and fairly superficial cases; what we do not recognise, I think, is that self-deception is the characteristic mode of existence in this society, nor that it is the combination of self-deception and our excessive over-valuation of words which maintain the objectifying structures of our culture.

To say that people deceive themselves is not to question the sincerity of their utterances – the element of dishonesty in self-deception exists more at the level of experience than at that of words. Indeed, dishonesty may not itself be the best concept to invoke in this context: on the whole, people deceive themselves through lack of courage rather than lack of honesty, or even simply through lack of clarity about the predicament in which they find themselves – one may deceive oneself because one lacks the courage to face the implications of one's experience, or simply because that experience is so confused and puzzling that one opts for a relatively non-threatening interpretation of it. But in either case there is no doubt that people believe the stories they tell themselves.

Janet had become an increasingly frequent visitor to her general prac- titioner over the course of two years or so. She complained of violent headaches, dizzy spells and bouts of vomiting. She had been examined by several specialists and tried on a wide variety of medicines, but all to no avail. The doctor's suspicion that her complaints were 'neurotic in origin' increased in proportion to the imperviousness of her symptoms to the usual treatments, and he therefore inquired after her psychological well-being – whether anything might be worrying her at home, etc. Janet immediately perceived what was in his mind, and angrily repudi- ated any suggestion that her symptoms were 'psychological' or 'imagi- nary'. The situation deteriorated when a friend of Janet's mother-in-law died suddenly of a brain tumour, some of the symptoms of which had been dizziness and vomiting – Janet became convinced that she had a tumour herself, and insisted on seeing a neurologist. Like the other specialists she had consulted, he also found no physical abnormality, and suggested to her general practitioner that Janet's symptoms were indeed 'neurotic'. Once again, the doctor's – this time slightly more insistent – inquiries into her psychological circumstances revealed nothing of significance.

Janet, as he knew, had been married for five years, and had two little boys, one four and the other two years old, of whom she was very fond (the doctor knew she looked after them well, bringing them to the surgery when they needed medical attention, etc., and he also knew that her home was well kept and carefully looked after). Her husband was a self- employed joiner, and worked very hard, and successfully, to provide for his family – he was in the process of building up his business, had recently taken on two workers, and in fact was making quite a lot of money. Janet was always smartly dressed, and had a new car of her own. Neither she nor her doctor could find anything in these circum- stances to suggest that her symptoms were 'psychological', but he never- theless persuaded her, considerably against her will, to see a clinical psychologist.

*Interviews with the psychologist – about an hour every fortnight –
extended over a period of eighteen months. At first Janet talked most
about her symptoms, and there was no doubting her fear that she might
have a brain tumour, nor that she viewed the hypothesis that the symptoms were 'psychological' with hostile scepticism. The picture she had
given her general practitioner of a happy domestic life was also at first
that which she painted for the psychologist. However, it emerged over
the weeks that a rather different view could be taken.*

*Her own family background had not, it transpired, been a happy one
(though Janet's initial statement had been that 'you couldn't have a
better Mum and Dad'). She had felt dominated by what she saw as a
more successful sister who was the apple of, in particular, her father's
eye. Her mother was a worrying, uncertain person, cowed by her
husband, who himself drank heavily and had been periodically violent
towards both Janet and her mother, though never her sister. It took Janet
some weeks to acknowledge that she had been miserably unhappy in this
household, and that the feelings she bore both her father and her sister
bordered on hatred. She still felt close to her mother, and visited her
often during the daytime, when her father was at work. It was evident to
the psychologist that Janet felt extremely guilty at voicing (putting into
words) the feelings she had so long avoided confronting.*

*She had married at the age of eighteen, largely, as she now saw it, to
escape from home, but also because she was moved by her husband's
affection for her, scarcely able to believe that anyone could prefer her to
her sister. It took several months before the psychologist could gain a
clear view of her marital situation: at first she represented it to him as
almost ideal. After an initially happy time, her husband became increasingly preoccupied with his work, and she only saw him briefly late in the
evening or on Sundays. Her two small children she found extremely
demanding, and sole responsibility for their welfare made her anxious;
she worried about shouting at them too often. She spent as much time as
she could with her mother, who seemed by now to be her only source of
support. As Janet grew to trust the psychologist, and indeed to allow
herself to review her own experience, she revealed further details of her
life – for example, that on two or three occasions, when feeling at her*

loneliest and most despairing, she had been to bed with her husband's best friend when he had called round during the day. This seemed to have done little for her other than make her feel guilty. Very soon after she had begun to confront her painful experience, Janet's concern about her symptoms began to diminish, though from time to time there would be a resurgence of anxiety about them, often, it seemed to the psychologist, when she was about to come face to face with further unpalatable truths.

Now it could not plausibly be maintained that, at the time she consulted her general practitioner, Janet did not in some sense 'know' about her unhappy family background, her loneliness in her marriage, her affair with her husband's friend, and so on. What was also clear, however, was that she *genuinely believed* that her physical sensations (of anxiety) were in fact symptoms of an illness, which her mother-in-law's friend's death eventually persuaded her to be a brain tumour. In fact, Janet restricted her knowledge of her predicament to what she *told herself* about it. She was not, so to speak, critical of her experience. After all, her mother and father and sister were features of an *unquestionable* experience which constituted her reality – they were her family, and one is supposed to love and honour one's family. She had no first-hand knowledge of what else a family could be. Similarly, her husband was doing only what husbands are supposed to do, and for her to take seriously her unhappiness would have been to raise questions which could not be raised without the most threatening and painful implications, and though her brief affair constituted an attempt to assuage her loneliness, it formed a part of her conduct which, again, did not have to be reflected upon with words. She could preserve her normality, her existence within the world in which everyone is expected to live, simply by not attending reflectively to her actual experience of it. She was married to a man who was by all standards doing his best for her and their children; there was no other life obviously available to her, no situation she could envisage which offered greater happiness without causing enormous distress to others and herself. Her pain and confusion thus demanded an explanation which, though apparently not to be found in the natural, immediate usualness of her day-to-day existence, was from her point of view afforded much more adequately by the hypothesis that she had a brain tumour.

As long as we restrict what we 'know' to what we are prepared to tell ourselves, we can (at the cost, of course, of some considerable discomfort) preserve the myths by which we wish to live. Our culture almost invites us to take a stance of bad faith towards our experience, since it provides us with a common verbal currency which is designed to protect us from the dangers and risks of subjectivity. In Janet's case, for example, there was no particular community for her to turn to which could provide for her a context in which to examine critically her experience. There was nothing so outlandish about her background or her marriage or her situation as mother (indeed, I have deliberately described a 'case' which typifies the existence of countless women) which seemed to justify pain on the scale she felt it. Our 'objective' standards would indicate, in fact, that she was particularly advantaged in relation to the majority of her social peers – she had a 'decent' upbringing and a 'good', hard-working husband and 'two lovely children', and she was financially well off. Having, as it were, put obstacles in the way of her analysing her situation according to her actual experience of it, however, the objectifying culture does provide alternative concepts by which it may be 'understood', e.g., through the concept of 'illness'. It takes particular courage and tenacity in these circumstances to reject the ready-made, objective framework in which one may conceptualise one's difficulties, and to advance instead an analysis based upon one's own subjective position.

To take a stance of good faith towards one's experience, to take heed of one's intuitive sensitivity, is to assert the values of subjectivity and to challenge the thick, heavy, objectifying verbal concepts which monopolise our reality. The emperor's mythical clothes are woven with words, and their close, heavy texture can be unpicked only through a courageous, isolating and often painful attempt to make articulate what one senses to be the case without becoming enmeshed in concepts already in the service of myth. Perhaps this is why those philosophers and others who have written in support of the subjective are so difficult – for the Anglo-Saxon mind, at least – to grasp: it is as if they need to dodge and duck their way between the ponderous, pinning-down objectifications of our common conceptual language in order to provide subtlety and space for the development of subjective insights. But this is not the concern only of philosophers: as I shall argue in the next chapter, our very anxiety is at least in part an insistence that our experience be taken seriously, a symbolic expression of the fact that our everyday language is not capable of taking true account of our pain.

There is no way of saying much of what we sense and feel, and it is probably our culture as much as ourselves which determines what can be said (in this respect Freud was perhaps unfair in emphasising so strongly the role of the *individual* in repression – i.e. in detaching words from actions – and suggesting that this is largely a pathological process). In fact, though we live, deceptively and self-deceptively, in a construction of reality depending heavily on our conscious, verbal accounts of it, our conduct towards one another, indeed our transactions with the world as a whole, take place very largely without the use of words. In this respect we are not so different from other animals as we think. A number of concepts which are built into our everyday language make it very difficult for us to appreciate the significance of this state of affairs – most of us see language as simply describing things, and fail to notice that it may embody an entire philosophy which is utterly misleading. Again, it may only be at moments of particular conflict or distress that one becomes aware that ordinary language does not do justice to experience.

For example, one particularly important area in which our everyday concepts fail us – and one which it is essential to clarify if we are to achieve any understanding of psychological distress – is that surrounding the idea of responsibility.

The attraction of self-deception is so great not least because the main alternative to seeing our distress as somehow inflicted upon us – as, for example, 'illness' – is to see it as being our 'fault'. Our language certainly affords us the possibility of being objective bodies open to attack by malign organisms or prone to mechanical defect, and on the whole illness carries no imputation of blame. Over the last hundred and fifty years or so, more and more 'behaviour' which was once seen as the individual's personal responsibility has been redefined as the effect of illness – for example (quite apart from actions definable as arising out of 'insanity'), alcoholism, some kinds of sexual aberration, and even some forms of criminality. Naughty children may now be seen as 'suffering from' 'behaviour disorders'. In part one can see the value of this kind of view – it is more humane than the otherwise punitive attitude which may be taken towards deviant conduct, and maybe, even, it contains a tacit acknowledgement of the fact that people are frequently at a loss to account for their own actions. But it is precisely this assumption – that if 'behaviour' is not 'caused' by, for example, illness, then the person must be able to account for it – which leads us into difficulty. As long as we believe that people's ordinary activity is carried out in response to a kind of internal monologue in which decisions are taken, intentions settled upon and consequences calculated, we are likely to conclude that when their conduct takes an undesirable course it has done so because of their deliberate perversity. If, in these circumstances, they insist on withholding from us an account of or an acknowledgement of their wrong-doing, we are likely to assume that they are compounding their guilt by lying or malingering.

Thus the patient who consults her doctor about acutely distressing symptoms of physical dis-ease, when told that these have 'no organic cause', is forced to consider the imputation inherent in our conceptual system that she is 'imagining' them. Many patients, having exhausted all the possibilities offered by physical medicine, say with a kind of hopeless despair, 'I know it must be me' or, 'I know it's my imagination', as if all they can reasonably expect (and, of course, they frequently get it from doctors of the 'old school') is a sharp reprimand or an exhortation to pull themselves together. But because they know that they cannot even tell *themselves* why they feel as they do, and because conceptually there seems no other possibility open to them, they continue secretly to believe that there *must* be some-*thing* 'causing' their complaints.

If, however, the arguments put forward in this chapter can be accepted – i.e., that our conduct does *not* have to be within the reach of words – then a third possibility opens up: that we struggle to understand our actions in the same way that we struggle to understand anybody else's; we try to see what reasons we might have for acting the way we do, 'read off' our intentions from our activity without assuming that we must know in advance what they are. This, certainly, implies an acknowledgement that our conduct is indeed our own, and nobody else's, and that the reasons for it are our reasons, and hence that we are responsible for what we do. But the concepts of 'fault' and 'blame', I think, legitimately apply only in situations where we do indeed know what we are doing, and *that* what we are doing is socially disapproved of. It is of course much easier to be aware *that* we are doing something than to be aware of *why* we are doing it. Thus in these situations, and in *some* respects, we can give an accurate commentary on our conduct. In most cases at least, when I park on the yellow lines I could give a clear account of what I'm doing, and how, though I know the significance of yellow lines, I calculate that in the ten minutes I intend to stay parked there no traffic warden or policeman is likely to pass by – if one does, I can scarcely claim diminished responsibility or maintain that I am not to blame. In this way, the law defines for us those situations in which we must take care to spell out *some* of the (social) rules applicable to our actions, and, indeed, limits itself by and large to those situations in which we can. In contrast, when driven by inarticulate terror to run screaming from an enormous bloated spider advancing across the carpet, I have no such coherent account to give of my actions (nor is there any *social* necessity for one), though I am still responsible for running and screaming, for these are nobody's actions but my own. Thus fault and blame are concepts relevant to situations in which we know *that* we are breaking rules in a *social* context.

To extend these concepts into the psychological sphere, by, for example, implicating them in a demand that we know *why* we are doing something, is neither useful nor legitimate.

The attitude which it is reasonable to adopt to the kind of responsibility I am trying to elucidate here is not one of blame, but rather one of interest, tolerance and concern. I presumably have my reasons for being afraid of spiders, and they may well be understandable; I am certainly not wilfully withholding them either from myself or anyone else, and I should actually quite like to know what they are.

Of course, 'spider phobia' is a fairly common phenomenon, and although one may feel rather silly about it from time to time, it is unlikely to make one feel a social outcast. Many people who find themselves tortured by either more severe or less familiar forms of anxiety, however, feel that, unless a suitably exonerating 'illness' explanation can be found, their apparently irrational fears – quite apart from being open to construction as their own 'fault' – render them absurd. This may again be put down to the myth that others are 'normal' and act always according to a coherent (verbalisable) analysis of their situation. Perhaps the anxious person's shame at his or her supposed 'difference' from others would be lessened by the realisation that all of us, most of the time, do not know why we are doing what we are doing.

The fact that any kind of answer is difficult to give does not mean that it is idle to inquire into why we do what we do, for in making such an inquiry we may begin to grasp the importance of our subjective stance in the world. Accepting responsibility for our conduct merely means that we acknowledge that we have reasons for it, and that those reasons are ours. This at least has the merit of ruling out the possibility that they are anybody else's reasons, or that, as passive objects, we are caused to do what we do by external forces. We thus remove one of the prevailing myths of an objectifying culture – i.e., that our conduct is *determined* by causes outside ourselves which can be revealed only through scientific analysis by appropriately qualified experts. Even our most incomprehensible actions, it may turn out, are the result neither of our badness nor madness (nor even helplessness) but rather arise from a perfectly reasonable and understandable construction (our construction) of our experience, even though that construction is lived out in our activity rather than transmitted through the medium of words.

In seeing how this can be the case, however, our language is once again sadly inadequate to the task. Most of the difficulty seems to stem from our deeply ingrained habit of thinking of mind and body as two qualitatively different kinds of thing, in which the latter depends for its proper functioning on the instructions of the former. Before, that is, the body can actually be got physically into motion, it is felt that something must be wished, or wanted, or decided by the mind, and, as I have already suggested, it is further often felt that the wishing and wanting and deciding which take place do so in some kind of verbal manner, or at least in a manner which can potentially be put into words. In this way we are led to suppose that we are in control of our bodies as a crane driver is in control of his crane, and that if we want to know the significance of our conduct, all we have to do is consult ourselves. Hence the puzzlement of people who 'find themselves' doing unaccountable things, or unable to do 'obviously' desirable things. It is, for example, characteristic of people gripped by anxiety that they may feel compelled to do things which they don't 'want' to do, or incapable of 'deciding' to do things which would appear clearly to benefit them. The severely 'phobic' housewife cannot, surely, *want* to live the life of a recluse, but though she sees the advantages of leaving the house to do essential shopping, she cannot 'decide' to open the front door, although that is what she 'wants' to do. If the crane appears to behave irrationally, it makes sense to inquire into the reasons from the driver, for here person and machine (mind and body) are indeed two separate entities, the one controlling the other. But one may harangue an anxiously conflicted individual endlessly without becoming any the wiser as to the reasons for his or her conduct. Nor is it that such people are exceptional by virtue of their predicament: in fact, they provide particularly clear examples of what is the case with all of us, and demonstrate the futility of our adopting an inquisitorial attitude to ourselves in seeking the explanation of our conduct. The language of 'explanation', in which the individual inquires into his or her own wants, wishes, intentions, decisions, etc., is a maze of hopeless confusion.

A person's desires, wants, decisions, etc., cannot be separated from their *bodily* enactment. We can only talk as we do about such concepts by abstracting them from the physical structures of which they are a part, and falsely turning them into nonphysical objects. This is a point well recognised by psychologists, particularly those of the 'behavioural' school; their mistake, however, was to conclude that because, say, 'purposes' could not be seen as non-physical *things* there could be no meaning to the term 'purpose' which was not reducible to something much more 'scientific' like 'behaviour', which could itself be seen simply as the 'response' to 'stimuli'. However, it is not the case that 'behaviour', or as I prefer to call it, conduct, cannot be seen as purposive, but merely that purpose cannot be abstracted from what people *do*. The woman who claims that she really *wants* to go out shopping when actually she always stays indoors is not taking full enough account of her conduct. The only way one can really be clear about what one wants is to look at what one does. Presumably she claims to 'want' to go out since that would accord best with what she thinks she *ought* to be doing, but in making the claim she fails to recognise that in fact being terrified is a very good reason for *not* wanting to go out, even though not going out has clear disadvantages of its own. While going out would solve some problems (and is therefore to that extent desirable) it would create considerably worse ones, not least of which would be the person's becoming inundated with fear. There is therefore nothing either shameful or puzzling in concluding that the fact that she stays in suggests that the 'phobic' person does *not* want to go out. Once this is agreed, she can perhaps begin to see that her conduct is not simply crazy or wilfully bad, but actually forms part of a stance she is taking for reasons which are perfectly understandable. We must read off the nature of our desires and purposes from the conduct in which we find ourselves engaged. To do this we need, as suggested before, an attitude towards ourselves of interest, tolerance and concern, in which it is far more fruitful, and indeed accurate, to assume the fundamental rationality of our conduct than it is to anticipate its moral reprehensibility. There is no shame attached to not knowing why one does what one does, and indeed no special credit to be accorded the person who can give an instant explanation.

As with 'wanting', so with 'deciding'. Many people feel alarmed at the idea that their activity is anything other than the outcome of a carefully monitored series of decisions, and their alarm can reach panic proportions if they find, as they are likely to, that at times of stress the control which normally they seem to have over what they do suddenly evaporates. But here again it is the 'abnormal' experience which points to the true state of affairs. I do not feel that there is any convincing case to be made for our activity's being the result of decisions which we settle upon from time to time as we conduct our internal deliberations. Our activity is or is not itself decisive, and our decisions are made in and through our conduct. The anxious woman who hovers inside her front door waiting for a 'decision' to go out is in fact *acting* indecisively, and the 'decision' to go out is only made as the activity itself is carried out. We can indeed abstract decisions from our embodied activity in order to talk about them, but we cannot *make* them in this way – no amount of talking to oneself can constitute a decision. Decisions come into being with their bodily enactment. Again, because we do not first 'make' decisions somewhere inside our heads before we actually act 'upon' them, this does not mean that our conduct must be somehow impulsive and unpredictable (which is a fear difficult to shake off if one is wedded to the 'internal commentary' theory), for it is not only language which is ordered and rational. The pianist's activity is no less controlled, purposive or decisive for being unattached to words. Here again we are easily misled by the 'crane driver' model of behaviour: if the crane were suddenly to start doing things not instructed by its driver, one could of course reasonably view its movements as in a sense dangerously irrational. But to account for our own conduct we neither need nor have 'drivers' sitting inside our heads telling us what to do; and, as many others have pointed out, even if we had it would solve no problems, for then we should have to account for how our 'decision maker' makes its decisions (presumably by having another 'decision maker' sitting inside *its* head), and so on and on.

Appraising, wanting, intending and deciding are all accomplished through our total embodied activity, in which verbal reflection plays a relatively insignificant part. If we want to achieve a verbal understanding of our conduct we must observe very attentively what we do. And if our available vocabulary is found inadequate to the task, or fails to do justice to what we see, or imposes upon us conceptual structures which distort our experience, we shall simply have to struggle to refine it.

I am convinced that these are no mere abstract or empty philosophical issues. Our inarticulate subjectivity is at work constructing our lives and our world at every level of social organisation, while our objectifying linguistic culture is busy articulating an almost entirely mythical version of what we are about. Language here becomes the tool of bad faith, its central function to deceive. At least in part the explanation for this is to be found in the defensive function of objectivity – its myths protect us from the threat, the pain, and the sheer hard work of getting to grips with what we actually do to and with each other. It is easy often for the psychotherapist to see this process at work in individuals, and to some extent, perhaps, to correct it. For example, the man who claims that all he wants to do to achieve lasting happiness is gain promotion at work, when in fact his every action sabotages that possibility, may be made aware that he has a deeper project of failure which is in fact much more important to him than is his avowed aim. At more complex levels of social organisation the same processes may be seen at work, though here it is less easy, but (desperately) more important, to become aware of them: governments, for example, assure their national populations, as well as each other, of their peaceful intentions, while at the same time moving towards the most aggressive and destructive (and self-destructive) confrontation imaginable. The child who knows that the emperor is naked also knows that the man of peace does not build an arsenal. If the analysis in this chapter is correct, the most terrifying possibility is opened up: it is not simply that governments are lying, or bluffing (or, indeed, deterring), or can be trusted to be in some kind of skilled control over their projects, but that they may be *deceived* about the aims of what *they themselves* are doing. Again, just as the individual can disclaim responsibility for acting upon the *reasons* for his or her conduct and can change them, through the obliging offices of objectifying language, into 'causes' which he or she 'cannot help', so societies can blind themselves to the institutions and interests ('pressure groups', etc.) which, *out of their awareness*, shape their policies. As the individual needs to wake up to his or her intentions by reading them off from his or her conduct, so collectively we need to see that our activities may betoken something quite other than what we *sincerely* avow, and that unknown to ourselves we might have the most appalling aims. The only way we can criticise or communicate about what we are, as subjects, making of ourselves and our world is to establish between our language and our experience a relation of good faith.

The conceptual vocabulary of objectivity, as has been observed by several critics of contemporary society,* pushes us more and more in the direction of seeing ourselves as containers or owners of objectified forces which, so to speak, pursue their own existence within us (rather as one might envisage the crane-driving decision maker doing). Partly this has come about through the gradual conversion of verbs – i.e. words to do with activity – into nouns. Thus, being unable to do something becomes 'having a problem', wanting something becomes 'having a need', making love becomes 'having sex', and being good at something becomes 'having a skill'. The human being thus becomes a kind of box of tricks (some good, some bad), a programmable automaton in which the needs, problems, skills, etc., can be slotted in or out like floppy disks in a computer.

The project to mechanise people (to which I shall give more detailed attention in a later chapter) represents the ultimate in objectification, and certainly, if successful, would absolve us from the demands of responsibility and the terrors of subjectivity. But we can assent to it, and to its manifestation in the use of language, only by standing to our experience in a relation of bad faith. Paradoxically perhaps, it is particularly in those situations where we are said to have 'broken down' that

*See for example E. Fromm, *To Have or to Be*, Jonathan Cape, 1978. Also, I. Illich, *Tools for Conviviality*, Calder and Boyars, 1973.

the inadequacies of our objectifying concepts are most apparent, and where the inescapability of our subjectivity is revealed. At these times, if we are honest, we may be able to see and accept that our conduct is constituted by our own assessment of and responsible reaction to our situation in the world, however painful that situation is, and however wordless our reaction to it. This is obviously not to suggest that we deserve what we get or that the individual is responsible for the predicament which gives rise to his or her fear and pain. The evils of the world are absolutely real, and not to be wished away as the maladjustment of individual people. How we deal with them, however, is up to us, personally and collectively. There is no 'them' to whom the job can safely be left.

CHAPTER FIVE

The Language of Anxiety

In using our everyday language and the concepts embedded in it, we tell each other and ourselves more or less what we want to hear. The comfortably familiar, objective and objectifying verbal structures with which we surround ourselves are designed to reinforce the myths by which we live and reassure us that the boat in which we all find ourselves, even if it rocks a bit at times, is fundamentally under firm (objective) guidance and control. If, occasionally, we find ourselves feeling more than usually queasy, this is likely to be regarded as the result of a malfunction somewhere in the system (most probably in the individual's 'adjustment' to the world) which, given the requisite expert attention, can quite likely be put right fairly painlessly.

The two chapters following this one will deal in greater detail with the ways in which our society meets the threat of psychological distress – and in particular anxiety – but here I want to consider first the possibility that the kind of 'symptoms' of which people complain are not merely indications of something's having gone wrong which can be put right, but rather are forms arising out of people's *experience* of the world, and constitute almost a language on their own, though a subjective rather than an objective one. Acute distress and anxiety are such ubiquitous and pervasive phenomena in these times that they can scarcely be dismissed as in some sense unnatural, unfortunate hiccups in the smooth running of our everyday lives, and I believe they are to be taken seriously, not by our trying to eliminate them as mechanical defects in an otherwise satisfactory system, but rather by attending closely to their *significance*.

It strikes me as a surprising fact that, although they have identified some of the most important features of 'symptoms' of distress, psychologists and others have failed to recognise the implications of their own observations. For example, 'neurotic symptoms' have (unlike symptoms of physical illness) been characterised as *learned* phenomena by a wide range of psychological writers, and as *symbolic* phenomena by, in particular, psychoanalytic thinkers. However, though, as I shall argue shortly, I think both these characteristics *are* typical of the phenomena in question, the latter have continued to be treated by almost all concerned *as if* they were curable symptoms. In other words, though many people have seen clearly that these 'symptoms' have features which make them quite unlike the kinds of symptoms of illness with which we are more familiar (like, for example, the symptoms of a common cold), they have nevertheless been so caught up in the 'symptom' analogy that they have continued to treat them as if the very features they have remarked upon do not exist. It seems to have escaped the notice of nearly all psychologists and psychiatrists that, for example, 'treatment' is not an appropriate procedure to apply either to symbolic or to learned phenomena, even when they have acknowledged that such is the nature of 'symptoms'. So great is the power of our myths that even when their falsity is laid bare we continue to be ruled by them. In this case, it seems, we simply cannot afford to give up the idea that anxiety is the remediable sign of mechanical breakdown, and so, in the manner typical of self-deception, we contrive not to pay attention to our own discoveries concerning its nature.

Far from being a mechanical fault, a 'symptom', a 'dysfunction' or an indication of 'maladjustment', the experience of anxiety constitutes an assertion of the real nature of our subjective engagement with the world. To fall prey to anxiety is, at least partially, to fall *out* of self-deception, since the phenomenon of anxiety is an insistence that the subject's experience be taken seriously, that the person's *actual* predicament cannot and will not be ignored.

Were words really as powerful as we would like to make them, we could indeed manufacture an endless series of alternative worlds in which to live. Merely by inventing a new way of interpreting the world – verbally remodelling it, so to speak – we could magic away any painful circumstance in which we found ourselves (there are indeed forms of 'psychotherapy' which attempt to do precisely this, as we shall see in Chapter Seven). Because different people have different perspectives on the world and describe it in different ways, and because the same person can also experience similar events in very different ways at different times, it is easy to be encouraged in thinking that there is no hard reality behind the seemingly infinite relativity of views which can be taken of it. But to suppose this would be as foolish as to suppose that, because we have free will, we could do *anything* we liked, and is to overlook the fact that, though we can describe an experience in very different ways and from many different perspectives, the experience has a reality of its own which cannot simply be talked away. The experience of anxiety indicates to us that there are features of our world which we can no longer afford to ignore. Nobody would suggest that the panic attendant upon your being charged by a bull in an open field would best be 'treated' by taking a tranquilliser, but rather that its prompting to you to take to your heels could usefully be heeded. Although anxiety has longer-lasting effects and less easily identifiable referents than does fear of charging bulls, its 'message' may not be all that dissimilar, and the threat to which it relates none the less real. Anxiety, I believe, tells us that the world is a place of real terrors which we ignore only at our greater peril. We mythify anxiety precisely because we *do* wish to ignore the terrors to which it points.

However clever we are at telling ourselves comforting stories, however sophisticated our ability to deceive ourselves, we actually *are* engaged *bodily* in a *real* world which cannot be wished (or talked) away. The evils of the world hurt us because they impinge upon our embodied existence, and they can be changed only through our embodied intervention in an actual world (not by 'thinking' of them in a different way, or by the 'treatment' of their effects on us through interference – either physical or mental – with the way we perceive them). Our involvement as subjects in an actual world affects us in ways we cannot escape, however unpalatable we might consider that involvement to be and however much we might wish it to be otherwise.

A married woman, referred because of her 'frigidity', confesses (or comes to see) after a time that she is not frigid at all, but is in love with someone other than her husband. 'But I don't want it to be like that,' she says, 'I don't want to have those feelings with Bill; I want to have them with my husband.'

Our feelings, then, insist on recognition even though, in our accounts, we can dissemble endlessly. Although we can fake our experience through the way we describe it, and even if we can blind ourselves to its significance, we cannot fake the experience itself.

As suggested in the previous chapter, that we talk about things as being 'imaginary' or 'all in the mind', etc., is the unfortunate consequence of a misleading philosophical split between mind and body. This gives us the chance to see 'worries' as things which take place somewhere inside our heads, and thus as of little consequence, while actual bodily sensations are seen as mechanical events most properly the province of medicine. Thus worry becomes a phenomenon internal to the individual – perhaps 'imaginary?' – and to be combated by, for example, positive thinking or pulling oneself together, while sensations of physical discomfort are to be dealt with by medication or surgery. In both cases it is quite easy to leave out of account the actual evils of the world which may well be – almost certainly are – playing a part; presumably these are to be coped with by those of us clear-sighted, level-headed and healthy enough to deal with them as 'problems'. To deal with anxiety as *either* mental (worry) *or* physical (illness) thus serves the myth that the evils of the world do not have the evil *effects* which in fact they do have (in giving rise, among other things, to the *meaningful* pain which is anxiety) and renders them as, at worst, practical 'problems' to be overcome in an otherwise well-functioning system.

Mrs Eliot has four children and an alcoholic husband who, though a pleasant and affectionate man when sober, can be verbally cruel and sexually brutal when drunk. They live in a small terraced council house on a 'problem' estate, and Mrs Eliot's neighbours are unremittingly noisy and aggressive. She has no close friends, and her relations with her own family are strained – her father used to beat her savagely, and her mother dealt with life by taking a submissive and thus rather ineffectual stance towards most difficulties; she is therefore little support to her daughter. Because of her childhood experience, Mrs Eliot's fundamental (inarticulate) view of herself is as worthless, and hence as extremely lucky to be taken notice of by anyone, however badly they might treat her. Two of Mrs Eliot's children are bed-wetters (though both she and her husband are clearly very fond of them, this is probably in part the consequence of the almost continuously high levels of tension in the household). Though he made good money when working, Mr Eliot has been unemployed for two years, and money is tight. Mrs Eliot works non-stop: shopping, cleaning, taking children to and from school, washing sheets, cooking for an endless succession of her husband's friends and relatives at all times of the day and night, managing the household budget as best she can, suffering the humiliation of those dependent upon the state for basic financial security. Occasionally she is overcome with 'symptoms' of anxiety (dizziness, headaches, breathing difficulties, burning sensations, etc.) and, puzzled and frightened by what she takes to be signs of illness, she consults her general practitioner fairly frequently at these times. She was once diagnosed by a psychiatrist as an 'inadequate personality' and heavily tranquillised. Nobody, least of all herself, saw that, in view of the circumstances of her life and her living conditions, she was in fact coping with almost superhuman adequacy, and nobody made the connection between what was happening to her and how she felt.

Psychological distress and anxiety are of course bodily feelings – i.e., physical sensations *with a meaning*. They are neither imaginary ('in the mind') nor purely the result of mechanical breakdown, but expressive of a certain kind of embodied relation with the world. Sadness at the death of a loved person is not (yet!) considered a treatable illness, nor is the physical experience of ecstatic happiness (at, say, falling in love, or winning the pools) taken as an indication of madness. We are used in these circumstances to ascribing people's *feelings* to the particular form of their engagement with the world, but the demands of myth-preservation mean that we are quick to abandon the conferring of any such significance to the moods and feelings created by the intractable evils of our social organisation. Somehow the Mrs Eliots are supposed to sort out their familial, marital, social, economic and housing (etc.) 'problems' without being seriously affected by them; if they are so affected, they are deemed to be 'inadequate' or 'ill'. Certainly, Mrs Eliot herself thought she ought to be able to cope, and *could not understand* why she felt so 'ill'.

All our feelings are *about* something, that is, are felt in relation to a real state of affairs or an actual experience. As the evening draws on, Mrs Eliot becomes increasingly tense waiting for her husband to return from the pub, because she can never be sure whether he will be sober, friendly and 'normal', slightly drunk and maddeningly, inappropriately (in view of her state of near exhaustion) jovial, or very drunk, shouting and wildly abusive. The tense anticipation with which she awaits his arrival is a *bodily* state – like everyone else, she experiences the world with her body, and, in view of her circumstances, there can be no mystery about the pain she experiences. Whatever the grounds on which one distinguishes signs and symptoms of illness from other kinds of distressed state, one cannot correctly advance the view that illnesses are so classifiable because of their physical characteristics – *all* experiences are physical, since it is with our bodies that we do the experiencing. It does of course seem to be possible that a person may become distressed solely because of *internal* mechanical (bodily) malfunctioning (as, for example – as far as one can tell – in the case of pre-senile dementia), but it is a grave mistake to suppose that *all* physical discomfort must originate in this kind of way. Human beings exist in a delicate and sensitive relationship of mutual transaction with their surrounding world, which itself can only be experienced, or indeed altered, through bodily engagement with it. To 'medicalise' indications of pain and distress which arise *between* people and their world is, literally, to dislocate people from the context in which they live and to obscure from them the possibility of their acting *morally* on the world to improve it. The same mistake is made by choosing to locate the 'problem' in the way the person sees the world (i.e., in his or her own head). Thus, when distressed or anxious people say either, 'it must be illness because the pain is real,' or, 'it must be my imagination because the doctor says I'm not ill,' they are falling for one of our commoner myths – i.e., that psychological pain is not bodily pain.

There are other myths which help to make it possible for us to deceive ourselves about the nature of anxiety. One, already touched upon in Chapter Two (p. 40) is what one might call 'the myth of spatio-temporal contiguity' – i.e., that one's sensations of anxiety must be immediately linked either in space or time to some kind of clearly definable stimulus. Thus it may be thought that you cannot possibly be afraid of something unless you know what that something is (that is, it is immediately present 'in your mind'), or at least unless that something is *there* *with* you at the time. Mrs Eliot, for example, might well say that she cannot understand why she should 'get these feelings' when she is sitting quietly in the empty house watching the television. To be overcome *then* with anxiety or feelings of distress, she might feel, must indicate that she is ill rather than anxious because 'there is nothing to be anxious about.' But, of course, Mrs Eliot's past and her future do not disappear simply because she is on the face of it able to have a moment's respite in the present. The pain of her parents' (at least perceived) rejection of her and, more importantly, the insecurity it generated, do not evaporate simply because she is in a different time and place, nor does the sickening dread occasioned by the near certainty of her husband's future drunken rage get blotted out (indeed, it is increased) by his temporary absence. These experiences and anticipations are part of the very structure of her body, and they do not go away just because she is 'not thinking' about them: that she does not rehearse her misery in words to herself does not mean that it ceases to be present in her embodied existence. Just as any chance event – a sight or sound, for instance – can remind one of a current, or even past preoccupation, so a word, a gesture (even something on the television!) can bring one face to face with the *state* of dread in which one lives.

There are schools of psychotherapy which attempt to use a variant of the 'spatio-temporal contiguity' myth to avoid the inconveniences caused by the fact that we are subjective beings engaged in a *moral* relation with our world. What we should do, these 'humanistic' psychotherapists suggest, is learn to live in 'the now', 'fully and richly experiencing' the world immediately present to us, shaking off our morbid preoccupation with the past and our gloomy anticipation of a future which might never happen. But this lotus-eating philosophy again takes us out of relation to our world just as surely as the 'medicalising' approach, and at least implicitly denies our moral concern, since the latter simply could not exist without an acute sense of past and future. For instance, the moral subject recognises that if a painful past is not automatically to be reduplicated in the future, some *person* will have to intervene. (It is interesting to reflect in this context that some parents insist on their children suffering the same privations that they did while others are determined to use their experience to shape a less painful world for their children. I would speculate that the former are among those who place their faith in the objective correctness of our institutions, while the latter accept the importance of their subjective role.) This kind of 'humanistic' therapy thus advocates, albeit unwittingly, a kind of solipsistic self-indulgence which makes the individual an end in him or herself, and the future of the world an irrelevance.

There are other questions raised by Mrs Eliot's predicament to which we need to pay attention – for example, why does she, particularly in view of the fact that in terms of capacity for hard work and practical ability she is by no means incapable, put up with her lot with such apparent docility? The 'experts' will quite likely point to her lack of 'social skills' and 'assertiveness' and may suggest 'programmes' of 'training' to make good the 'deficits'. But here again, I think, we find ourselves in the world of myth, dealing this time with a version of the myth of 'cure'.

Those who advocate the overcoming of 'problems' through appropriate courses of 'training' would probably reject the idea that they are in fact caught up. in the myth of cure, and would want to point out that theirs, far from being a medical approach, is one based on psychological ideas concerning the nature of learning (Chapter Seven will deal with some of these issues in greater detail). However, 'official' psychological ideas about learning are on the whole far from enlightening, and have paid almost no attention to features of learning which are starkly obvious to the most casual reflection. Because psychological views of learning as applied in the field of 'mental health' rest largely on the theory that people learn through a process of 'conditioning' (i.e., the automatic establishment of habitual connections between 'stimuli' and 'responses') it seems to follow that people can be 'deconditioned' and 'reconditioned' if the original 'conditioned responses' turn out to have unfortunate or unwanted consequences. It thus becomes possible to think that Mrs Eliot could be put through a course of training which would replace her old faulty and inadequate ways of coping with her 'problems' with new and more effective habits. This, I think, is as an approach scarcely distinguishable from more overtly mechanistic notions of cure or repair, in which the person is seen basically as a machine which can be adjusted to optimal functioning through the requisite expert tinkering.

Mrs Eliot does indeed live her life the way she does because of what she has learned. But what she has learned she has learned as a living, embodied subject in a difficult and often cruel world, and the significance of her experience is unlikely to be erased or eroded through intervention based on the inane theories and practices of those indoctrinated by a half-baked and myth-infused 'official' psychology.

Some of the earliest lessons which Mrs Eliot learned were those which taught her insecurity. For reasons already explored in earlier chapters, she cannot rehearse those lessons in words, but her body knows the feeling of living under the Other's cold and rejecting eye. She does not complain about her lot because she sees no reason to: the worthless have no right to complain, and it is easy to see (though, of course, she could not say it) that Mrs Eliot counts herself lucky that *any* man should take an interest in her, and that her children do not openly revile her for the useless reject she knows herself to be. It will take more than a course in 'assertiveness training' from some brightly confident, earnest young psychologist to convince Mrs Eliot that the world is not a place which can easily do without her, and that the best thing she can do is stay inconspicuous and get what appreciation she can through service to others.

In talking about learning, psychologists have failed to take note of learning's nature. One learns insecurity in the same way that one learns to swim or to speak English. Even though one's ability may get a little rusty with time, one does not forget how to do the breast-stroke, nor can one be 'deconditioned' from knowing English or, for example, 'cured' of riding bicycles. One learns through committing oneself bodily to an engagement with the world, and the very structures of one's body are changed thereby. Though you might live abroad all your life and never meet a fellow countryman, it is likely to be your mother tongue which comes to your aid at times of pain or stress, or forms the words you whisper on your deathbed. Similarly, the person who knows the annihilating blows which the Other can deal is likely to be thrown into an all too familiar state of dread whenever life ceases to run more or less smoothly.

The myth that we can with ease free ourselves of the lessons of the past is constantly reiterated and reinforced by our official institutions as well as by the organs of popular entertainment. How many film or television villains, for example, are talked out of their black past and evil ways in a five-minute chat with a wise priest, a well-meaning policeman or a worldly-wise, tough-but-loving *pater familias*? Even though they must know better, haunting the back of many psychotherapists' minds, I bet, is the seductively magical idea that wise, or clever, or technically brilliant words will change patients' lives. This myth lurks behind the search for, and offer of, a thousand kinds of cure, from those of the conventional doctor to the faith healer, the brain surgeon to the spiritual guru. Behaviour therapists, hypnotists, counsellors of every kind and description, psychiatrists and psychologists, teachers, advisers, dieticians, experts in meditation and relaxation, all make the same implicit offer – to rid you of your experience of a painful world. If I am right when I suggest that we can no more be cured of insecurity than we can of knowing English, then it seems clear that that offer is bogus.

The anxious or insecure person has good reasons for feeling that way: reasons which spring from his or her bodily engagement in a real world and which will not for long remain obscured, however thick the blanket of myth which covers them. This is not to say that one can do nothing about the reasons for one's dread, only that the solution to the 'problems' they pose is not to be found in somehow juggling the individual's interpretation or perception of his or her experience. Though such juggling may usefully and validly form *part* of a process in which people begin to gain a subjective purchase on their predicament, it is, in the end, their actual embodied relation with their circumstances which counts. And, even then, new experience does not obliterate old. If a naturally acquired knowledge of English ceases to serve your needs, or if the crawl becomes more essential to your purposes than the breast-stroke, you may commit yourself to a relatively difficult and effortful process of learning a more appropriate language, or the new stroke, but in doing so you will not lose your former abilities. Our bodies do not acquire experience as does magnetic tape, but rather than being erased our earlier and more fundamental experiences provide the foundations on which (and the framework in which) later experience is built. Thus people whose insecurity is fundamental to their experience will, except perhaps in only the most unusual of circumstances, almost certainly *never* become fundamentally secure, though they may come to be able to acknowledge their insecurity in ways which mitigate its intensity and minimise the effects it has on the actual conduct of their lives.

The view that insecurity, and the anxiety it gives rise to, are acquired states of being rather than curable 'symptoms', and are as indelible as other learned acquisitions such as language or physical accomplishments like swimming or riding bicycles, has not occurred to me solely as the result of any kind of theoretical reflection, but has been imposed upon me as the result of my experience, particularly, but not by any means only, with patients. As part of a bureaucratic system of hospital treatment (which was for many years my role) it was easy to persuade oneself that patients who came for some form of psychological treatment – referred, often, through a long chain of medical practitioners – had been successfully 'treated' once they had been 'discharged' from care, for they rarely represented themselves for further attention. As much as anything, however, this was probably the result of their being absorbed by some other part of the referral chain if they sought further help on subsequent occasions. Working, in more recent years, closer to the community in which they live, I have been struck by how patients, even when they have made very great therapeutic progress, may well re-present themselves for further consultations perhaps on several occasions, but never with quite the same 'problem'. It seems likely that they come back to me because, in contrast with the hospital situation, they know how to find me.

Just as a person whose native language is English may, when living abroad, fall back on it when knowledge of the foreign language is inadequate to meet some particular task or challenge, so the insecure person falls back into the fundamental experience of insecurity whenever events arise to challenge his or her competence in dealing with them. Quite apart from anything else, even the most painful fundamental experiences have the advantage of familiarity. The rejected child at least learns to cope (enough to survive) with rejection, and so may in later life even *seek it out* in preference to an altogether more risky relationship of closeness and confirmation. Better the pain of loneliness than the risk of a new experience of annihilation. One need not have recourse to psychoanalytic jargon ('repetition compulsion') to understand such a process: people deal with the present in terms of the methods and concepts they have learned in the past, and, because of the sheer effort involved if for no other reason, are reluctant to learn new ways. It is as misguided to invoke 'psychopathology' to account for the repetition of 'maladaptive' behaviour as it would be to accuse someone suddenly abducted to China of being mentally ill because, being unable to speak Chinese, they insisted on speaking their native language.

The myth of cure infects our thinking even when we profess

to have rejected it, and as one consequence we have an altogether superficial and unsympathetic view of personal change: we overlook the difficulty of change and the pain it demands, as well as the impossibility of eradicating experience. Our view of man is based on objective (largely mechanical) concepts, and we have developed almost no understanding of a subjective psychology appropriate to these issues, even though many of its principles are as obvious as the ground we walk on.

There *are* forms of change which are painless and which may result in such radical improvements in a person's condition that they appear almost to have undergone transformation. But such changes do not come about through the manipulations of doctors or the imprecations of therapeutic gurus: they arise out of changes in the person's *world*. I have known people undergo such radical transformation through events as diverse as being moved to a new council house (which gave a view from its main windows of an open street rather than a smoke-blackened factory wall), learning to drive, and falling in (reciprocated) love. The last of these conditions is perhaps the most common cause of transformation – people who have for years depended on professional help while they struggled with loneliness and despair, may suddenly glow with life, health and optimism if somebody they love falls in love with them. It is certainly something moving and warming to see, even if one trembles a little in anticipation of what may happen as the relationship matures. It is ironic that some research investigators of psychotherapy feel that improvements in patients due to 'significant life events' outside the therapeutic situation should be carefully excluded as cases counting towards success of a particular therapeutic 'technique', for in so doing they exclude the only possible cases which could remotely resemble cure. What strange, mythifying arrogance it is of psychotherapists to feel that they, in the seclusion of their consulting rooms, can undo the ravages which their patients have undergone in their embodied transactions with the world, and that nothing the world does during the course of treatment should be construed as counting towards improvement.

The evils of the world are much too real to be talked away by the myth carriers of our time. And supposing they weren't – what sense could then be made of the struggle of our species to establish itself and its cultures over even those centuries of which we have some knowledge? We are deceived by our magico-religious lust for painless solutions which absolve us from responsibility for our condition into an implicit devaluation of all that is admirable about mankind. For there would be no point in painful struggle, in heroic battle against injustice, in the painstaking achievements of culture and learning, in courageous stance against cruelty or adversity, in loving self-sacrifice for others, if in fact the experience gained by just one tortured and despairing individual could simply be 'adjusted' or 'modified' by the appropriate expert. Our current attitude to suffering would suggest that Jesus Christ could have saved himself a lot of trouble had he had the chance to consult a good psychotherapist.

We are *not* programmable or erasable; our experience of the world is gained through and often at the expense of our living tissue; whether we wish to acknowledge it or not, we are subjects who have wrung a perspective on the world from our embodied experience of it, and our moral evolution, as individuals as well as groups, nations and races, depends upon our making what sense of our experience we can and putting it to the best purpose we can find. There is something about the lessons they draw from their experience of life which human beings are reluctant – indeed, often almost unable – to abandon, and it is senseless of us to praise the courage and integrity of, say, pioneers of science or great moral reformers at the same time as condemning, at least by implication, the views of those who, though equally insistent on the validity of their experience, draw less uplifting conclusions from their knowledge of rejection and brutality; they too may have much more to teach us than we think. It is profoundly, contemptuously disrespectful of individuals for us to characterise the uses to which they put their experience as 'pathological', or to attempt to alter the stance towards the world which they have gained, at great cost, in accordance with some ill-considered professional notion of 'normality'. We can have no clear idea of the shape which moral evolution will take, though we may indeed endeavour to give shape to it, and we need therefore to approach the ways in which other people live their lives with a kind of tentative moral respect if we are not totally to miss the significance of their living at all. Even (indeed, especially) the 'agoraphobic', housebound housewife – the all too familiar patroness of every general practitioner's surgery and psychiatric clinic in the country – constitutes living, embodied testimony to (and protest against) the failures of our social organisation; simply to try to 'cure' her, or to talk away her pain, is to dismiss the meaning of her life and to negate her lived moral significance, even though, of course, she herself would be astonished at the idea that her life gave evidence of any such significance. I do not mean to romanticise the life of the 'agoraphobic' – it has no great nobility. But it does have a meaning, it points to a *real* state of affairs, and its pained and distressed aspects cannot be eradicated out of the context which gives rise to them.

Our objectifying language gives us little chance to gain a purchase on the predicaments in which we find ourselves engaged as subjects, so that the experience of distress or anxiety is virtually constrained to take on forms which constitute a kind of language in itself; the expression of our painful relations with the world is to be found in the symbolic aspects of our dread. Whatever the form in which we choose to represent our experience to ourselves, it is inevitably symbolic, just as, of course, language is itself a symbolic medium, and this applies no less to the ways in which our anxiety presents itself to us. Anxiety has a *meaning* which points to a state of affairs in our experience.

Although they seem often absurd, the 'symptoms' of anxiety may actually be speaking a language much more succinct and eloquent than the conventional words we would use to describe the same state of affairs. Moreover (and this is a point to be considered in greater detail towards the end of this book) anxiety as a language may be quite well *understood* even though it cannot be translated into conventional words. However, we should be careful not to mystify the meaning of anxiety by making of it an esoteric symbolism accessible only to those experts initiated into its secrets. The point, rather, is that the way anxiety presents itself is individually meaningful to the person who experiences it, *whether or not* that person can spell the meaning out in conventional language, or, better, *precisely because* he or she cannot.

John (p. 27), though sensitive to his own and others' feelings, thoughtful and very good at his job as an apprentice joiner, was neither philosophically reflective nor unusually articulate when reviewing his own experience. Even had he been, it is unlikely that he would have found a neater, more economical or accurate metaphor (and it may of course be argued that all language is metaphor) for his predicament than that expressed in his fear of falling off the face of the earth. From an objective point of view of course, this is a crazy idea which makes no apparent sense, though it hit him with the force almost of revelation. For many reasons, I do not believe John could have said to himself, 'I am fearful and uneasy because I have never experienced the confirmation of another person and feel therefore fundamentally insecure, and I live in dread that the few tenuous connections I have established with others may disintegrate or be snatched away from me. Life seems a terrible risk in this way to me, and I dare not take any kind of step which might jeopardise my fragile security.' All that was a feeling which, very probably, had its origin in the days before he could remember (the days, that is, before he had developed the power of language with which to encode and objectify his experience to himself) and which he experienced as a mysterious dread. A few days before his fear took him over in the middle of the park, he had seen a television documentary which had propounded a number of physical principles, including the law of gravity. Here, suddenly, was a concept which fitted his feeling better than any other he had come across. His disconnectedness and isolation were experienced as if the pull of gravity was about to cease to exist. He experienced his fear as absurd, and kept it a shameful secret for some years. He did not understand his fear in the conventional sense, and yet it carried a conviction for him which he could not ignore. His predicament insisted on recognition in this way, even though the symbolic form taken by this insistence ignored all the rules set by objective discourse; nevertheless, it was more true than anything that discourse had to offer.

The form taken by 'symptoms' of anxiety is by no means always as neat and eloquent as this, nor as easy to understand. The situation which establishes the subject's painful relation to the world is usually (to the outsider) much more easily identifiable, and probably more important to focus upon, than the symbolic form it takes in the subject's consciousness. In this way, it may well be much more easy to see that Mr Y's fundamental experience of insecurity is leading him to avoid any kind of situation at work which might involve him in angry confrontation with someone in authority than it is to explain why this should present itself symbolically to him in the form of an intense fear of travelling in lifts. The meaning of his fear is clear, but the choice of symbol is less so, though it could probably be found through an investigation of his subjective experience. Not that the fear of lifts need be a *direct* symbol of fear of authority (as may well be assumed by those influenced by the more mechanistic theoretical excesses of psychoanalysis), but rather it is the form seized upon by Mr Y's fear (for what might be quite idiosyncratic reasons) in which to present itself to his consciousness. He (unlike us, who can see much more clearly what he is really afraid of, and why) has to deceive himself about the actual nature of his fear, and, so to speak, look around for something which seems to justify it. 'Phobias' may be of almost anything, from bumblebees to factory chimneys. The point is that they are not absurd, but on the contrary, given the need for self-deception, constitute the best guess (the most sense) the individual can make as to the nature of his predicament, that is, are as near as he can get to a coherent symbolic form or 'description' of his feeling, and satisfy his need for meaning even though they fly in the face of objective factuality.

Jane (p. 32) would be diagnosed in orthodox psychiatry as suffering from a compulsive-obsessional state, the content of her 'symptoms' being seen (if thought about at all) as a kind of meaningless spin-off from a pathological condition. Her central 'symptom' is a compulsive wish that people she loves should meet with a fatal accident. Particularly with her parents, but sometimes with her children as well, she experiences this wish as popping unbidden into her mind, and she finds it very distressing, feeling both guilty and wicked, and full of a superstitious dread that she might actually have a supernatural power to damage people. It is not difficult to see the significance of this 'symptom': as a child, any kind of negative feeling remotely resembling belligerence or hatred, hostility or rebellion was vetoed, obscured or denied by her parents, who so swamped her with their cloying 'love' that she had scarcely any chance to develop as an individual, own her own feelings or express any independence. Least of all was she able to protest against and attack the 'love' which threatened to destroy her, although she would find herself from time to time doing aggressive things in secret, but without knowing why. But her subjective anger could not be shut out, would not be banished by her verbal denial of it: her 'symptom' was really her telling people to 'drop dead' while she deceived herself that this, though clearly 'a' wish, was not 'her' wish. The possibility for such a self-deception is given by the kind of conceptual structure of our language outlined in the previous chapter: Jane could apparently quite sensibly talk about wishes 'popping into her mind', as if by a faulty electrical circuit, as this is the way we tend to conceptualise wishing, i.e. as a mental act preceding some kind of bodily activity. She was thus permitted not to take responsibility for her anger and hatred even as she gave (though still, of course, in secret) the strongest vent to it.

'Symptoms' reveal the person's subjective experience of the world, and we fail to read and acknowledge their meaning only because of our desperate need to cling on to the defensive structures of objectivity. 'Symptoms' are as powerful a refutation of myth as one could wish to find.

Despite her apparently 'successful' life style and all its objective indications of comfort and security, Mary (p. 18) is 'suffering from a depressive illness', as the psychiatrists would say. The very fact that, outwardly, her life is so well ordered and easy seems to point to the 'pathological' nature of her 'condition', and, indeed, she spoke to psychiatrists over many years without one of them ever making any other assumption: not one of them made any kind of serious inquiry into whether her lethargy, her weeping and her despair might indicate unhappiness. If, of course, one accepts the objective mythology concerning what is and is not conducive to happiness, then it is clear that Mary could not be unhappy, and Mary herself is as convinced a subscriber as anyone to that mythology: she does not believe that her subjective experience can possibly be important enough to contribute to the way she feels. She believes that if the objective circumstances demand that she should be interested, then she should be interested (for example, in the conversation of guests at a party given by her husband for his golf club acquaintances); she believes that if her role as housewife and mother demand cooking and shopping, then she should of course carry out these activities cheerfully and efficiently. In fact, from a very early age, Mary was discouraged from acknowledging and taking account of her own feelings, and, like the other members of her family, was constrained to give precedence to those of her eccentric and demanding father, who, under a cloak of fake but almost frenzied concern, tyrannised all those over whom he had power. The family itself was confused and confusing, and included six children from a collection of marriages, Mary being the youngest and only child of the union then current. At the age of seven-

teen she had a stormy, unhappy and greatly disapproved-of love affair with a man many years older than herself, and at the end of this married on the rebound a man who seemed to represent the stability, security and confidence she felt she had always wanted. In fact, as she soon discovered (but did not acknowledge), he was a pompous bore who had no interest in women other than as sexual partners, and was afraid of any kind of display of emotion. The marriage declined into a state of guarded coexistence, devoid of warmth and soon enough even of sexuality. Mary deferred to her husband's view that their daughters were best educated in private boarding schools, and did not even 'notice' (i.e., failed to tell herself) how bitterly she missed them. At every point, she regarded the wishes and feelings of others, as she had first learned to do with her father, and disregarded her own. Her subjective, emotional life was a desert, and yet she was simply unable to recognise her own unhappiness. Her 'depression', however, apart from expressing her unhappiness in a manner recognisable at a glance to all those capable of seeing the emperor's nakedness, also provided her with a means of rebellion, for when she was 'ill' she was also prevented form cooking, shopping, and otherwise giving the kind of attention to others which they and she expected of her.

'Symptoms', then, issue from a subjectivity that will not be gainsaid, and reveal a world which is full of cruelty and pain. Even the 'psychopath', with his 'shallow affect' and his 'incapability of acting in relation to long-term goals' in some ways authentically embodies a statement about the world in which he has lived, for it has been a world in which there was no long-term gain, but one in which rewards were few and fleeting, and punishments frequent, violent and brutal; his 'affect' is 'shallow' because he has learned to fake feelings (like love) he has never experienced, and also that to invest emotionally in anything is a risk taken only by mugs.

Our subjective experience of the world tells us the truth about it, even if the language it has to use to do so is cast in forms we have come to see as 'symptoms'. We live in anxiety,

fear and dread because these constitute a proper response to the
nature of our social world, and if we continue not to take
account of the message they give us, we shall make it even more
impossible than it has already become to act upon the reality
that threatens to imprison and destroy us. So far, however, we
have met the challenge of our experience by ever more feverish
attempts to objectify ourselves.

CHAPTER SIX

The Magic of the Machine

Several influential thinkers of widely differing persuasions have suggested – in my view convincingly – that it is *in principle* impossible for individual people to give a complete account of their own intentions,★ if only because that 'part' of them which is giving the account cannot fall under its own scrutiny: the eye cannot look directly at itself, as it were. As I have already argued, this certainly seems to be the case with people who seek to make sense of their own psychological distress: the conscious (articulate) mythology in terms of which they provide an account of their actions and intentions contrasts strongly with the truer motives which may be inferred from their conduct. Thus their explicit assumptions remain unquestioned until their attention is drawn to the *significance of their conduct*. Their discovery of the falsity of what they had explicitly believed about their intentions is, naturally enough, often attended by pain, confusion, and, at first, almost certainly resistance: one does not willingly or enthusiastically give up beliefs which, however self-deceiving, have protected one from harsh and uncomfortable realisations about the nature of the world and one's own projects in relation to it.

It is my experience, however, that despite its being a relatively unusual idea, individuals do not on the whole have too great a difficulty in eventually accepting, at least provisionally,

★I am thinking here of people as contrasting in their approach as, for example G. Ryle (*The Concept of Mind*, Hutchinson, 1949) and J.-P. Sartre (*Being and Nothingness*, trans. H. E. Barnes, Methuen, 1969).

the view that what they say about their motives and intentions has no special claim to accuracy. I have already suggested once or twice that exactly the same state of affairs may obtain at the *collective* level, i.e. in terms of what we tell ourselves as social groups, and even much larger units of organisation such as nations and cultures. This, I think, is making much heavier demands on the reader's credulity, since our explicit cultural values (as, for example, the virtues we assume to inhere in science, technology, objectivity, etc.) are strongly reinforced on all sides, and receive the authoritative endorsement of our most respected social institutions. However, it does seem to be the case that with societies as with individuals there is often a striking contrast between our stated aims and the actual results of what we do. Just as the individual's basic assumptions and projects are almost inevitably buried, uncommented upon, at the centre of his or her conduct, so what we *claim* to be doing collectively may be quite different from the actual achievements of our tacit cultural objectives. We *assume* the rationality of our common activity (necessarily, for if we consciously questioned it, we should presumably be doing something else), and there-after fail to examine it with any degree of critical detachment, even though our activity may show every indication (as, surely, in many areas of our communal projects it does) of utter irra-tionality. Though societies of course have their critics, they have nobody much in the role of 'societotherapist', and it is usually only the historian who can provide anything like a convincing account of our true intentions some time after events have revealed what they must have been.

In this chapter, then, I want to suggest a number of quite closely related ways in which, I believe, cultural aims which we take completely for granted contribute to the destructive objec-tification of individual people and weaken the possibility of their being able to take an effective subjective grasp on the conduct of their own lives and the shaping of their own world. Possibly people may find my observations implausible, or perhaps even offensive; if so, I suggest that this *may* be analogous with the situation in which the individual, faced with a challenge to his or her own version of what he or she is trying to do, will react incredulously or with hostility to the challenger's view. Of course I have absolutely no guarantee that much of what follows may not be the product of an altogether misconceived pessimism, although I find some encouragement in the fact that others who have considered the issues far more thoroughly than I★ have arrived at not dissimilar conclusions.

The need to consider issues at this rather general level arises out of an overemphasis in Western psychology and psychiatry on the part played by *individuals* in the generation of their psychological distress. In fact, the nature of such distress cannot be understood anywhere near fully unless it is placed in the context of our general cultural assumptions and aims, and it is certainly not the case that the processes of objectification which I have tried to identify as lying somewhere near the centre of our malaise are merely the products of individual people who just so happen all to react in rather the same way at this particular point in our development.

Few of us question that the concepts we find ready and waiting for us on our entry into the social world do anything but reflect an 'obvious' reality. A twentieth-first-century baby destined to be an astronaut is about to imbibe a cultural world very different from that of a fourteenth-century baby about to become a monk, but, whatever we may think from our supposedly enlightened vantage point, not one which *at the time* carries any more conviction for the individual. With hindsight (and *only* with hindsight) we can criticise aspects of the monk's naturally accepted beliefs, and few would question the sense and value of our doing so. But it takes an act of imagination to criticise our own values and beliefs, and there is, of course, no guarantee that our criticism will be proved justified. However, it is

★See, for example, L. Mumford, *The Pentagon of Power*, Harcourt Brace Jovanovich, 1970.

the inevitable lot of human beings, as inescapably *moral* beings, to take that chance, for otherwise our world will not evolve at all, or at least not under our own guidance.

The cultural phenomenon which I particularly want to consider in this chapter, because of its special centrality to the theme of objectification, is that of the cult of the machine. There are several subsidiary reasons for focusing on this particular aspect of present-day existence, most of which, I hope, are also germane to my thesis in one way or another. For example, the machine (at present, in particular, the computer), in representing the most developed extent to which objectification has so far been carried, reveals, I believe, something about our *intentions* towards the world and ourselves. The machine is a ubiquitous feature of our environment, and is accepted as an inevitable (unquestionable) development, even though *in fact*, as a mere product of our activity, its existence could in principle become subject to our conscious control; on the whole, we unhesitatingly endorse the value of progressive mechanisation in our explicit consideration of the processes involved, though we fail to take account of what it *actually* does to us and our environment, and express bewilderment and surprise when things turn out to be different from our avowed expectations. We all acknowledge, for example, that many of the fundamental deprivations and injuries suffered by our species could be greatly alleviated if we devoted to them the resources we devote to the refinement of our technological achievements, and we all know that the depletion of our natural resources and the pollution of our world on the scale we at present find necessary to maintain our mechanised way of life cannot be allowed to continue without disaster. And yet we ignore this utterly reasonable assessment of our predicament in favour of a correspondingly *ir*rational belief in the viability of what is in fact a mythical ideal. There are thus, I believe, several parallels between our society in relation to the machine and the individual in relation to his or her personal mythology. The person's mythology forms the very framework through which he or she looks out at the world; our machine culture reflects our values and shapes our experience in ways of which we are unlikely to be aware, and for reasons which are on the whole opaque to us. The largely man-made world which we inhabit did not come about merely by chance, nor by the inexorable unfolding of progress, but by the designs of men and women. These designs, however, are no more conscious and explicit than are the motives of the individual, and if we want to know what they are we must examine the nature of the world around us with a vision which does not simply take everything for granted.

The machine culture, then, does us great damage because it constitutes the mythology which prevents us from getting to grips with what ails us collectively in exactly the same way that the individual's personal mythology prevents him or her from even seeing what features of the world need subjective attention and intervention. Just as the individual in distress will look round for something on which to blame that distress (as, for example, 'illness'), so it is common at the societal level to look round for something, probably a group (capitalists, Marxists, 'extremists') seen as consciously malign, on which to lay the blame for socio-economic breakdown. However, it is usually hard to identify any *actual* malign groups of this kind, just as it is hard to identify the 'illness' thought to be causing the individual's distress. It may be, rather, the *unacknowledged needs and interests* embedded in our social existence, and the defences against their recognition, which cause us trouble, just as it is individuals' unacknowledged aims and strategies which cause them theirs.

Since there are some needs so fundamental that they are shared by all of us, it will scarcely be surprising if we find defences against the vulnerabilities to which they expose us built into the very foundations of our social institutions. If we are not to allow our communal defensiveness to run out of our control, with possibly extremely destructive consequences, we must make strenuous efforts to become aware of (make explicit) the ways in which it dictates our conduct.

Take, for example, the very basic need for security which is shared by us all. It is fairly obvious, perhaps, that the initial experience of all those members of our species who survive infancy is likely to be one of *being looked after* when in a state of utter passive dependency. It is therefore not surprising that for the individual growing up is an *inevitably* painful process since built into his or her *bodily experience* is a 'memory' (the knowledge of a feeling) of a time when there was no pain, no frustration or difficulty which could not be solved by a force (in fact, what H.S. Sullivan called 'the mothering one') outside the self, and this 'memory' remains always with us for longing comparison with the painful present in which *nobody* is going to have one's interests that much at heart. All of us therefore know the struggle to escape the pains of maturity and adulthood and the yearning search for dependence on the Other, and we fear also the dangers, indeed terrors, which such dependence implies, since we know that it cannot last. While it may be relatively easy to appreciate the significance of this for the individual, it may be less obvious that we have a *cultural* investment in perpetuating the blissful warmth and safety of the infantile state; even if we can see elements of collective need in, say, 'primitive' religions, we are less ready to see them at work in the revered institutions of our contemporary society.

Again, at the less fundamental level of *interest* (as opposed to need), it is customary in the traditional psychotherapy of so-called 'neurotic' individuals to point to the results of their 'denial' of (i.e. self-deception concerning) their less praiseworthy enterprises, which may for example involve elements of aggression, lust, envy, etc. Collectively, though, we seem less alive to the fact that our self-interest, our economic apprehension and greed, may offer unseen (but much more satisfactory) explanations for our social organisation than do the official formulae to which we give quite sincere, if self-deceiving, allegiance. If we do detect such motives, we tend to impute them to some section of society other than that occupied by ourselves.

Thus the pursuit of objectivity, in finding the purest form of its realisation in the mechanisation of the world and most things in it, including ourselves, serves a number of unstated and unexamined purposes, which include our need for security as well as a number of our less creditable interests.

For example, one of the central security-serving functions of objectivity, in particular as it is embodied in our scientific and technological dogmas, is to relieve us of the painful necessity for making mature, subjective and *ethical* judgements. The ideal world for the kind of 'positivistic' view of science which has dominated the English-speaking intellectual communities in this century is one in which the clarity of 'evidence' and the indisputability of 'facts' obviates the necessity for judging whether one course of action is *better* than another. It is but a short step from here to attempt to realise the removal of the 'human element' of uncertainty and moral choice through the construction of machines (computers) which appear to be concerned solely with the 'facts', and with 'deciding' on the basis of an appraisal of these what is the best course to adopt. To believe in the possibility of any such mechanical solution to our dilemmas is, however, to perform a kind of self-inflicted confidence trick upon ourselves, in which we turn a blind eye to the fact that the computer has been programmed by human beings who have built into it their own human purposes.

Of course there is an essential place for the balanced consideration of matters of fact and of questions of evidence for, and justification of, judgements and propositions, for respect for experience and knowledge and the (as far as possible) disinterested pursuit of truth. It is also the case that the appraisal of facts and the calculation of probabilities can often be carried out very efficiently and quickly by machines (the speed and efficiency with which computers perform what would for people be utterly tedious and laborious tasks – and that is *all* they do – in no way accounts for the awe in which they are held; for that we must seek other explanations). It is clear, however, that none of these laudable operations, however successfully achieved, obviates the necessity for ethical judgement and moral concern, and the exercise of these faculties can, *in principle*, never be detached from human beings, nor ever escaped by them. It is a philosophical truism that however much is known about the factual aspects of any particular issue, it is still always possible to ask whether it is *right*, and to that *ethical* question there can be no certain answer, no deliverance from the necessity of making a fallible human judgement. A child, certainly, may leave the exercise of such judgement to its parents, but for the adult there is no such escape.

The cult of objectivity, in trying to make us secure from the necessity for taking account of the subjective, ethical aspects of our intellectual and social culture, simply becomes blind to their actual influence, which then runs out of control giving unchecked *moral* fervour to our pursuit of the objective, and making it impossible for us to identify what *particular* moral concern might be lurking behind so-called 'value-free' objective investigations and 'factual' pronouncements. On the one hand this kind of approach embodies a fervent hope which, however attractive, is really as obviously and as absurdly naive as any belief in witchcraft, and on the other it sets up a kind of inverted moralism★ of its own which views any kind of assertion of subjective or ethical values with (in 'non-factual' areas) contempt or derision, or (in areas which could be regarded as 'factual') deep hostility and disapproval.

One effect of this, as far as the man-in-the-street is concerned, is to make personal judgments about the desirability or otherwise of states of affairs or courses of action something which he can no longer see as his prerogative, if indeed he does

★The concept of 'moral inversion' was developed first by M. Polanyi in his book *Personal Knowledge*, Routledge and Kegan Paul, 1958.

not see them as actually reprehensible. You have no right to a view if you 'don't know the facts', and to expound one is impudently to usurp the function of 'experts', or even more reliable machines, from which, so it seems, every last possibility of error has been removed. Not only do 'ordinary people' feel they have no right to comment on 'things they don't understand', but, particularly significantly for the focus of this book, they come to feel incapable of judging even the significance and sanity of their own conduct.

Thus, in our society, balanced judgement, knowledge of facts, 'scientific' and technical expertise become the property of an elite class of professionals, who alone are seen as being in a position to judge the uses to which such knowledge should be put. Subjective, ethical judgment and conduct become inverted and out of sight. This then leaves the 'ordinary person' with very little role at all, except as object and consumer, for he or she has neither the 'training' nor the 'expertise' to make balanced, objective judgments, and depends utterly on the professionals – academics, scientists, medics, lawyers, technicians, etc. – for the exercise of these capacities. Thus a faith in objectivity which serves to preserve our security also comes to serve the interests of those who become its conceptual custodians. It is not that the experts maintain their monopoly with any conscious malice or greed – in fact most would feel as well as profess a pride in their reputation for probity and a genuine satisfaction in their service to others. It needs a painful effort of 'consciousness-raising' even to begin to see what, for example, Ivan Illich means when he writes about the 'disabling professions'.* To take the most severe view, however, it is possible to see professional experts as being on the one hand like intellectual usurers who, as it were, hire out their concepts to the uninitiated, and on the other hand like a priesthood which mediates the mysteries of objective knowledge to the masses, but does not permit them entry to them.

*I. Illich *et al.*, *Disabling Professions*, Marion Boyars, 1977.

To pursue for a moment the first of these analogies, it certainly seems that a large part of the *actual activity* of professional academics, scientists, etc., is aimed at keeping their knowledge as a kind of intellectual capital which may be employed to make money at interest without itself becoming dissipated into the beliefs, practices and preoccupations of ordinary people – hence perhaps the enormous energy put quite overtly by professional groups in these fields into protecting their rights and claims to exclusive knowledge and competence, etc. The economic basis of production and consumption in which we are all, willy nilly, caught up, is thus reflected in the structure and functions of our scientific and intellectual institutions. Psychotherapy, for example, is as much an industry as is steel manufacture or entertainment; universities have in many fundamental respects become factories for the production of 'knowledge' the primary function of which is to perpetuate the academic industry itself by manufacturing the raw material which keeps it going. If this latter seems a harsh judgment, one need only reflect that both teachers and students in universities are in their own (not consciously perceived) interest forced to act (produce) *like* teachers and students if they are to justify their continued existence in an overcrowded and competitive academic world. It is obvious that in these circumstances mere quantity of output will become more important than quality of work (it is also, let it be noted, more easily objectively measurable). Thus I have seen academic boards set up for senior university appointments make preferences for one candidate rather than another on the basis of the *number* of publications listed in the candidate's curriculum vitae, *without any attempt being made* to consider the content or intellectual quality of the publications. Similarly, considerable debate has taken place in the pages of the main professional journal of British psychologists (*The Bulletin of the British Psychological Society*) seriously advocating the measurement of psychologists' academic worth by the *number* of publications they produce. The parallels of this kind of approach with industrial production seem to me inescapable, as does its irrelevance to anything one might naively have associated with academic excellence. Again, students have complained to me that their teachers, though sometimes representing extremely opposed intellectual positions, will not confront each other in public over their differences, but instead advocate a kind of tolerant eclecticism in which the concept of truth quietly disappears. This seems hard to understand as anything but a function of the setting in which teachers depend heavily for their academic advancement on winning research grants from both public and private bodies, so that they *cannot afford* to be wrong, and hence unconsciously suppress public disagreement amongst themselves, as well as the opportunity for outsiders to criticise their activities. This is highly understandable (which of us would not do the same?) but nevertheless militates against traditional (possibly even mythical?) values of intellectual honesty and debate, and at the same time subtly appropriates knowledge as the *production* of a particular professional group.

That self-interest and greed play a large part (albeit unconsciously) in these processes, as indeed they do so obviously in our more overtly economic institutions, is perhaps easy enough to see. What may less readily be appreciated is the extent to which the general population becomes intellectually subjugated thereby. One result of this is the enormous gullibility and unreflectiveness of the 'ordinary' person in matters which have become professional property. For example, laymen's expectations of science and medicine are almost boundlessly naive (and their surprise when confronted personally with medical and scientific failures correspondingly exaggerated) since they have, in a sense, given up their right to consider or criticise. Consideration and criticism have become part of the *professional's* special prerogatives; for laymen, theirs is only to wonder and consume.

Lurking behind the sheer economic self-interest of intellectual and technical professionalisation is, I believe, an inverted form of the moral zeal which once fuelled our religions. The science-based professions are not simply cynically out to feather their own nests and make monkeys of those to whom they sell their services. More fundamentally, they are gripped, like the rest of us, by a dream of how the world might be, and inflated with a sense of their own mission in bringing it about. Just as the priest interprets to the laity a reassuring vision of love and redemption, or at least the possibility of salvation, so the scientist conveys to the lay populace the possibility of a world in which all 'problems' are soluble, all need for subjective judgement potentially redundant, all pain and despair in principle curable. Like the priest, the scientist expounds these mysteries in terms incomprehensible to the layman, but socially authorised and hence believed. Our attitude to scientific and technical matters is soaked through with awe, and the uninitiated will drink in the banalities and fake profundities of, say, televisual scientific acolytes with a credulity quite as blind as that of any newly converted religious zealot.

'Scientists think . . .' and 'scientists have shown . . .', etc., form the preamble to countless statements of almost infinite implausibility, to which, because of their apparent scientific legitimation, the layman is expected to give immediate credence. This, moreover, is not simply the result of a popular corruption of matters surpassing lay understanding, but a clear reflection of attitudes held by many scientists themselves. At least in the social sciences (I have no first-hand experience of others) it is common for practitioners and theoreticians to spend considerable amounts of time and energy in admitting or excommunicating fellow members to or from the scientific club on the grounds of whether or not their work conforms to *dogmatic* rules concerning what it is to be 'scientific'. For the most part, these are the rules of objectivity and mechanism, and bear only the most distant relationship to questions of importance, interest, or truth.

It seems to me fairly obvious that at least in part science had its origin in a reaction *against* a view of knowledge as dogmatic or established by authority, insisting instead that personal experience, or at least those aspects of it which can be shared with others, provide the grounds upon which claims about the nature of the world can be made. This enormously liberating position almost immediately (as seems so often to be the way with great moral or philosophical insights) became itself ossified into a dogmatic orthodoxy which by now holds sway in our intellectual institutions with an almost unassailable repressive force. Just as a religion may become obsessed with its forms and its rituals to the complete neglect of its moral content, so science has become utterly preoccupied with its methods (for example, objectification, quantification, mechanisation) and almost indifferent to the content to which its methodology is applied. For example, it is far more important for a Ph.D. student of psychology to employ the officially approved methods of measurement and experimental design than it is for him or her to apply them to any particularly interesting issue or question. In part, no doubt, this is because interesting questions, seriously addressed, would not provide enough raw material to support a large academic industry, but it is also true that recitation of the dogmatic scientific creed is a virtually necessary act for admission to a priesthood dedicated to upholding the values of objectification. This again is, I believe, a largely unconscious process (in the sense of not being explicit or avowed): it is not the case that those who embody 'the system' – e.g. academic teachers of psychology – see themselves as guardians of a repressive orthodoxy. I am sure they would be appalled at any such suggestion. Rather is it the case that this is the result of their conduct, whatever they may claim to be doing.

As with the self-deceptive manoeuvres by which individuals attempt to defend themselves from painful recognition of their predicament, so the culturally embedded defences of objectivity frequently defeat the very aim which they profess to be pursuing. While the explicit aim may be an altogether laudable one of furthering a commonly acknowledged cultural value, the implicit one (judged by what in fact we manage to achieve in our cultural institutions) may well be once again to prevent us from catching a glimpse of our own vulnerability. For example, medicine, and too often nursing, rather than cultivating the arts of tenderness and concern, may tend to foster a kind of stony indifference to the emotional vulnerability of those they 'care' for (there is no institution less comforting than the 'traditional' hospital). Our school system, in its obsession with 'techniques' of teaching and the relatively narrow definition of curricula, becomes blind to the complexity of the processes and content of learning, so that while a school may indeed be a most potent source of learning for children (e.g. in terms of what they learn about each other), *what* is learned may have almost nothing to do with the official curriculum, and what is learned outside school hours, because it falls under no official or objective demarcation of 'training', is unlikely to be conceived of as learning at all. The way in which learning actually does take place is likely to be very different from 'official' views concerning the 'acquisition of skills', etc. I have already suggested ways in which the achievements of some of our institutions of higher education may depart from those traditionally associated with them. All in all we pay a heavy price for the reassurance we gain from the conviction that the automatic progress of science and technology will ensure a satisfactory future while removing from us the necessity for personal, subjective judgement or intervention in the world's affairs, since we alienate from ourselves our ability to determine the quality of our social existence.

Almost the only visible shred left of anything approaching moral concern in the actual conduct of our official institutions has come to be couched in (objectively measurable) financial terms. For example, it is taken as *self-evident* by many National Health Service psychologists (whom I single out only because I know them best) that 'cost effectiveness' should be their primary consideration when evaluating the 'treatments' they apply. To question whether what is good for patients must *necessarily* be connected with what is relatively less expensive is to be regarded with slightly disapproving non-comprehension. Literally not to count the cost of what one does for patients is to invite *moral* disapproval. Money thus becomes an objective substitute for more subjective qualities like concern, interest or care. (This is not, of course, to suggest that financial questions are *irrelevant* to the provision of services.)

And yet this investment in an apparently cool practicality, this hard-headed invocation of objective and 'scientific' standards, is in truth only a mask for a form of idealism which, if it continues to go unchecked and unnoticed, threatens to degenerate into an uncontrolled yearning for a magical state of freedom from pain and threat, in which human beings become the invulnerable and immortal foetuses of an enormous, impersonal, technological womb. The longings and illusions we once hoped to realise through religion we now see, through a kind of greedy haze of mounting excitement, as being obtainable – thanks to 'science' – here on earth. Through the use of drugs, and spare parts, processes of conditioning or hypnosis, the ever more 'miraculous' discoveries and promises of science, our fantasies of everlasting life, unmitigated ease and plenty, seem tantalisingly to approach ever closer to our grasp. And in pursuit of this we abandon our subjectivity, and retreat from our reason.

So blind is our faith that objectivity will deliver us from evil, that we become incapable of seeing the evil around us; so much more vivid are our dreams than our perception of reality that we can only gaze fondly upon them as, unconsciously, we embark upon the destruction of our world. Soberly we contemplate the Frankensteinian reveries of 'scientists' who speculate with barely suppressed excitement about the implications of 'breakthroughs' which offer to halt the processes of ageing, restore or erase memories, activate 'pleasure centres' in our brains, and in other ways spare us the boring necessity of actually having to deal with the world. Mouths agape like the dupe of Bosch's mediaeval conjuror, we credit these and other self-deceiving illusions with infinite plausibility just as long as they are offered to us by our accredited scientific priests, never once pausing to reflect that, for example, our experience of the world depends on more than the mere mechanical processes of our bodies, and that if we were to succeed in encapsulating ourselves off from the world outside our skins, ceasing to take responsibility for what we do to it, we should simply be destroyed. Tinkering, however 'scientifically', with our minds and our bodies will never make the *world* a better place.

The solemn surprise with which we point to the 'prescience' of futurist writers like H. G. Wells, the naivety of our ponderous astonishment at the coming to pass of the erstwhile fantasies of science fiction, are surely pointers to the extent to which we have blinded ourselves to the nature of our own undertakings. Sublimely unaware that our science and our science fiction are but aspects of the *same* subjective impulse, the latter providing the blueprint for the former, we act as if those who first give words to our imaginings somehow 'foresee' the awe-inspiring achievements of 'objective' developments which come about apparently untouched by human minds. The vast mechanical world which we have created is, of course, not the inevitable achievement of a value-free science and technology, the necessary result of the unlocking of nature's secrets, but rather the concrete realisation of our seemingly relentless urge to achieve our wildest dreams. (This fusion of the objective with the religious, hard fact with wild fantasy, dry mathematical efficiency with a kind of half-conscious, slightly decadent lack of moral restraint, seems often to be found in science fiction, and may go some way towards accounting for its often compulsive quality, and for the slightly dazed and sickened feeling with which one surfaces from it!)

Naturally, we take for granted our attitude to our own technological achievements, and yet, if something like the analysis
offered here is not correct, *some* explanation has to be found for
our fusion of the scientific with the magical and religious. Why
else, for example, do we so often speak of the 'wonders' of
modern science, the 'miracles' of medicine; what explains our
awed fascination with technical developments and electronic
machines? After all, such achievements are in fact extremely
prosaic, absolutely explainable and understandable (since we
have constructed them ourselves) down to the last detail. It
must be, I think, that we infuse them with the wordless longings of our infancy, and with inarticulate religious hope. (The
very day following the writing of these words, a television
programme describes in one breathless sentence an American
clinic for plastic surgery (!) as: 'A *Mecca* to which *pilgrims* trek
who are seeking medical *miracles*'.) Through a kind of generalised Myth of the Machine, into which we project all our
unacknowledged craving for comfort and security, we seem to
have found a way of actually constructing for ourselves the God
in whom our hopes had begun to founder.

There seems little doubt that most people are only too happy
to conceptualise themselves in mechanical terms – the most
recent fashion in academic psychology, for example, is to
develop theoretical understandings of 'human behaviour' from
analogies based on the workings of computers. Almost no
attempt to understand human nature in 'scientific' terms has
paid serious attention to man's subjectivity and essentially moral
nature – indeed to do so would (ludicrously, in my view) in
itself be considered 'unscientific'. The 'computer model' is but
the latest in a long line of mechanical analogies in psychology,
earlier versions of which (like Freud's) based themselves on
concepts more appropriate to hydraulics or steam engines.
Today, as before, any attempt to understand human nature
through even a commonsense appraisal of people's *experience* of
their world is rejected in favour of theoretical positions which

invoke psycho-biological mechanisms of one kind or another. On the one hand this kind of approach leads to a gross distortion of the meaning of our experience; on the other it specifies the conceptual moulds into which we have to fit ourselves and thus determines the limits within which we are able to understand ourselves. The more we feed the mechanistic myths which govern our thinking about ourselves – the more, that is, we appear to have an acceptably 'scientific' understanding of our nature – the more, in fact, we become unable to acknowledge, interpret, or talk about our own experience.

For example, because we treat sex as largely a mechanical 'drive', placing great emphasis on its 'optimal' functioning and being constantly vigilant for breakdowns or 'dysfunctions' in the sexual machinery, we pay virtually no attention to people's *actual experience* of their sexuality. We find it more important to preserve and foster the myth of sexuality as mechanical process than we do to develop any kind of detailed or sensitive phenomenology of sexual experience (i.e., establishing how *in fact* people experience their sexual needs and feelings). I suspect that a vast proportion of people live in secret unhappiness about their sexuality because they are unable to meet what are in truth entirely mythical 'norms' of 'performance'. In this context, for example, I am struck by how many women seem to find sex a less impelling need after some period of married life, usually after the birth of their children, and how they endeavour to disguise this fact from their husbands, who they rightly suspect will wrongly interpret their lack of sexual interest as lack of love. Aspects of this situation are of course far from unnoticed in our culture, and indeed are a reliable source of comic material, but I know of no 'official' movement to take what people feel seriously enough to suggest that an open appraisal and discussion of what seems to be a common experience might ease some of the tensions which so often lead to marital disaster in middle life. Rather, women who feel this way may guiltily conceal what they fear to be 'sexual dysfunction' while men continue to be haunted by fantasies of what a 'real woman' would be like. As one of the primary 'drives' fuelling the entire mechanical process which life has become, sex develops into an increasingly undifferentiated, urgent preoccupation, a kind of life-long, meaningless lust, ready to be tended and if necessary stoked by a horde of experts if it shows any signs of flagging.

If, however, we were prepared to examine the meaning of people's sexual experience, to acknowledge the fluctuations and changes it undergoes at various times in our lives, the differing experiences of men and women in relation to their sexuality, we might not only learn to feel more comfortable with ourselves and each other, but sex itself might become a slightly less prominent cultural obsession, and take its place alongside other important human preoccupations. This, of course, is speculation based on my experience of being able to talk to people about their sexual feelings with a degree of honesty. It would be foolish of me to claim on this basis any kind of expertise on sexual matters, but it does prompt me to wonder what we might be able to know about ourselves if we were not constrained to see ourselves as machines: if, that is, we could talk about our experience rather than our myths.

Because the Myth of the Machine has gained such sway over our outlook, we can only think in terms of things 'working' in a well-oiled, predictable, comfortable way. We cannot easily conceive, for example, of life being *necessarily* painful: if we are not 'happy', something must have 'gone wrong'. I suspect, for instance, that the occurrence of so-called 'depressive illness' among the middle-aged and elderly (the 'endogenous depression' particularly likely to be regarded by psychiatrists and others as physically caused disease) is especially poorly understood because of our failure to pay serious attention to our experience and to develop a language in which it can be discussed. Gradually to become old can for many people be a particularly painful experience, and one for which life, however well ordered, 'successful', etc., offers little compensation. The loss of one's children, one's influence and social and economic status, the decline in one's physical and mental powers, the ever more certain knowledge of approaching death, the experience of the death of others, are, to be sure, part of a natural and 'normal' process and cannot therefore reasonably be complained about without placing an unfair strain on those around one. And yet to glimpse these factors – which can scarcely be ignored for long – in a world in which all the explicit emphasis is on ease and pleasure, happiness, youth, sex and 'success', in which the ideal is to be passively nurtured in a giant mechanical womb, is to find oneself in an almost unthinkably lonely and frightening condition which one is simply not prepared to face. Thus our ability to confront, acknowledge and come to terms with this *inevitably* painful state of affairs is seriously depleted, so that almost the only possibility open to us is to slide into a kind of numb 'depressive illness' which will give us licence to be stunned by drugs or electricity into a state of relative indifference to our circumstances and our future.

John (pp. 23, 115) has not complained of any of his 'symptoms' for over a year, but on this occasion keeps returning to the feeling of dizziness and nausea which has been troubling him for the past few weeks. He says he cannot understand it, is worried that it might be something serious, and though willing superficially to accept the idea that it is just a touch of tension, shows no interest in talking about anything else. He looks ill at ease, and his insistent focusing on 'symptoms' becomes quite irritating to the therapist. John cannot identify anything that is troubling him – 'things are all right, nothing's wrong.' Only when the therapist, on a hunch, asks him how his daughter is does the truth begin to emerge. 'They don't seem to need you so much, do they?' says John, and goes on to talk about how his daughter, now fifteen, is going out more without him and acting more often on her own initiative rather than seeking his advice. Hobbies which they had shared she now pursues quite often on her own, and she tells him less about the events of her life. It has always been clear that she is the apple of John's eye, and he has been an involved, but lovingly encouraging and non-intrusive parent. His expression is full of a kind of diffident pain as he describes his daughter's growing up. 'For a moment', he says, 'you wonder if you've done something wrong, don't you?' He and the therapist then discuss issues to do with the intense sadness which a parent may feel over a child's growing up, and as a result, it seems, John is able to integrate and accept a feeling which until then had just been an unexplained physical nausea; he feels able to feel his feelings and accept himself as normal. (I know of no psychiatric or psychological text which acknowledges such feelings as real, profound, in a sense 'incurable' sources of pain, i.e. as legitimate causes of distress. It is therefore no wonder that people misinterpret their feelings as 'symptoms' and cannot for themselves find the words to describe them.)

A sensitive, subjective appraisal of the world in which we live, as well as of our own nature, uncovers misery which cannot be escaped, risks which cannot be side-stepped. As we struggle to avert our gaze from these, they become, in the corner of our eye, terrors which must be avoided at all costs, and so we construct our semi-magical machine world which promises to ward off evil for ever. To fit into this machine world we must also make machines of ourselves, and we do so with enthusiasm. We become plastic, standardised, passive consumers, intent upon deadening our own unease. Patients who for one reason or another have perforce stumbled across their subjectivity are apt tremulously to ask 'are there other people like me?', as if the experience of pain, fear or doubt is about to place them outside the bounds of humanity, as if the only safe way of 'being' is as one of millions of identical units all of whom act and feel similarly and predictably. Every secondary school child knows that to be 'different' is to invite suspicion, hostility and ridicule; the Other's eye is naturally drawn to the conspicuous (the feeling of conspicuousness is often the most salient component in the experience of 'phobic' anxiety). The attraction of machine status, of serfdom in its modern form, is protection from an unkind world and from the Other who strikes you down if you dare to become a person; and so we invent a mythified 'force' of impersonal objectivity (invested in 'science' or 'progress') which promises to look after our interests far more reliably and impartially than any Jehovah could have managed.

There is one particular mechanical medium – television which shapes the nature of our reality more than almost any other, though most of us, I suspect, hardly notice the pervasiveness of its influence since it has become such an established part of our experience. In fact, television is the near-perfect expression of our self-deceiving urge to take our mythology for the truth. Its greatest asset in this respect is its plausibility: seeing is believing, the camera cannot lie. And yet, in so credibly putting before us the world in which we wish to believe, it distorts and betrays just about every truth and value of the non-magical, non-mechanical world in which, unless we actually do turn into machines, we are still constrained to live. Television pacifies, deludes and bemuses us to such an extent that we can scarcely even look at the real world without wanting to adjust its contrast and colour balance (looking at some slightly purple-coloured fields not long ago, I found myself actually thinking that something must be wrong with the colour control).

Television fulfils our wildest magical dreams while appearing to present us with reality. Everything which offends our mythology can be laundered out of what is presented to us through the process of editing: the aged and ugly, the sick and deformed will not be invited to appear as contestants on the quiz shows; the unscripted outburst can be cut out of the recording, the camera pick and choose what it wants us to see. The relatively unbounded money and power available to television production, combined with its technical possibilities, mean that we are bombarded with magical images – ordinary people can be transported from their ordinary world and find themselves suddenly confronting their relatives in Australia, being flown to New York, or presented after fifty minutes of inane entertainment with a shining new car which is driven into the very room where they stand by a girl in a bikini.

If asked, of course, we would claim to have 'insight' into our addiction to this cultural diet, would claim to know that it is 'only entertainment'. But this is as self-deceiving as saying that one knows one's 'symptoms' (of psychological distress) are 'silly', for what we fail properly to notice and take account of is that we are indeed addicted, and that there must be reasons for it. Why, for example, does so much highly expensive 'peak viewing time' get spent on presenting to us the odd and the quirky: astrologers who foretell the lives of royal babies, eccentric ladies who feel that they can communicate with their cats, vicars who imitate the sounds made by railway trains? Could it not be because these and others like them have their own special place in constructing for us a kind of comfortably whimsical world in which we like to believe (continuous perhaps with the fairytale world we like to create for our children)?

Television is not, however, particularly concerned not to offend our traditional moral values (it is our *mythology* it preserves at all costs): the endless stimulation of voyeuristic sexual interest, prurience and violence (epitomised in the official speculation that, with the advent of cable television, shift workers could have the benefit of one or two channels of non-stop pornography) testify to the fact that television's is not a *conventional* moral concern. The tacit aim of television, rather, is to keep us from catching a glimpse of the world in which we actually live, the world in which real pain, real love, actual death, loss and despair, real struggle and conflict, economic and social deprivation play such a prominent part. Instead, television feeds our passive torpor by permitting us to sink into the semiconscious world of our most primitive dreams and fantasies, in which we may indulge the half-formed urges for personal, tribal and sexual conquest which slosh about in the sumps of our minds. Any visiting Martian anthropologist intent on gauging our values from the way we spend our spare time would surely be appalled at what television reveals as our major pre-occupations.

Time and space are, in television, also given distorted, magical dimensions, the unspoken aim of which seems to be to insulate us from, and eventually blunt, our natural emotional reactions. Images of corpses crawling with flies will be followed in a flash by one of an old lady winning the football pools. Hardly has one had time to focus one's eyes on a scene in which desperate citizens are being bludgeoned by riot police when the image is replaced by that of the arrival at some airport of an international superstar dressed in a glittering suit. We may be reassured that none of this is real because it flits across our consciousness so rapidly that we have no time to digest its significance before our emotions are jerked away and engaged in some quite different sphere. With a kind of convoluted hypocrisy, television can even remove from us the responsibility for looking at what it shows us – I remember a news reporter, even as the cameras dwelt on the tattered remnants of people and their personal effects at the scene of an appalling air crash, berating in tones of the highest moral indignation those 'ghouls' who had driven out to inspect the event for themselves.

The exigencies of programme timing mean that no issue, however complex or interesting, can be aired beyond its allotted span. In fact, this means that complexity and interest become extinct qualities: the pundits and personalities, the 'experts' who will be invited and reinvited to present their views, are those for whom interest, profundity, scholarship, moral sensibility and complexity can be sacrificed to 'image'. The real people may only be glimpsed occasionally, and then by mistake, but the images we see are of instant people with instant ideas and instant reactions to the imperious demands of television technology; they bear as much relation to real people as instant potatoes do to real potatoes. Our mythical world demands blandness in all things, easy solutions, the ability to flit as fast as light from the potentially painful to the reassuring.

Television feeds our passivity through its ability to remove from us the need for patience and attentiveness. Because of the technical possibilities offered by editing, replays, etc., the actual texture of experience is altered, both on and off the screen. For example, sporting events become 'action-packed' series of incidents, and real, non-televisual sport has to be changed – simplified, made more 'spectacular', less 'boring', more instantly consumable – in order to accord with the expectations generated in both spectators and players by television. Again, we approach in this way the binary, all or nothing world of the computer, in which there is no time for subtlety, patience or ambiguity.

Attending to detail, effortfully trying to understand, is an active process, and like all active processes relatively painful. Attention to content, to detail, is in television sacrificed to fascination with style. Politics becomes a gladiatorial spectacle in which the struggle for power or the occurrence of 'splits' absorbs all the interest which might otherwise be invested in how and for what that power might be used. What people have to say becomes far less important than how they say it. Partly to preserve us from the 'heaviness' of their subject matter, and partly perhaps to enhance their status as magicians, the pundits must display strange gestures, quirky mannerisms or funny voices if they are to be able to 'explain' to us the mysteries of botany, or astronomy, or 'science' is general. There is no place on the television screen for the serious and the concerned (unless it is mock seriousness and concern) for these are the kind of qualities of spontaneous subjectivity which demand hesitant, often ambiguous complexity. The fabricated personae of television 'people' are the necessary outcome of the posed self-consciousness which the medium demands, and yet for most of us these are the 'people' we 'know' best, the acquaintances we have in common with millions (this, of course, gives a quite bogus, simplified structure to our socal existence, distracting us from the painful complexity of our relations with real people who, in comparison, are likely to be enigmas to us).

The pace of 'serious' programmes is, in terms of what we are asked to digest, extremely easy. Again, the lumps are ironed out, the contentious issues ignored. Even with the aid of a video recorder, you cannot easily flick back and forth through the material (as you can with a book), so that the effort has to be taken out of understanding through repetition and oversimplification, and your being offered nothing which demands questioning or reflection. The television viewer exists in a world which is complete and finished, ready to be transmitted in easy stages. He or she is there to consume the world, not to create it.

Because we may consider the camera lens as objective and impartial, we may feel it scarcely rational to entertain the idea that television embodies values of its own (ultimately, of course, these are the values with which our split-off and denied – inverted – subjectivity has invested it). Television imposes, certainly, its own unwritten etiquette, and its unstated but almost absolute power to determine our reality leads to a quite general and apparently unquestioning acceptance of its manners. Central to these is precisely television's implicit claim to objectivity, so that the interviewer, who, largely unseen, becomes the camera's voice, is enabled to ask questions which would in any other context be considered offensive, impertinent, or stupid. But, so it seems, his (or hers) is the voice of objective inquiry, and may not itself be questioned. The objects of such inquiry, transfixed by both camera and voice, thrown perhaps suddenly into the bright arena of '*real*' reality (as against the shoddy world of everyday life), stutter and stammer and search their verbal repertoire for any kind of idiocy or irrelevance rather than fail to answer, or ask a question of their own. The camera, in other words, exacts the instant and willing abandonment of the person's last shred of subjectivity. The grief-stricken widow will actually pause in her weeping to tell the voice 'how she feels'; the cornered politician will overlook the hectoring moralism of the voice in order to try to justify a position which, between them, the voice and the camera have already rendered untenable. Association with a television camera seems to justify almost any kind of intrusion. Occasionally, presumably, a person may rebel against the insolent impositions of the camera-voice (by asking it a question, for example), but if so, no doubt this evidence of subjective power will be edited from the tape before it gets a chance to subvert us.

The passivity of the person in relation to television is expressed in almost beautiful symbolism by the development of cable television. Like a great umbilical cord, the cable snakes to your set from some huge central placenta, promising to relieve you of the necessity for activity, creativity, thought, or even, eventually, movement. Passive consumption as opposed to active involvement is already the keynote of pre-cable television, but the multiplicity of channels offered by the cable means that you can be almost infinitely capricious with the choice of your diet if too heavy demands are made on your digestion. And even literally, once the potential for 'information technology' has been realised through your cable, you will not have to move from your sofa to order your breakfast.

Television's is the world of the 'image', and the camera constitutes the eye of the Other which renders self-conscious all those who become aware of its gaze. Television's ability to turn us into objects – to realise, that is, one of our most profound magical wishes – may go some way to explaining our readiness to accord *its* world a fundamental reality and to accept the necessity it imposes upon us to make the world of our experience fit in with its technical constraints and demands. People will distort the natural space-time of their experience in order to accommodate the needs of television – even 'spontaneous' expressions of joy or sorrow may be delayed until the cameras arrive on the scene. The dimensions in which ordinary activities take place, the timing of celebrations (as in pre-recorded

'Christmas' shows), the appropriateness of human conduct (as when junior school children are taught – no doubt as part of a 'training' in 'media skills' – to smile at cameras or talk to 'people' they will never meet) may all be altered to conform to what once might have seemed the *limitations* of television technology. But those limitations now come to be accepted as the prestigious accoutrements of a manufactured reality which promises to provide us with objective being. We are ready, it seems, to trade in the natural world of our experience, to sacrifice spontaneity and unreflective absorption with each other and the world, for a self-consciously fabricated image of how we should like things to be. In doing this we have failed to notice the quite untrammelled licence we have given to our magico-religious dream of escaping from our subjectivity. We smile indulgently at those 'primitive' peoples who refuse to be photographed for fear of losing their souls, when in fact we might envy their still having souls to lose. As for us, we become the mechanical terminals of the machines we have created.

Indeed, it is hard now to believe that in many ways we have not actually achieved the state of affairs in which the machines control us rather than we them. Quite apart from television, which hynotically draws people out of interaction with each other, there seem to be endless ways in which we become plugged into machines which render us oblivious to our human surroundings. It is scarcely possible any longer to find a pub in which conversation is not drowned out by the juke box, the electronic explosions of the space invaders and the bleeping of the fruit machines. Like automata ourselves, we stand in front of these machines, the movements of our eyes and limbs stereotyped and repetitive, controlled by a mechanical program which determines precisely the limits of our freedom. Already quite possibly slightly deafened by discos, young people walk or cycle down the street with headphones clamped to their ears ('wired for sound', in the words of a pop song), cut off from any possibility of mutual relationship with their world. Girls in offices sit with docile attentiveness before the balefully glowing green screens of computer terminals and word processors which type fake 'personal' letters to potential customers whose names have been swallowed up into the software (no 'neurotic' dislocation of words from reality could be more poignant than the way in which we have learned to speak about the 'personalised' communications of computers).

Almost every human ability and characteristic which can be mechanised has been syphoned off from our subjectivity and translated into plastic and electronic circuitry. And we, enslaved to the machines, passively consume from them the fruits of the very abilities of which they have robbed us – more accurately, of which we have robbed ourselves and built into them. With our willing connivance, the machines, and of course the professionals and experts whose interest it is to tend them, have taken over and objectified the subjectivity of 'ordinary people', who become emptied-out objects unable to reintegrate what is rightfully theirs, but who can, for a price, effortlessly consume what once they might have been able effortfully to create. No longer needing, for example, to make music, people can surround themselves with stacks of stereophonic gadgetry from which they can hear music as digitally faultless as technology can make it. 'Entertainment', as well as 'communication', have become the prerogatives of a tiny minority of professional experts (the globally familiar celebrities and pundits) whose already highly practised abilities are electronically perfected and offered for mass consumption to us, the public, who no longer see music, art, discussion or even thought as any part of our own 'skills', and who, as unprotestingly as battery chickens (themselves, let it be noted, animals we have mechanised), accept an ever more narrowly standardised cultural diet fed to us through our brushed aluminium hoppers.

In this way we become mere shells, passively consuming via a highly evolved technology an artificial world which is increasingly insulated from any effort we might make to impinge upon

it. This is not the result of the evil machinations of any particular group or class (though clearly some people's interests will
be served by this state of affairs more than others'), but rather
the upshot of a magic-infused mythology in which to a greater
or lesser extent we all collude, and which may well have its
roots in the greedy passivity we all experience as infants.

Since, however, the real world continues to exist, we find
ourselves from time to time rudely awakened from our wishful
dreams to confront issues which cause us unexpected and
incomprehensible pain. Far from being an indication of our
own malfunctioning, this may yet provide us with the spur we
need to recognise and confront the reality of the world, to
accept responsibility for the mechanised impoverishment of our
lives, and to reassert our subjectivity. But, predictably, our first
impulse is to look for technical solutions to our troubled
dreams.

CHAPTER SEVEN

The Experts

When the myth-infused structures which support the objectified individual's sense of security split open to reveal the threats
of the real world, he or she is likely to interpret this as a form of
mechanical breakdown. In this chapter I want to consider –
necessarily only in outline – those forms of professional help
which are most widely available to those who seek it when they
feel in need of a degree of repair which they cannot effect for
themselves. In doing this I shall stay as close as possible to my
own experience, particularly as someone working with people
who have sought or been offered psychological help within the
facilities of the British National Health Service. I shall not on
the whole be considering the predicament of those thought to
have 'broken down' so seriously as to justify the label
'psychotic' and to merit admission for in-patient treatment (for
example for 'schizophrenia') in psychiatric hospitals – not
because I believe their condition is in any way fundamentally
different from that of the rest of us, but rather because my experience in that kind of area is not particularly great. For the most
part, the people I have in mind may be experiencing quite acute
distress, in which 'anxiety' and 'depression' both feature to
some extent, perhaps taking a particular kind of form ('phobias',
'obsessions'), or seeming to them to indicate some kind of –
perhaps serious – physical illness. These are the kinds of 'symptoms', in other words, which have been under scrutiny
throughout this book, and which will in some degree be
familiar to almost everyone.

The objectifying categories of thought which determine the

'symptoms' also, of course, determine the 'cures', so that the mythology of 'breakdown' in the lay mind is complemented in the professional mind by a mythology of 'treatment'. There is something about operating within a common mythology which seems in itself to have a kind of efficacy and to satisfy the expectations of those involved whether or not there is any independent evidence of anybody's really benefiting thereby indeed, the satisfaction of mythological expectations may in itself constitute a certain kind of benefit. For example, one can read accounts of medical treatments having been administered throughout the ages to the obvious relief and satisfaction of patients, even though, from our own scientific standpoint, the treatments can at best have been neutral in terms of their physical effects on patients. It would, I suggest, be simplistic to assume that physicians of previous ages were just wrong, while ours, with their superior 'scientific' insights, are right, and a sober consideration of history might well suggest that in any case ours may not be half as right as we like to think.★ Science has become our own particular dogmatic mythology, and it is my belief that, while it may well perform the same kind of social functions which were served in previous times by magic, it now stands in the way of our achieving an accurate understanding of the origins and significance of psychological distress. There is a sense, then, in which the recognised professional approaches to 'breakdown' *work*, in that they provide a conceptual framework in which people's distress can be contained and dealt with. I do not wish to dismiss the significance of this kind of efficacy, but nor am I particularly interested in it, for whether or not the orthodox approaches 'work', they still, I believe, obscure the nature of our reality.

The kinds of help available to people whose distress drives them to seek it nearly all have their roots in a mechanistic (basically medical) view of 'illness' or 'breakdown'. In the long

★See I. Illich, *Medical Nemesis*, Calder & Boyars, 1975.

run, I think, this is bound to have negative effects since it serves the aims of a defensive objectification which can only mask from us realities of our world to which sooner or later we shall have to pay attention. But it also seems clear that there are good humanitarian reasons for the development and endurance of the mechanistic approach, and at least patients may expect to be able to reveal their distress without receiving an immediately moralistic or condemnatory response – although there is a small (and diminishing) risk that the person they are likely to consult first (their general practitioner) will respond with a 'pull yourself together' homily.

There are two main approaches to 'treatment' which are likely to be encountered once the plunge has been taken and the doctor consulted. The first is frankly medical, involving the prescription of physical treatments (particularly tranquillising and anti-depressant drugs), and will be administered either by the general practitioner or by a psychiatrist to whom the patient has been referred. Prescription of treatment of this kind is likely to take place in a setting in which the patient will be expected to talk about 'symptoms' and personal diffficulties, but probably not in any great detail or depth (as much, perhaps, as may be fitted into the odd ten- or fifteen-minute interview). The other main approach will focus more on the psychological 'causes' of the patient's difficulties, seeing them as the outcome of his or her life history and current situation, and is more likely to be taken by a psychiatrist or clinical psychologist to whom the patient has been referred. Although on the face of it less obviously 'medical' or mechanistic, these forms of treatment, as I shall argue in more detail presently, still depend heavily on inexplicit but distinctly medical assumptions.

The various schools and shades of opinion within these two broad approaches – in particular the variations to be found in the psychological therapies – are bewilderingly numerous, and the uninitiated sufferer, unless unusually well equipped with a knowledge of the field permitting insistence on a particular type of treatment (which even then may well not be available locally) is likely to receive nothing more reliable than pot luck once he or she enters the 'system'. The most predictable aspect of the treatment system, as well as the most prevalent, is that offered by orthodox psychiatry.

British psychiatry has on the whole stayed much closer to the traditions of physical medicine than has, for example, psychiatry in the USA, and those who rely for their expectations of psychiatrists on trans-Atlantic films or television programmes will be in for a surprise. Psychiatrists in Britain are trained in the orthodox methods of medicine, in which great emphasis is laid on the accurate identification (diagnosis) of illnesses, or 'disease entities', so that established methods of treatment can be applied almost automatically. Although many voices both within and outside psychiatry have been raised to suggest that this approach is not appropriate to much of the field of what has come to be called 'mental illness', the very rigidity of the deeply embedded practices and assumptions of medicine has meant that psychiatrists have been slow to react to doubts about the viability of their undertaking, and even when they have acknowledged that there may be conceptual difficulties about seeing 'problems of living' as illnesses, have not seemed able to think of anything more effective to *do* than administer superficial reassurance along with the tranquillisers.

There are, however, several factors which contribute to the maintenance of orthodox psychiatric practice other than simple lack of imagination on the part of psychiatrists. For example, it undoubtedly is possible to 'discover' systematic similarities and differences in the way people cope with distress, and it is therefore *plausible* to treat the revealed regularities as 'syndromes' resembling those more fruitfully identified in other fields of medicine. It is, however, frequently overlooked that the reliable identification of such 'behavioural' syndromes does not *necessarily* imply the presence of actual disease. Again, it would be quite wrong to pretend that 'psychotropic' drugs of the kinds prescribed by psychiatrists do not alter the way people experience the world through their bodily engagement with it, and that the contact they have with it may not by this means be rendered less painful. In some senses, at least, it is thus quite reasonable to acknowledge that physical treatments 'work', and it is also possible that the degree of relief experienced, apart from the obvious welcome it may be given by patients, may provide people with the opportunity to examine and deal with their predicament more effectively than they could when overwhelmed by anxiety or distress. It is also true, however, that many patients experience psychotropic medication as in itself a further source of confusion and discomfort, since it may alter their perception of the world in an idiosyncratic way, so that their experience seems to bear no relation to the meaning of the actual events of their world. Most patients whom I have seen, even when they have found the consumption of such medication helpful, seem to have a guilty sense of dependence on an almost illicit form of comfort of which they feel they should rid themselves.

I suspect that the argument that temporary reliance on tranquillisers or anti-depressants may permit patients to take a more effective grasp on their diffficulties, while occasionally justified, in fact reflects an infrequent occurrence. The effect of such drugs seems on the whole to make one care less, not more, about the circumstances of one's life (which are in any case often extremely resistant to easy alteration) and hence to encourage an attitude which is even less likely than before to confront them. A little later in this chapter I shall be discussing factors common to *all* forms of psychiatric and psychological treatment which may result in the achievement of positive 'therapeutic gains' for patients, but for the present one might speculate that one of the central reasons for the continuing 'popularity' of orthodox psychiatry is the close correspondence of its assumptions to those of our cultural mythology.

There is little that is compellingly rational in the historical development of psychiatry's treatment techniques – the history of ECT (electro-convulsive therapy), for example, is a grotesque tale of mistaken assumptions and fortuitous observations (to do with the electrical stunning of Italian pigs before slaughter), from which emerges, in our day, the 'scientific' use of ECT on patients suffering from some forms of 'depressive illness'. Psychiatric treatments seem always to have been particularly prone to vicissitudes of fashion, underpinned by superficially plausible rationales that quite quickly turn out to be untenable. (Psychosurgery for schizophrenia, for example, once all the rage, is now virtually never used for this purpose, and indeed is, mercifully, not greatly in vogue for any psychiatric condition at present.) There is no convincing evidence that this is any less the case now than it ever was, and psychiatric theories about the causation of 'illnesses' such as 'schizophrenia', let alone the more heterogeneous 'neuroses', are signally lacking in scientifically persuasive force. In relation to their colleagues in other medical specialities, most psychiatrists are uncomfortable and defensive about the insubstantial basis of their discipline, and yet probably few of them (and few of their patients) doubt that they are on the right lines, since it seems 'obvious' that one day 'mental' and 'behavioural' 'disorders' will be shown to have physical causes which can be accurately diagnosed and effectively treated by physical means.

This reasoning is of course at the very centre of our self-characterisation as machines, and the promise that our unhappiness can be relieved with little effort from ourselves by the administration of drugs, electricity, or brain surgery has a particularly strong appeal to our longing for passive objectivity. However, as has been pointed out by critics of the psychiatric orthodoxy such as Thomas Szasz, the cogency of this undertaking rests on the assumption that what are in fact 'disorders' of conduct, i.e. *moral actions*, can be traced to 'dysfunctional' mechanisms rather than accepted as the natural outcome of a person's transactions with the world. The man-as-machine analogy may be a fruitful one to apply in some areas of physical medicine, but there is certainly nothing necessarily compelling about its use in psychiatry.

The 'objective methodology' of research in psychiatry, as well as in other areas of the 'treatment' of 'mental disorder', precludes any radical criticism of the approaches involved since it assumes their conceptual validity at the outset – i.e., it only *looks for* entities of the type it *expects* to find. Briefly, methods of research perhaps most useful for determining, say, the relative usage of instant versus real coffee in different social *groups* or geographical areas (and therefore for suggesting likely marketing strategies), are used to supply inferences about the significance and reaction to treatment of an *individual's* personal psychological pain. Objective research deals almost exclusively with groups, statistical averages, artificially numerical measurement and predetermined categories of meaning (for example, diagnostic 'inventories' allow only a narrow range of answers to predetermined and usually highly specific questions). Within this framework there is no scope for voicing a *subjective* criticism of the procedures involved, and so what people actually think of themselves, their difficulties, or their treatment, is almost impossible to discover. (The reader may well be familiar with the related phenomenon which dictates that what is seen as being medically the matter with individuals depends far less on their subjective experience than on the 'objective' findings of X-rays, etc., so that people may even *themselves* discount their only too vividly experienced pain because it does not receive 'official' – objective – confirmation.) The 'scientific' studies of psychiatric procedures which fill the libraries to bursting point with ever-increasing numbers of 'learned journals' on the whole simply ignore how patients perceive their treatment, in favour of, for example, displaying a 'statistically significant difference' in some kind of 'objective measure' (such as a rating scale, questionnaire, psychological test score, etc.) between two or more groups of patients. The 'findings' of this huge volume of research literature are almost wholly equivocal.

My impression is that people on the whole are not greatly appreciative of the official methods of psychiatry, though this is not to say that many psychiatrists are not compassionate and experienced people who have at the very least the ability to offer support and reassurance to, and the power to arrange for a respite for, those in their care who have been particularly battered by their life experiences.

Those forms of 'treatment' which rest on a psychological rather than physical brand of mechanism constitute, as already mentioned, a very wide range of approaches which are not all that easily classified. Crudely, they may perhaps be split into two main strands: the 'psychodynamic' therapies which developed out of a tradition first established by Freudian psychoanalysis, and the 'behavioural' approaches which were developed more recently and have at least a significant part of their origins in the academic discipline of experimental psychology. There are also, however, many hybrid psychotherapies which draw their inspiration, often somewhat indiscriminately, from no particularly pure intellectual strain.

In the public mind 'psychotherapy' is often synonymous with psychoanalysis. However, despite the crucial role played by psychoanalysis in establishing a 'psychological' approach to the 'treatment' of 'mental disorder', orthodox Freudian analysis is not widely practised in Britain, and is only within the reach of a tiny minority of people who can afford the time and expense incurred in visiting an analyst several times a week over a period of years. There is a very small number of specialised clinics within the National Health Service which do owe particular allegiance to Freudian methods (though in a somewhat modified form), but it is extremely unlikely that the average patient will get anywhere near one.

It is much more likely that patients who are referred for specialised psychological therapy will find themselves receiving individual or group psychotherapy from psychiatrists (i.e. medically trained specialists) who have received instruction in psychotherapeutic 'techniques' loosely related to the Freudian approach, but considerably less intensive in terms of frequency and duration, or a form of 'behavioural' psychotherapy which is most likely to be dispensed by a clinical psychologist (i.e. a non-medical practitioner who has under- and post-graduate training in psychology).

Although it is the later developed of the two broad strands of therapy to be considered here, it will be more convenient to consider the behavioural approach first; in any case, I think it probably true that this approach constitutes the most 'popular' and widely practised form of non-physical treatment likely to be encountered by the average patient.

Behaviourist psychology, from which behavioural psychotherapies derive many of their ideas and principles, was the ruling dogma in academic psychology in Britain and America for at least the middle forty years of the last century (it seems fairly clear that in the academic, non-clinical field, this dogma has now given way to slightly less simplistic, but still just as 'objective' variants on the man-as-machine theme). The central claim of behaviourism is that all those concepts which we connect with 'mind' (lumped together in the contemptuous term 'mentalism') are false, misleading, and (worst of all!) 'unscientific' because subjective and not measurable. We cannot therefore talk meaningfully of wishes, intuitions, desires, thoughts, feelings, intentions, etc., as long as these refer to people's subjective experience, since there is no way of demonstrating or measuring their existence objectively. If we are to be 'scientific', what we must do, therefore, is restrict ourselves to those aspects of people's *behaviour*, and the factors in the environment which impinge upon it, which are objectively observable and quantifiable. At the time when this view was being formulated, the concepts of the physiologist Pavlov were readily to hand to provide just the kind of objective characteristics which were needed to 'explain' 'behaviour' – i.e., stimulus, reponse, and the 'conditionable' connection between them. The hope was that the behaviour of an individual person (referred to as 'the organism' in experimental jargon) could be predicted and controlled once a full understanding had been reached of the operation of the environmental stimuli which provoked from him or her what were seen (again according to Pavlov) as reflex responses.

For a number of reasons which are likely to be quite obvious to even the most unreflective layman, this attempt at producing an exact, experimental science of psychology was doomed to failure, not only because of the complexity needed to give a full account of human conduct in these terms (some very ingenious attempts were made to handle this) but also because, *in principle*, any such analysis is impossible unless the psychologist manages to become a different order of being from those whom he or she is studying (only God could be a successful behaviourist psychologist); the subject's *awareness* of the experimenter's predictions concerning the former's behaviour is, of course, often sufficient to change the very behaviour predicted. However, these philosophical stumbling blocks, which follow from the fact that psychologists are not gods and those they study are not machines, have not prevented the thriving development of behavioural methods in the clinical field.

Despite behaviourism's quite spectacular failure to produce a psychology which was either practically useful or intellectually convincing, psychologists' repetitious insistence on its 'scientificness' earned it a kind of superstitious credibility among those who had been brought up under its sway, and it was belief in this dogmatic claim which allowed some of its methods to be applied, and then vociferously advocated in the treatment of so-called 'neurotic' disorders. The field of non-physical treatment had up to that point (the late 1950s and early 1960s) been dominated by the medical, psychoanalytic approach, which, it is true, had maintained its dominance partly on the grounds of a mystique-laden appeal to what had become the rather convoluted theories which had been developed by his followers from Freud's often profoundly important insights. Behaviourally inclined clinical psychologists used the dogmatic appeal to scientific objectivism to challenge some of the more esoteric and impenetrable notions of the analysts and to offer instead a much simplified and altogether more obvious account of what caused, and what might cure, 'neurotic disorders'.

Rather than referring to, for example, the unconscious reaction to the Oedipal and castration complexes attaching to the repressed traumas of childhood, the unrecognised 'transference' longings of the infantilely fixated patient which it was the special business of the trained analyst to unravel, the behavioural therapist suggested that the neurosis consisted of nothing more than responses which had become faultily conditioned to inappropriate stimuli. The triumph of 'behaviour therapy', as it swiftly came to be called, was, under the guise of a 'scientific' technique of treatment, to appropriate the methods of common sense, and to turn the latter with good effect against some of the more mysterious, implausible and unhelpful practices of a psychoanalysis which had wandered too theoretically far from a basis in clinical experience.

In claiming to apply to clinical phenomena the 'laws of learning' which had been 'scientifically established' in university departments of psychology (claims almost laughable in their implausibility to all but the converted), behaviour therapists developed such 'techniques' as 'systematic desensitisation' and 'implosion therapy'. Though set in a suitably impressive 'scientific' context which, for example, warned solemnly of the importance of the exact timing of 'reinforcement' (reward and punishment of 'responses'), etc., these proved to be nothing more than the time-honoured methods of overcoming anxiety either by a) being introduced very gradually to whatever causes it, or b) being thrown in at the deep end.

There is no doubt that there was a good deal that was helpful about this kind of approach, for example in demystifying some of the supposed powers of 'the shrink', and in (inadvertently) emphasising the importance of bodily confrontation of those aspects of the real world which cause us distress. What was not helpful (and yet, ironically, lends behavioural methods much of their cultural acceptability) was the overtly, and even crassly, mechanistic nature of its theoretical claims.

Behaviour therapy, and related approaches such as 'behaviour modification', have enjoyed great popularity, spawning a wide variety of 'techniques' and a reputation for technical respectability which, though in my view entirely undeserved, is the envy of all its theoretical competitors. Of course, behaviour therapists' success, such as it actually is, may have very little to do with their theoretical position. While purportedly defining their patients' difficulties objectively, designing appropriate courses of intervention with scientific precision (for example by isolating those 'contingencies of reinforcement' – rewards and punishments – which maintain the 'dysfunctional behaviour' and replacing them with more appropriate ones) behaviour therapists are of course developing a relationship with patients which contains all kinds of elements which cannot *in fact* be conceptualised in the same aseptic and 'rigorous', 'non-mentalistic' terms as the theory itself. Behaviourist language, certainly, is as spotless as the scientist's proverbial white coat, studiously avoiding anything which smacks of imprecision or value judgement, but what behaviour therapists *do* is entirely another question – many of them are warm and concerned people whose conduct in the therapeutic setting bears only passing resemblance to their theoretical claims.

However effective behaviour therapists may be in their treatment of so-called 'neurotic disorders', they are to be numbered among the most prolific myth-makers of the age. The idea of the sufferer as a passive victim of a faulty 'learning history' (i.e. the inappropriate pairing of stimuli and responses), in principle repairable through a kind of re-programming not unlike that one might consider for a recalcitrant computer, clearly goes straight to the heart of our longing for machine status, as well as of the 'expert's' dream of technical mastery. It permits us also to continue to live uncritically in a world in which, it appears, people only go wrong more or less by accident. 'Evil' (if one may be permitted to use so emotive a word) thus becomes a technical, not a moral problem. Behavioural approaches share with most others which the sufferer is likely actually to come across an emphasis on the *individual's* malfunctioning in relation to a world which is taken as in essence objectively given and unalterable. That the world contains real evils which cause real distress which cannot simply be 'adjusted' out of individuals is countenanced as little by the behaviourists as by the other approaches under consideration, and indeed in its pure form behaviourism is perhaps the least likely of these approaches to allow any such possibility to be theoretically posed.

We must acknowledge, however, that the behavioural approach, having successfully masked common sense with a suitably 'scientific' façade, has in recent times modified its theoretical bases in order to try to avoid the embarrassment caused by some of its more obviously unacceptable simplistic assumptions. Behaviourally inclined psychologists have now had to acknowledge the importance of *meaning*, since they could not ignore for long the fact that, for instance, the same stimuli and responses may signify different things for different people, or to the same person at different times. The result of this is that there now exists a school – unthinkable to the pure behaviourist of old – known as 'cognitive behaviourism'. Where once 'mentalistic' concepts were anathema, 'cognitions' are now welcome, and behaviourists are happy to acknowledge that people think, and even to some extent initiate activity rather than simply react passively to 'environmental contingencies'. What has been preserved is a suitably impersonal, jargon-ridden, 'objective' language which gives proper regard to the dictates of mechanism. By taking compromising steps of this kind it seems to me that from a theoretical standpoint the approach has become less rather than more respectable, since now it is merely inconsistent, and the recognition of 'cognitions' seems to do little more than acknowledge, and then place far too much emphasis on, the fact that people 'talk' to themselves about what they are doing. Behaviourism would, I think, have done better to shift from 'behaviour' to 'conduct' (i.e. to acknowledge the moral possibility of *intention*) than to readmit under a new guise the mentalistic ideas which in some important ways it had been right to reject.

Therapeutically, the practice of cognitive behaviourism results in some fairly common-sense ideas about how patients may work at correcting faulty expectations or unduly pessimistic interpretations of their experience (for example by 'monitoring' and altering their 'self-talk'). This kind of approach seems to rest on assumptions to be found more generally in other forms of psychological therapy – e.g. that what matters (and what causes distress) is not so much the way things are, but the way things *seem*, and that by changing one's attitude towards them one may come to feel a good deal better. Since this is indeed a central aspect of most forms of psychological treatment, it may be as well to consider the more 'dynamic' approaches in somewhat greater detail before making any judgement about the usefulness of 'attitude change'.

As has already been pointed out, Freudian psychoanalysis, despite the familiarity of many of its concepts and even of its therapeutic method to the general public, is unlikely to be met with in anything like a pure form by those seeking help within the National Health Service. There are some psychiatrists (a minority) who practise group or individual therapy based loosely on psychoanalytic principles, and patients who fall into their hands may find their actions and utterances being 'interpreted' in the light of the unconscious motives which are supposedly to be detected beneath them, as well as a good deal of attention being paid to the 'transference' relationship between patient and therapist (i.e. the degree to which the patient carries over to that relationship feelings and expectations learned in earlier, particularly parental, relationships). The 'insight' to be gained from this therapeutic procedure will, it is hoped, lead either directly or indirectly to changes in the patient's actions.

Psychoanalytic theory is neither simple nor simplistic, and embedded in it is a view of human nature the implications of which have probably yet to be fully appreciated. A critique of psychoanalysis itself would take us too far beyond the purposes of the present book – suffice it to say for the moment that in my view only the foolish or the naive would treat psychoanalysis as a *theory* with anything but the greatest respect. As a practical technique in the hands of the less reflective therapist, however, it may leave a good deal to be desired. The temptation, of course, is to treat it as a technique which, mechanically applied, will lead automatically, and possibly mysteriously, to a 'cure' of the patient's 'neurosis'. Even more than with most forms of therapy, the analytic therapist may find it hard to resist the role of awe-inspiring expert, since so much of the theory is easily (if wrongly) seen as esoteric knowledge available only to a privileged few. For patients, this inscrutability of both theory and practitioner may be somewhat intimidating, or perhaps irritating, or possibly just baffling. However, there is, again, nothing to suggest that therapists claiming a theoretical allegiance to psychoanalysis may not be sensitive and concerned individuals whose experience over the years has given them a profound understanding of people in distress and has led to their developing helpful therapeutic practices which may or may not be related to Freudian theory.★

Post-Freudian psychotherapies, developed mainly by

★For the views of a psychotherapist who has developed a very coherent account of his theoretical progress beyond his origins in psychoanalysis, see P. Lomas, *The Case for a Personal Psychotherapy*, Oxford University Press, 1981.

psychologists and psychiatrists in the USA, have probably had more influence on the kind of non-medical, non-behavioural, psychological help available through official channels in Britain. Among these are Carl Rogers's 'client-centred therapy', George Kelly's 'personal construct therapy', Albert Ellis's 'rationalemotive therapy', Eric Berne's 'transactional analysis' and Fritz Perls's 'Gestalt psychotherapy' (the two latter approaches probably enjoy greater popularity beyond rather than within the 'official' setting of the National Health Service). It is not easy to generalise about these approaches, not least because it is usually one of the central aims of any 'school' of psychotherapy precisely to *differentiate* itself from other schools. However, most of them do, I think, share a particular focus on the *individual* and the way he or she experiences the world.

This exploration of how the person sees his or her predicament takes place in a setting in which the importance of the *quality* of the relationship between therapist and patient is explicitly recognised, and there is no doubt that this is an advance (attributable in particular to Rogers) over those 'techniques' which (like orthodox psychoanalysis) advocated in accordance with the best mechanistic principles a deliberately impersonal role for the therapist. Thus the therapist's personal way of relating to the patient – for example, to use Rogers's terms, with warmth, empathy and genuineness – becomes central to the therapeutic process rather than an aspect of it deliberately to be expunged.

It is a central point of all psychotherapies that patients' views concerning what ails them will be questioned by the therapist, perhaps even disputed quite hotly (many therapies lay emphasis on the importance of *confronting* patients with the falsity of their views). This I see as a necessary part of *undeceiving* people about the mythological accounts of their difficulties which they have come to tell themselves, but it is easy to slip from this position to one which takes an almost entirely relativistic view about the way people see the world. Undeceiving someone is, usually, to present them with a view of the world which is clearer, more accurate, than the mythified (defensive) view with which they deceived themselves, but also a *painful* one which requires some kind of active (bodily) response from them; it is *not* simply to replace a 'maladjusted' or somehow distressingly misconceived view of their circumstances with a more reasonable (rational) one which shows them that things are not so bad really, or that all their difficulties have been due to their mistaken way of looking at things. This latter, and, I think, misguidedly optimistic view of psychological distress is a characteristic of many of the lighter-weight psychotherapies at the 'cognitive' end of the spectrum. At the root of such approaches, again, is an almost entirely mechanistic view of man, in which adjustments to *individuals* (changing attitudes or perceptions, training in 'skills') are, even if no more than tacitly, seen as the way to tackle what are in fact absolutely *real* difficulties arising *between* people and the world. If taken at their face value, such approaches are cruelly mythifying, since the person is left in a painful world with nothing more substantial than the belief that if only he or she could see it differently things would be better.

It is no surprise that any seriously conducted psychological investigation of people in distress will quickly run across the importance of the way such people interpret their world (i.e., what they tell themselves about it), and in this is to be found the defensiveness (self-deception) which Freud's inquiries so clearly revealed. That such investigation has almost always taken place in the context of fundamental assumptions having their origin in medico-mechanistic habits of thought (including, for instance, ideas of 'breakdown' and 'cure') means, however, that the significance of what is being defended *against* is overlooked. The individual defends against a painful world, and it all too easily happens that the therapist concentrates on the 'maladaptive' nature of the defences, aiming to 'cure' the person of reliance on them, but ignoring the moral problem presented by the world's real dangers and injustices against which they have been erected. Whether they know it or not, and however much they might wish to repudiate such a role, psychological therapists almost inevitably become instruments for the adjustment of individuals to a social *status quo*.

It is perhaps implicit in the work of those who, like R. D. Laing and Thomas Szasz, have criticised the 'mental health' approach to psychological distress that any therapist who accepts that something is *wrong with* those who seek help is likely to be implicated in a moral–political confidence trick. Only the therapist who adopts the position that there is *nothing* wrong with those in distress (i.e. no mechanical or even 'cognitive' fault identifiable), but that their response is a *natural* one to a painful world, stands a chance of not enmeshing people even further in the strands of myth.

Enormous efforts have been made to determine what if anything is useful and helpful in the various kinds of treatment available to those who seek it. Almost all this research has, as one might expect, been carried out within the 'scientific' tradition which asserts the values of objectivity and mechanism. The search has thus been for techniques, stimuli, controllable and generalisable therapeutic strategies which will lead to predictable improvement in the identifiable 'conditions' 'presented' by patients. Everything about the therapeutic effort, from the construction of technique-specifying theories to the painstaking effort to demonstrate their effectiveness through objective research, testifies to the fundamentally mechanist assumptions involved. There are undoubtedly very many people so embedded in this perspective that they would consider it barely sane to question it – it seems to them simply *self-evident* that the kinds of 'symptoms' which those in distress display just must be due to specific causes which can at least in principle be understood and eradicated by technical experts. Even the most 'humanistic' psychological theories tend to betray an allegiance to this kind of belief, even if they do not profess it.

In the final analysis it is only a profound mechanistic faith of this kind which can explain the extent to which the professionalisation of psychological help has taken and is taking place. Professional helping organisations sprout and mushroom in direct proportion to the rate at which people embrace a conception of themselves as mechanical objects. Experiencing themselves as unloved and without resources, drained of energy, powerless, blistered by the omnipresent gaze of the threatening Other, unable to meet the standards objectively established for beauty and effectiveness, struggling with conditions of life which, if accepted as objectively immovable, appear to a view unclouded by myth as almost unbearably malign, people naturally turn hopefully to the only kind of remedy their cosmology permits them to imagine: i.e., one which offers mechanical modification to adjust them to the world.

The fundamental social conceptions of our time of course play straight into the interests of the 'helping professions', and the search for security in objectivity offers those of us involved in mediating its delivery an opportunity for profit which only the most self-denying could refuse. As long as therapists can see themselves as 'change agents', possessors of 'therapeutic skills', 'trained' and 'qualified' in technical procedures firmly grounded in a scientific 'knowledge base', able to offer 'programmes' of 'treatment' and courses of 'training in social skills', to correct 'sexual dysfunction' through behavioural 'techniques' of established effectiveness, and so on and on, they can scarcely be chided for taking money for their services.

In fact, however, there is not a shred of convincing evidence in support of these or similar claims, and there can be no doubt that they continue to be asserted not least because the interests of a professional helping industry have become a barrier to appreciating the truth. Again I would wish to stress, however, that this is not the sole reason for the way things are, or even the most important (even those who advocate 'self-help therapy' as an alternative to over-professionalised approaches still for the most part see 'therapy' as a *technical* undertaking). The helpers have as big a 'religious' stake as the helped in the mythology of objectivity, and most would feel a quite sincere pride in the humanitarian nature of their calling. To question the motives of therapists' conduct is no less challenging and painful – possibly outraging – to them than it is for them to do the same with their patients in the course of therapy, but neither is it intended to carry any greater imputation of blame. If patients can only get to grips with the world by becoming aware of the context from which their experience stems, so therapists cannot in the long run afford morally to ignore the significance of their conduct *as* therapists while priding themselves (not unjustifiably) on their conduct in easing people's pain *in* therapy.

Despite what I take to be the fact that there is no consistent evidence for the effectiveness of psychiatric and psychological intervention as technical treatment, there can be little doubt that many of those offering such treatment are in fact experienced by their patients as helpful. The reasons for this are clear enough for all to see, but have largely been ignored because they do not accord with our mythology. Even many of the most 'objective' research studies of therapeutic methods have acknowledged, often with a kind of apologetic puzzlement, that the personal qualities of therapist and patient, and the nature and quality of the relationship between them, are influential in determining the degree to which 'treatment' is found to be useful. Because such factors form no part of the technical procedures held by most (but not all) therapeutic theorists to be important, they are often more or less dismissed as 'non-specific' by research workers and commentators. It also seems likely that the realities of the situation in which therapy takes place encourage therapists to conduct themselves in ways more consistent than the theoretical differences between them would seem to permit: in other words, people of reasonably good will whose professional lives expose them to the kinds of experiences of people and their difficulties which are in fact familiar to therapists are likely to end up doing much the same kinds of things with patients no matter what they tell themselves they are doing. There is as evidence of this, research work which suggests that experienced therapists of different theoretical allegiances in fact conduct themselves more similarly in therapy than do experienced and inexperienced therapists of the same school. For these and similar reasons it may be sensible to seek a 'de-mythified' account of what people in distress do actually find helpful, rather than straining our credulity on accounts which seem to be aimed more at supporting the structures of objectivity than articulating our experience.

In fact there is quite a large, but also largely neglected, literature which attempts to take therapists' and patients' experiences seriously.* The basic lessons of therapeutic experience, seriously reflected upon, can, I believe, be stated in outline quite succinctly, though they have implications for a long overdue renewal of interest in subjectivity which need to be spelt out in considerable detail, and will in fact form the focus of the final two chapters of this book. There is, however, one particular problem presented by the professional practice of an 'honest' psychotherapy (i.e. one which, among other things, starts out on the basis that there is nothing *wrong with* the individuals who are helped by it) from which even the most serious and socially committed of its practitioners have tended to deflect their attention. Before addressing this particular difficulty, however, it would be as well briefly to sketch what appear to be the main features of psychological therapies which seem actually to be of help (though much of this will I hope by now be apparent from previous discussion in this book).

Psychological help, then, is gained by those who seek it first and foremost in the context of a *relationship* in which they are *undeceived* about the nature and significance of a real, often complex and possibly insolubly difficult, painful predicament or

*For two recent attempts of this kind see P. Lomas's book, already referred to, and my own *Psychotherapy: A Personal Approach*, Dent, 1978.

set of circumstances, and *encouraged* to confront *bodily* those
aspects of the predicament which admit of any possibility of
change. In essence this procedure is a moral, not a technical
undertaking, since at every point it necessitates judgements'
being made by both therapist and patient about what is *right* and
what is good for either or both to do, not only in the immediate
therapeutic setting, but also in the wider social context (particularly, of course, that of the patient). I do not believe that this
process can be stated, evaluated or understood in the conventionally objective terms which determine our orthodox habits
of thought, and therefore all sorts of questions must be raised
and revisions made concerning what we usually take to be the
nature of responsibility, learning, 'breakdown', etc. Some of
these questions have already been addressed, others will be
shortly. What needs to be considered now (and raises the particular difficulty mentioned above) are the implications of the
nature of the *relationship* upon which effective 'therapy' seems to
depend, and how this can be reconciled with a *professional* stance
on the part of therapists.

   In the semi-technicised jargon of some of the more 'humanistic' therapies, it has, as already indicated, been recognised that
personal qualities of therapists like 'unconditional positive
regard' (warmth), 'accurate empathy', and 'congruence'
(genuineness), seem conducive to positive change in 'clients'.
That these are seen as 'qualities' *possessed* by therapists (thereby
stimulating attempts to 'train' people in their acquisition) testifies to the tacit influence of the philosophy of objectification,
for they are of course qualities of *relationship* which may be
abstracted from people's *conduct* towards each other, but which
cannot be turned into things or possessions. However, the
central conclusion to be drawn from such observations is that
people are most likely to be influenced positively by those
whom they trust, and have *reason* to trust. This has, indeed,
been acknowledged quite unflinchingly by several psychotherapists of great distinction (C. G. Jung being among the earliest),

and the bravest have gone as far as venturing the view that the
most important 'healing' force in the therapeutic equation is
love.★

The very breath of such a notion is of course enough to send
the orthodox technicians of psychotherapy scurrying behind the
ramparts of objectivity, from where it can safely be regarded as
preposterous nonsense. If true, however, we come face to face
with the difficulty (alluded to above) which I think even the
bravest therapists prefer not to confront: is it morally justifiable
that patients should (directly or indirectly) *pay* for the professional provision of love?

Once all the technical mystique has been stripped away from
psychotherapy, it does seem that a likely explanation for its
almost explosive expansion over the last few decades is that it
provides something which is otherwise in very short supply in a
world in which a kind of watchful defensiveness against our
vulnerability has replaced any kind of spontaneous generosity
which people may more often once have felt for each other. As
Peter Lomas, particularly in *True and False Experience*, has very
cogently argued, the good therapist's stance towards his or her
patients may be likened to that of good parents towards their
children. This may perhaps be described as a kind of unselfish,
loving concern and interest under the benign influence of
which the child (or patient) can grow into an adult person. It is
precisely this kind of intense, concerned, caring interest which
is in such short supply in our objectifying social world – even, if
not especially, in the place where one would most hope to find
it, i.e., between parents and children. The demands of our social
organisation, the threat of annihilation which necessitates the
toughening of our defences, the unrelenting competitiveness

★See, for example, I. D. Suttie, *The Origins of Love and Hate*, Penguin
Books, 1960, and P. Lomas, *True and False Experience*, Allen Lane, 1973. Paul
Halmos, in an important but now largely overlooked vork, *The Faith of the
Counsellors*, Constable, 1965, examined in considerable detail the importance
of love in therapy.

which the need for objective status provokes, all militate against
our addressing each other spontaneously with the kind of open,
subjective, personal, intuitive, honest lovingness which we find
so warming but so scarce.

So depleted are our resources, so needy are we of the sort of
loving attention which is like rain to a meadow, that we cannot
find the strength to offer this kind of attention to others in our
personal lives, but feel an almost overwhelmingly insistent
demand to receive it from them which is of course never met,
since they are like us. The only times we are likely to experience the warmth we crave is for those relatively fleeting periods
when our interests appear to coincide with those of another (as
may be the case with mother and infant, or between lovers).
Almost everyone is desperate to be recognised, confirmed,
approved. Just as it can annihilate with a cold stare, so can the
Other through a loving glance infuse the flagging spirit with
life-giving warmth. But our neediness prevents us from being
Other for others.

The psychotherapist, in fact, offers a commodity available
almost nowhere else (not, that is, with any consistency or
predictability). Quite regularly, for about an hour at a time, you
can go to your psychotherapist and be listened to, concentrated
upon, thought about, puzzled over, understood, questioned,
encouraged. Here is someone who will take an absolutely
exclusive interest in you (or so, certainly, it is likely to seem to
you), who will attend to and remember even apparently trivial
details of your life, who will sympathise with your pain even
when gently remonstrating with instances of your intransigence, who will blame you for nothing and demand nothing
from you, fob you off with no superficial or impossible advice,
but open the way for you to tackle the difficulties in your life.
Put like this, surely, it is not hard to see the attraction of
psychotherapy nor to understand its popularity, and scarcely
necessary to invent for it any spuriously technical justification.
The more therapists' interest and concern is genuine (as

opposed to the rather coldly distant professional posture which some earlier psychotherapists took to be proper), the more they appear as real, recognisable people, the more they are likely to be trusted, and the more effective their influence – just as loving, and lovable, parents will have more influence over children than punitive, forbidding, or indifferent ones. Just such inferences as these are to be drawn from research revealing the 'non-specific' factors in psychotherapy.

There are of course qualities brought by good therapists to psychotherapy other than *merely* concern and warmth, just as the good parent will need more for the successful upbringing of children than simply benignly approving affection. Love, perhaps, is more than just a *component* in a 'therapeutic package', but rather the *spirit in which* one person places his or her resources at the disposal of another. Just as parents place at the disposal of their children, among other things, their knowledge of the world, in a way which maximises the usefulness of that knowledge, bending their concern to the child's interests, so therapists use their knowledge of, say, the nature and significance of distress, in their patients' interests. As professional people therapists are not more effective than laymen because of any greater capacity to love (and certainly not because of any esoteric technical knowledge), but rather because of the opportunity open to them to draw on their special experience in a loving way. That they can *afford* to be loving in this way may at least in part be attributed to the undemanding and uncomplicated nature of the emotional setting in which professional therapy takes place. If their relationship with patients extended beyond the times at which they made themselves professionally available, therapists would then end up in the same boat as all those who find *mutually* demanding relationships so threatening and draining.

Therapists are naturally quick to point out the importance for successful therapy of the professional nature of their engagement with patients, but are on the whole less comfortable about acknowledging the moral incongruity of offering, in essence, love for money. Psychotherapists in private practice often profess a convenient belief that patients are only properly 'motivated' to make the kind of efforts necessary for therapeutic progress if they pay for their therapy, but few of those who fully appreciate the importance of love to their calling are quite as brazenly and unreflectively self-interested, though they would still, I think, be reluctant to admit that their activities served any but the highest of motives. However, my own feeling is that it may be salutary for those of us who make a living as psychotherapists to consider the wider implications of what we do, for there is no obvious reason to suppose that ours is less disabling as a profession than any other.

Almost anything in our society which can be turned into a commodity and marketed, will be. Love is no exception to this rule, and it can come as no surprise that in a world in which its free availability is so strictly limited there should be found a flourishing profession engaged in its supply. This is again, of course, not the result of a conscious plot on the part of unusually greedy or unscrupulous individuals, but rather the inevitable outcome of the interplay of supply and demand, needs and interests.

In this way, then, I think it not entirely shocking to suggest that psychotherapists are to be found in a role closely analogous to that of prostitutes. As a professional group prostitutes may not commonly be held in great social esteem, but probably few would claim that, in a less than perfect world, their activities are entirely without social value. (If nothing else, prostitution has the merit of honesty; for this reason it is sad to learn that there are apparently prostitutes in the USA who have now begun to call themselves 'sex therapists'!)

Just as prostitutes supply sexual favours to those who find them difficult to obtain in any other way, so psychotherapists provide for a price the kind of individual attention many of us need to get from someone in order to survive in a cruel world.

Therapists may feel that the attention (love) they give their patients is more genuine, more worthwhile and respectable than the sexual 'love' dispensed by prostitutes. But this, I think, is debatable. The prostitute's is a very specific and very frank service – though she may not feel love for her clients, she unequivocally makes her body available to them on terms which are clearly understood. She may well feign an affection or enthusiasm she doesn't feel, but such deception, even if necessary for the successful conduct of her business, is perhaps relatively innocent and uncomplicated. The psychotherapist, on the other hand, may be helping patients through the provision of what they experience (even if inarticulately) as love, but under the guise of performing a psychological service of a technical nature. In this way psychotherapists may be appropriating their patients' ability to understand their own situation and think clearly about themselves, and by technicising, and in fact mythifying, psychological understanding they make it the property of a professional class – that is, they become 'professional usurers' in the way discussed in the previous chapter. Furthermore, the love through which their therapeutic function is *actually* achieved is but a pale and uncommitted version of what it would be in an ideal world, but is not acknowledged as such. Patients, it is true, may sometimes ruefully comment that 'you wouldn't put up with me if you weren't being paid to', and most therapists would be unlikely to deny, at least to themselves, that this is indeed the case; however, when not faced directly with this element of hypocrisy, therapists are quite likely sentimentally to deceive themselves about the 'deeply meaningful' significance of the therapeutic relationship.

It is certainly true that the therapist can become a figure of enormous importance to patients, often because he or she seems to them to be the only person who cares, and most competent therapists are aware of the dangers and responsibilities of this role. Almost none of them, of course, assume that in *reality* they could be this important or would be willing to shoulder the responsibility of so being – rather, they have convenient psychological 'mechanisms', such as 'the transference', readily at hand to 'explain' their patients' degree of dependence, infatuation, etc. No doubt it is possible for therapists at least unconsciously to abuse their role – to become a kind of paid friend and confidant to patients, endlessly taking their money in exchange for an available ear, a tolerant acceptance of their transgessions, an interested but morally uncritical acceptance of their interpersonal and sexual preoccupations and worries, offering appropriately mysterious psychological 'interpretations' which provide a kind of scientific justification for an anxious or tedious, or even profligate or futile life. Much more likely, however, is the kind of situation where the therapist simply slides into the role of substitute parent or friend, thereby indirectly syphoning off from the world – absolutely without meaning to do so – people's ability to support and look after each other. To turn love into a commodity, especially without realising that that is what is being done, may turn out to be one of the most disabling professional feats of all. On the other hand, to recognise that the provision of therapeutic love in a far from perfect world may be better than nothing at all, to accept, that is, that psychotherapy is like a form of prostitution, may be to achieve a quite healthy perspective.

If one accepts our present social organisation and ways of thinking about ourselves as more or less immutable, and if one can see no alternative to the structure and mode of influence of our social and intellectual institutions, then it seems likely to me that the only palliative to what appears to be an increasingly psychologically distressing and painful existence for most people is going to be an ever-expanding profession of love-givers of one kind or another. Apart from this, presumably, our only recourse may be to strengthening our defences by reinforcing our mythology (to a point at which we shall be in danger of becoming subjectively detached from the external world), or simply blowing ourselves up and starting, if possible, again.

However, after only a few hundred years of anything like care-fully recorded and reflective intellectual and moral develop-ment, it may seem premature to presuppose that radical changes in our understanding of ourselves and our relations with each other and with the world are not possible. Contemptuous though one might be about utopianism (and it is certainly the case that we cannot foresee with any accuracy at all what conceptual turns our descendants may take), we certainly have no reason to be self-satisfied about the present, as anyone who has the courage to examine the reality behind the myth must, in my view, acknowledge. It may not therefore be entirely idle to consider ways in which the experience of some of those involved in often very painful self- (and other-) examination point to revisions we may profitably make in our approach to the world and what we tell ourselves about it, even if some of these cut across our most cherished and 'objectively well estab-lished' beliefs. Perhaps one of the most pressing problems confronting us is to conceive of ways in which people may regain personal dignity and effectiveness in a social world in which there is not, and never will be, enough love to go round.

CHAPTER EIGHT

The Possibility of Undeception

Before it is possible to formulate even a vague idea of how one may be able to live one's life constructively (though certainly not painlessly) and *relatively* free of the paralysis which anxiety and psychological distress often impose (though certainly not free of fear, uncertainty and worry), it is necessary first to be able to expose the falsity of our usual way of looking at ourselves in relation to our world.

The equipment needed for undeceiving ourselves is not readily to hand, since culturally we have for centuries put all our conceptual eggs in the basket of objectivity, and it is the concepts of objectivity which we have used as the main means of our self-deception. To find our way back to judging ourselves and the world from a defensibly subjective standpoint means entertaining ideas and exercising faculties which we have all but forgotten how to name. But there *are* ways of knowing which are independent of objective language, and there *are* meanings other than objective meanings; one *can* make valid judgments on the basis of evidence unendorsed by 'experts', indeed one can appreciate truths which are unavailable to objectivity. Most important of all we can *share* subjective forms of knowledge, meaning and truth: it is one of the crasser, and most harmful, notions of objectivity to identify subjectivity with solipsism, to suggest, that is, that subjective experience is necessarily idiosyncratic, untrustworthy and incommunicable (on our first day as first-year psychology students, a lecturer told us, with almost savage satisfaction, that from that day forth, if we wanted to be scientists, we must forget our own personal experience as far as the pursuit of psychological understanding was concerned). It is of course true that subjective, personal opinions, beliefs and explanations can have no particular claim to truth, and are certainly of little interest to science; subjective *experience*, on the other hand, is in the long run the only ground upon which truth can rest.

Perhaps our greatest frustration is caused by our inevitable failure to achieve the goals which our myths tell us must be achieved. We believe in love (of the 'object–confirming' kind), we believe in 'relationships', we believe in 'fulfilment' (material, sexual, and sometimes even spiritual), we believe in happiness, and we see all of them as objective, obtainable possessions without at least some of which our lives will be rendered barren and meaningless. When the failure to achieve such goals leads our subjectivity to nudge our awareness with dread, when we find ourselves frozen under the gaze of the Other or threatened with annihilation by the withdrawal of love, there seems to be no refuge, nowhere to struggle to where existence can be continued. In the final chapter of this book I shall make some tentative suggestions about alternative ways of dealing with our predicament, but first of all, in this chapter, I shall try to draw together themes, many of which have been introduced earlier, to make a little clearer how we may at least begin to think about ourselves in ways which are not determined by our deep-seated penchant for objectivity and machine status.

I have already tried to establish that there is nothing particularly trustworthy about the words with which we consider our experience, and indeed that what we tell ourselves about our experience is more rather than less likely to serve the aims of self-deception. 'Anti-subjectivity' may make use of the fact that the possibilities for self-deception are infinite to suggest that the experience which underlies them is itself untrustworthy. But this, I think, is wrong, and in fact robs us of the only chance we have to *share* experience. The only acceptable form of objectivity is that which arises out of the overlapping of our individual subjectivities. Even for physical science, the ultimate test of whether or not something is true lies in the individual's experience, not in some objectified, dogmatic set of rules. The sensory experiences which are predictable from natural scientific 'laws' permit agreement between individuals because those individuals share very similar physical structures, are persuaded by the same kinds of logical reasoning, and operate with a similar set of values. It is easy to forget that, for example, it is only because scientists *value* the evidence of their senses that science itself hangs together; for a religious person who values, say, only the authority of holy writ, scientific statements need not be in the least compelling. The nature of our embodied presence in the world, i.e., the structure of our bodies in relation to the structure of the world, must in large part determine what one considers it important to know as well as the means of our getting to know it. We are able to build a shared body of scientific knowledge only in so far as we share this kind of common structure. Were they given the opportunities for self-conscious reflection conferred by language, other types of being (bees, say, or fish) would presumably construct a very different kind of science, because the nature of their engagement with the world is very different; the evidence of *their* senses would in many important respects differ greatly from the evidence of ours.

Science is thus not the creation of some kind of mysterious contact with or insight into ultimate reality, but the upshot of our own very human, and even culturally local, interests, concerns and values. I suspect, also, that we are ready to give particular weight and credence to the 'evidence of our senses' only because it is not in our interests to deceive ourselves about its nature (though it is certainly *possible* to do so). It is unfortunately much *more* in our interests to deceive ourselves about our subjective experience of our relations with and conduct towards each other, and indeed our intuitions of our own motives. We have, for example, as I have tried to suggest earlier, developed ways of considering, talking about and investigating our own motives which allow us the maximum scope for deception and self-deception, and we have almost entirely obscured from ourselves the insight that our motives are quite easily discoverable from our *conduct* (as opposed to our language).

In fact, I believe that our psychological, moral, social ways of experiencing are fundamentally *just* as shareable as our more obvious sensory experience. In other words, what I have called our 'intuitive sensitivity' is, I believe, just as reliable as the experience which provides the ultimate justification for natural scientific statements, but that, because of the problematic and painful nature of the world it reveals to us, we have chosen almost completely to suppress and ignore it in favour of a false objectivity. No doubt many would consider this an extreme claim, if not just a foolish one, but there does seem to me to be some evidence for it. For one thing, if it were not the case that we shared an extremely elaborate, fine, delicate awareness of the interpersonal, moral, unsayable currents that flow between us, and between us and the world, we should not in fact be able to sustain any kind of orderly conduct towards each other. How, for example, could one possibly negotiate the role of lover, or parent, or even buy a box of matches in the corner shop, according to the rules and precepts of objectivity alone? Even the most elaborate computers would not be able to cope with the subtlety of the *reality* which infuses even the simplest of human exchanges. For another thing, I have found that it is possible, even in the face of the most determined efforts at self-deception, to appeal to what people know, to ask people to *trust* their experience.

In the conduct of psychotherapy, for example, it is possible over and over again to see a patient struggling to deny what both he or she and the therapist know to be the case – the *reality* of the denied, the rock-solid certainty of what the patient is seeking to obscure, cannot for ever go unacknowledged precisely because it is so obvious, lying across their subjectivities at least as surely as the walls and windows which occur in both their visual fields, even though not 'objectively' demonstrable according to the tenets of 'scientific' dogma. I *know* if you are afraid of me, and I know you know I know, even should we deny it with our language and seek to cancel it out with our gestures. Centuries of effort to gainsay knowledge such as this means that we have lost the concepts – or failed to develop them – with which to consider it, but that does not alter the certainty of our knowledge. This is not, of course, to say that such knowledge is infallible or cannot be mistaken, just as the evidence of our senses can at times be misleading, but it *is* just as good as any other kind of knowledge.

We could, I think (and do in certain protected settings such as that found in psychotherapy), check, evaluate and elaborate the knowledge given by our intuitive sensitivity, but for that we need to be able to stand to each other in a relation of good faith, and our difficulty in achieving that constitutes the major stumbling block for the development and appreciation of intersubjective truth. For a variety of reasons (which owe as much to chance as to any impersonally objective reality) you will be hard put to it to deny that there is a telephone on my desk, but if you wish to deny that you are afraid of me (when you are) you have every chance of obscuring the truth. In principle, the exercise of bad faith is equally *possible* in either situation, but much more in our interests to permit in the sphere of intuitive sensitivity. To be able to acknowledge the truth which is to be gained in this sphere, one has to *want* to find it.

To the objectivist mind there is no doubt something absolutely maddening about suggesting that one should *trust* one's 'intuitive sensitivity', since such a statement seems to lack all the verbal and 'operational' exactness which objectivity demands. The objectivist can tolerate such a concept only if the phenomena involved can be converted or translated into concrete and manipulable commodities (hence the attempted translation of some of the more subtle features of social interchange into a 'body language' which can be used consciously to manipulate or dissemble). However, the very nature of intuitive knowledge is such that it need not, and *cannot*, be translated in this way without the immediate loss of its essentially subjective character: as soon as you become unspontaneous in some particular sphere of conduct, your spontaneity slips away to some other sphere, where again it operates, as it were, out of self-conscious sight.

There is really nothing surprising about suggesting that there can be fields of communicable meaning which cannot be made articulate in language. Even if language bears almost the entire weight of our (objective) intellectual culture, it is by no means the only meaning-system with which we are familiar for example, musical experience is known, understood, communicated, evaluated and validated, in its own terms, quite satisfactorily and fully without ever having to be put into words. We feel no particular embarrassment about acknowledging and sharing musical meaning outside the context of language, and its essentially non-linguistic nature does not lead us to dismiss music as somehow unreliable and misleading. We can of course *talk about* music, consider it verbally in every aspect, but in doing so we do not feel we have to reject the wordless experience of music itself.★ I see no reason why we should not extend the same validity to the experience rendered us by our intuitive sensitivity.

Our objective habits of thought also demand that some account be given of what could possibly be meant by 'intuitive sensitivity' – for example, on what objective or mechanical structures could it depend? Though I certainly mean to invoke no mysterious or magical faculty, and while I am happy to acknowledge that the exercise of such sensitivity must depend upon the structures of our body and the evidence of our senses,

★The implications of this argument are spelt out in extremely interesting detail by Susanne Langer, *Philosophy in a New Key*, Harvard University Press, 1942.

it does seem to me that perhaps it *cannot* be analysed in the way which objectivity demands, since it lies at the very basis of our knowledge of the world. Perhaps it is true that one can know everything (or, at least, a great deal!) except how we know – for as soon as we knew how we know, the process of our knowing would again slip out of sight. Put at its simplest, subject (knower) cannot simultaneously and for itself be object (known). This kind of thought, familiar enough – indeed positively banal – in Continental philosophy, is by and large anathema to the Anglo-Saxon mind, and yet it is hard to see how it can be escaped, even if it seems to outrage what we have been taught to consider reason.

This philosophical problem is more than just an intellectual puzzle, and it is very easy to see how it translates into concrete reality. For as soon as objectivity unearths what it takes to be the fundamentals of our ways of knowing, it seeks to put them to practical use without noticing that *what* is putting them to use is again, inevitably, an unanalysed subject.

Not only, then, is it possible for us to trust in our subjective experience, but in the final analysis we have no alternative to doing so, though we can of course fail to acknowledge that we do so. Trust in one's experience, however, carries with it no objective guarantee of correctness, and as much as anything else it is probably the risk of being wrong which generated our desire for absolute objectivity. The objectivity which we created ended up, ironically, by dogmatically removing us – the knowers – from the scene altogether.

Where objective knowing is passive, subjective knowing is active – rather than giving allegiance to a set of methodological rules which are designed to deliver up truth through some kind of automatic process, the subjective knower takes a personal risk in entering into the meaning of the phenomena to be known. In learning to read, for example, the child takes a risk with those words he or she is unacquainted with, relying on the context for clues which *might* be misleading (it strikes me that children of the television age are often particularly reluctant to take this kind of risk – their reception of meaning needs somehow to be 'authorised' before they will risk 'knowing' it). One of the most 'subjectively risking' people I know tells with puzzlement how she is the only person in her particular circle who seems able to understand the West Indian patois of one of her neighbours. Needing to judge correctly means risking foolish mistakes, and trusting one's intuitive sensitivity demands a quality – courage – not normally associated with purely 'cognitive' activity. Objectivity, again, attempts to remove from our ways of knowing the necessity for courage.

When the risk is successfully taken, one reaches an intersubjectively shared reality which is as concrete as any other, even though it may not be 'demonstrable' in objective terms. Seven members of a therapeutic group may know with absolute certainty that the eighth is falsely disavowing anger, but there is no really satisfactory way of 'proving' the case objectively; nevertheless, the *strength* of their case leads the eighth member to acknowledge its truth. He *could* of course be giving way to 'social pressure' (in which case the more sensitive members would probably know he was) but there can be no way of deciding this which depends on anything more solid than subjective certainty.

Those who have some time for the validity of subjective experience but intellectual qualms about any kind of 'truth' which is not 'objective', are apt to solve their problem by appealing to some kind of relativity. For example, it might be felt that we all have our own *versions* of the truth about which we must tolerantly agree to differ (I have already discussed some of the implications ofthis kind of view for psychotherapy in Chapter Seven). While in some ways this kind of approach represents an advance on the brute domination of the 'objective truth', it in fact undercuts and betrays the *reality* of the world given to our subjectivity. Subjective truth has to be actively struggled for (just as, in psychotherapy, the truth of the patient's predicament has to be painfully negotiated): we need the courage to differ until we can agree.

Though the truth is not just a matter of personal perspective, neither is it fixed and certain, objectively 'out there' and independent of human knowing. 'The truth' changes according to, among other things, developments and alterations in our values and understandings. It is an act of unbelievable hubris to suppose that we have, or could have, a kind of contact with absolute objective Reality which guarantees us a truth which is independent of our interests. The idea of something approaching absolute or objective truth is one of the main weapons with which to defend dogma and to subdue those who wish to evolve our understanding. But the 'non-finality' of truth is not to be confused with a simple relativity of 'truths'. Truth changes in a *direction*, and it is not just the case that one view is as good as another. It was once 'true' that the world was square and became (more) true that it was round. What will be true of it in a thousand years is, obviously, impossible for us to say.

Nowhere is the necessity for courage and good faith more evident than in the search to establish the truth about relations between people, for in this process lies the threat of annihilation. As A struggles with B to lay bare the meaning of their conduct towards each other, bravely trying to stay clear of the slide into self-deception, to confess and accept his fear and vulnerability, to acknowledge his defensive strategies, his meannesses and malignancies and desperate cravings, so B can with a single act of bad faith betray the reciprocity of this process, perhaps by 'closing down' A with some kind of objectifying label which sends him spinning like a deflating balloon into the distant, icy, sterile reaches of isolation. For these reasons the exploration of subjective truth needs usually to be tentative, gentle, delicate; a process of negotiation which, to proceed satisfactorily, has first to construct a basis of trust. By its very nature, there are no rules which can be formulated for this procedure, since it takes place at, as it were, the very forefront of our conduct, involving our total, integrated effort; it leaves out no part of us which can sit back and conduct the proceedings self-consciously. There are some things, certainly, of which we should no doubt beware – for example, of self-justifying or comforting verbal constructions, of labels and diagnoses, but in the end it is only trust in one's subjective knowing that will inform us of success or failure. Many of the myth-creating properties of our everyday concepts could be avoided if we attended in our relations with each other to what we do rather than to what we say. In this way intuitive sensitivity deals with reality rather than with misleading verbal constructions of it. But this again cannot be turned into any kind of *method*, for method inevitably becomes once more a tool of objectivity.

It is, in fact, precisely the methodological dogma of objectivity which has to be rejected if we are to be able to acknowledge and pursue subjective truth. That is, we have to get used to the idea that we can do without – indeed to some extent *must* do without – the very things we have always understood to be indispensable for the reliable establishment of truth, if we are indeed to establish it. If it *suits* us, we may make use of the canons of reasoning or methods of quantification thought to be essential to science, but they can never on their own be enough to ensure a path to the truth, and may as often as not block it completely. But this does *not* mean that the end result of our search has no inter-subjective validity. In fact, the result of our negotiations concerning our subjective experience, where they have been successful, is a freely entered into commitment to the reality which we find we have in common.

Our culture makes it almost impossible to think of knowledge other than in terms of acquisition. Scientific knowledge, for example, is, especially in the current technological climate, treated almost exclusively as a kind of weapon, a powerful possession which we can use to subdue nature and add to our material well-being. We do *not* seem to use the knowledge we

gain in this way so that *we may do things better*. Subjective knowledge may, on the other hand, carry more this latter kind of
implication – it contributes to part of a flowing process of
conduct or activity which is not just about making use of things,
but at least *may* be about how *we* may be useful. In this way, the
knowledge which we achieve inter-subjectively does not *need*,
as does scientific knowledge, to be fashioned into a monument
to our own acquisitive cleverness, does not need to be spelt out
articulately, studied academically, hoarded in books, appropriated by experts, but rather contributes, uncommented and
uncommentable upon, to our efforts to fashion a world we
cannot predict, but can only try to achieve. Such knowledge is
to *some* extent safeguarded (though certainly not totally
immune) from abuse precisely because it *cannot* be objectified
and manipulated.

In pursuing the painful process of undeception there is no
doubt a sense in which *self*-knowledge becomes important, but
this, again, is not the kind of self-knowledge which most of us, I
suspect, think will prove useful. It is all too easy to interpret the
injunction 'know thyself' as a recommendation to become
aware of that which one is in a kind of finished, objective way,
so that one can, for example, put oneself to better use in the
business of acquiring things while subduing the opposition.
Knowing yourself, on this kind of view, means knowing yourself as an object which you can manipulate, knowing your
strengths and weaknesses, knowing how to use yourself as a tool
for getting what you want and keeping out of psychologically
troublesome situations. Self-knowledge thus becomes yet
another kind of 'skill' which marks its possessor as in some way
superior to or more valuable than those who remain relatively
ignorant of their 'selves'. There is no doubt that many psychological thinkers advocate this kind of objective self-knowledge
as one of life's major goals, and it may puzzle many people to
suggest that, because we do not 'possess' things like 'selves', it is
not only undesirable to pursue knowledge of them, but the

pursuit itself is doomed to failure. Claims to this kind of knowl-edge constitute the very essence of bad faith, since the one 'thing' that cannot be known is the subject who makes the claim. These, of course, are themes already met with in Chapter Three, but it still remains to clarify what *could* usefully be meant by 'self-knowledge'.

'Know thyself' might I think best be interpreted as a warning that one should, as part of a kind of continuous process of self-suspicion, keep a wary eye on what one is up to. This would *not* mean listening to the self-justifying accounts which we are always ready to tell ourselves, indeed it means specifically disregarding them, but rather attempting to divine from our own conduct what might be the nature of our undertakings. Unlike knowledge of self-as-object, this kind of process would never arrive at finite knowledge of any*thing* in particular, but would represent a kind of running battle not to fall into self-deception. This is not acquisitive knowledge, but knowledge which contributes to one's functioning in the world as a subjective influence within it; it keeps one in touch with reality. Again, one must frustrate the habitual objectivist urge to lay down a *method* whereby the pursuit of such knowing can be maintained – there is no certain method beyond the effort itself. It does seem however that, for example, patients who have begun through the process of negotiation in psychotherapy to see through their self-deceptive strategies do with practice often become better at recognising what they are up to and learn to regard the stories they tell themselves with increasing scepticism. But if the threat is strong enough, if the painfulness of the world again becomes too much to contemplate, the slide back into self-deception is easily achieved.

To 'know yourself', then, involves a constant effort to maintain your integrity and honestly to acknowledge the projects which are revealed as the meaning of your conduct. There is no way of ensuring the success of this effort, and the knowledge which results from it is of no permanent use. No wonder, perhaps, that we are individually and collectively so reluctant to abandon the seductive promises of a much less personally demanding objectivity.

Slowly, then, we begin to find ourselves in a world without the familiar reference points supplied by objectivity, sharing knowledge which cannot be proved or put to use, losing the selves which we had always thought we had, discovering that even 'simply' knowing something demands of us the courage to take an active risk. But these are not new demands which are placed upon us, we are not required suddenly, like infants, to learn an entirely unfamiliar way of life, for all these are things which, to some extent at least, we have been doing all the time, though without taking account of them or taking them seriously. What happens, then, if we *trust* our subjective experience of ourselves and the world?

A number of 'humanistic' psychologies have extolled the virtues and benefits of being 'open to experience' as if the myths by which we live were *personal* creations which distort not only a clear, but in many respects a reassuring, view of the world. Thus the implication is that openness to experience will somehow bring about a more personally rewarding life in which, free of the 'hang-ups' which we have somehow fool-ishly created for ourselves, we will see that the world is not such a bad place after all. The 'fully experiencing' person might be seen in these psychologies as likely to find as reward for his or her honesty, 'immediacy', etc., a 'deeply meaningful' related-ness to others in 'the here and now', a satisfactory flow of 'peak experiences', 'individuation', fulfilment, and a lot more besides.* Were this really the case, it would be difficult to understand why our objective mythology is maintained with such all-pervasive tenacity, since relinquishing it would appear to bring such easy benefits.

In fact, though there are no doubt liberating aspects in

*R. D. Rosen, in *Psychobabble*, Avon Books, 1979, has exposed the shal-lowness of several of these approaches to psychological well-being.

trusting one's own experience, there are many more which are painfull, disturbing, and even terrifying. Objective mythology, as well as personal ('neurotic') self-deception, do not arise merely out of our having made a few silly mistakes about the nature of the world or ourselves – they protect us from a vista we can hardly bear to behold. However, the price we pay for self-deception, for too eagerly grabbing the opportunity our linguistic capacity gives us for misrepresenting our reality, is in the long run likely to be greater than the pain and panic afforded by subjective insight. Personal self-deception is likely to lead to confusion and anxiety upon which the individual can simply gain no purchase, and collective mythology is maintained at the expense of the gradual disintegration of the social world and the physical environment. It is only as subjects that we can influence or alter anything, and it is only by taking the risks involved in acknowledging our subjectivity that we can hope to improve our condition. The point of acknowledging subjectivity is not to achieve 'fulfilment', but to be able to act upon the world.

It is true, I think, that people may experience a sense of relief in admitting to themselves a vision of their reality that they had fought to deny. The 'agoraphobic' housewife, for example, who is able eventually to acknowledge, say, her loneliness and insecurity, her anger at her husband, her occasional murderous rage towards her children, at least no longer needs to pretend that her distress arises from mysterious sources beyond her experience; she is no longer a passive victim of the inexplicable, though she does of course find herself in a world full of real difficulties. Breaking free of myth may also allow one a refreshing appreciation of *meaning* – the wordless fears, unpleasant physical sensations, the 'symptoms', the uneasy and inarticulate preoccupations and forebodings which, perhaps, overshadowed daily existence, suddenly become linked to actual experience, pointing, as it were, to something out in the world (a situation, perhaps, or a relationship) which is an intelligible source of distress. People who permit themselves to acknowledge the significance of what they are subjectively, bodily informed of, are suddenly able to believe what they have always tried not to know, and if nothing else that tends to clear up a good deal of confusion.

Clarity, however, brings with it a series of further difficulties which may seem almost insuperably daunting. These involve not only the disturbing nature of what is revealed about the world, but also the consequences of being prepared to acknowledge that things may not be quite as one had thought.

Most of us withdraw confidence from our subjective experience of the social world at a fairly early age once it becomes apparent that relations with others are fraught with danger. To keep track of the truth of what is passing between oneself and others is both intensely threatening and very complex, especially as it demands the kind of sceptical attitude towards one's own stance which is necessitated by the untrustworthiness of what one tells oneself. Worst of all, recognition of the threats, demands, embargoes, pleas, severances and dependencies, hopes and fears we place upon each other, puts us in a position where we feel almost impelled to *do* something about aspects of relationships which can no longer be ignored. Recognising what is the case leaves one suddenly unsupported by the myths which maintain a comfortable blindness. The married woman, for example, who finally admits to herself that she no longer has the unqualified support which she had thought to be the meaning of her husband's love, that in fact he needs her to provide him with a kind of unstinted mothering of which she feels simply incapable, who begins to see that behind the apparent mutuality of their courting days and early married life there lurks the separateness of two people whose experience leads them to widely differing expectations of human relationships, who begins to see, perhaps, that she originally married her husband as an escape from a particularly uncomfortable relationship with her father – this woman is faced with some very disturbing possibilities indeed, and is thrown into a region of uncertainty in her personal life for which our culture provides almost no signposts. Is, for example, her situation unusual? Does she leave her husband in the confident expectation that, with hindsight and more mature judgement, she can make a happier and more suitable relationship? Does she, on the other hand, conclude that her situation is the rule rather than the exception, and that her insight into it in fact gives her a better than average chance of being able to work for its betterment? Our objective culture operates precisely to obscure from our view what goes on in our own lives, and hence offers us no help when we start to discover for ourselves the nature of our predicament.

Those people who opt for a self-deceptive strategy for avoiding this kind of discovery may do so partly out of a dimly sensed anticipation that to acknowledge what in their heart they know to be the case would be to bring about catastrophe. To draw attention to the emperor's nakedness is to initiate the collapse of the entire social system. Or so one may fear. Part of the feeling of relief with which people find that their 'symptoms' are in fact indications of a state of affairs that they had formerly not dared to recognise is probably due to their realising that no catastrophe has taken place, however daunting the need to act upon their insights might be. The objective (for example, 'illness') view is often maintained through a kind of blackmail which conjures up a superstitious terror in those who even contemplate calling its bluff. The child who innocently threatens to expose the secrets of its parents' vulnerability is likely to experience the full blast of this reign of terror in its original and most powerful form. For adults, however, acknowledgement of the subjective truth is not often met by the disaster they expect in imagination.

There is no doubt that to be honest with oneself is to recognise a terrible vulnerability and to see that there is no escape from the risks which involvement with the world entails. One can never become a safe success, never, without monumental self-deception, bask in the security of having become the satisfactory object of everybody's esteem. Every new enterprise, every new relationship carries with it the possibility of failure; nothing is guaranteed. As a subject, one is, as it were, inescapably dedicated to living out the meaning of one's own ineradicable experience. We of course differ from each other in terms of the content of that experience, though our manner of experiencing may be very similar – more similar, as I have argued, than we are usually prepared to admit. He whose parents nurtured his early years with wise and loving concern is likely to have more confidence in himself and others than she whose father subjected her in her first ten years to an unremitting sadistic battering. Each is likely to draw different lessons from experience, and to pursue different projects. There is a loneliness about this which is very hard for most of us to take. How much easier it would be to be a standardised unit in a vast impersonal machine!

There is an added complication to a belated trust in one's own experience, to acknowledging, say, that one is not the passive victim of an illness ('anxiety state') but rather the vulnerable contributor to a network of complicated and dangerous relationships. For in making any such acknowledgement, which entails beginning to take responsibility for those aspects of one's own conduct which contribute to one's predicament, it becomes immediately apparent that time formerly spent in self-deception was *wasted* time. Admitting that one was wrong, even over trivial matters, is never a particularly comfortable experience; admitting that one has made life-long mistakes and entertained entirely misleading assumptions about matters of vital personal importance is all the more painful, and constitutes often a major stumbling block to the development of a more accurate perception of the meaning of one's conduct.

It helps with the *painfulness* of honesty to extend to oneself the same kind of compassion one would extend to others. Many people confronting for the first time what they see as their own futility and contemptible vulnerability, realising with a rush of shame the cowardliness of their self-deception, are comforted a little by the suggestion that they should look at themselves as if they were someone else, and remember that the world they live in gave them good reasons for doing what they did. Having reasons, furthermore, is not the same as being to blame or being at fault. The self-disgust of the shy man who begins to see that he is afraid of people rather than 'ill' does not usually constitute the kind of feeling he would see as applicable to other shy people, and it may in fact be possible for him to regard himself with the same kind of reassuring warmth that he would want to offer them.

However, whatever crumbs of comfort may be gleaned from breaking free of objective mythology, the immediate consequences seem not at first sight devoutly to be wished. Among other things, thus, the person finds him- or herself vulnerably adrift with no more guidance than his or her own convictions in a world full of pain and danger, isolated in a standpoint which most seem unwilling to share, and faced with having to do something about it. It is hardly surprising that in these circumstances most of us would feel that we can scarcely be expected to cope.

CHAPTER NINE

The Confrontation of Reality

There is no doubt that, in facing life's difficulties, it helps to be loved. When the gaze of the Other becomes warm and approving, when we are confirmed as good, or as beautiful, the freezing winds of isolation and despair give way to a glowing self-confidence, a kind of amniotic security which, perhaps, formed the basis of some of our very earliest experiences, and which, again perhaps, we may have been seeking to recreate ever since.

It is scarcely possible, however, to conceive of love in our own time as anything but conditional and 'object-directed'. Love is both our salvation and our greatest danger: he or she who loves reciprocally and without defences takes the most terrifying risk of annihilation. Love confirms you as a satisfactory object, but its withdrawal may destroy you. Whether or not you are loved is likely to depend on your behaving in accordance with your lover's needs and expectations. Lovers must watch each other warily, fake, dissemble, and be ready at a moment's notice to defend themselves.

To be relatively confident and free of the tortures of self-doubt and self-disgust, it helps to have been loved as a child usually, of course, this means to have had loving parents, i.e. parents who approved of and took an interest in you. Again, in sexual and marital relationships, it helps if the partners like and appreciate each other, take a real interest in each other, confirm each other's embodied presence in the world (it helps if they find each other beautiful and desirable). Being loved helps so much, in fact, that we try to establish it at the very centre of our interpersonal culture, so to speak. Love is all; all you need is love. We proclaim the importance of love, we sing about it and dream about it and advocate it as the only possible basis for marriage and family life. We see the desperate need for it so clearly that we pretend love we cannot feel, we attach ourselves to eviscerated religions in which we lie hysterically to each other about the extent of our mutual loving. We turn love into a commodity which can be bought and sold. We lie and cheat for love, we steal and extort it, for only love assuages the lonely terror of empty objectivity. You are nothing if you are not loved.

It helps to be loved, but not many people are. Hence, no doubt, our concern to increase the supply of love, to professionalise its provision and advocate its universal desirability. But we fail to see that this is the conditional love of the market economy. As objects, we are victims of the laws of supply and demand. Love, like gold, must be scarce if it is to retain the meaning we give it. It must be competed for, and there will be many losers. There are, certainly, those who are rich in love, and who consequently are happy, but it is as realistic to aim for a society made up of such individuals as it would be to aim for a society composed only of millionaires. Those who have been deprived of love, but get, as it were, a sudden windfall, may well find that the tenor of their lives changes from dull, aching self-hatred to undreamed-of joy. The supply of love is not equitable or even; unfairly, like money, it can probably be inherited.

Love is not to be sneezed at. In a society in which we have all become objects, it is the best and most fulfilling mode in which to conduct our relations with each other. Love and happiness go hand-in-hand. Love protects us from the sheer brutal savagery otherwise so apparent in our social intercourse. Love is our emotional currency, without which we cannot, it seems, exist.

I do not wish to disparage love, indeed I am sure that we

should be loving towards each other, but I do think that, in allowing love to have become inextricably enmeshed with the values of objectivity we have created a threat (the withdrawal of love) which, combined with the fact that there can never be enough love to go around, forces us to defend ourselves with such desperation that we become almost incapable of conducting our lives sanely and safely. We stand in danger of making love indispensable to our survival. That would be fine if there *were* enough of it to go around, but there isn't. Not even by buying and selling love on a vast scale, not even by faking and fabricating it on every side, will we be able to meet the need for it which we have created. Most people most of the time are facing a difficult and frightening world with only very little if any at all of the protection afforded by love, and the only other ways in which they can survive involve the pretence that things are not as bad as they know they are. Love is at the same time our highest salvation and our greatest myth, and it is mythical to the extent that we see it as the answer to our 'problems'.

Apart from straightforward self-deception, which has perhaps by now received enough attention in this book, there are a number of other answers, not depending solely upon the acquisition of love, which our culture allows for the attempted solution of the problems it poses us.

Because individual, personal adequacy plays so central a part in determining a person's worth, to self as well as to others, it is not surprising that the cultivation of adequacy – or indeed of *in*adequacy – may become the ruling preoccupation of our lives. Here again it is the individual self-as-object which is the focus of attention. How adequate we may feel ourselves to be depends on the extent to which we have achieved personal happiness and fulfilment through material success and satisfactory 'relationships'. Our psychological as well as our material goals are defined in terms of acquisition rather than instrumentality i.e., what we 'end up as' is considered much more important than what we do.* Though we may pay lip-service to half-remembered religious precepts such as 'by their works ye shall know them', we are for the most part utterly impervious to the moral intention or significance of our conduct, and on the whole what we do is evaluated mainly in terms of what it achieves for the enhancement of our image and the augmentation of our power, status and material advantage. It would be hard for us to conceive of a life as being fulfilled or successful unless it terminated in a roseate glow of comfort and love, material well-being and social respect. It seems to us at the very least somehow unfair that Christ should have died on the cross, that Mozart should have been buried unidentifiably in a pauper's grave, or that Tolstoy should have breathed his last at a tiny provincial railway station amid the chaotic and bitter emotional turmoil of his family relations. Not that we have to look to such exalted regions to find evidence that life is not as we should like it to be. It is virtually only the mythified diet of 'fact' and fiction fed to us by the 'entertainment media', the reassuring pomp and circumstance of the occasional state funeral, which prop up the 'credibility' of our cherished ideals. The truth is to be found near at hand in hospital wards, old people's homes, and indeed within our own families. The happiness and fulfilment upon which we suppose the meaning of our lives to depend in fact constitute an illusion to which our collective cowardice in the face of the truth leads us to hang on desperately even though for each of us in our individual experience it is an illusion which is shattered over and over again. Of course there is a tiny minority which does appear to achieve the goals so assiduously pursued by the rest of us, but their success *depends upon* our failure. All this is only a cause for despair if we are incapable of conceiving the meaning of our existence in anything other than individual and objective terms. Though it may be frightening to penetrate the myth, to do so

*This, of course, is the central theme of E. Fromm's book, *To Have or to Be*, Jonathan Cape, 1978.

may be preferable to spending an entire lifetime in fruitless pursuit of mythical goals.

After all, what is one supposed to do with, for example, 'fulfilment' and 'deeply meaningful' relationships? The cultivation of self, the acquisition of confidence and self-esteem, the occupation of a central point in a network of warm and loving relationships, the final, if brief, satisfaction of having rounded off one's life in the achievement of all one's major aims – is it really self-evident that these are the best goals we can imagine for ourselves? Most psychologies which are concerned with anything more than the relief of 'symptoms' do seem to suggest that there can be no more desirable outcome to a life than the achievement of some such *personal* satisfaction. The fact that nobody ever actually achieves it does not seem to deter us from continuing to pursue it or from persuading ourselves of its desirability; nor do we notice that our failure to achieve it leaves us more and more confused and desperate. The psychological and spiritual problems we set ourselves (in regard to 'fulfilment', 'individuation', etc.) share all the banality of that presented by our material acquisitiveness: what do you do when the novelty of the new car wears off?

There are, of course, those who recognise quite early on that they are doomed to lose in the race for fulfilment, and see no alternative but to carve out for themselves a career in the cultivation of inadequacy. The painfulness of trying when you are virtually certain you will fail should not be underestimated: one cannot live perpetually with the shattering anticipation of disaster without eventually simply falling apart, and in these circumstances it is almost with relief that one can opt for failure. Indeed, the role of failed, inadequate object can become so (relatively) comfortable that people may hang on to it very tenaciously even when life offers them a sudden unexpected opportunity. The young woman who has accepted a definition of herself as ugly, fat and bad and pursues a series of degrading relationships with men who treat her with callous indifference and contempt may actually turn down the attentions of a concerned, gentle and attractive lover partly because she simply cannot bear the potentiality for hurt in the hopes which start to stir within her. The man who has always seemed to stake his self-esteem on getting promotion at work, perhaps resentfully pointing out the inferiority of others who seem unfairly to have beaten him to it, may suddenly succumb to a host of debilitating and mysterious 'symptoms' when he is himself unexpectedly offered the promotion he always coveted. Fake martyrdom is a far more attractive role than most of us like to think: it appears morally unassailable, and it carries no risks. For the price of a little suffering (which with luck may have the advantage of drawing some sympathy from others), one may live quite safe from the awful threat of annihilation which is incurred by taking risks. In real life Cinderella will continue to scrub the floor on her knees even when nobody is standing over her, will develop an immobilising illness on the day of the ball, and will in any case disclaim vehemently any suggestion that the slipper is her size.

There is of course much more to this kind of phenomenon than simple cowardice: as I have argued earlier, we cannot just erase our early experience, but most likely spend our lives doggedly pursuing its significance in every aspect. Contrary to what many people, including many psychologists and psychiatrists, seem to think, we cannot slip from role to role, even with the most massive amounts of help. Our language, literature and drama can project for us infinitely variable 'realities' and modes of being; we can so easily *think* of being different that we may be forgiven for supposing that actual change is really not all that difficult to achieve. But it is perhaps precisely because our experience, and our conduct in relation to it, are so concrete and resistant to manipulation that we are so fascinated by the fantastic possibilities offered by language. Those of us who offer professionally to change lives and alter experience are in this aspect little more than conjurors paid to reinforce some of our culture's more comforting myths.

Most of us, I suspect, live our lives bewildered by the pain in which we find ourselves, discovering over and over again that our actual experiences – whether concerning childhood, work, love, marriage, parenthood, old age, death – fall far short of those our mythology leads us to anticipate, or at least hope for. Desperately we may try to shut out our recognition of reality, smile through our despair, by becoming enthusiastic mythologisers ourselves. And despair and isolation increase in direct proportion to the fatuity of our myths. Those who have been stamped 'reject' early on – and one wonders whether they may not be a majority – live lives, if not tortured, then haunted by a kind of hopeless, aching pain which never seems to be assuaged for long, and which, even if expressible, is hardly ever expressed because our mythology does not permit its recognition. One's 'inadequacy' can be experienced as a dreadful secret which may suddenly be exposed at any time; 'anxiety' often stems from a sense of the imminence of such exposure.

Another apparent way out of the dilemmas posed by our existence as objects in a threatening world is to attempt to preserve indefinitely that state in which we felt most safe – i.e. infancy or childhood. The responsibility and isolation of adulthood are things very few of us manage to accept, and in view of our early experience of dependency and protection, this is hardly surprising. The hierarchical and fundamentally authoritarian nature of almost all our social and political organisations reflects our continued need for parental supervision. However resentfully and vociferously we may demand independence, it is usually the last thing we really want, and we may actually find it terrifying. To find oneself as an adult in an adult world is rather like waking as a child unexpectedly to find the house on fire and only one's brothers and sisters on the premises. How can one organise, cooperate, take responsibility, decide what to do, without a parent (leader) to point the way and keep the others under control? Those politicians, I suspect, who appeal to the electorate, even if patronisingly, as parents who know best start with an enormous psychological advantage over those who address us as brothers, sisters or comrades – who would trust the running of the country to their brothers and sisters? It is a tragedy built into the very structure of our experience that we must eventually perform the function of adults while feeling like children, and it is no surprise that we may try to escape the conflict involved by offering our childish allegiance to some mythified person, social structure or idea which represents Authority. We may also reject our own adult status by refusing to exercise the authority which inevitably falls to us, for example in bringing up children.

It is part of objective culture to reinforce the idea that on almost every question of factual or moral importance there are others (experts, professionals) who 'know best', and in this respect objectivity plays straight into our need for parental reassurance and escape from adult responsibility. One of the most threatening things to be experienced by many people is to be called upon suddenly for an opinion, especially in the presence of a judging Other, for in being asked without warning to take up a stance the possibility of exposure of one's inadequacy is increased a thousandfold. But objects do not make judgements, and 'science' is value-free and therefore ethically neutral. The spiritual parent of the 'scientist' is the methodological dogma to which he or she subscribes, and association with scientific culture therefore frees one from some of the uncomfortable features attached to being an adult person.

The only hope of our recognising the truth of our predicament, becoming a part of as well as being able to influence our reality, lies, I believe, in our making the transition from object to subject. For most of us this is a far from painless process, and many never even dream of its possibility. Paradoxically, it is in our 'symptoms' of anxiety, distress and malaise that encouraging signs are to be found of the insistence of the subject on being recognised. It is thus in our capacity to be disturbed by the false objectivity of our world that the greatest hope lies for our being able to do something about it.

Many patients talk with puzzled longing of the days when they felt 'all right'. People who feel that their confidence and ability to cope have utterly ebbed away may remember nostalgically a time when they could do anything and go anywhere. Many interpret this as an indication that something has 'gone wrong' in a way which could in principle be mechanically repaired. On the whole, however, it seems more likely that the myths and distractions they were able to live by can no longer disguise the gravity of their predicament; the accuracy of a subjective view, breaking through as panic or dread, can no longer be denied. To make proper use of the opportunities opened up by the acknowledgement of distress is to take one of the few paths open to us to develop and assert our subjectivity. It is those for whom the myths are not working, the 'unsuccessful' and painfully self-conscious (as opposed to the successful image-makers) who, paradoxically perhaps, stand one of the better chances of becoming aware of the real world around them. Psychological distress and anxiety are thus not indications of illness or abnormality, but the inevitable experiences of anyone who begins to become aware, however dimly, of the disparity between myth and reality. Our culture, it is true, offers them almost no hope at all of understanding their experience, but even so their experience is more a sign of the culture's failure than of theirs. I do not mean to romanticise or ennoble suffering – there are enough 'martyrs' as it is – but only to emphasise that there is a *meaning* to our misery, and one which we may take note of. Again, this meaning need not be one we have to spell out laboriously in words: as always, it is only the literal-minded objectivist who insists on being able to say what things mean. As with our dreams, for example, our despair, our sense of dread or our 'symptoms' may move us and have significance for us in ways which we cannot articulate but which nevertheless alter quite profoundly our stance towards the world.

I do not wish to suggest that the experience of psychological distress and anxiety is *necessary* for the transition from object to subject. Those who remain true throughout their lives to the significance of their personal experience (the reality revealed by their intuitive sensitivity) may never experience anything like a 'symptom' of the kind which stems from failing self-deception, but nor will they be likely to find life comfortable. The gradual falling away of myth, the process of becoming adult from infant, of travelling from birth to death with one's eyes open may involve a continual (and literal) process of disillusionment as agonising as having the skin slowly stripped from one's body. This, again, is only really a problem if one regards one's personal comfort, 'fulfilment', etc., as particularly important. One may instead be distracted from these latter concerns by attending to the effectiveness of what one does. This is not asking for any special saintliness – there are many people who unself-consciously live out a life of absorption in activity without ever realising, or needing to realise, that this is what they are doing.

What happens, then, to the person who, by whatever route, comes to discover that, contrary to all previous expectations, he or she is a subject rather than an object?

The world which is revealed to the subjective gaze is in almost all aspects the opposite of how it seemed under the rule of objectivity, and to confront it unflinchingly may at first be a vertiginously frightening experience. Where before one had a defined role in an articulated social structure which operated largely automatically and mechanically, where one was more or less literally a cog in the machine, suddenly now one finds oneself in a fluid, evolving world full of untagged, unarticulated meaning, in which one's own conduct may alter the course of events in unpredictable ways, in which one has no feeling for what kind of an object one is, and which seems to present undreamed-of threats and dangers. To catch such a glimpse of reality is enough to send some people into a kind of perpetual frenzy of anxiety in which they insist on the validity of myth to the point of resorting to the basest emotional blackmail of anyone around them who threatens to blow the gaff. Not only may people in this state drive their children crazy through their insistence on a false reality of their own construction, but they may even succeed in establishing myths which generalise beyond those immediately closest to them. I suspect, for example, that the phenomenon 'poltergeist' has in some instances gained credibility only through the ability of one member of a family who has succumbed to personally unacknowledgeable violent rage to terrorise the rest into silence and pretended ignorance concerning the havoc that has been wrought. In any case, one is unwise to underestimate the lengths to which people may go to hide from themselves and others the unpalatable truth. However, such extreme reactions to the sight of reality are the exception rather than the rule.

People I know who have through a long process of negotiation been able to edge their way into acceptance of their own subjectivity are often indignant at their inability to be able to deal immediately with what they find. Our existence as the passively consuming termini of a huge nurturing machine, our lifetime of experience of being trained but not learning, being acted upon but not acting, being chosen but not choosing, ill prepares us for the new terrain in which we find ourselves. To the object newly become subject it seems almost an outrage to be placed in unfamiliar territory without a map. Sometimes it helps people in this circumstance to think of their task as analogous to that of the explorers of old, who presumably did not depart for darkest Africa expecting to recognise the landscape when they got there. If, say, you have spent the last three decades thinking of yourself as the worthless victim of fate in a world which is otherwise populated by happy and effective people who will only look upon you with pity or disgust, it is not easy to know how you set about your relations with them once you have realised that you are as much Other for them as they are for you. How do you cope when you realise that your 'illness' was despair, or rage, or hatred, or longing or confusion?

How do you calm your terror at finding yourself the centre of a network of relationships which does in fact reverberate to *your* conduct? Suddenly you are faced with the reality of concepts which objectivity had promised to render obsolete. Concepts, that is, like courage, loneliness, difficulty, uncertainty, faith. Learning becomes slow, painful and risky, the conduct of relationships delicate and dangerous, the future in principle unpredictable. At times like these the allure of hypnotism or electric shock is not hard to understand.

To find oneself a subjective adult rather than an objective infant, to do without the comforting myths which seemed to point the path along which one could be ushered through life, to take responsibility for what one does knowing that the outcome of one's conduct is uncertain is likely at first to be experienced, by those who are able to face it at all, as that kind of pain which is often called 'depression'. To be uprooted, isolated, confused and uncertain is a physical experience the meaning of which is clear enough to a subjective view, though its clarity makes it none the more pleasant. For many people in this position, life for a while becomes a kind of Pilgrim's Progress in which they stumble from despondency to terror as unfamiliarity and directionlessness are replaced by unknown obstacles looming unanticipated round the turn of a corner.

There is no doubt that one needs courage – and wherever possible encouragement – to pursue this course, and that courage can probably only be summoned up in the context of faith, i.e. faith that somehow what one is trying to do is worth doing. Objectivity, of course, attempts to replace faith with certainty through the exercise of 'scientific prediction and control'. But since we ourselves are, through our conduct, determiners of our world and our fate, and since we cannot know ourselves and each other as fully analysable and therefore completely understandable objects, we are in reality doomed to operate without certainty. Our conduct is inevitably uncertain precisely because we are not, and cannot be, machines, and it is

this uncertainty and unpredictability which in large part constitutes the *moral* nature of our conduct. We are absolutely
unavoidably faced over and over again with having to do what
we think is right rather than what we know will be effective,
and the more we try to hide this truth from ourselves the more
blind, and probably destructive, will our influence on the world
actually become.

It is not inconceivable that in the course of progressing with
the pilgrimage of newly discovered subjectivity initial fear and
despair may give way to something more like elation as the realisation dawns that one is not an object labelled, anchored and
evaluated for all time, but rather a freely flowing focus of action
through which one may to *some* extent take charge of one's
own fate. At the very least, having recognised that in fact the
way courses of events become altered is through the intervention of people, one might hope to bring one's subjective influence to bear on those courses of events with which one is
directly engaged and which formerly seemed objectively unalterable. This is not the same as saying, as some 'humanistic'
psychologies do, that the subject can become *anything* he or she
wants, or do anything he or she likes. Indeed, subjects may have
to recognise and take responsibility for a quite narrow line of
conduct which is likely to bring them little personal satisfaction
or happiness. As always, one must beware of confusing the
projects and possibilities which one can construct in words with
those in which one is actually engaged. Reality lies in what we
do, not in what we tell ourselves, and what we do arises, often,
out of our passionate (even if tacit) commitment to the lessons
of our experience. The nature of that commitment does not
necessarily change just through our being able to put it into
words and imagine it otherwise.

People who see the possibility of taking some kind of subjective charge of their lives will not be able simply to erase their
previously painful experience, and learning new ways of
responding to circumstances or people with whom they find

themselves in a new, probably more responsible, relationship, will not be easy. The whole message of the professionalised management of human relations and 'problems' such as that found in psychiatry and psychology is of relative ease, passivity and painlessness, and so most people are not expecting to encounter the degree of difficulty in learning to conduct themselves in this kind of sphere that they might consider reasonable enough were they trying to acquire competence in, say, a particular sport, craft or art. For example, a patient who gets to the point where she is determined to 'take on' her shyness, suddenly baulks at going to a small social gathering because she realises that she does not 'know what to do'. There are two aspects to her difficulty, one being a mistaken assumption that other people *do* know what to do (i.e., that they have some kind of prepared map for how the evening will go), but the other a more reasonable sense of her own lack of practice in such situations. Even in this latter respect, having pursued a fairly conventional existence in the world for thirty-five years, she is more competent than she thinks she is, but she has always defined herself as utterly worthless and incapable. Ultimately she will only gain in confidence through risking herself in threatening situations and discovering thereby that no catastrophe of major proportions results. Just as sportsmen or artists could never acquire competence without its becoming built into their bodies through practice, so experience of situations or events that used, probably out of fear, to be shunned, just must now be physically acquired if the fear is to be overcome. Even learning to play the piano demands a degree of courage the necessity for which may be avoided by listening instead to a CD.

The avoidance of *difficulty* has become a kind of imperative in our age of passive objectivity. We take it as a self-evident technological (invertedly moral) axiom that 'less difficult' equals 'preferable'. To say that a course of action is 'difficult' is to condemn it as inferior or unworkable, to offer a seemingly unchallengeable objection to it. From the subjective viewpoint such a stance is utterly fallacious: the bodily engagement of the subject with the world is inescapably difficult, if only because of the at least mildly painful adjustment to its demands that the world exacts from the body. In precisely this way learning the piano is for most people, among other things, a painful experience. Not only does one have a heart-sinking awareness of the steadily increasing complexity of the task before one (which makes the mastery of a five-finger exercise, once it has been achieved, seem absolutely paltry), but the sheer physical frustration of trying to discipline one's fingers to conform to the unnatural dictates of the keys while having to coordinate this with the maddeningly abstract significance of the musical notation, is a seemingly endlessly repeated challenge to one's capacity for self-imposed torture. Why should facing and, as far as possible, learning to deal with the complexities and difficulties of one's personal world be any easier? Just as the child sits before the piano weeping with frustration and screaming 'I can't do it,' so people who emerge from a fog of self-deception to find themselves beset by absolutely concrete tasks 'out there' in the world, fall back in horror at their initial incompetence to take them on. But it is equally as unreasonable for them to *expect* to be competent as it is for the child to expect to be able to play the piano without having learned. Again, the fusion of 'science' and magic in our culture frequently makes the validity of this argument almost impossible to maintain: over and over again people will be seduced by the blandishments of those 'experts' who offer easy solutions to the 'problems' which in actuality necessitate painful bodily involvement with the world. So out of touch with our reality have we become that, for example, many people find reasonably plausible the idea that one could while asleep learn a foreign language 'subliminally' from a tape-recorder under one's pillow.

Perhaps the most difficult myth of all to give up is the myth of togetherness. Although there is much that is subjective which can become inter-subjective, there is almost certainly some that isn't, and in any case the more that one departs from the tenets of popular mythology the more isolated one becomes. Whoever dares comment on the emperor's nakedness is likely to become part of a very small minority indeed, and one which provokes the hostility and derision of the majority. Furthermore, if we find ourselves unable to conduct our lives and understand our experience in accordance with the utterly banal precepts and expectations provided by our mythology, we are likely to find the almost total absence of any more helpful source of wisdom doubly disconcerting: in the entirely unexpected set of circumstances in which we find ourselves there is no one to tell us what to do, and no body of knowledge readily to hand to reassure us that we are not alone in our predicament. The emperor's nakedness is a discovery which can only be made personally and individually; imperial schools and libraries will be concerned only to suppress recognition of this phenomenon. Hard to bear though this isolation may be, it does have the advantage of conferring upon those who experience it the dignity of being human and the possibility of making some kind of personal contribution to the moral evolution of the species. As mechanised units we are safe in that we need not ever individually stick our necks out, but we are also expendable and interchangeable, condemned to eternal objectivity; we may be programmed, but we may never expect to programme. But in so far as the unique aspects of our experience force us into areas of exploration where, so it seems, nobody else has been, we may at least hope that our discoveries may be of help or illumination to others who find themselves in the same kind of isolation. We can make as well as follow maps.

Some aspects of the discomfort of subjectivity may be directly related to the extent to which one is still unable to abandon one's needs as object, and it seems unlikely that anyone could ever abandon these entirely. Because self-consciousness entails becoming the object of one's own awareness, to be completely subjective would be, among other things, to be completely unselfconscious, and any such being is hard to imagine, though no doubt there are some people who come close. As soon as one becomes aware of oneself as under the gaze of the Other, even where the Other is oneself, awareness of one's objective shortcomings gives rise to pain. Utter selfless absorption in some kind of active, bodily engagement with the world excludes experience of the kind of psychological distress which has been the focus of this book. Small children totally taken up with what they are doing – no doubt in part because they have no words to represent themselves to themselves – can be touchingly unaware of the extent to which they are exposed to the mockery of an observer (though, of course, what in adults we would see as absurd, in them we see as sweet). People absorbed in the performance of an art or a craft may be utterly free of the pain which floods back once their awareness of their 'selves' returns.

The subjective person is concerned not with being (anything in particular) but with doing. *People* are not to be evaluated, but their *deeds* may be. What one does at a particular point does not at *any* point define what one is – for example, one might make music without 'being a musician'. In relation to other subjects the subjective person pursues his or her activities in what Roger Poole calls 'ethical space':* what we do to and with each other becomes part of an ever-evolving moral process in which there is no objective guarantee of prediction or control.

Since everything about our culture tends towards turning people into objects and estranging them from their own conduct and activity, what you do is of almost no significance alongside the importance of what you are, and in any case what you do can probably be done better by real machines. To attempt to upend these values by laying on subjectivity the emphasis we now lay on objectivity would seem on the face of it to be almost insanely utopian (and would, incidentally, no

*Roger Poole, *Towards Deep Subjectivity*, Allen Lane, The Penguin Press, 1972.

doubt also undermine the social, cultural and economic foundations of our way of life far more radically than any merely political revolution). And yet, paradoxically, to acknowledge our
subjectivity is doing no more than acknowledging what is
already the case: in fact what evolves our world and seals our
fate is nothing other than our own activity. This is even more
true of our collective activity than it is of the self-deceiving,
'neurotic' activity of individuals, since the causes of their distress
more often lie outside their control. Where we act in bad faith,
in the collective as in the individual case, the authorship of our
actions is denied, and we become the helpless objects of what is
in fact our own conduct. To free ourselves of the illusion of
objectivity is therefore as much an acknowledgment of truth as
a merely utopian gesture.

Were we able to live our lives focusing only on the value of
what we did, unaware of ourselves as certain kinds of objects in
the eyes of other people, engaged bodily with the world in
order to realise our projects within it, relating to each other in
'ethical space' rather than in terms of an objective struggle for
relative power or status, we should be unlikely to be suffering
the kinds of psychological malaise to which our current society
gives rise. The opportunities given us by language to misrepresent the meaning of our conduct to both ourselves and others
no doubt renders impossible the attainment of a subjective
social world in anything like pure culture. It would be absurd to
suppose that we could use language solely in the 'vernacular'
mode discussed by Ivan Illich★ – i.e., as facilitating unself-
conscious cooperation in the course of doing or making things
together and one must no doubt resign oneself to the fact that
the capacity of human beings to posture before a linguistic
mirror in which they can excite their greed and self-importance
with all kinds of insubstantial images of greatness will never
allow them to develop the kind of business-like sobriety with

★I. Illich, *Shadow Work*, Marion Boyars, 1981.

which animals not possessed of language conduct their lives. Nevertheless, it may be of some comfort to those whose very distress allows them to glimpse the falsity of our objective values to realise that in fact they *can* do things, and indeed that there may be some things worth doing.

There are some very tangible benefits to the acceptance of subjective as opposed to objective values. For example, in a world in which doing was valued over being, those millions of people who now live in more or less continuous pain and shame over the size and shape of their bodies would suddenly find that that issue simply became irrelevant. In the 'being world' the body is an object in competition for approval with other objects; in the 'doing world' the body becomes an instrument, and while the effectiveness with which it achieves its aims may come under scrutiny from time to time, its physical properties are of scant interest. This again is no mere utopian ideal – in fact, of course, despite the objective bias of our aesthetics, beauty *is* conferred by the loving or appreciative eye of the beholder. Though even in the most rarefied areas of our cultural development we are not free of the polluting influence of objectification (in classical ballet even the most sublimely gifted dancer will be rejected if she departs by an inch from the standard mould), it is still the case that the experience of beauty in another person, if it is to be more than a fleeting, split-off acquisitive interest, arises from the relation *between* people. Whether or not people experience or are experienced by each other as beautiful depends on what they do in relation to each other and to the world, and in this respect it is the very individuality of the person's body which the other experiences as beautiful – not its conformity to a standardised cultural norm of some kind. Unfortunately, the fact that this is a truism does not prevent people from trying desperately to achieve a mythical objective standard of beauty, and feeling hopeless misery when, as inevitably they must, they fall short of it.

Even love itself is transformed in a world imbued by subjective values, for it ceases to constitute the bestowal of approval or confirmation upon a person-as-object, and becomes instead the facilitation of a person's embodied activity. By the latter I do not mean some kind of bloodlessly distant engineering of the person's environment, but rather the kind of loving attention some gardeners might give to the contents of their gardens, as opposed to, say, the acquisitive pride some collectors of art or antiques might have for the items in their collection. Subjective love involves the loving subject in the active taking of risks of a kind which are particularly threatening and repugnant to those who place their faith in objective being, since they necessitate taking a stance and making judgements which depend on little more than the individual's personal assessment and intuition of the concerns, possibilities and needs of the loved person. One can see the operation, or indeed the lack, of this kind of active loving particularly clearly in situations where one person or group of people is responsible for the care of another person or number of people. Subjectively loving parents, for example, watch their children's conduct with an attentive eye, not judging them as objects, but identifying and where possible encouraging and facilitating the nature and extent of their engagement with the world. In practice this might among other things mean, for example, noticing and nurturing their children's interests, competences and passions, using their greater power and experience as adults to clear space for and remove obstacles in the way of their children's own development as subjectively active beings. In this way parents may place all their resources at the disposal of their children, so that the latter may actively use them in their personal understanding and elaboration of the world. This involves a collaborative effort, a fusion; not a standing-back.

To attempt, as many people seem to do, not to 'influence' children morally for fear of impeding their growth is as foolish as it would be not to speak English to them for fear of biasing their linguistic development; parents cannot escape passing on a culture and adopting a range of attitudes towards the world, but this does not mean that they have to be punitively moralistic or unnecessarily constraining of their children's possibilities for developing different understandings. Of course a gardener might insist that marrows should be raised like radishes, and if he does no doubt they will be harmed, but it is also possible for him greatly to facilitate the growth of marrows through devoting himself to the study of their nature, needs and preferences and assisting these wherever possible. Nobody can escape self-consciousness, but the child whose parents focus open-mindedly and with interest on what he or she does rather than on what he or she is stands a better chance than most of being able to function in the world as a subject relatively free of the threat of paralysing anxiety.

In many of the institutions we have established for the longer-term care of social casualties – for example, children or people regarded as handicapped in some sense – the care we in fact offer is almost always of the objectifying rather than 'subjectifying' kind. Usually, certainly, there is no lack of the kind of concern and good will which most of us would probably hope to receive in these circumstances, but what is often lacking is any recognition of the subjective needs of people whose only real hope of salvation is (like all of us) to be able to stand in an *active* relation to the world in a way which lends *meaning* to their existence. Children in care, for example, may (at least, that is, while they remain in care) in fact be deluged with the kind of material advantages which the average kind-hearted citizen might expect them most to lack and appreciate, and are likely to be surrounded by concerned and dedicated professional staff who take every opportunity to show warmth toward and take an interest in the 'relationships' of their charges. Well-meaning local charities collect money for televisions and computer games for the children while social workers attempt to puzzle out and identify the traumata which have marked their experience so that this can be 'talked through' or otherwise taken account of to their benefit. Our collective need towards such children is often an almost desperate one to make up to them for the appalling blows to their objective existence we know them to have suffered, and one can scarcely take exception to the self-denying dedication with which this need is often expressed. What tends not to happen, however, is any real attempt to take seriously the lessons a child may have learned from its experience (however 'deprived' we see this as having been) and to facilitate the possibilities for it to act on its knowledge. We attempt (and inevitably fail) to repair objects rather than help the development of subjects; in trying to 'normalise' those who arouse our compassion we inadvertently deny them the significance of their own experience, and in trying to replace their bitter knowledge of a cruel world with belief in the myths we would prefer to be true, we do them, perhaps, the greatest violence of all.

To heap approval, confirmation and love-as-object upon people, to provide them unstintedly with what so many of us think we want – i.e., to be 'loved for ourselves alone' – may in fact be to do them no great favour since it does nothing very directly to facilitate their development as subjective agents, and leaves them as well vulnerable to annihilation should the source of such love be for any reason withdrawn. To love somebody conditionally as an object is cruel, and to love somebody unconditionally as an object results in empty futility. The individual can only function smoothly when he or she is able to escape from the crippling glare of self-conscious evaluation to make his or her active contribution to the evolution of our world.

There *are* no ways that we *ought* to be other than those which we determine for ourselves. The abandonment of our myths, even though it may free us of the anxiety which arises from self-deception, will not bring us peace of mind, but it may enable us to engage with a real world which we have allowed to get dangerously out of hand.

Taking Care

An Alternative to Therapy

New Preface

Of all my written works, *Taking Care* provides the clearest statement of issues concerning psychotherapy and society which I have been struggling with all my professional life. Less ambiguously than previous books (*Psychotherapy: A personal approach; Illusion & Reality*), it sets out what I see as the limitations of conventional approaches to psychotherapy. At the same time, it lays the ground for subsequent works (*The Origins of Unhappiness; How to Survive without Psychotherapy* both available in a combined volume, The *Nature of Unhappiness*, also published by Robinson) to elaborate, respectively, a detailed theoretical analysis of psychological distress and a kind of manual for 'ordinary people' to understand the significance of their own suffering.

Principally because, in my view, it became a victim of publishing takeovers in the 1980s, *Taking Care* was not as widely read as its predecessor, *Illusion & Reality*. I have always regretted this: for me, it is the profounder and more mature of the two. I am therefore particularly grateful to Carol O'Brien and Constable for bringing it out in this edition.

It is, to put it mildly, a bracing read, bucking the trends of fashion, I have to admit, almost foolhardily. For the most part, works of popular psychology – and many academic approaches too, come to that – seek to reassure their audience that all is not as bad as it seems and that their ills can be overcome through the exercise of some kind of technique or other discovered, or at least propounded, by the author. Such, I think, is the secret of the success of much of the bestselling literature in the psychology and psychotherapy field: it feeds on the hopes and fantasies of people struggling against very difficult odds and only too ready to jump at relatively painless solutions.

No such Panglossian philosophy underlies this work, I fear. Reading it ten years on, even I was slightly taken aback in places at the bleakness of the view of society it portrays. The message is that, far from things being not as bad as they seem, they are in fact worse, and the (largely commercial) apparatus of social control through which the relatively more powerful maintain their advantage over the relatively less powerful has become perfected to the point where it is virtually insuperable. So far as *repairing* the damage done by this society is concerned, psychotherapy is an irrelevance: at best it is a temporary comfort, at worst a distraction. There is no substitute for taking care, and in the long run how a society takes care of its members is a political, not a therapeutic matter.

Uncompromising though this message undoubtedly is, I do not regret it, and indeed I have since retracted no part of it. And although it is stated in these pages with some ferocity, in places, it carries with it a level of reassurance for those in psychological pain more profound than that provided by any form of 'treatment'. For the whole point is that emotional suffering of the kind which comes to be labelled 'neurotic' or 'clinical' is the result not of the individual's inadequacies, shortcomings, personal or genetic weaknesses, but of the *inescapable* infliction on vulnerable bodies of noxious social influences which have their origin, most often, far beyond the orbit of our personal lives.

The issues of responsibility and blame, of what we can and cannot will (spelt out in most detail, perhaps, in *How to Survive Without Psychotherapy*), constitute a theme which recurs throughout my written work, and though I have been hammering away at it in one form or another for twenty years, it is still, I think, the one most people find hardest to grasp. The core of our problem is stated about as clearly as I can manage in Chapter Four, where I try to show that it is the apparent indubitability of our personal experience – our intimate knowledge of our feelings – which makes it so difficult for us to conceive of the source of our difficulties as outside ourselves. We *feel* it inside, so we think that that is where it must indeed originate, and we are, therefore, easily persuaded that it is we who are responsible for what ails us.

We give up this notion, if at all, only with the greatest reluctance, for we feel that to do so robs us of our freedom and our agency. In my subsequent writing I have tried to elaborate the point that we do have freedom and agency, but only to the extent that they are *accorded to* us. The power(s) to choose and to act are not God-given, personal attributes, simply matters of 'will-power', but social acquisitions dependent on the availability of essentially material resources in the world outside our skins. Though some may find it paradoxical, I resolutely maintain that this is, for those who are suffering, a counsel not of despair, but of comfort. Certainly, in my work as a clinical psychologist, I have met many people who have found it comforting; better to be suffering than to be sub-standard.

This book is, therefore, more a critique of the society which gives rise to psychological distress than of the approaches to therapy which have been spawned to assuage it; the focus has shifted from individual experience (as in *Illusion & Reality*) to social structure.

It was not difficult to see ten years ago how pervasive make believe and wishfulness were becoming as ways of interpreting experience and constructing means of social control – I claim no prophetic powers- but even so the true prophets of 'postmodernity' (Jean-François Lyotard, Jean Baudrillard) may have seemed to be over-stating their case. Where I wrote in Chapter One of our failure to distinguish between emdodied reality and dream-like imagery, the representation of war as an aesthetic, electronic experience was still almost five years off. The 1980s, however have seen the extension of imagery and make-believe right into the core of the body politic and the threats to our embodied hold on reality which were identified in the earlier chapters of this book are now represented within the official institutions of our society more as a virtue than a night-mare.

The further disintegration of any idea that politics could be the proper concern of the citizenry is particularly to be deplored. In what has become a kind of apolitical, almost 'virtual' government, issues affecting the mate-rial reality of our lives, along with concepts of economic fairness and social justice, have been set aside in favour of, for example, variants on the theme of 'responsibility'. Rather than either the regulation or the overt exercise of oppressive power, there is an attempt to maintain control (whether of scapegoats, such as the teachers, or of corrupt commercial institutions selling pension plans) through shaming and admonishment. The manipulation of image, the frank abandonment of actuality for appearance (for example the celebration of fashion as an 'industry') have become not just ideological tools of government but the very process of government itself. Government has thus become the management of appearance; what is done to people is considered indistinguishable from what they think has been done to them (hence the successful politician's obsession with 'focus groups' and the consequent inevitability of dema-goguery); magic is officially rehabilitated at every cultural level – science and soothsaying are seen as but alternative ways to 'the truth'. The collapse of the distinction between public and private which so concerns me in these pages is now virtually complete.

And yet, of course, reality will not be gainsaid. We are still embodied creatures in a real world even though the concept of a 'real world' has been hopelessly undermined by marked rhetoric. What has happened, of course, is that the demands of global Business have put out of sight and beyond the reach of our criticism – beyond, most significantly, the power of national governments to control – the actual levers of power which constistute the ultimate influences on our lives. A 'Labour' Prime Minister can smugly extol the virtues of a 'flexible labour market' because the 'reality' of his world does not include being able to influence the policies of huge multi-national companies – he can only dance to their tune. And for the men and women thrown out of work in the interests of 'flexibility' there are no officially authorized words with which to criticize their condition; if their distress is not simply dumb, it can be given form only in the language of personal responsibility and inadequacy. The unemployed are 'jobseekers' or 'welfaredependants' and rather than being able to earn the means of their livelihood they are offered either moral exhortation or counselling.

We need more than ever before to rescue the reality of our world if only because of the pain which is inflicted on the lives of so many 'ordinary' people. Our virtual reality is bought at too high a price. Even in relatively prosperous Britain the suffering of those at the bottom of the heap – and they are no small minority – is a social outrage. Though not exactly a secret (ask any inner-city teacher or health worker) the extent of this suffering is resolutely obscured by the official institutions of society, not least the therapy and counselling industry. The very first thing we have to do, therefore, is to establish with fearless clarity what the nature of our predicament is, and that may indeed prove a somewhat harrowing process. Our real problem, however, is in knowing where to go from there. It is easy enough to construct formulae for how our personal lives should be lived – the philosophy of life sketched in Chapter Seven, for example, still seems to me a fair enough ideal – but turning insight into action is not simply a matter of the exercise of personal will, for as individuals we are not in control of what we do. In this book I make the case for taking care rather than providing therapy, *but* how that is to be achieved requires a political analysis and understanding beyond the scope of these pages. One thing, however, is certain: it will require the exercise of social power.

David Smail
Nottingham, 1997

Introduction

Our accustomed ways of looking at the world suggest that we all live in an unalterable, shared reality which exists quite independently of any feelings we might have about how it *ought* to be. Equally, our accustomed view of knowledge – especially scientific knowledge – is that it gives a dispassionate, disinterested description of the way things *are*, again independently of how we might like them to be.

These accustomed ways of looking at the world and viewing knowledge have long been known – at least by many of those whose business it is to think about such things – to be false.

In fact, the 'reality' we believe in is an illusion. In fact, our 'dispassionate' knowledge is highly partial and selective: it has aims and purposes inextricable from the *interests* of power. We use knowledge to subordinate nature, and that includes ourselves.

These issues may seem a long way from the concerns of a psychologist whose job it is to try to understand and if possible alleviate the emotional distress of individual people. However, having worked for a number of years in the field of psychological 'treatment', I have become convinced, in the first place, that these issues are central to an understanding of human despair, and in the second that they should no longer remain the particular property of 'those whose business it is to think about such things'. These issues are everybody's concern, and though it may be in the professional interest to limit serious consideration of them to the experts, to do so would not be, and is not, for the public good.

The central argument of this book is a very simple one, but, obscured by my professional blinkers, it took me nearly three decades to see it: psychological distress occurs for reasons which make it incurable by therapy, but which are certainly not beyond the powers of human beings to influence. We suffer pain because we do damage to each other, and we shall continue to suffer pain as long as we continue to do the damage. The way to alleviate and mitigate distress is for us *to take care of* the world and the other people in it, not to *treat* them.

Although (to me, but I am sure also to many others) this 'insight' has now become blindingly obvious, it is extraordinarily difficult to marshall the arguments and evidence which support it, since they so often run counter to our customary ways of seeing and thinking about things. It is, however, my belief that one cannot expect people to give up the hope (not to mention the resources) they invest in 'treatment' until they have gained access to and had a chance to consider for themselves what the arguments and evidence are. And one cannot expect the sum of human distress to diminish until we give up our investment in treatment, and address instead the daunting task of taking care.

In *Illusion & Reality* my basic concerns were not different from those informing the present work, but my focus was particularly upon individuals and their experience of anxiety within the compass of their own lives. My aim was to try to offer encouragement to people (that is, all of us) who have been bludgeoned out of their understanding of the world by a remorseless 'objectivity', to risk trusting themselves to become the 'subjects' that, in fearful secret, they somehow know themselves to be. This time my focus is wider; having, as it were, stated the dilemma in terms of the way it presents itself in our immediate experience, I want now to broaden the view to show how that experience is formed and influenced by the social and cultural structures which we inhabit, and to suggest what the implications of that may be for the way we should conduct ourselves towards one another.

An attempt to understand the influence of social and cultural

structures takes one beyond present times and places, and challenges familiar and unthinkingly accepted views of what
'society' is about. In the following pages I shall suggest a
number of things which may well seem at first – or even second
– sight hard to swallow: for example, that the world we seem to
know, and which seems so unalterably hard, and real and resistant to our will, is in several important ways the illusory creation
of our wishes, the fabrication of our dreams. Indeed, there is a
sense in which dreaming, even when awake, is *inescapable*. We
are, as it were, doomed to 'grasp' reality only through our *interpretation* of it, and hence we cannot really grasp it at all. But we
can, as I shall also argue, have *respect* for it: we may dream reck-
lessly, or we may go carefully because we know we are
dreaming.

Again, I shall argue that what we take to be dispassionate
knowledge is in fact suffused with *interest*; that is, our knowledge is inseparable from the uses to which we wish to put it –
we *exploit* our knowledge in order to *exploit* the world's
resources (including people), and because so much of that
exploitation is fundamentally dishonourable, we hide its nature
from ourselves (we 'repress' it). My particular concern here will
of course be with psychological knowledge, and again I shall
have the difficult – and to many people perhaps unpalatable –
task of suggesting that the main use to which psychological
knowledge has been put has been the exploitation of some
people by others for purposes which, though they do not appear
in those others' conscious awareness, nevertheless suit them
rather well.

Furthermore, if one is to understand the workings of interest,
particularly in relation to psychology and 'treatment', one must
investigate the sources of the plausibility in which it manages to
clothe itself. In part, I believe, these are to be traced to an age-old
and ever-present attraction to magic (which also shapes much of
our dreaming). Magic, indeed, is not at all a relic of the past, but
is found at the very kernel of our enthusiasm for science.

These factors (our wishful dreaming, magic, and interest) combine with what we take to be the point of our lives – the 'pursuit of happiness' – to enslave us within a society in which exploitation and indifference are the norm. In this society also, the intellectual and conceptual means whereby we might get a purchase on our predicament are largely obscured from us. Nowhere is this more so than in the case of psychological distress and its treatment, in which our ideas about why we suffer as we do, and whom we are to 'blame', as well as how we may change or be 'cured', are shaped by our social and cultural concerns much more to justify and permit further exploitation than to allow us an insight into the true reasons for our ills.

Far from being repairable machines, human beings are embodied organisms on whom damage will at best always leave a scar. We simply cannot get away with using and abusing each other as we do, and it is small wonder that the ways of life into which we have uncritically fallen, and which we take for granted as the natural response to an inescapable reality, reverberate so disastrously in our conduct towards and experience of each other – that is, in our 'relationships', where, again without noticing, we have carried exploitation to the very heart of our social undertakings, placing it between man and woman, and parent and child.

The sense of 'therapy' which the subtitle of this book calls into question is that in which therapy is 'officially' offered (and undoubtedly widely accepted in the public mind) as a *technical* procedure for the cure or adjustment of emotional or psychological 'disorder' in individual people. There are 'unofficial' aspects of psychotherapy – recognised at least implicitly by many of its practitioners – which I would not want to question, and indeed in pursuance of which this book could be said to be written. These aspects, however, are, in contrast with the grandiose claims and aspirations of most 'schools' of psychotherapy, extremely limited (sadly necessary palliatives in a disordered society) and not justifiably professionally 'patentable'. Elaboration of them should in no way distract us from the much more essential task of trying to understand and prevent the processes whereby we come to inflict upon each other so much incurable damage.

As a matter of fact, though their stated profession and unstated interest may be to offer cure, most therapists of good will also play an inadvertently subversive role within the society which damages us so profoundly. As I tried to show in *Psychotherapy: A Personal Approach*,* what most often psychotherapists *actually* (as opposed to professedly) do, is to *negotiate* a view of what the patient's predicament is about which both patient and therapist can agree (which is to establish, as closely as one ever can, what is the truth of the matter), and then to *encourage* the patient to do what he or she can to confront those elements of the predicament which admit of some possibility of alteration. This almost inevitably means that patients begin to criticise aspects of a social 'reality' which before they had always taken for granted, and, with courage or grace, to learn actively to dissent from and oppose the constraints it had placed upon them: to overcome the tyranny of objectivity. I would now lay more emphasis than I did in that book on the value of *comfort*: for many people, psychotherapy provides the only source of comfort they are likely to find in what has been, for them at least, a predominantly cruel world.

The *actual* possible achievements of therapy may thus be summarised very briefly as establishing what is the case ('demystification'), and providing comfort and encouragement. Inasmuch as this book is addressed primarily to people trying to make sense of their own and others' distress, it is my hope that lessons I have learned from the experience of psychotherapy (as I have come to understand it) may to some extent transfer to these pages.

The process of demystification, the examination and clearing

*Dent, 1978.

of the confusions which surround the person's deceived or self-deceiving view of what lies behind the 'symptoms', often forms the longest part of the therapeutic enterprise. There are, it is true, therapists who feel that, as long as *they* are sure of how they can make patients confront the difficulties which beset them, there is really no point in spending much time in demystification: what matters, they say, is getting on with tackling the problems, not investigating the reasons why they arose in the first place. I do not myself agree with this view, though I have no doubt that it may sometimes 'work'. It seems to me essential for people to enter into, to have the full opportunity to alter and argue with the processes whereby someone else arrives at a formulation of 'the problem'; the alternative constitutes reliance upon an authoritarian or 'parentalist' elite which in the long run infantilises and makes dependent – embodies, indeed, a form of tyranny.

It is of course not possible in a book to enter into a dialogue with the reader, and hence the *negotiative* element of attempts at 'demystification' has to be missing. I shall, then, have to rely upon arguments which I hope will persuade, and forego the opportunity of *listening* which is so essential to reaching an understanding. Nobody, I am sure, who is fundamentally antipathetic to any particular view is persuaded of its truth by argument. I shall, therefore, be preaching to the at least half converted; in any case I believe that the most a writer can hope for is to illuminate and articulate ideas and views which are already partially formed in the reader.

It is then in a *kind* of demystification process that the first six chapters of this book (those, that is, whose contents have been briefly sketched above) are intended to be engaged. The intention is to suggest that our ordinary ways of considering our lives and 'relationships' (i.e. the other people in them) obscure a view of how corrupt, exploitative and emotionally impoverished and damaging our social organisation, and hence our conduct towards each other, have become. In the course of making my argument I cannot rely on cast-iron 'evidence', but will have to trust to the all-too-fallible methods of persuasion (as for example occasional reference to what may turn out to be entirely idiosyncratic elements of my own experience) by which I may hope to strike in the reader a sympathetic chord. Some of the arguments I shall marshall are based on ideas I know I have gleaned from others, and some, no doubt, on ideas which I have forgotten that I have gleaned from others. Whatever their source, all of them are ideas which illuminate and make sense of my experience during the conduct of psychotherapy: they clarify, for me anyway, the nature of distress.

The final two chapters are written in the hope that some *encouragement* may be derived from them. There are in fact no magic answers to our predicament, no dreaming away of our real, embodied, presence in the world. There is no escape from the necessity to give up an infantile longing for blissful ease, to grow to maturity and to take care both of our environment and of each other. We have to rediscover a morality which is not moralistic, and construct a society which both acknowledges and makes what provision it can for the *difficulties* involved in creating tolerance, forbearance, justice and care. We talk a lot about love, but (as I suggested in *Illusion & Reality*) there is not a great deal of it about. We cannot, therefore, simply love each other better; we have first to make a society in which love may take root and thrive.

I cannot claim to be optimistic about the prospects of attaining any such society (could anyone, who sees the lack of restraint in our history and the destructive intent of our technology?), but it might, with the very greatest effort, just be possible.

There is probably not very much of *comfort* in all this. However, my experience both personally and professionally is that the greatest comfort derives from having one's view, however despairing it may be, confirmed by someone else who is not afraid to share it. As long, then, as this book helps some people in their quest to identify the roots of their unease, I hope it may even be comforting. It would certainly comfort me to think that here or there it might find an echo.

There is one central and essential point I wish to emphasise above all others in this introduction, and to beg the reader to bear in mind throughout what follows: it is neither my wish nor my intention to engender in him or her any sense of guilt or blame. It is extremely difficult, perhaps impossible, seriously to criticise our society and our conduct toward each other without challenging very fundamental and widely shared assumptions, without showing anger and having at times almost deliberately to shock. Even the most constructive criticism, if it is to avoid superficiality, necessitates seeing some very familiar things in some very unfamiliar ways. There are thus some elements of trying to 'negotiate' a view which just cannot be at all times measured and reasonable and cool. But it is part of the very heart of my argument that no body – singular or collective – is to *blame* for the predicament in which we find ourselves. We are all, certainly, *responsible*, in the sense that nobody but we ourselves wreak on each other the havoc we do, but the concept of blame is one which mystifies and obscures the processes whereby this comes about. (Blame is an effective means of manipulating people and groups, not a valid concept for understanding them.) As anyone who has an intimate concern with human misery knows, blame and guilt, invoked as explanations, are simply ways of evading the difficulties involved in tackling it. The same, it seems to me, is likely to be true of misery on a societal scale.

CHAPTER ONE

Dreaming and Wishing: The Individual and Society

'All life is a dream, and dreams are just dreams.'

What seemed to me as a schoolboy no more than a poetic affectation useful for quoting in exams, comes to mind years later as a statement of the simple truth.

Perhaps all that signifies is that literature is wasted on some schoolboys; perhaps anyway Calderon* meant something entirely different by his words from what I now understand by them. However that may be, it seems to me that we may be sunk more deeply into our dreams than at any previous time in our recorded history, and in any case more deeply than we can afford to be, for our dreams are full of a destructive rage and hatred, a frustrated craving for omnipotence, a desperation for satisfaction beyond the bounds of mere greed, through which we may dream ourselves to our own annihilation.

We can see the world only in the ways that human beings, with their own particular ways of sensing and experiencing (and *interpreting* sensation and experience) *can* see it. Whatever reality there may be beyond the 'reality' which filters to us through our individual, historical and cultural ways of seeing, we shall never be able to say what it 'is'. We have, of course, a naive belief in a scientifically establishable, objective reality, but subscribing to that belief is in truth doing no more than taking, in a very grandiose way, what is merely our best guess so far

*In his play *Life Is a Dream*, 1635.

about the nature of things *as* the nature of things. We have yet fully to accept that we can *never* get beyond guesswork.

So we are dreamers within a reality we cannot ever completely know, but which is nevertheless vulnerable to our conduct. Our lives are dreamt within a world, indeed a universe, which *permits* our dreaming and exists independently of it. Though we cannot know our world, we can certainly dream its destruction (and thereby put an end also to our dreaming).

That 'primitive man' lives in a dream is easy enough for most of us to grasp as we read of his nervous transactions with a world of ghostly ancestry and dangerous magic. What we find less easy to see is that our own world is to just about the same extent constructed out of superstitious fantasies, centring, in our case, mainly around images of conquest and wealth. Furthermore, our naive belief in a scientifically establishable objective reality renders us dangerously blind to the influence of our dreaming. Less wise than the Australian Aborgines, we do not acknowledge our origin in a 'dream time', and have not traced its contribution to our 'scientifically established reality'. We mistakenly trust our reality, therefore, not to be affected by 'primitive' dreaming: we are not sufficiently on our guard against the influence of our dreams.

Dreams vary in the degree of their 'primitiveness', but this is to be judged more by the extent to which they are infused by wishful self-concern than by any lack of correspondence they may have with what we assume to be 'objective reality'.

Human beings are, so to speak, engines of symbolism. We turn the reality we cannot finally know into a kind of endlessly enriching compost of symbols, of which our wide-awake, conscious words are only one, and by no means necessarily the most profound, aspect. Anyone who has 'watched' his or her thoughts (i.e. self-addressed speech) turn at the point of sleep into 'pictures' cannot fail to be astounded by the economy, complexity and beauty of the process of symbolic transformation. Since it tends not to have words attached to it, and since we find it very hard to 'remember' without the use of language, this process is an extremely difficult one to capture. Although I know I have experienced it quite frequently, I can only think of a couple of examples.

Sitting in a London underground train, for instance, I watch the cables writhe past along the tunnel wall. Some are thicker than others; they run neatly parallel, until suddenly they switch position, cross over, alter their height, branch unexpectedly, swerve a little. I just catch myself 'realising' that the cables 'are' an argument; they are a complex logical discourse; in some absolutely *direct* way they display the nature of an intellectual thesis. Again, one hot afternoon, I look slightly sleepily out of the window down at the car park outside. Suddenly the car park – the arrangement of the cars, their colours, the way the sunlight reflects off them – is absolutely *full of meaning* (I cannot say what, for I am surprised into wakefulness and have no time to put words to the meaning before it has gone).

I suspect that our world – the world, that is, of 'developed' Western civilisation – is as saturated with our dream-meanings as are the cave walls of any Stone Age hunters. We live with the world we cannot know (in the way we think we would like to) in a relation of symbolic reciprocity. We extract from the world meanings and metaphors which we then project back into it as objective characteristics, though of course there is nothing truly objective about them.

At any moment, waking or sleeping, experience reaches us through an accretion of meaning, all of it to *some* extent individually and culturally idiosyncratic, which has, as it were, become wired into our bodies from previous experience. This accretion of meaning thus gives form and colour to everything we experience in the present, providing a kind of symbolic background to what we take to be reality. In this sense, we dream all the time. Perhaps the underground cables have more

in common with the caveman's bison than we might suspect.★
More than just dreaming inside our own heads, we dream *into*
as well as *out of* the world: our psychological relation to the
world is one of continuous symbolic interchange. The depth,
complexity and significance of that relation is quite awe-
inspiring; symbolisation of this kind, asleep or awake, is the very
opposite of primitive. There is no shame in our being dreamers.

'All life is a dream', if true, seemed to my schoolboy self a
potential reason for taking life less seriously than otherwise one
might. However, the reverse now seems to me the case. If I
dream you, and you dream me (and, of course, we *do*: how else
explain the rapid shifts in perception of each other we undergo,
the discovery in time that we are more separate than we
thought, that wife is not mother, husband not knight?), then
how careful we must be with each other. For if all there is for us
is dreaming there is no possibility of waking to find that the
harm we have done each other was *just* a dream. Over and over
again, as a species, we 'awake' from our dreams to find our
hands covered in blood.

There are all kinds of dreaming, and it is important not to get
carried away by the metaphor of 'life as a dream' to the point
where we lose a conception of reality. Even though we cannot
directly know reality as something 'in itself', existing quite
objectively apart from our symbolic understanding of it, we can
attempt to 'unwind' it as far as possible from our wishful
fantasies.

This, no doubt, is what science, at its best, achieves. But all
too quickly science itself becomes enmeshed in our autistic
reveries of power, so that we use it as a vehicle for our covert
aims and borrow its authority to justify our ravaging of the
world and each other.

The wishful fantasies we dream in our beds at night – the

★This line of thought is pursued with great, if at times rather oppressive
erudition by Susanne Langer in her three-volume *Mind: An Essay on Human
Feeling*, Johns Hopkins University Press, 1967–82.

kind of which Freud began, at least, to articulate an understanding present no great problem of themselves. (In fact, they
need no articulate understanding since their whole meaning is
*in*articulate and in most respects quite sufficient unto itself.) As
we sleep, we may fantasise any kind of satisfaction or horror
with no more illeffect than, perhaps, a slight feeling of unease or
embarrassment for half the following day. But, awake, only a
faithful respect for the unknowable reality of the world and the
other people in it will prevent our enacting our dreams in
potentially catastrophic ways. For what else is the man who
takes an automatic rifle to mow down the shoppers in an
American supermarket doing but dreaming?

If we are to unwind ourselves from the strands of base magic
which are so thickly interwoven in our dreams we need to
remind ourselves that we are not simply pictures, or shadows, or
images, but *bodies* in a *world*. In the second half of the twentieth
century there grew an increasing awareness of the dangerous
seductiveness of the image, though interpreted differently by
different writers.* At times, even, it is unclear which is more
important to us – the image or the actuality. In the political
sphere particularly, though by no means solely, the explicit
concern of the actors (some of them trained as such!) as well as
the commentators is with the adequacy of their image, the
effectiveness of the 'P.R.' battles which seek to present us with
credibility as a higher value than truth. The awful danger, of

*Daniel Boorstin, for example, in *The Image* (Penguin Books, 1963) simply
bemoans the usurpation by vulgar and synthetic imitativeness of values once
the hallowed property of an appreciative elite. His thesis that the populace
demands the trash supplied to it by an almost reluctant commercial world is
absurd, though his exposure of the nature of the trash itself is brilliant. Guy
Debord's *Society of the Spectacle* (Black and Red, 1983), born of the Paris riots
in 1968, makes an altogether more plausible link between image and interest,
though with great Gallic opacity. Most compelling of all is Christopher
Lasch's *The Minimal Self* (Picador, 1985) in which the depths of our confusion
between reality and illusion, and its dangers, are described with considerable
power.

course, is that enactment of the fantasies which such 'images' create can, and does, result in the mutilation of our bodies and our world.

Contributing to this state of affairs, no doubt, is the fact that our very experience of the world is becoming increasingly insubstantial and disconnected from any bodily involvement in it. For example, whether presenting 'fact' or 'fantasy', the television – on which most of us depend for any kind of understanding of world affairs – deals solely in images. It thus becomes increasingly difficult to differentiate the images of our dreaming sleep from those of our waking televisual experience, and gradually the laborious, uneditable nature of our bodily experience of the world seems to become a kind of irksome, obsolete burden. Our dreams are so much more attractive, and it seems that technology makes them attainable.

At no time in our previous history can it have been so possible for people to 'experience' death and destruction – the actual death and destruction of real people – on such a wide scale but in such a disembodied and dislocated form. The danger is that we get so used to them in this form that we think we know what they're like and that they don't really hurt. Hence perhaps the numbed amazement written on the face of people who discover that 'it' has indeed 'happened to them'. Hence perhaps also the unhappy moral confusion and uncertainty surrounding the deaths of forty spectators at a televised football match – do we treat this as a real event demanding a flesh-and-blood response to the sensible agony of those involved, or do we sweep up the bodies like so many discarded cardboard containers of fried chicken and get on with the game? Our confusion is *genuine* – already our world is such that the values of embodied presence seem not necessarily to outweigh those of disembodied image.

And yet it is inconceivable that we shall ever be able to achieve what seems to be our covert aim – that is, to etherealise ourselves to the point where we become pure, disembodied images, as unencumbered as an electronic pulse. We are creatures of bone and tissue in a world upon which we depend for our bodily existence. If we persist in actually involving each other in the pursuit of our dream images, we shall discover that they are indeed dreams from which we cannot awake and that the sacrifices we make will be made not in pictures, but in tears and blood.

In our eagerness to escape the vulnerability to pain to which our nature as embodied beings exposes us, we construct a variety of technological and therapeutic 'solutions' which share a common origin in the wishful magic of dreaming. But no matter how hard we may try and how fervently we may believe in it, magic still does not work. The reluctant conclusion to which I have been driven after having worked for some years in the fields of psychology and psychotherapy – fields which are, as I shall argue later, deeply imbued with magic – is that human suffering arises from our embodied interaction with a world whose reality, though it cannot be known, cannot be wished away. A very significant part of the psychologist's role is contin-uous with that of the 'cunning man' and the astrologer, and as such is a sham. The evil that we do each other cannot be undone, at least not so easily as we like to think, and the ravages of the world cannot be erased.

Not for nothing, I believe, are so many people these days oppressed and frightened bv a sense they have that 'things have got out of control', that people are the powerless victims of impersonal forces which are experienced as a strange and barely analysable mixture of malignity and inevitability – even neces-sity. It is as if these forces are uninfluenceable: we wait for them to crush us and to destroy our environment with the kind of hopeless resignation one imagines prisoners awaiting execution to feel.

Thirty or so years ago, it was quite common for people who expressed a sense of impending doom, and who perhaps coupled this with some kind of untutored critique of the societal or technological influences they took to be responsible, to be diagnosed as mentally unstable in some way. I have several times in the past observed at first hand the label 'schizophrenic' being attached to someone on no better grounds than that they accounted for their emotional unease in terms judged by their psychiatrists to be 'pseudo-philosophical'. Nowadays, it seems, this sense of helplessness and threat has become much more general, and though the 'pseudo-philosophical' constructions of and reactions to it have become both more shared and more focused (e.g. in environmentalist movements and an upsurge of fundamentalist religious feeling) there are still many people who feel unable to formulate a clear idea of exactly what is wrong.

It is no longer plausible to suggest that people who feel this sort of unease are unstable or even mad (though this is a possibility that they themselves often consider with great trepidation). Our feelings seem rather to be indications of a social, not an individual, 'disease', and are to be taken absolutely seriously. 'Ordinary people', it seems, are swiftly becoming dislocated from any sense at all that they can influence or even identify those forces which shape their lives, and this both engenders a despair which is reflected in their relations with others and stimulates forms of defensiveness (such as denial, apathy, or ostrich-like optimism) which only serve to make things worse. The state of affairs, in any social community, in which people find themselves being carried along by forces which seem both destructive and out of reach of their influence, is a recipe for disaster.

'There have always been prophets of doom,' you may say, to which the answer must be that doom is prophesied only that it may be avoided. What I find much more chilling than prophecies of doom is the fact that doom has often enough already occurred with only one or two observers (out of millions) brave enough to say what they saw and to draw lessons for the future. The prophet of doom may indeed be an optimist alongside the observer of doom, who could under the circumstances scarcely be blamed for pessimism.

Take, for example, just one fragment of the experience of the psychoanalyst Wilfred Bion, who as a youth of barely twenty found himself blown into a shell-hole in a First World War battlefield, drenched in mud, water, and bits and pieces of other people's bodies – 'a kind of human soup'. It is surely not surprising that, having observed the 'progress' of humanity for the ensuing sixty years he should write:

> When the super clever monkeys with their super clever tools have blown themselves into a fit and proper state to provide delicate feeding for the coming lords and ladies of creation, super microbe sapiens, then the humans who cumber the earth will achieve their crowning glory, the gorgeous colours of putrescent flesh to rot and stink and cradle the new aristocracy.*

What is perhaps much more surprising is that so many people who have experienced similarly horrific circumstances to those Bion describes in his book, and so many of the rest of us who may in one way or another learn of them, continue, either by forgetting them, excusing them or even glorifying them, to believe in any future at all.

This may seem an unnecessarily drastic theme by which to illustrate our apparent inability to learn from our mistakes, and one far removed from the usual concerns of psychology. However, I make no apologies, since it seems to me that the everyday violence we do each other, the waste of human talent and squandering of human resources, the suspicion of and indifference toward each other which are such features of our alienated existence, all of which lead to a wreckage of human life which in its own way is quite bad enough, may eventually – perhaps quite soon – terminate in a frame of mind in which we really don't care if we try to destroy ourselves outright. This is

*W. R. Bion *The Long Week-End*, Fleetwood Press, 1982.

not fanciful; it has happened before. The difference now is that 'we have the technology' to guarantee success.

Perhaps the most tragic aspect of human nature lies in its vulnerability to wishful magic. Perhaps, ultimately, it will prove to be its fatal aspect. Over and over again we abandon a rational intuition of our embodiment in a real world for passionate belief in alternative modes of existence in worlds created out of our imagination. Our genius as symbolisers and as users of language enables us to disregard the lessons of our bodily experience, and to construct acceptable versions of all our lowest motives and actions, in ways that, fortunately for them, are not available to less 'gifted' species, which are by contrast firmly anchored in an ineffable reality from which no flight of fancy can release them. A dead cat is a dead cat, and could never become, for example, posthumous martyr to some warlike feline cause.

The cultural miasma that we have created inside our heads to preserve us from catching a glimpse of the mess we make of our world leads us also to be not easily moved by pity. If our response to physical pain and death is frequently uncertain, our awareness of frustration, deprivation and waste seems, on the face of things at least, largely absent. It was, for example, what he saw as the appalling waste of youth which inspired Paul Goodman to write a bitter critique* of American society of the fifties.

> In our society, bright lively children, with the potentiality for knowledge, noble ideals, honest effort, and some kind of worthwhile achievement, are transformed into useless and cynical bipeds, or decent young men trapped or early resigned, whether in or out of the organised system.

> In despair, the fifteen-year-olds hang around and do nothing at all, neither work nor play . . . They do not do their school

*P. Goodman, *Growing Up Absurd*, Vintage Books, 1956.

work, for they are waiting to quit; and it is hard . . . for them to get part-time jobs. Indeed, the young fellows (not only delinquents) spend a vast amount of time doing nothing. They hang around together, but don't talk about anything, nor even – if you watch their faces – do they passively take in the scene. Conversely, at the movies, where the real scene is by-passed, they watch with absorbed fantasy, and afterward sometimes mimic what they saw.

It is sad that Goodman's book, apart from its forlorn thread of optimism more relevant today than ever, has not become a bible for anyone (i.e. all of us) who has responsibilities to the young. One wonders what Goodman would have made now of the dead-eyed hopelessness of so many young people whose only permissible aspiration is to acquire the plastic junk they appraise so listlessly in shopping-precinct windows, and one despairs that so passionate and articulate a warning should have gone so apparently unheeded.

No one is likely to become more aware of the extraordinary ingenuity possessed by human beings in the business of magically falsifying their experience than the psychotherapist. It is in the way we try to deal with the anguish arising from our existence in the world that one may see most clearly our reluctance to recognise its causes and get to grips effectively with its consequences. One of the earliest lessons learned by any moderately observant therapist is that what the patient says about his or her predicament is, for a number of reasons (often outside the patient's knowledge or control), systematically distorted so as to hide its real significance. In fact, psychological malaise is the inevitable sequel of difficult or unfortunate aspects of the individual's relation to his or her world, but (conveniently for the person, society or both) is not recognised as such. To recognise the real reasons for psychological distress would, usually, be too painful or threatening, present difficulties too apparently insuperable, uncover hatred and recrimination too seemingly unbearable, reveal too much guilty subterfuge, or simply expose to view social injustice which would be too insupportable for the attendant difficulties to be kept within manageable bounds. Patients therefore magically interpret 'the problem' as something altogether more amenable to professional intervention; a lifetime of misery becomes an illness with a cure.

So far, psychotherapists, in seeing accurately enough that patients distort their experience so as to minimise the difficulties of its implications, have failed to realise that they themselves are playing a complementary part in this process of mystification by implicitly offering magic solutions for the 'problems' encountered. These are points upon which I shall expand in subsequent chapters, but what I want here to emphasise is that the therapeutic situation *as a whole* offers a rare insight into the way *collectively* we try to use magic to repair the damage we do to each other. Although it may be true that psychotherapists (and this was the abiding achievement of Freud and his colleagues) are able to remove some of the mystery from the individual person's anguish, they may end up only making matters worse lf they set about trying to put things right merely through a process of, in the broadest sense, interpretation. We shall make, and in my view have made, no progress at all by *interpreting* human misery *merely* as the outcome of the individual's *mis*interpretation of his or her circumstances. What is so instructive about the therapeutic situation taken, again, as a whole, is that it shows clearly how we collude with each other in trying (on the patient's side) to falsify our experience and obscure our motives, and (on the therapist's) to offer magically painless ways out of the predicaments we create. A further instructive feature of the therapeutic situation, again one which I shall criticise in greater detail later, is that it seeks to understand and explain human distress precisely in *individual* terms, as well as implying that it may be 'cured' or ameliorated through efforts of individual consciousness.

For the moment, then, there are two lessons in particular

from the experience of psychotherapy which I should wish to be borne clearly in mind. The first is that human beings easily misrepresent the reasons for their own anguish. The second is that those supposed to be most expert in the understanding of that anguish, being no more than human themselves, easily succeed in obscuring its nature even further. As a partial explanation of this I have concentrated so far upon our wishful fantasies, our greedy, magic-infused dreams. But at the centre of these is something altogether harder and more mundane: our interest.

Interest is the method in our madness, the force which pushes our dreams in some directions rather than others, the guilty secret which collectively we do our best to keep. It is by dragging interest into the open, I believe, that we shall most readily be able to understand the damage we do each other and the pain we cause. Not that in many ways interest is not perfectly manifest – indeed in these days in particular it shows itself in some of its aspects quite boldly – but still, of all our mystifications, the mystification of interest is the most developed and most defended at every level of society.

Among other (and more important) reasons for 'neurotic' self-deception is frequently to be found the individual's camouflaged interest – the rather base and shameful motive which is satisfied by the 'illness', the weakness, perhaps, which permits one person to tyrannise another. Indeed, almost any form of disability can be turned to the person's interest, and it is only the most unusual people who do not find *some* advantage to be gained from their lameness, deafness or blindness. However, our shameful weaknesses, if we are to put them to the fullest use, must be disguised, or, best, made unknown to ourselves, and for this the process of repression is most suitable: we *do* things, but we do not acknowledge (spell out in words) what we are doing. But this, and other reasons for 'neurotic' conduct identified as residing somehow within individuals, are not enough to explain their suffering. The operation of interest and repression at the individual level is useful mainly for offering us a clue to the understanding of their operation on an altogether wider scale.

In our everyday considerations of how societies work, repression is of course used in a rather different sense from that above. Groups or classes of people are repressed, it is thought, when the instruments of power are used quite consciously on the part of the ruling group or class to 'deal with' those it considers for one reason or another undesirable. And yet it is not only unhappy individuals who hide from themselves, by failing to acknowledge them, the operations whereby their interests are furthered. Through manipulation of the media of mass communication – the means whereby they spell out their intentions to their members – whole societies, and especially their governments, pursue the interests of those who wield power while claiming or appearing to pursue the welfare of all. In part this is of course quite conscious – few people these days, and least of all politicians, are unaware of the importance of 'image' – and yet, I suspect, most would feel (i.e. articulate to themselves) that the manipulation of image is aimed only at finding the 'best', most palatable way to present an entirely honourable policy. In fact, however, it is probably the case that societies no less than individuals successfully hide from themselves the dishonourable pursuit of their own interest by an exactly analogous process of not spelling it out. Furthermore, those people within a given society who threaten to discover the hidden interests and expose them to public criticism are likely to be repressed in *both* senses of the word: if they are not simply ignored or forgotten by public consciousness, they will be put down by power. They will be resisted just as bitterly as the psychoanalyst's interpretation of the individual patient's baser motives are resisted.

Nobody I know puts the issue of our interestedness with greater directness and simplicity than Leo Tolstoy. In a book (perhaps unsurprisingly in view of the nature of social repression) no longer widely read,* he suggests that the major cultural preoccupations of society have always been used in the service of the interests of the ruling group, covert vehicles for the unworthy motives of the powerful. First the Church, then what he calls State or 'professorial' philosophy, and now science have been used as justifications for some people to exploit others. With the clarity and percipience which are so characteristic of his writing, and with a relevance which has if anything increased in the hundred or more years since he wrote it, he suggests, for example, that the much-vaunted impartiality of science is merely a smokescreen for the operation of interest:

> Contemporary science investigates facts.
>
> But what facts? Why those particular facts and not others?
>
> Scientists of today are very fond of saying solemnly and confidently: 'We only investigate facts,' imagining these words to have some meaning. One cannot possibly only investigate facts for the number of facts available for investigation is *innumerable* (in the exact sense of that word). Before investigating the facts one must have a theory on the basis of which such or such facts are selected from among the innumerable quantity.

And, of course, as Tolstoy goes on to point out, the theory is one which happens to justify the social *status quo*. A few pages further on, he also indicates the selective nature of our intellectual interests. Citing the influence of Comte's philosophical positivism on the new enthusiasm for science, he writes:

> What is remarkable . . . is that of Comte's works, which consist of two parts – the positive philosophy and the positive politics – the learned world only accepted the first: the part which on the new experimental basis, offered a justification

*L. Tolstoy, *What Then Must We Do?* First published 1886.

for the existing evil of human societies; but the second part, dealing with the moral obligations of altruism resulting from acknowledging humanity as an organism, was considered not merely unimportant but even insignificant and unscientific.

I do not believe that anyone who attends closely to the nature of ordinary people's distress – even if it appears to be 'purely psychological' – and confronts honestly the resistance of its causes to our efforts at magical cure, can ultimately ignore the fundamental part played in our suffering by the disavowed (repressed) operation of interest on a societal scale. Explanations of distress which rely simply on concepts of the malfunctioning or intransigence of individuals in fact lead nowhere, unless, that is, explainers and explained manage to collude in an illusory version of a world which has no substance outside our own heads. We have developed and exhausted just about every variation on the theme of either individual mechanical breakdown or personal moral inadequacy to account for the anxiety, isolation, fear, depression and frustration which are endemic in our society, so far with no convincing success. There is, for example, no satisfactory evidence that 'mental illnesses' are illnesses at all, but there is every indication that our pain, confusion, suspicion and hostility, the vulnerability which we try to disguise in so many desperate and crazy ways, arise out of our conduct towards each other.

No matter how appalling the circumstances in which people live, it seems that sooner or later they grow accustomed to them. Not only that, but it seems quite quickly that these are the only possible circumstances which *could* exist. When one thinks of the contrasts which are to be found in the world between the ways of life of the people in it, it is in many ways astonishing that people so readily accept their lot. For example, both the most and the least privileged are quite likely to view their circumstances as both inevitable *and* somehow deserved. In this manner, when people seek an explanation for their unhappy situation, they tend to seek it in some kind of *natural* rather than *social* order. This propensity of human beings, whatever its fundamental explanation, is one which it is very easy to exploit, often unconsciously, in the interests of those so disposed, and one of the best ways of exploiting it is by creating institutions (like 'scientific psychology') which reinforce our readiness to believe that our unhappiness is the natural result of our personal shortcomings.

It is strangely difficult for the naive investigator (and no investigators are to be found more naive than those in psychology and psychiatry) to uncover the principles by which modern Western society seems to render so many of its members so desperately unhappy. One reason for this difficulty is that the naive investigator is as prone as anyone else to take society as given and to focus on the problem of how individuals may be brought to 'adjust' to it. However, naivety may to some extent be overcome by an (all too rare) combination of experience and honesty, in which case it becomes clear that the individuals cannot be taken out of the context of the society which they inhabit.

Slowly one becomes led to see that the hostile defensiveness which so often characterises our relations with each other, the heartless ways in which we exploit and use each other, the extent to which we accept and reject ourselves and each other as commodities, *entirely inescapably* reflect the culture in which we live. One can no more easily opt out of a culture than one can opt out of a physical environment, and a poisonous culture will affect one just as surely as will a polluted atmosphere.

Encapsulated in our belief that the reasons for our conduct are to be tracked down somewhere inside our own skulls, most of us assume that, if life becomes uncomfortable, it must be some individual's 'fault'. Most psychotherapy patients, for example, are quite surprised, if greatly relieved, to discover that their predicament is not unique in the therapist's experience. What, to the attentive therapist, comes as even more surprising is the discovery that not only are patients' experiences and 'problems' often not unique, *they are general*, and more than likely pretty familiar in the therapist's personal experience as well. As I shall discuss in greater detail in Chapter Six, this is nowhere clearer than in our 'relationship problems'. What seems to millions of men and women a singularly personal and isolating misery, a purely private mixture of hate, rejection and despair, is in fact being experienced (or repressed) in one form or another in practically every household in the land. We are caught up in the movements of our culture as droplets in a wave. This is not to say that we have no unique difficulties or purely individual 'problems', but that very much more often than it seems our predicament is created by circumstances we all share but none of us is able to) see or to acknowledge. Recognition of this state of affairs has the most profound implications, since it opens the way for hatred, bitterness, recrimination, guilt and self-disgust to be replaced by, at least, a kind of sympathetic tolerance for those who are, in Dickens's phrase, our 'fellow passengers to the grave'.

Culture does not come about by accident. Just as the psychotherapist may after long and patient inquiry, perhaps with the aid of one or two fortuitous discoveries, slowly begin to be able to formulate an idea of the patient's unacknowledged reasons for his or her conduct, so may one at the wider, societal level begin to see – almost by becoming aware of the factors we explicitly *do not* refer to – what some of the reasons may be for our adherence to our 'psycho-noxious' ways of life. Most of these reasons, it seems to me, cluster around a collective aim to maximise, at more or less any cost (to others), personal interest. We are united nowhere more than in our selfishness.

When our fundamental collective aim is less than worthy, we construct special institutions for the more or less sole (if quite unconscious) purpose of repressing its recognition. Psychiatry and psychology largely fulfil this role, and so it is not surprising that the discussion of interest forms virtually no part of their concern. One has, rather, to turn to social criticism within history for the beginnings of an understanding of what our inarticulate projects may be.

It is almost certainly as misleading to look back on former times as less problematic or destructive than ours as it is to regard our own times as the inevitable achievement of progress. However, there seems to be a strong case to be made for the reflection that for the past four to five hundred years Western society has become less and less concerned with a social order based on moral principles and more and more concerned with one based on economic principles. It would of course be utterly false to regard the Middle Ages as a period when no one had an interest in power and riches, but there seems to be at least a measure of agreement among historians that some coherence was then lent to society by an explicit, largely religious philosophy which aimed at the moral regulation of people's conduct towards each other, and which indeed had some success in defining a social order in which everyone had rights as well as obligations. Though exploitation and corruption may have been rife, it is still worth noting that, as R. H. Tawney pithily puts it:

> If it is proper to insist on the prevalence of avarice and greed in high places, it is not less important to observe that men called these vices by their right names, and had not learned to persuade themselves that greed was enterprise and avarice economy.*

It seems a long way from the experience of distress of individual people in psychotherapy to reflections concerning the undermining of ecclesiastical authority at the time of the Renaissance and the subsequent rise to power of a class of merchants and financiers who were to change the sin of usury

*R. H. Tawney, *Religion and the Rise of Capitalism*, Penguin Books, 1938.

into the virtue of profit. And yet I believe that the connection is inescapable, and I find myself unexpectedly grateful to historians who, like Tawney, throw light on the societal conditions in which our experience is set, and which go some considerable way towards exposing the reasons for its so-frequently distressing nature. For while it would be at best tendentious and at worst entirely misleading to attempt to derive a psychology of individual experience from an account of historical processes, it seems much more intellectually reassuring to find in the historical account explanations for individual experience which would remain otherwise quite unexplainable.

Most psychologists work within a ludicrously short time scale. The 'literature' of research and 'laboratory experiment' by means of which most British and American psychologists orientate themselves tends to be compressed within – to put it on the generous side – the most recent twenty years. Satisfaction with this state of affairs depends upon a confidence in the relative infallibility of the 'scientific' methodology of 'objective' measurement and 'quantification' of human 'behaviour', and an indifference to the influence of historical, social and political factors, which seem to me to be becoming increasingly hard to maintain. The necessary alternative is, then, to stray outside the bounds of one's own discipline, and gladly to accept from whatever other sources offer themselves the kinds of conceptual help which contribute to making sense of one's experience. At a time when intellectual specialisation is so narrow that 'education' in one branch of 'knowledge' qualifies one not at all to judge the validity of argument in other branches, such straying beyond one's 'legitimate' boundaries is not without risk. However, since this kind of specialisation is one of the consequences of the workings of interest in the very way that I am seeking to criticise, it is a risk I shall from time to time have to take.

In trying to understand the frequently quite unconscious aims of individuals it often helps to ignore what they say, to themselves as well as to us, and to look as ingenuously as possible at what they seem to be trying to do, in which case the aims may become quite surprisingly obvious. In the same way, if one wants fully to comprehend the impetus behind our collective, social conduct, one need often do no more than ignore the rhetoric and look instead at our actions. Such ingenuous observation only goes to confirm the ubiquity of interest. We have carried the commercial values developed over the last five centuries, at first with shame and later with enthusiasm, to a point where all our dealings with each other, at the institutional as much as if not more than at the personal level, are based on the advantages which are likely to accrue in terms of power and money. Socially, politically, recreationally, intellectually, educationally and academically, in every sphere and department of life, it is towards money and its power that our conduct is orientated.

There is still a *touch* of shame about this. Though our fascination with the struggle for money-power is only too evident to the most casual observer, we still often tend to hide it behind a moralistic screen of judgements of good and bad, and in this are not unlike our Puritan ancestor described by Tawney:

> Convinced that character is all and circumstances nothing, he sees in the poverty of those who fall by the way, not a misfortune to be pitied and relieved, but a moral failing to be condemned, and in riches, not an object of suspicion – though like other gifts they may be abused – but the blessing which rewards the triumph of energy and will. Tempered by self-examination, self-discipline, self-control, he is the practical ascetic, whose victories are won not in the cloister, but on the battlefield, in the counting-house, and in the market.

In recent years, our love of money and confidence in the values of the market place, the primacy of cost-benefit analysis to moral questions of right and wrong, have become more overt, as has our readiness to expend each other, sacrifice our young and discard our old in our personal interest. But even still there is a tendency to disavow our intentions, or at least to draw a veil of repression over our most basic inclinations.

The crude, 'value-free', 'objective' and mechanistic preoccupations of 'modern science' have of course done much both to obscure the nature of our enterprise and to lend it an authority which might otherwise be less easy to establish. This is certainly the case with psychology, which serves with studied innocence to divert our gaze from our least creditable undertakings. An examination of the indexes of the nine textbooks of psychology to be found in our local university book shop reveals that only three mention 'power' and *none* mention 'money'. How seriously should one take a 'science' which claims to deal with 'motivation' and the 'prediction and control of human behaviour' and yet which fails to mention the one most powerful motivator in every Western person's life? (The answer should probably be *very* seriously, since psychology is clearly about something quite other than a *disinterested* examination of 'what makes us tick', and it is presumably important to know what that something other may be.)

It is my belief, then, that to trace the sources of what we feel as our individual distress, we shall need to turn to a critical examination of what our collective enterprises are. The inter-twining of our interest with our dreams is leading us into a progressive carelessness of each other's welfare, to an extent indeed which will, *at the very best*, damage us for generations to come.

CHAPTER TWO

The Pursuit of Happiness

It seems a matter of self-evidence to most people (indeed I
wonder if, in our hearts, *any* of us can escape such a view) that
the point of life is to be happy. If, in an attempt to tap a relatively selfless opinion, you ask people what they would most
want for the lives of their actual or hypothetical children, they
will usually say 'happiness'. They may also specify other conditions, like health, material success or a modest degree of fame,
upon which happiness may be taken to depend. Not everybody
chooses happiness, but most people do, and in the highly
informal 'experiments' I have made in asking people this question there seem to be no unusual patterns to the responses they
give in terms of age, sex, class, etc.

And yet, in some ways, to hold happiness as the ideal of life
seems to me to involve a number of difficulties and paradoxes,
not the least of which is the extreme infrequency with which,
despite all our best efforts, it seems to be achieved. We appear to
be surprisingly undaunted by disappointment. Infrequency of
achievement does not in itself, of course, render the ideal of
happiness invalid in any way, but it does among other things
add an element almost of cruelty to the pursuit of our elusive
goal.

Further reflection leads one to wonder whether the attainment of happiness may be so infrequent because in fact it is not
even possible. How, for example, does one know that one has
reached the point in one's life where happiness has been
achieved? What does one do with it when one has got it? Can
one specify the conditions in which it may be retained? Can

one see what other people need to do to gain it, perhaps being able to draw up a kind of blueprint for the achievement of general happiness?

Even if one cannot easily arrive at a formula for the capture of happiness in the present, it may be misleadingly simple to imagine what a human life in which ultimate happiness has been reached might look like, and those of us who have found the early and middle years of life less rewarding in terms of happiness than perhaps we had hoped as children, can still probably fantasise how we may yet grasp it in our declining years. The 'happiness' which throughout our lives stayed just beyond our reach becomes, in the nick of time, the 'fulfilment' of old age. Our faded gaze rests with contentment on the persons of those who love us and who accept from us with gratitude the fruits of a mellowed wisdom as they enact in our autumnal world the little dramas we ourselves have known so well. I have read about such old people, but I have never met one, and unless it is possible that a lifetime's isolation in some privileged enclave could somehow preserve a person from knowledge of the world outside, any such 'fulfilled' departure from this earth would seem to me to involve, at the very least, an extraordinarily egocentric self-satisfaction. Perhaps a merciful old age would temper our 'rage at the dying of the light', but I hope would not obliterate it, or transform it into a kind of fatuous contentment simply because there is no further chance of influencing events.

And so, a further paradox: if we got 'happiness', would we want it? To take for a moment the extreme case, it is hard to conceive of any version of everlasting, perhaps heavenly existence (in this world or the next) which would not become intolerably burdensome; there could be no more boring place than paradise. The enormously powerful attraction of 'happiness' lies in the fact that (in the commodified form in which we conceive of it) we never experience it, it is always just beyond our grasp. Happiness, of the kind which can be pursued, is an illusion.

One may ask people a slightly more awkward question than that concerning what they would want in life for their children. Imagine that you are visited shortly before the birth of your only child by an archangel who offers you a choice you cannot decline: either your child will grow to a great age, loved and respected by all, having done no wrong or mean thmg to anybody, successful, rich, healthy, and, above all, happy, *but* will have made no memorable contribution to the future of the species beyond the immediate good works of a lifetime. *Or,* your child will have a short, bitter life, full of spiritual pain and bodily ill health, will be universally misunderstood and rejected, *but* will make through his or her work a contribution which will prove to be of fundamental, beneficial significance to the culture for centuries to come. Which would you choose?

My own experience is that people have little hesitation over choosing one or the other of these hypothetical futures for their hypothetical offspring, and that the vast majority plump for the happiness option. To get a reasonably honest answer, the question has, obviously, to be posed innocently, but even those people who angrily sense some moral disapprobation of their choice of happiness, still, very understandably, defend it on the grounds that *whatever* their hypothetical child's potential achievement, they could not wish upon him or her the kind of unhappiness the archangel promises.

Hypothetical games such as these are of course predictive of nothing and revealing of very little, and though one can add a surface plausibility to this example by, for instance, citing the life of Mozart, there is in fact no *necessary* connection between ill health, rejection, etc., and creativity. Indeed, it is a central contention of this book that constructively creative and socially valuable conduct is most likely to be fostered by the kind of concern for their children's well-being which loving parents characteristically show. In other words, the archangel's offer forces a *false* choice, and it is probably that which causes a measure of irritation in some of those who respond to it.

Nevertheless, what *is* revealed, I think, by the large preponderance of happiness choices people seem to make, is the extent to which we implicitly believe in the values of an illusion. This is, of course, no surprising discovery, but merely confirms what is already entirely obvious to the most casual observer of our ways of life. What seems to motivate us, to keep us going from day to day, is the pursuit of happiness; and yet, if 'pursuable happiness' is necessarily an illusion which can only melt in one's grasp as soon as one's fingers close around it, how can its enormous force as a motivator for human conduct be accounted for? Why is it so hard for people to be able even to imagine any other point to life than the personal satisfaction of the individuals living it?

Among the many factors which might contribute to an answer to these questions, there are two to which I want to give prominence. The first refers to an inevitable feature of every person's embodied experience – the memory of bliss. The second refers to a practically inescapable feature of our society, and one without which it would rapidly crumble and be transformed – the profitability of illusion.

It is a fact not lost on students of individual psychology – most notably Freud – that our first and most blissful experience of happiness is probably also our last. It is a virtually universal tragedy of human experience that the very earliest impressions we have should be those of such perfect warmth and protectedness and oneness (with the mother), both inside and for a while probably outside the womb, that we may be tempted to spend the rest of our lives trying to recreate what is in fact an unrepeatable situation. By the time we have become reasonably competent in the use of language, that experience of perfect happiness has probably been overlaid by much harsher realities, and since what we normally consider as memory depends upon our ability to rehearse experiences in words, our 'memory' of bliss is not something we can get to grips with in our thoughts, but remains in our bodies as a kind of aching absence. Those of our experiences which are beyond the reach of words, when their bodily 'memory' is stirred by some perhaps fortuitous set of circumstances, tend to be rekindled in a kind of awe-filled burst of inexpressible, unnameably familiar ecstasy. (Such an experience is falling in love, but, in some ways sadly, as we must grow out of infancy, so we must grow out of being-in-love.)

Those psychologists who tend towards a view of human development as a kind of mechanical unfolding of an inevitable series of stages of experience are likely to see the tragic frustration of the infant's initial experience of bliss as a *particularly* inescapable and particularly constant feature of our psychology, and in this they are unlikely to be wrong. But even so we would do well to remember that the individual's experience is set within a social context, and the extent of his or her disillusionment, and certainly the degree of its painfulness, will depend quite largely on the provision which is made for it.* Does one, for example, speed the process of severance from maternal love in the belief that the sooner the child learns to cope with a hard, tough life the better, or does one gently protect its tenderness and vulnerability until it has matured to a point where one feels that it can take on for itself the unkindnesses of the world? No doubt both answers, as well as complete indifference to the question, have been popular at various junctures in our recent as well as our more distant history. For the moment, however, what I want to highlight are the *uses* to which we have put our 'memory' of bliss. It seems to me, indeed, that assiduity in *making use of* the aching absence of fundamental happiness has been far greater than any attempt rationally to understand the painful passions associated with it and to construct a social world which treats them with sympathetic kindness; the brave efforts of some psychologists in this latter direction have, after all, met with little respect.

The very unrepeatability of that first experience of radical

*In this connection see I. D. Suttie, *The Origins of Love and Hate*, Penguin Books, 1960.

protectedness and passivity, the effortless achievement (for a while) of unlimited warmth, gratification and love, has been exploited in our culture to fuel an endlessly tantalising hope. We know, in some sense, that that state is attainable (for once we really did experience it) and so we easily fall prey to the promise of its reoccurrence. It is precisely the 'pursuit of happiness' – culturally sanctioned at the very highest levels – which holds out this promise to us. But the actuality of its nature as an illusion, the fact that our infantile experience is unrepeatable, ensures that we do not attain it, and so we are left in unending and empty pursuit. All the time we see as just beyond our grasp what is in fact not there at all. And the more that 'happiness' and 'success' elude us, the harder we strive to overtake them.

There is a bleak view to be taken of this state of affairs, which, as with Freud's 'death instinct', suggests that our futile pursuit of effortless gratification leads us eventually to seek the everlasting, if negative peace of death. Nor is this view to be dismissed lightly, for there is much that argues in its favour. We do indeed seem to pursue our fantasies of inert, passive satisfaction beyond the boundaries of fiction and dream. 'Scientists' actually have experimented with the idea of stimulation of 'pleasure centres' within the brain as an attractive way of passing our time,* and there are people who do not regard as preposterous or even disturbing the idea of a *totally* self-sufficient person living a life of sensual bliss alone in a glass bubble. One only has to look at the world-wide success of the American junk food industry,

That is, the drink-down, quick-sugar foods of spoiled children, and the pre-cut meat for lazy chewing beloved of ages six to ten. Nothing is bitten or bitten-off, very little is chewed; there is a lot of sugar for animal energy, but not much solid food to grow on†

*For a particularly disturbing account of one such experiment, see Chapter 2 of my *Psychotherapy: A Personal Approach*, Dent, 1978.

†Goodman, op. cit.

to see the attractions of a return to infancy, and by extension to the womb. And it is by no means implausible to project one further step to complete oblivion as part of our unconscious craving.

And yet – I hope, at least – this is not a *necessary* feature of our individual psychology, but an only potentially fatal weakness brought about by our early experience of bliss. For if this is a weakness to which the very structure of our bodies exposes us, it is still one which occurs in a world which may or may not encourage it. Though weaknesses are indeed likely to be exploited, they may also be acknowledged, understood, and even, eventually, turned into strengths.

It does indeed seem that we pursue an illusory happiness with all the futile enthusiasm of a tame mouse in a treadmill – but how is it that we could be so blind? Rather than simply being misled by some intrinsic weakness of psychological structure, we are, I believe, blinded by interest. There is money to be made from the pursuit of happiness.

I do not wish to suggest that there is anything *fundamentally* wrong with the idea of happiness: it is clearly preferable for people to be happy rather than unhappy, and there is no *necessary* connection between virtue and misery. There have been times in our history when the pursuit of happiness seemed an altogether less hollow undertaking than it does today. For example, it is not difficult to detect in the writers of the Enlightenment and in the philosophical and political works of the British Utilitarians (i.e. those late eighteenth- and early nineteenth-century thinkers who believed that 'good' could be measured in terms of 'happiness') a spirit of real hopefulness and generosity as they glimpsed the possibility of constructing an unprecedentedly equitable society in which happiness – freedom from want as well as political representation and influence – might be spread as widely as possible.

It seems, however, always to be the case that significant movements in our cultural and political history, particularly those which open up liberating vistas of change, even 'progress', last but a brief instant before their motivating ideas and the institutions they create are put to the use of those who have the power to turn them to their interest. One can think of several examples. Christ's revolutionary teaching concerning personal responsibility and love, and the example of his life, were almost immediately turned into an oppressive church orthodoxy which established a doctrine of myth and magic and a coercive political power which were to betray truly Christian values for centuries. Relative freedom from the sclerotic and corrupt power of a decadent Church offered Renaissance man a glimpse of what it would be like to organise life on the basis of scientific reason and subjective authority, but it was not to be long before science – at least in terms of its intellectually liberating vision – became a travesty of itself, and man's momentary apprehension of self-responsibility was quickly usurped by the State in combination with a 'reformed' religious hypocrisy, and turned against him. Much the same seems to have been the case with the Enlightened vision of happiness.

It seems as though the new-found freedom of a prosperous middle class for a while imbued it with a generous impulse to share its good fortune with those who were, as in contrast with the landed aristocracy it had itself also so recently been, less privileged. John Passmore puts it well:★

The Enlighteners . . . thought they knew who was bound to come to overt power in the State – the commercial classes. And there was, they were convinced, a natural alliance between the new governors and the spirit of enlightenment. Overt power to the middle class, actual power to the intellectuals – that was the future of society as they envisaged it. The 'honest man', the merchant, the 'civically good' man, replaced the aristocrat and the hero – in England especially – as the 'ideal type' of humanity.

★J. Passmore, *The Perfectibility of Man*, Duckworth, 1970.

And:

> Commerce and liberty, so Voltaire maintained in his
> *Philosophical Letters*, are intimately associated. The close link
> between literature and finance was, he thought, one of the
> glories of the eighteenth century. No Rotarian could be
> more enthusiastic about the benefits of commerce than was
> Joseph Priestley. By bringing the merchant into contact with
> other places and people, he tells us, commerce 'tends greatly
> to expand the mind and to cure us of many hurtful preju-
> dices'; it encourages benevolence and a love of peace; it
> develops such virtues as punctuality and 'the principals of
> strict justice and honour' . . . 'Men of wealth and influence',
> so he sums up, 'who act upon the principles of virtue and
> religion, and conscientiously make their power subservient to
> the good of their country, are the men who are the greatest
> honour to human nature, and the greatest blessing to human
> societies.'

A connection between big business and philanthropy would
be unlikely to be one impressing itself upon modern intellectual
observers of society, although of course it is one which big business seeks, through procedures of 'image building', to create.
Once again, those processes which at the time looked to constitute a liberating move and were advocated with enthusiastic
optimism by those caught up in it, came very rapidly to be
exploited in the sole interests of those – now the 'bourgeoisie' –
with power.

It is instructive in this respect to reflect upon the career of the
most 'official' sanction we have to pursue happiness. It was of
course Thomas Jefferson who first articulated 'the pursuit of
happiness' as one of the rights of men in the American
Declaration of Independence. According to Hannah Arendt,*

*H. Arendt, *On Revolution*, Penguin Books, 1973.

however, Jefferson himself may at that time not have been entirely clear about what he meant by the phrase, and his idea of happiness and ours may well have diverged considerably in the intervening two hundred years. She argues that by 'happiness' he may have meant, at least partly, what he meant elsewhere when he wrote of 'public happiness', that is the freedom of people to take part in their political self–determination. However, as she points out, the phrase

> was almost immediately deprived of its double sense and understood as the right of citisens to pursue their personal interests and thus to act according to the rules of private self-interest. And these rules, whether they spring from dark desires of the heart or from the obscure necessities of the household, have never been notably 'enlightened'.

Arendt suggests also that in debates in the Assembly

> none of the delegates would have suspected the astonishing career of this 'pursuit of happiness', which was to contribute more than anything else to a specifically American ideology, to the terrible misunderstanding that, in the words of Howard Mumford Jones, holds that men are entitled to 'the ghastly privilege of pursuing a phantom and embracing a delusion'.

Arising out of this discussion, then, are two possible views, or versions of happiness: happiness as something which may attend or follow from our actions (as for example in the conduct of our political freedom, our ability to take part in the affairs of our own government), and happiness as something 'in itself' which may be pursued. In fact, Arendt suggests that the (illusory) pursuit of happiness as a thing in itself, and of the associated ideals of 'abundance and endless consumption', are the product of a vision conditioned by poverty, and it is for that reason that they are so characteristic of American culture, since it was that country which seemed to promise so much to the poor emigrants from Europe:

> The hidden wish of poor men is not 'To each according to his needs', but 'to each according to his desires'. And while it is true that freedom can only come to those whose needs have been fulfilled, it is equally true that it will escape those who are bent upon living for their desires. The American dream, as the nineteenth and twentieth centuries under the impact of mass immigration came to understand it, was . . . unhappily, the dream of a 'promised land' where milk and honey flow. And the fact that the development of modern technology was so soon able to realise this dream beyond anyone's wildest expectation quite naturally had the effect of confirming for the dreamers that they really had come to live in the best of all possible worlds.

Now that America has successfully sold its dream to most of the rest of the world, those of us in Europe who have become, as it were, the all-too-willing subjects of an economic and cultural empire based on the values of which Arendt is rightly so contemptuous, can no longer stand by (as we seemed only a few years ago to be able to do) with amusement or disbelief as we watch the tasteless antics of our trans–Atlantic relatives. For we are now busily performing the self-same antics. We have bought, lock, stock and barrel, the idea of happiness as commodity, and we pursue it with singleminded dedication.

The increasing affluence and freedom from want of 'developed' Western society has, however, not resulted in our seeing through the illusory nature of our pursuit of happiness, and the reason for this lies presumably in the changed nature of our enslavement. The interests of power no longer lie, as until recently they so transparently did, in extracting from an oppressed work force the maximum production at the minimum cost, but in stimulating from a dazed and pacified population the maximum consumption at the greatest price the market will bear. The chief means by which this may be achieved are through the promotion of happiness as a commodity and the prevention of happiness as a consequence, or epiphenomenon, of activity.

Anyone who has tried to do it – and that must, surely, include everyone – knows how impossible it is to manufacture happiness. Whether or not one is happy depends entirely upon events and circumstances which one cannot will, and usually the more selfconsciously one attempts to be happy, the more signally one fails. When happiness does arise, it does so spontaneously and unbidden, and often unexpectedly, as a concomitant, usually, of our absorbed and unselfconscious activity. It arises out of doing things, or out of our doing things together, and it is often only after we have ceased doing them that we realise we were happy. Those who recognise this are easily led to romanticise the lives of people who are necessarily committed to endless hard work, punctuated only occasionally by simple festivals or the innocent pleasures of family celebrations, but such is not my intention. I rather doubt if the peasant's long-awaited appointment with a happy Christmas is any more often successful than the culmination of our own harassed and jaded preparations for that same event. Unremitting drudgery is likely to be no more rewarding than the apathetic killing of time and invention of 'pleasurable' sensations necessitated by satiated affluence. Happiness comes, rather, from having something useful and absorbing and demanding to do which can be valued by the doer as well as those for whom he or she is doing it.

It is this form of happiness which has become vanishingly rare in our world, and in my view it is the lack of the possibility for this form of happiness which, at least as much as anything else, lies behind our despair. We have constructed a society which is in essence a vast machine designed for the maintenance and development of an illusion. We believe that the value of our lives may be measured by the degree of their happiness and that happiness in its turn may be understood as personal satisfaction and fulfilment, to be gained, if not *through* the acquisition of things, then certainly as the acquisition of things. In these beliefs we are misled on the one hand by the technological pragmatism we have developed over the past four centuries and on the other by our enthusiasm for greedy exploitation. Our technological bent has led us to isolate the happiness we have rightly observed as occasionally accompanying our activity, to posit it as the point of life, and then to try to manufacture it as a commodity. Our greed has led us, freed from the repressive moral strictures of a 'parental' religious authority, to throw ourselves upon the world's bounty with all the lack of restraint of a group of adolescents at their first party. And, of course, our genius for exploitation has quickly revealed that our unrestrained adolescent greed offers a market for ever more 'exciting' and 'satisfying' commodities which may be tended and stoked and stimulated more or less endlessly. Rather than being, as it were, encouraged by our social and cultural institutions to grow out of our infantile craving for the delights of the womb and the breast towards a mature and sober undertaking of a contribution to the life of our society and the continuation of our species, it has become our aim to benefit in every way possible from a concerted pandering to our longing for blissful satiation. We all believe in happiness, and most of us have a stake in its production and consumption. We thus become caught up in a frenzied pursuit of happiness which, being illusory, renders us ever more dazed and out of touch with our embodied reality, and ever more vulnerable to and injured by the abuses of our exploitation of each other.

People suffer bitterly, go crazy and even kill themselves because (among other reasons) they are unhappy. It is easy to see why: to be unhappy means in our society to have lost the point of living. (In making this point I do not wish to justify unhappiness nor to advocate the policy of the stiff upper lip. All too often unhappiness is seen as something some people have to get used to so that other people can escape it. This constitutes a version of moralism about which I shall say more in the final chapter.) The *inevitable* non-achievement of the greedy individ-ualistic satiation which we take to signify happiness, means that we suffer from a kind of collective, chronic frustration.

In the very midst of a kind of lunatic celebration of symbolic satisfactions, a mirage of pleasures excited and achieved, people are in fact almost beside themselves with need. A sense of despairing neediness seems to me to be endemic at all levels of our society – experienced just as much by the 'helpers' as by those they seek to help – and to lie curled at the centre of most 'relationships'. For our frantic search for happiness meets only emptiness, and if we could we would all scream like abandoned infants as our mouths fail to encounter the promised breast. We are, however, not infants, but rather adolescents who don't know our own strength, and the response to our frustration is more likely to be a destructive lashing-out than an infantile scream.

Happiness – of any kind, commodity or 'epiphenomenon' – cannot be the point of life. Indeed, the very expectation that there must be a discernible point to life constitutes the first step towards a life-denying individualism in which the future of the species becomes sacrificed to personal immortality.* Among the reasons for our reluctance to abandon our pursuit of happiness, however, is the fact that so many of us make a living by encour-aging it. But abandon it we must if we are to progress beyond a struggle with illusory unhappiness, grief at the lack of blissful satisfaction, to a struggle with the causes of real unhappiness –

---

*It is significant in this respect that even so humane and critically gifted a believer in the greatest happiness for the greatest number as William Godwin (see his *Enquiry Concerning Political Justice*, 1793) should have fallen for a Utopian fantasy of man as non-reproductive and immortal. There are no doubt millions today who would see nothing the matter with that as an ideal for the future.

the injuries we do each other as we exploit and compete with each other for what we take to be the good things of life.

Whatever their circumstances in life, it is, as I have already noted, hard for most people to imagine that they could be otherwise. Even people living in squalor and misery do not necessarily *know* that they are, and anyone proclaiming a vision of a better life may have considerable difficulty persuading unhappy people that they are indeed unhappy. This is not as paradoxical as it seems, as any psychotherapist, for example, should know: the 'neurotic' patient's suffering is most often inarticulate and its causes unacknowledged; he or she has to be *brought to see* what the trouble – with the world and with his or her relation to it – really is. A condition of political repression has always been that it is able to thrive on the unawareness of the people it oppresses that they are indeed oppressed, and those of broader vision who are able to envisage a life of liberty may have to struggle hard to get their view accepted.

To suggest, therefore, that our current ways of life distort almost beyond recognition what human existence should look like, and that our relations with each other and the world constrict and mutilate our experience, our potentialities and our actual living presence, is likely to be met by blank incredulity and scorn. To protect us against any such view (apart from the usual processes of resistance to change which will be discussed in Chapter Five) we have on the one hand the whole apparatus of marketing of an illusory happiness and on the other such a familiarity with the conditions of our crippled lives that we take them for an ineluctable normality.

Nevertheless, almost anyone, if he or she can bear to look, will catch a glimpse from time to time of the ways in which we have sold ourselves into slavery, of the sad results of having done so, and indeed of the devices whereby we prevent ourselves from seeing what we have done.

Just at the most obvious level, a weakening of our individual- istic and tribal values would allow us to see how our personal, commodified happiness is bought, and always has been bought, at the expense of others. The evidence of the results of our having unloaded our want and discomfort on to others – other classes, races, nations, even continents – is absolutely plain for us to see, if only in our own inner cities. Sometimes, certainly (as in the case at the present time with starvation in Africa) our compassion is stirred, but even then only rarely do we see that 'their' problems cannot be disentangled from our conduct. Hannah Arendt points out* how even the civilised prosperity of revolutionary America was built upon the grotesque values of slavery. Again, it is common to represent the 'problems' of Western 'civilisation' as those which naturally follow upon affluence: we have conquered want, and must now concentrate upon our spiritual and therapeutic needs and cultivate the values of 'fun' and leisure. This kind of view, probably wearing a little thin now after its particular popularity in the sixties, is plausible only if we manage to disregard, i.e. repress, at least half the consequences of our actions: we have not conquered want, but merely discovered ways of exporting it.

The peculiar dishonesty of repression also haunts our more personal experience, numbing the pain we would otherwise feel at the destruction of human potential we witness in our lives more or less as a matter of course. How easily, for example, the middle-aged person comes to accept with only a minimum of sorrow the almost standard transformation of the children he or she once knew: open, inquisitive four- and five-year-olds, bearing the clearly visible buds of whole ranges of ability and concern, become now uniform, already half-hopeless nineteen- and twenty-year-olds, cynical devotees of commodified sex and bad music, defensive about their feelings and encapsulated in a world bounded by consumption. I know there are exceptions, but too few, surely, to justify anything other (if only we could but feel it) than a sickened rage at the sort of society we have created.

*On Revolution, op. cit.

One has often to make a special effort of the imagination to see quite how mad and destructive the world we live in has become. This is only a seeming paradox, indicating more a deep and usually unquestioning familiarity with our environment than any reassuring possibility that things are not really all that bad. The effort of imagination needed is like that which dreamers make in order to wake themselves from a nightmare.

Insights sometimes present themselves at the most unexpected times and places. For example, a young waiter in one of those mass-produced Italian restaurants paces across the fake ceramic floor, gliding from narrow hips, swaying broad shoulders. He tosses his thick black hair so that it quivers on the collar of his open shirt, and glances semi-boldly and semi-defensively at the two girls who are waiting for their food at a corner table. He has perhaps ten paces to walk from the centre of the restaurant to the bar where the pizzas are being made. Every step of the way he is utterly conscious of himself, of his luxuriant mane, his olive skin, his narrow hips. He is a tall, strong young man caged in a pretend environment, serving day in and day out the same junk food to an endless stream of customers for whom the most he may hope to be is the object of an idle admiration or desire.

In those rare moments when the familiar world (for example of waiters and restaurants) breaks open to reveal how much worse things are than they appear, the accompanying emotion seems usually to be one of sadness. The waiter is not obviously hurt by his world, and one feels neither sorrow nor contempt for him, nor even anger at the circumstances which have conspired to make a mockery of a life which would, one feels (no doubt sentimentally), have been more suitably spent less self-consciously among vines or olive groves. For a moment, rather, he becomes a symbol of us all, and his (and our) unawareness of his (and our) plight, our acceptance of what we all too easily see as 'reality', is above all *sad*.

I remember, years ago, watching the chimps at London Zoo.

A small crowd had gathered to watch them disport themselves in their 'outdoor' cage. Two of them swung into a smoothly practised routine: in an almost single movement of flowing synchrony one ran along the upper branch of a dead tree which lay in the cage while the other entwined itself gracefully round a horizontal branch perhaps six feet lower. The reclining chimp arched back his head, and at that precise moment the chimp on the upper branch, with pin-point accuracy, urinated into his open mouth. The crowd gasped with surprise and laughed with a mixture of disgust and admiration at the virtuosity of the performance, and the chimps looked towards their audience with unmistakable delight and pride.

I suspect that a lot of what passes for 'human nature' is really the result of our having to deal with a certain *kind* of world. Self-consciousness, for example, whether in the form of vanity or shyness (both of which are *characteristic* of our time), might not seem so inevitable in a world which gave us space in which to *do* things.

If the possibility is denied you of doing anything of value in the world, you have to use your ingenuity in order to feel alive while passing the time. If your activity counts for nothing your *person* is likely to become salient – it will become important what you look like (you could decorate yourself, dye your hair) and what you feel like (you may become absorbed in the state of excitation or satiation of your nervous system, stimulation and satisfaction). In his savagely constricted and inexpressibly sad little environment at the zoo, Guy the gorilla passed much of his time in a rather distractedly off-hand indulgence in masturbation. Unlike the chimpanzees, he did not seem to mind what people thought, apparently not noticing their blushes and giggles.

It is really not the case that we treat animals differently from the way we treat each other: what is most disturbing about factory farming is its revelation of the mentality which lies behind it, and which is the same as that lying behind, for example, high-rise building. Point for point, the life of a battery hen is no different from that of the high-rise tenant. Both are victims of the same cruelty, indifference and greed, and in all probability neither is aware of it. Furthermore, the suffering occasioned by their enslavement will be met not with liberation, but with treatment.

Cruelty, indifference and greed are distributed throughout our society, and are not to be identified solely in the intentions or malicious motivation of any particular individuals or groups; I shall return to this question in future chapters.

I think I can remember a time (but perhaps I am deluding myself) when advertising was a distinctly suspect but sometimes faintly amusing undertaking in which fairly transparent lies were told about products which could not be relied upon to get sold on their own merits. Nowadays, however, we have developed a kind of commitment to the illusory nature of the artificial 'satisfactions' in which we imprison ourselves, and we seem therefore to stoke up a more and more frenetic and hyperbolic language by which to sell ourselves our self-deceiving vision. The advertising man becomes a symbol of the only kind of respectability which counts – the respectability of success – and his power to manufacture images is regarded, if not quite yet with awe, then certainly with uncritical admiration. The language of advertising and marketing infects just about every area of our activity as we persuade ourselves how 'important' and 'major' and 'exciting' our undertakings – academic and artistic as well as social and personal – are. The very language of international negotiation, in which 'front' men occupying jobs which might once have been filled by statesmen conduct 'propaganda battles' for the conquest of 'public opinion', becomes one of 'offers' in which 'fifty per cent reductions' (for example in nuclear weaponry) are bandied back and forth with all the gravity of cynical marketing executives whose function in life is to 'hype' poorly selling breakfast cereals. Even our most serious and vital concerns become in this way sucked into a kind of make-believe world in which 'credibility' counts more than life itself.

One's consciousness is relentlessly battered by the weaponry of image creation and fabricated excitement. Even a simple announcement of forthcoming programmes on the radio or television is uttered by a voice frenzied with fake enthusiasm, and our language is progressively emptied of subtlety and depth as every kind of activity possible or imaginable becomes reduced to its significance for how nice it will make us feel (you don't any longer so much 'have' or 'drink' a cup of coffee, for instance, as 'enjoy' it). It is impossible, particularly perhaps for a male, to walk through any city shopping or entertainment centre without coming under a kind of unremitting sexual assault: at every turn and corner another sexual image snatches at his flagging nervous system to associate with a flash of excitement some utterly sexually irrelevant object or service for sale. And the more habituated we become, the more lurid, basic or fantastic the sexual pitch is made. The everyday world we move in thus becomes one of ceaseless, frenetic, raucously euphoric promises of bliss. But we get used to it, and there are probably very few of us who do not take this crazy detachment from our actual embodied reality as normal.

> Commodity production and consumerism alter perceptions not just of the self but of the world outside the self. They create a world of mirrors, insubstantial images, illusions increasingly indistinguishable from reality. The mirror effect makes the subject an object; at the same time, it makes the world of objects an extension or projection of the self. It is misleading to characterize the culture of consumption as a culture dominated by things. The consumer lives surrounded not so much by things as by fantasies. He lives in a world that has no objective or independent existence and seems to exist only to gratify or thwart his desires.*

*Christopher Lasch, *The Minimal Self. Psychic Survival in Troubled Times*, Picador, 1985.

So that nothing may stand between us and the consumption of happiness, we are stripped of our functional activity and, like battery animals, lifted from the course of time to be located in an endless present.

'A function may be defined as an activity which embodies and expresses the idea of social purpose.'* If life is not simply something for oneself, to be enjoyed and indulged and spun out as long as possible (its dream-ideal thus being some form of solitary immortality), then its most profound value (and satisfaction) may come from the individual's being able, along with others, to make a contribution to – perform a function within – something infinitely larger than him- or herself. As part of an ever-evolving social process the individual is shaped by a largely unknown past and projected towards a totally unknowable future. Thus the individual becomes a tiny particle through which the course of social evolution moves; the meaning of our lives cannot be understood outside the context of the social and cultural processes in which they are embedded. It is probably misleading to speak of our bodies as having been designed *for* anything, but certainly if there is anything for which the design of our bodies is *suitable*, it is for contributing to a process far too great for us to be able to understand and a future far too distant and impenetrable for us to be able to divine. To see our bodies as being designed merely for the experience of pleasure or 'happiness' is surely to trivialise human existence to the point of utter despair.

. . . to say that the end of social institutions is happiness, is to say that they have no common end at all. For happiness is individual and to make happiness the object of society is to resolve society itself into the ambitions of numberless individuals, each directed towards the attainment of some personal purpose.

Such societies may be called Acquisitive Societies, because their whole tendency and interest and preoccupation is to promote the acquisition of wealth. The appeal of this conception must be powerful, for it has laid the whole modern world under its spell.*

Human functions are, sadly, extremely vulnerable to exploitation by interest. Almost anything that people can do in the way of productive or creative work can be mechanised, objectified, appropriated and then sold back to them as passive consumers. The social activity of making music, for example, becomes the solitary reception of mass-produced sounds through headphones. Production becomes consumption, activity becomes spectacle. Even relatively privileged functions of a service or professional nature (privileged in the sense that they are themselves not without an element of exploitation) may fall prey to the 'managerial' stratum of society which seeks to objectify and manipulate for profit just about any identifiable and potentially saleable form of human conduct. Anything people can do for themselves is the waste of an opportunity to make money, and it therefore becomes important to find ways of annexing the fruits of their activity and putting them up for sale. The medium through which the trick is performed is, of course, our fatal penchant for passivity, the blissful ease of inert consumption, but this would not have anything like the power over us it does were it not sanctioned by the values of a society (maintained through the more or less willing complicity of us all) which posits the making of money – 'the creation of wealth' – as the highest good, the necessity of necessities.

One can sell things only in the present. The past, from the salesman's point of view, is certainly a dead loss (hence the cultivation of obsolescence, the frenetic insistence on the 'now' and the 'new'), and the future is uncertain (hence the desperation to close the deal *today*). Happiness, therefore, becomes a phenomenon of the here and now. You must be satisfied, be

*R. H. Tawney, *The Acquisitive Society*. First published 1921, Wheatsheaf Books, 1982.

excited, enjoy, have fun *now*. Every moment that passes in which your nervous system is not perceptibly going through the cycle of sensations involved in excitation/satisfaction is wasted, mis-spent (and unprofitable) time. Only new things matter; our pursuit of fulfilment *now* uproots us from our past and disconnects us from the things we knew, enabling us endlessly to recycle the past but preventing us from developing it. This applies to ideas as well as to goods. The thoughts that people had in previous times become either objects of study from which, via the machinery of a vast 'knowledge' industry, academics may churn out endless exegesis, or they are left behind in the pervasive fetish for 'novelty', only to be reiterated as new discoveries by people for whom true scholarship is a lost art. The future is important only for how it affects our buying habits *now*; it may thus be used as a stimulus to anxiety – something we must provide for before it's too late ('while stocks last') – but it is unlikely to be seen as something worthy of sacrifice. We do not postpone satisfactions, we anticipate them. Our attitude to the future is symbolised by the credit card – access to it is now. We no longer have posterity, only children.

The person becomes stripped of function, confined in space and restricted in time to a ceaseless present, and all in the name of happiness. The world which is thus created is quite grotesquely unsuited to our actual embodied existence, but we are used to it and do not, any more than blind fish in subterranean pools, complain of circumstances which are hard to imagine as otherwise.

But if the damaging nature of the environment we have created slips easily beneath the attention of our critical awareness, we certainly do not escape the painful 'symptoms' to which that damage gives rise. The process of symptom formation is quite easy to understand in the case of 'neurotic' suffering: for the onlooker who stands outside the personal predicament of individual patients, it is more often than not quite obvious that their puzzled, inarticulate sense of pain –

frequently explained as 'illness' or expressed in actions distressing to self or others – is directly understandable in the light of circumstances which they cannot see (because these circumstances are not in their field of vision) or do not wish to see (i.e. repress or deceive themselves about). But this is not the sole or even special problem of 'the neurotic', who merely provides the paradigm case for a predicament shared by us all.

Frustration, neediness, chronic irritation, suspiciousness, agonised self-concern, feelings of unreality, nausea, dizziness, a whole host of 'psychosomatic' afflications through which our bodies 'protest' at the treatment we give them, nagging anxiety, rage and panic: few of us escape for any length of time from some or several of these. (And in order to try to deal with them we assemble medical, therapeutic, counselling and other 'helping' professions whose membership would threaten to outnumber potential clients were it not for the fact that the helpers themselves need help.)

Apart from the symptoms, there are the signs – i.e. indications of the injuries done to us by our condition which, however, may not themselves be experienced as unusually uncomfortable. Since we have no world to pour ourselves into, no possibility of spontaneous absorption in a society within which we may use the concepts and implements of a tradition to work towards an unknowable future we may try to make worthwhile, we become collapsed in on ourselves, not so much introspectively (a cultivable 'inner world' is in any case the invention of a romantic individualism) as self-regardingly. We observe ourselves with minute attention, alert to the sensations of our bodily organs, monitoring carefully our state of satisfaction. We have, like Guy the gorilla, only our bodies to play with, so we strut and posture in an endless parade of fashion, or we shrivel and shrink under the glare of our own self-conscious gaze. We pamper and weigh and tend ourselves, worrying obsessively about the damage to our health which our self-indulgence may create. It is utterly characteristic of our society that it supports side-by-side a huge mass-produced food industry and a huge dietary and health industry, the latter profiting from the damage caused by the former. This is reflected at the individual level by the increasing prevalence of 'bulimia' – i.e., the compulsion to voracious eating followed by self-induced vomiting. Again I must emphasise that we are caught up in these phenomena, whether at the societal or at the individual level, quite uncomprehendingly. As I hope to show later, the operation of the influences and interests involved does not appear within our personal consciousness nor under our personal control.

And yet, I suspect, beyond the reach of words, we hate this world which we have created and which force-feeds us with its happiness until we choke. There is a deadness in our eyes and an anger in the air and an almost tangible contempt for each other which seep more and more overtly from the fantasied televisual lives of the 'rich and successful' into the everyday transactions of ordinary men and women. The more sensitive among us may be so disturbed by observation of this process that they feel they are going mad – more and more people who come to see me as patients, and from all walks of life, have literally been unnerved by an increasingly commonplace brutality and indifference they cannot believe they are seeing around them.

The hatred of the less privileged for their enslaving environment is obvious – spray paint and urine are fitting enough adornments for the walls of battery housing, and who with any spirit, having too often waited shivering outside it to phone their mother or an ambulance at the dead of a winter's night, would not want to vandalise the phone box which stands almost insolently on the corner to proclaim their subjugation? But perhaps the case is little different when it comes to those who seem more obviously to profit from our society: the *fact* is that we wreck the landscape, pollute the earth and poison the seas, and treat our fellow beings with a callous unconcern. However much we may be able to deceive ourselves about the nature and consequences of these undertakings, there is still really no doubt that they are ours, and, as with the individual 'neurotic'? the only sure way of determining intention is to infer it from action. From the way we treat the world and the other people in it, from our carelessness of tradition and posterity, from the official endorsement given at the very 'highest' levels to self-interest as the only possible motive and to the threat of annihilation as the legitimate ultimate goad, it seems obvious that our obsession with an entirely self-indulgent 'happiness' has as its obverse hatred, suspicion and total unconcern with what may lie, in space or time, beyond our individual lives and the satisfactions they may afford.

This is not, I am sure, a state of affairs that any of us *wants*. In order to get to grips with this paradox, one must attempt to gain a view of the way in which social forces operate *through* rather than within individuals, how *personal* conduct can only be comprehensible in the light of *collective* aims.

CHAPTER THREE

Magic, Interest and Psychology

Throughout our culture there are, I believe, widely shared and deeply held misconceptions about human psychological makeup, particularly concerning 'motivation' (or why we do things) and 'change' (or how in the course of our individual lives we may become happier, more 'adjusted' people). These misconceptions make it very difficult indeed for us to get a helpfully explanatory purchase on the reasons for psychological distress and the chances of avoiding it. So solidly are they embedded in our culture, however, we can scarcely even see them. In order fully to expose their foundations, I believe that one must approach them through what might at first seem like a detour: one must examine the nature of 'official' psychology itself.

For while there may be no very direct relation between, on the one hand, what people-in-the-street consider the causes of their actions and the possibilities for their self-improvement, and, on the other hand, the speculations of the professionals, there is little doubt that both will reflect a general cultural impetus, and this latter, for me at any rate, is easier to detect in the relatively well formulated 'official' views than in the often unspoken or more tentative assumptions of the 'ordinary person'. Though it would certainly be a mistake to suppose that 'the experts' *determine* what the 'lay' person thinks, it is altogether more likely that those forms of psychological preconception to which our culture inclines us will find their most exact expression in 'expert' opinions and procedures. More important than this, clues as to the *reasons why* we think about ourselves as we do are, I think, most clearly revealed by a clarification of the *reasons for* our having 'a psychology' at all.

In trying, then, to understand (in the two chapters following this) how we have come to adopt ideas about 'motivation' which in fact enslave us, and ideas about 'change' which delude us, I think it may be illuminating (even if only by indirect lighting) first to gain some insight into how official psychology and psychotherapy came about, and what purposes they serve.

Whether as individuals or groups, people seem particularly prone to construct for themselves a myth of origin – i.e. a story about their beginning. Psychologists are no exception. We are the children, so the story goes, not of Adam and Eve, nor even of their simian substitutes, but of science.

Though psychologists and other professionals and academics of the 'psycho-' variety quarrel bitterly amongst themselves about the legitimacy of their claim to scientific respectability, virtually all of them trace their origin to a period during the second half of the last century when scientific method came to be applied to matters of psychological concern. Most of us, in this way, live with the happy myth that, intellectually speaking, we arrived but recently on the scene, bringing with us a clear and virginally pure scientific gaze with which to peer through the murk of metaphysics and superstition which had until so recently obscured our understanding of the workings of the human mind. It took the world a long time to get round to the one true belief – science – but as its children we are unsullied by the ignorance and incomprehension of the past, and (especially those of us in Britain and America) we now have the infallible canons of 'objective scientific method' which, as long as we remain true to them, will guide us through a future in which freedom from the errors of former times is guaranteed.

However, the very failure of psychology in its 'applied' and therapeutic forms to cope with the emotional distress and confusion which are so prevalent in our society exposes the fallibility of our 'scientific' dogma and indicates the falsity of our myth of origin. And in fact, of course, psychology did not undergo a virgin birth in the last century, but, like any other human endeavour, evolved out of, and still serves, concerns and interests that have been identifiable within our culture for as long as its intellectual history has been recorded. Indeed, not only are psychology's claims to an *objectively valid* understanding of and a *therapeutically effective* concern with the ills which beset us false, but it is more than possible that psychology, far from minimising, actually compounds our difficulties.

If I am not to be really seriously misunderstood, however, I must at the outset make one thing very clear, and that is that I do not regard psychologists, or psychotherapists, or practitioners of psychological medicine, as charlatans, nor do I wish in any way to impugn their motives. A charlatan is one who knowingly pretends to knowledge and ability he or she in fact does not have. As far as psychology is complicit in the social evils and self-deceptions of our time, it is so without (except perhaps for a very small minority) the knowing connivance of its practitioners. Almost without exception, the psychologists, psychotherapists and psychiatrists I have met are, professionally speaking, honest, concerned and conscientious people who work in what they see as the best interests of their clients and patients, and who do much, at the very least, to offer comfort and support to people who have no one else to turn to.

It is, however, an irony instructive of the very points I want to make in this chapter, that (with some very important exceptions) it is the 'psycho-' disciplines themselves which have led us (misguidedly) to seek the reasons for human conduct in the individual (and often conscious) motivations of those who enact it. It thus becomes extremely difficult to call into question the effects of somebody's *actions* without apparently implying an insult to the *person*; it is hard for me to suggest that what you do has an effect contrary to what you say your intention is, without seeming thereby also to suggest that you are a liar. But if we are to be able to engage with good will and mutual respect in a search for the truth of the matter, it is essential that we be able to distinguish the meaning of an action in its widest social context from the verbal account of his or her intentions the individual actor gives. The fact is that often, perhaps most often – and arguably even always – we do things for reasons of which we are not only unaware, but *could* not be aware (more will be said about this later), but of which we are understandably tempted – and easily able – to give a plausible account.

So-called neurotic symptoms are frequently the experience or expression of a distress for which individuals cannot accurately account through an examination of their own conscious purposes. This of course does not mean that their conduct and experience itself (as opposed to their conscious articulation of it) is *irrelevant* to an explanation of their distress – indeed it is likely to be crucial. In exactly the same way, psychologists must acknowledge that what they *say* they are doing may have very little relevance to what they actually are doing, and that a more satisfactory explanation must be sought elsewhere. With individuals, one has to formulate explanations (as well as evaluations) of their conduct (a) from a consideration of their history, and (b) by inferring their intentions from the actual fruits of their activity. The case is no different with collective human undertakings such as psychology.

The definition of psychology which was taught to me was 'the scientific study of human behaviour', and the chief aim of its most representative school – behaviourism – 'the prediction and control of behaviour'. I am not sure how far academic psychologists have in recent years modified the expression of this aim, but in so far as they have softened somewhat its rather stark outline, I suspect that this would stem less from any embarrassment over its almost touchingly ingenuous revelation of a dubious interest than from an uncomfortable awareness that psychologists have, over the last hundred years or so of psychology's existence as a 'scientific', laboratory discipline, been singularly unsuccessful at predicting anything of much intrinsic intellectual merit. However, what is worth noting for the purposes of the present discussion is that, despite its association with the rigours of a disinterested scientific objectivity, 'the prediction and control of human behaviour' is, as an aim of human inquiry, no new phenomenon: it expresses an intellectual aspiration as old as magic, and restates a practical interest dear to the heart of tyrants ever since time began.

One of the central arguments of this book is that, far from 'curing' people's distress, psychology too easily serves to provide us with an excuse for continuing, as a society, to inflict it. Psychology flourishes not through any truly scientific demonstration of its validity, but because, on the one hand, it feeds an age-old dream of the magical conquest of unhappiness and the achievement of power, and, on the other, it serves the interests not only of its practitioners, but more importantly of those who have actually achieved power within society and constructed an apparatus to maintain it (this, again, not *necessarily* with any consciously evil intent). Very much more than most of its practitioners would be willing to concede, then, psychology offers magical solutions to human distress which is in fact created by abuses of the very power whose interests psychology also serves. When 'ordinary people' accept that psychology represents a 'disinterested' body of 'objective' knowledge giving the best available account of their nature and difficulties – as soon, that is, as people abandon their experience of themselves in favour of the alienating dogmas of 'experts' – then the process of mystification becomes complete.

Traditionally, 'applied' psychologists – i.e. those working in the fields of health, education and industry – have claimed for themselves two principal functions: the scientific measurement of aspects of behaviour, 'personality', etc., relevant to their concerns, and a therapeutic function in dealing with 'mental disorder', 'maladjustment', and so on. Although a continuity between the witch's incantation and the psychotherapist's 'talking cure' could perhaps be established plausibly enough, it seems that even the 'scientific measurement' aspect of the modern psychologist's role also had its counterpart in what would now be considered less respectable historical precedents.

In his masterly study of religion and magic in the sixteenth and seventeenth centuries,★ Keith Thomas points out that magic to some extent filled a *therapeutic* vacuum created by the disappearance of the confessional and the emergence of a note of puritanical disapproval on the part of the clergy of the kinds of problems for which people might seek help. Indeed magic, Thomas argues, 'may have provided as effective a therapy for the diseases of the mind as anything available today'.

People have always sought to influence by magical ritual what they could not control in any other way. 'Witchcraft was thus generally believed to be a method of bettering one's condition when all else had failed. Like most forms of magic, it was a substitute for impotence, a remedy for anxiety and despair.' There is of course an element of pure wishfulness about this, but, again as Thomas notes, there are *facilitative* aspects of much magical ritual which, though they form no part of its central rationale, have the effect of encouraging people to make up their minds concerning a particular course of action, or of comforting the person who distractedly seeks a solution to his or her dilemma. Divination, for example,

> could help men to take decisions when other agencies failed them. Its basic function was to shift the responsibility away from the actor, to provide him with a justification for taking a leap in the dark, and to screw him up into making a decision whose outcome was unpredictable by normal means.
>
> The diviner's predictions, therefore, did not deflect his clients from their original intentions; on the contrary, it was the process of consultation which forced them to know their own minds. Divination could set the imagination free.

★K. Thomas, *Religion and the Decline of Magic*, Penguin Books, 1973.

In this respect, magical procedures acted precisely in the way that, as I suggested earlier, psychotherapy acts today. Psychotherapy also makes claims to technical processes of cure which are *in fact* invalid, but in the course of doing so dispenses comfort and encouragement which are far from ineffective.

Apart from the directly therapeutic significance of magical modes of thought, one may note that, for example, both in its methods (which were to a surprising extent 'objective' and statistical) and in its concerns (which included the study of 'individual differences' and human typology, vocational and educational guidance, etc.), seventeenth-century astrology bore resemblances to 'modern' psychology so strong that one can scarcely believe one is reading about a different discipline. Actually, of course, one is not:

> As Auguste Comte was to recognise, the astrologers were pioneering a genuine system of historical explanation. In their confident assumption that the principles underlying the development of human society were capable of human explanation, we can detect the germ of modern sociology.

Astrologers, apparently, even justified their failures in precisely the same way as do present-day applied psychologists. In both cases, practitioners point out that their 'scientifically established' procedures are based on an assessment of the *probability* of a particular finding, or outcome, or 'behaviour', so that one may expect there always to be a proportion of cases in which matters will go astray. Furthermore, both astrologers and psychologists confess a degree of human error: the procedures and tests used, they say, have to be to some extent *interpreted* and the accuracy of this will depend on the correct following of rules, 'clinical experience and judgment', and so on. In both cases, then, large loopholes are provided in the event of the 'scientificity' of the system being attacked. The similarity of concerns between astrology and more modern disciplines is clearly noted by Thomas:

> In the absence of any rival system of scientific explanation, and in particular of the social sciences – sociology, social anthropology, social psychology – there was no other existing body of thought, religion apart, which even began to offer so all-embracing an explanation for the baffling variousness of human affairs.

As is the similarity of clinical application:

> The attraction of having one's horoscope cast was not unlike that of undergoing psychoanalysis today. The reward would be a penetrating analysis of the individual's innermost attributes, the qualities which he should develop, and the limitations against which he should be on his guard.

Astrology's 'pretensions to be a genuinely scientific system' again remind one strongly of the insistence of present-day psychologists that their scientific orthodoxy must give them a right to respect and credibility, and they too would argue that their findings are based 'on the meticulous study of cause and effect'.

As far as 'modern psychology' is concerned, I see no real evidence that its findings and predictions, its so-called 'laws of behaviour', and so on, are any more soundly established or firmly based than were the claims to effectiveness of the astrologers. In my own field of clinical psychology, for example, it seems to me that scientific method has merely provided a rhetoric through which psychologists could (a) introduce ideas and practices which they *felt* to be beneficial and probably valid, and (b) create for themselves a credible professional role. Having largely succeeded in both these aims, psychologists have now for the most part abandoned the 'tough-minded' scientific stance by means of which they bought their respectability, and which would indeed now work *against* their interests because there is in truth so little scientific evidence that their procedures do in fact work. Having become firmly established professionally, psychologists now simply *assert* their effectiveness in the confident and correct expectation that this will be sufficient to maintain their standing.

But when all is said and done, it is of course a mistake to regard magic and science as *opposing* points of view, for our scientific procedures are informed by our wishful magic. As Thomas points out: 'the magical desire for power had created an intellectual environment favourable to experiment and induction: it maintained a break with the characteristic mediaeval attitude of contemplative imagination.' Science, in this way, evolves from magic.

There is indeed a sense in which scientific observation and procedure need to be dispassionate: the scientist must take note of what actually happens, as the result, for example, of experiments which have been conducted, rather than what he or she would like to happen. But it is only in a relatively limited and technical sphere that scientists need to maintain this kind of objectivity: the true scientist needs to pay proper respect to the 'embodied otherness' of the world and the things and people in it, to recognise that they are not to be *wished* in or out of existence, but this does not mean that he or she is not *passionately involved* in the search for knowledge. Above all, however dispassionate science may or may not be, it is certainly not disinterested. Francis Bacon, whose role in laying the grounds of scientific procedures is reverentially acknowledged by philosophers of science today, clearly associated his aspirations for science with the kinds of powers which at the time only magic could hope to achieve:

Francis Bacon listed as *desiderata* the prolongation of life, the restitution of youth, the curing of incurable diseases, the mitigation of pain, the speeding up of natural processes, the discovery of new sources of food, the control of the weather, and the enhancement of the pleasures of the senses. He wanted divination put on a natural basis so that it would be possible to make rational predictions of the weather, the harvest, and the epidemics of each year. His aspirations were the same of those of the astrologers, the magicians and the alchemists, even if the methods he envisaged were different.*

This is not the pursuit of knowledge for its own sake, but of knowledge in order to dominate nature and increase the power of men. And in truth, of course, science has not made a bad job of this enterprise (even if at a cost, in terms of pollution and impoverishment, etc., which we have yet to count). There is, however, much less hard evidence that the sciences of man, the 'psycho-' disciplines, have achieved even a tiny proportion of their aims. The evolution of natural science from magic – of, for instance, chemistry from alchemy – may be an interesting illustration of the constancy of our wishfulness and a sobering indication of our lust for power, but it is also an example of a real evolutionary movement (whether for good or for ill) in the nature of our search for knowledge. Whether the same can be said for psychology is another question, and how far it represents a distinct advance upon magic, in terms of evidential, objective knowledge, is entirely debatable.

It is my belief that, in terms of their capacity to develop and apply conceptual thought and practical action, human beings are broadly equal partners in the creation of a *moral* world (i.e. a world which cannot be technically known in advance, but must be created out of conduct we can characterise only as good or bad). If this is so, they cannot then expect to be able to understand or treat each other as if *some* of them were *objects*; methods of objective, natural science cannot be expected to bear fruit

*Thomas, op. cit.

when applied to a community of subjects (which is the only proper, and in the long run possible, way of regarding the human community).

Psychology then, it seems to me, is still much more closely related to magic than is, say, chemistry. Partly, no doubt, one can explain its continuing success because like magic, in Thomas's words, it 'lessens anxiety, relieves pent-up frustration, and makes the practitioner feel that he is doing something positive towards the solution of his problem'. But I think that there are more powerful reasons which support the practice of psychology quite apart from its convincing use of scientific rhetoric and its incidental provision of comfort and encouragement to those who lack more effective remedies for their ills, and consideration of these will once again involve us in an examination of the operation of interest.

Thomas himself notes the role played by some magical procedures in associating misfortune with moral blame, and hence contributing to forces of social control. It is precisely this aspect that of social control through the establishment of *individual* guilt and accountability – which has become, in my view, the principal function of psychology, and which serves to maintain it in so flourishing an existence within our society.

Modern psychology's aim to 'predict and control human behaviour', as well as its investment in the theory and practice of conditioning (particularly strong in the behaviourist school and the associated 'behaviour therapies'), may claim a significant part of their ancestry in the writings of the seventeenth-century philosopher John Locke. Showing the same kind of innocence which was noted in the last chapter in the case of the Utilitarians writing a century later, Locke seems unaware that his proposals for the effective education, or perhaps rather shaping, of the individual would ever be put to any use other than the perfecting of mankind. To our ears, however, there is already a rather sinister ring to his proposals. In advocating the establishment in children of habit through the judicious use of praise and blame (encouragement and shame), Locke writes:

> If by these means you can come once to shame them out of their faults, (for besides that, I would willingly have no punishment) and make them in love with the pleasure of being well thought on, you may turn them as you please, and they will be in love with all the ways of virtue.★

From this, as Passmore notes:

> It will at once be obvious that Locke has opened up, in principle, the possibility of perfecting men by the application of readily intelligible, humanly controllable, mechanisms. All that is required is that there should be an educator, or a social group, able and willing to teach the child what to pursue and what to avoid.

Here lies, in a nutshell, the whole point and purpose of the vast enterprise which present-day psychology has become: the location of the means of social control *inside the heads of the very individuals who are to be controlled*. Compare Locke's benign view of what has come to be known as 'behavioural shaping' or 'behaviour modification' with the altogether less palatable perspective of Servan, who wrote in late eighteenth-century France of the necessity to link the *ideas* of crime and punishment in the *minds* of people such that they

> follow one another without interruption . . . When you have thus formed the chain of ideas in the heads of your citizens, you will then be able to pride yourselves on guiding them and being their masters. A stupid despot may constrain his slaves with iron chains; but a true politician binds them even

★Quoted in Passmore, op. cit.

more strongly by the chain of their own ideas; it is at the stable point of reason that he secures the end of the chain; this link is all the stronger in that we do not know of what it is made and we believe it to be our own work; despair and time eat away the bonds of iron and steel, but they are powerless against the habitual union of ideas, they can only tighten it still more; and on the soft fibres of the brain is founded the unshakable base of the soundest of Empires.★

Already one begins to see why, having considered the associationist psychology which grew out of Locke's philosophical analysis, Passmore should judge that:

It is not surprising that, under Pavlov's influence, such a psychology won official approval in the Soviet Union and wide acceptance in the United States, both of them countries which are deeply involved in the technological 'management' of human beings . . .

Independent testimony to the success of this enterprise is lent by the words of two modern American writers, who in the course of a disturbing analysis of the uses to which 'therapeutic' psychology has been put in the United States to control the behaviour of children who are in one way or another troublesome to authority, note that 'behaviour modification can make the effects of such authority more painless than, for example, the use of a club or the threat of punishment, but in its ideal form it will erase all awareness of its existence and thereby make it absolute.'†

Nobody has done more than Michel Foucault to show how the development over the last few centuries of the human sciences has become saturated throughout with the interests of

★Quoted in M. Foucault, *Discipline and Punish*, Penguin Books, 1979.
†P. Schrag and D. Divoky, *The Myth of the Hyperactive Child and Other Means of Child Control*, Penguin Books, 1981.

power. In his magnificent book *Discipline and Punish*, for example, he argues that 'all the sciences, analyses or practices employing the root "psycho"' have arisen in the course of a process in which the punishment of illegal *acts* by otherwise anonymous malefactors, has turned into the maintenance of discipline in *people* by means of an ever more finely differentiated analysis of their individual characteristics. Where once the state discouraged threats against it through an ostentatiously terrifying recourse to spectacular tortures and execution, it now does it through a scientific technology of power – i.e. discipline. Through the use of scientific observation, the objectifying 'gaze' which seeks to see without itself being seen (a necessity well known to every student of psychology in search of 'uncontaminated' observations), social scientists become practitioners of a discipline which dissects, orders and normalises individuals, and documents and traces the roots of their differentiation or dissent.

The establishment of such discipline is aided by several factors. There is, for example, the actual apparatus of observation, corresponding to the microscope of the physical scientist: in this respect Foucault writes particularly interestingly of the 'panopticon', i.e. the physical structure whereby human beings could be observed or studied in large numbers by as few as one unseen watcher. The prototype of this design is the circular prison, in which cells are constructed around the circumference, facing inwards in such a way that one warder in the centre would have a direct view of all prisoners. This kind of structure, several examples of which were built in the last century, has its parallel today in the one-way glass screens to be found in every university department of psychology. (It is characteristic of Foucault's genius to bring one suddenly face to face with a question at once blindingly obvious and excruciatingly revealing: if psychologists' intentions are honourable – as we have always felt and asserted them to be – why *do* they need to shield people from their gaze?)

Apart from the physical paraphernalia of observation, the technology of power has other tools of its trade – for example the concept of delinquency, which allows the punisher of *acts* to become the disciplinarian who, as it were, invades the internal space of individuals in order to establish and track their *reasons*; instead of punishing the wrong-doer's action, you thus control his or her biography. There is also the procedure of the examination:

> The examination combines the techniques of an observing hierarchy and those of a normalising judgment. It is a normalising gaze, a surveillance that makes it possible to qualify, to classify and to punish. It establishes over individuals a visibility through which one differentiates them and judges them. That is why, in all the mechanisms of discipline, the examination is highly ritualised. In it are combined the ceremony of power and the form of the experiment, the deployment of force and the establishment of truth. At the heart of the procedures of discipline, it manifests the subjection of those who are perceived as objects and the objectification of those who are subjected.

For modern men and women who have never experienced what it is like *not* to live under the 'normalising' gaze of educational, medical and scientific experts of one kind or another, and who have been subjected from their earliest days to a rhetoric which emphasises the benefits of living in a 'free world', the suggestion that we are seriously constrained by the unseen discipline of our social institutions may seem simply incredible. Examinations, for example, seem to be the 'natural' and 'obvious' ways to test educational achievement, and indeed the educational system itself seems the 'natural' and 'obvious' way to impart knowledge to the young. At the same time, I think, we all of us have the evidence of our own experience to suggest that Foucault and others are not wrong to alert us to the extent to which our social institutions do curtail our freedom and cripple our potentialities as human beings. For example, who does not know for him- or herself the savage tyranny of the 'norm'? Being different, standing out, *feeling* differently from others, experiencing oneself as conspicuous in some way – feelings such as these are at the very core of much of what gets called 'psychiatric disorder', and indeed of the everyday terrors of us all. That such feelings are so familiar a part of our ordinary experience leads us to consider them as 'human nature', but much more likely, I suspect, is that they are the internalised values of a society which depends for its smooth economic functioning on the willing obedience of the individual. *Punishment* of illegality has become, through the processes so brilliantly described by Foucault, individual *guilt* over non-conformity.

Although the vast majority of those involved professionally in the technology of discipline (and ultimately in the engineering of *self*-discipline) tend to be quite unaware of their contribution (feeling instead that their role is merely one of scientific inquiry or therapeutic service), this is not true of all, and Foucault's insights find their echo in the observations of some of those much more directly engaged at the professional level. Not surprisingly, however, the most trenchant criticism tends to come from those who obtain a clear view of the 'psycho-' disciplines from outside. It takes, for example, two journalists, Schrag and Divoky,* to point out what the actual effects of 'screening' programmes for American children may be. A combination of parental anxiety, professional self-interest and undercurrent concern over social unrest resulted, they write, in a situation in which:

Between 1971 and 1974, thirty states passed special education laws and more are doing so each year; many of these mandate the screening of entire school populations not only for defec-

The Myth of the Hyperactive Child and Other Means of Child Control, op. cit.

tive vision and hearing, for malnutrition and bad teeth, but for 'oedipal conflicts', 'ego disturbances' and 'normalcy' in 'impulse control', 'withdrawal' and 'social behaviour'. Such screening is now common, even for four-year-olds.

While procedures such as these are justified by a rhetoric of welfare, their actual effect is that

> this generation is learning at a very young age that there is nothing unusual about being watched, questioned, tested, labelled and 'treated', or about the fact that the results of all that watching and questioning are being stored and processed in machines over which the individual has no control. It is hardly worth saying again that the existence of such a record can have a chilling effect or that privacy is 'the right to be left alone'. But for those who have become habituated to such records and treatment from the age of five, that chilling effect may never occur because they have never been left alone, and they will therefore never suspect that there might have been another way.

And so:

> An entire generation is slowly being conditioned to distrust its own instincts, to regard its deviation from the narrowing standards of approved norms as sickness and to rely on the institutions of the state and on technology to define and engineer its 'health'.

If one is to understand the processes whereby 'scientific psychology' comes to cooperate with the state in the realisation of the latter's interests, one must, I think, guard against the temptation – at times very strong – to attribute to those involved, i.e. the economically powerful, the politicians and the 'scientific' professionals, implication in some kind of malevolent conspiracy. Although it would no doubt be equally mistaken to rule out the possibility that there can be quite deliberate and conscious components to the exploitation of the weak by the strong, the process of exploitation as a whole is probably facilitated most of all by our having been overtaken in recent times by a general lowering of moral and political awareness. 'Politics and religion', together perhaps with too indecently direct reference to money (as in the question of how much a person earns), have become subjects which many people feel it indelicate to inquire into too closely or too publicly. This constitutes a form of repression the effect of which (as is, after all, commonly the case with repression) is to allow the interests which might otherwise be challenged by, in this case, moral and political awareness to operate all the more unrestrainedly. Professional collaborators with such interests have in this way no particular consciousness of the significance of their collaboration. Economic values have largely replaced moral and political ones in the public awareness, so that anything which appears to be conducive to the 'creation of wealth', or at least to economic stability, is taken as self-evidently desirable.

'Ordinary people', moreover, feel powerless to challenge an oppressive system partly because the channels of moral and political *understanding* which were once available (for example in the days when political pamphlets would be read in hundreds of thousands) have largely become closed off to them. (As noted earlier, this feeling of powerlessness is, these days, *very frequently* a complaint of people suffering from 'symptoms' of psychological distress, many of whom explicitly recognise that the information that would enable them to make judgements about socially significant and disturbing issues – for example 'the bomb', racial unrest – is not available in those 'media' to which they have ready access.)

It is thus with almost disarming political naivety that H. J. Eysenck – Britain's best-known psychologist– could write of a 'technology of consent':

which will make people behave in a socially adapted, law-abiding fashion, which will not lead to a breakdown of the intricately interwoven fabric of social life . . . a generally applicable method of inculcating suitable habits of socialised conduct into the citizens (and particularly the future citizens) of the country in question – or preferably the whole world.*

Psychology's most significant contribution to modern society is less 'scientific' or 'therapeutic' than managerial. The task shaped by the economic interests of the twentieth, and twenty-first centuries has been to shift the ordinary person's orientation from production to consumption, and this has been achieved by expropriating his or her knowledge and skill so that they can become mechanised and managed in a mass market. Indeed, this programme has at times been put into operation entirely consciously in the name of 'scientific management':

The managers assume . . . the burden of gathering together all the traditional knowledge which in the past has been possessed by the workmen and then of classifying, tabulating and reducing this knowledge to rules, laws and formulae . . .

Because:

. . . all the planning which under the old system was done by the workman, as a result of his personal experience, must of necessity under the new system be done by the management in accordance with the laws of science.†

---

*H. J. Eysenck, The technology of consent. *New Scientist*, 42, 688–90, June 1969. For this and the following quotations from Taylor, I am indebted to Dr John Shotter.

†F. W. Taylor, *Scientific Management*, Harper and Bros., 1947 (first published 1918).

The prestige of 'science' becomes associated with whatever social processes are necessary for the achievement of the economic interests of power, and to this purpose the 'social sciences' lend themselves admirably. As Schrag and Divoky put it:

> The normative assumptions and natural order invoked by the new modes of control are, in one sense, disciplinary replacements for Social Darwinism. Each in its own time was (or is) 'scientific'. But while Social Darwinism was almost entirely an economic 'law' concerned with the individual's fitness for the labour market (and particularly the factory), its contemporary substitute is concerned with every aspect of the individual's life and, most particularly, with his potential as a client. The system no longer requires his muscle, but it needs his obedience. It no longer must train him to be a reliable worker, but it must condition him to be managed.

What Christopher Lasch calls the 'tutelary complex' – i.e. the amalgam of educational, social and therapeutic agencies concerned with our 'adjustment' – has in fact become the instrument of managerial discipline. In a passage strongly reminiscent of Foucault, he suggests that the tutelary complex:

> . . . both reflects and contributes to the shift from authoritative sanctions to psychological manipulation and surveillance – the redefinition of political authority in therapeutic terms – and to the rise of a professional and managerial class that governs society not by upholding authoritative moral standards but by defining normal behaviour and by invoking allegedly non-punitive, psychiatric sanctions against deviance.★

★*The Minimal Self*, op. cit.

Interest is at once the most powerful and the least honourable motivation of human conduct. Unchecked, its operation is likely to be extremely destructive, since its long-term effect is to wear away the ligaments which bind a society in *communal* purpose. If, into the bargain, its operation is repressed – i.e. unnoticed and uncommented-upon – the destructiveness to which it gives rise may turn out to be uncontrollable. That psychology – supposedly the 'scientific study of human behaviour' – concerns itself not at all with the operation of interest (though it is itself heavily caught up in it), testifies, in, as it were, silent eloquence, to the extent to which we *do* repress awareness of the operation of interest. We simply do not talk about nor even notice the degree to which our conduct, at all levels, is aimed at the exploitation of the world and of each other purely for selfish gain, nor do we see that a great deal of the distress we experience *personally*, in our everyday lives, is traceable to the currents of interest in whose destructive vortices we *are* caught up.

We have in our present society largely dismantled the moral structures by means of which the operation of interest may be checked, and through the acceptance of mass-market economies as somehow inevitably *necessary* we have reduced almost to vanishing point the degree to which political opposition can expose and cancel out the operation of competitive interests. In these circumstances, it becomes all the more important to increase *awareness* of the degree to which we are under the sway of interest – i.e. to lift our repression of it.

There are perhaps some signs that the appeal of cupidity and self-interest is becoming less disguised than even a few years ago, but this seems to be happening not so much through a frank acknowledgement of greed as through an association of 'market forces' with a kind of unexamined moral imperative: interest is breaking free of moral restraint by linking itself directly with an *assertion* of moral authority – cost-benefit analysis becomes the *fundamental* measure of right and wrong.

(The technique of assertion is, of course, itself characteristic of the marketing society, and replaces now almost outmoded methods of what one might call 'evidential' persuasion. When what matters is *whether* rather than *why* you buy – the economy *must*, after all, expand – attempts to convince you of a commodity's value by a rational appeal to *evidence* of its qualities give way to an almost ritual *assertion* of those qualities, a kind of authoritative confirmation that it is indeed up for sale, and therefore *ought* to be bought. As I have already indicated in the case of clinical psychology, the technique of assertion extends far beyond the boundaries of what we have traditionally considered the 'market-place'.)

The extent to which the workings of interest are cloaked in repression is still, however, very great, and represents a process in which we are all implicated. Disavowed interest, one might say, is the barely visible oil which keeps the cogs of the acquisitive society turning. Interest works, indeed, not by the brutal oppression of one section of society by another, but through the interlocking of many types and sub-sets of interests. I may achieve what *I* want (which may easily be against your interest) by recruiting you to my cause through making the attainability of what *you* want appear dependent upon your falling in with my desires. This is of course nothing other than the ancient art of manipulation long known to politicians and horse-traders, but I think we fail to acknowledge how large a part it plays in our conduct, as well as how unrestrained and dangerous the game becomes when it is fuelled by an individualistic pursuit of happiness and unchecked by any overarching moral purpose.

In the context of the interlocking of our interests, our conduct tends to slide always in the same direction of exploitation and maximisation of perceived personal gain, harnessing as it goes baser and baser and coarser and coarser motivations in order to increase the saleability and consumption of our 'products'. This slide takes place in an almost infinite number of finely graded steps. The space between our potential and our actual actions may well be occupied by *feigned* considerations of right and wrong, but it is *in fact* occupied by the promptings of interest. One might almost formulate a 'law of human behaviour' in this respect (and one, I fear, more accurate at the present time than many advanced by experimental psychologists over the last hundred years): 'faced with a number of courses of action having roughly equal probability of achievement, a person is likely to choose that which conforms most to his/her self-interest'. Furthermore, what the individual *sees as* in his or her interest will be manipulated by higherorder interests, with the degree of superordinacy of an interest or set of interests being determined by economic power. We are thus led more or less automatically into forms of relationship and communication which are entirely manipulative. The more power a person or a group has, the more will it be able to determine the perceptions of their interest held by those lower in the power hierarchy, so that what low-status people *see as* in their interests will probably not be so, but will *in fact* be in the interests of the relatively more powerful.

Because the workings of interest are impersonal in the sense that they do not spring from the conscious intentions of particular people, it is very hard to find a language in which to express them. In this respect, one is reminded of nothing so much as the 'invisible hand' which Adam Smith described as responsible for the workings of the market economy, and which is extolled so enthusiastically by his present-day admirers. Thus, individual people *appear* to be absolved (since they are unaware of it) from complicity in a process in which some of them are subjugated to the interests of others while all *believe* that they benefit.

Since we are so unaccustomed to locating *ourselves* within this process, and have no real concepts with which to do so, it is hard to think of succinct or sharply drawn examples of its operation. At the simplest and most direct level, however, most people capable of honest reflection on their own conduct will be aware of how easy it is to slide towards rationalisations of actions which are beneficial (to themselves) rather than right (this is a distinction which will be taken up in greater detail in the final chapter of this book). Two apples are left in the bowl; though I am better fed and richer than you, I take the larger one, perhaps guiltily acknowledging to myself my greed and perhaps not, but in any case telling myself more emphatically that the slight blemish on its skin in fact makes it less desirable and nutritious than the other which I graciously leave for you.

At a less personal level, it may be easiest to see how, for instance, interest can disguise itself as necessity by examining the conduct of people other than ourselves; let me take directly from my own experience an example which I think at the same time illustrates processes typical of the 'managerial' ethos of so-called 'post-industrial society' on a much wider scale. The activity of some National Health Service administrators has in recent times undergone a striking change from the concerned, meticulous support of procedures of clinical care once charac-teristic of them to a kind of swashbuckling managerial bravado in which cuts in services to patients and jobs of staff are made with apparent indifference or even satisfaction. The same people whose conduct not long ago would have been cautious, balanced, concerned for fairness, now speak the hard, almost macho language of 'the real world' and of the need for 'effi-ciency and effectiveness', and actually express pride in cutting costs by measures which, ironically, are clearly neither in their own direct interests nor in those of the staff and patients for whom they are responsible. But there *are* ways in which their interests are caught up in this process. Their *perceived* interest lies in their 'image' of themselves as 'managers' – no longer are they seen by 'colleagues in industry' as bumbling clerical func-tionaries doing a second-rate job of administration in an over-protected public service: they are *managers* making the kinds of hard but necessary decisions made by executives of oil compa-nies. They conform to a style and rhetoric which has been sanc-tioned and endorsed from high above them by governmental power aimed at dismantling public health care. Their *negative* interest lies in the feeling that if they did not so conform there could be a threat to their jobs, though apart from this there is no tangible advantage to their conduct,* and indeed considerable impairment to the moral quality of their work. These are decent people whose conduct springs not from some kind of illusory personal autonomy, but from a social context structured by interest.

It would certainly be entirely misleading to locate the reasons for interest-shaped conduct in the gullibility, perversity or 'self-ishness' of people themselves: as I shall try to elaborate in greater detail in the course of the next two chapters, people react in relation to a world which impinges directly upon them, but which is largely shaped by forces not in their sight. The profound and pervasive significance of this process has become most obvious to me through working with 'patients' whose conduct is inexplicable, to themselves as well as to me, in terms of conventional understandings of personal autonomy. Why, for example, does someone with a serious physical condition such as diabetes or kidney failure make precisely those dietary preferences which create an otherwise avoidable threat to life or limb? (Why *do* people smoke, or work in asbestos mines?) Why do people fail to take measures which would quite obviously result in improvements to their personal condition or circum-

*Since these words were written the British government has adopted an altogether more workmanlike approach to the manipulation of managerial interest. The *Guardian*, 3 September 1986, reports that: 'Health authority managers could be denied an annual pay rise if they fail to achieve their individual targets under the Department of Health's new merit pay system . . . But those "consistently exceeding short-term objectives and making excellent progress towards long-term goals" will be awarded an extra 4 per cent on salary in the first year . . . Health service unions have attacked the plan as an incentive scheme for accelerating hospital closures and service cuts . . .' The article goes on to describe how each tier of management will be 'assessed' by those next highest in authority. This provides as good an example as any of how interest can be manipulated via a pyramidal hierarchy ('management') in order to achieve higher-order political goals.

stances? Above all, it has dawned on me – all too slowly – that the straight distress people feel cannot be explicated by the traditional conceptual paraphernalia of psychology and psychotherapy, etc., but arises out of a highly complex interaction between the economic coercion which bears directly upon them (you work in asbestos mines rather than starve) and the availability to them of information, ideas and language which would allow them to develop an understanding of their position. This picture is further complicated by the fact that information, ideas and language, once acquired (according to processes again to be elaborated in the following chapters), are not easily altered. This entire complex of interacting factors is shaped by the invisible handiwork of interest into a disciplinary network from which there is virtually no escape.

Take, for example, a gentle and sensitive man of thirty who is thought to be suffering from a 'mild depressive illness' because of his 'unrealistic fears' of contamination at work and a preoccupation with bronchial discomfort, his gloomy concerns about the state of the world and his 'undue absences' from work. He works in a machine shop clouded with industrial dust; he is worried about the bomb, the frequency of rape and racial tension; he is afraid that the vegetables in his garden have been polluted by fallout from the Chernobyl nuclear accident, and further afraid that this must mean he's crazy. On the face of it, it may well seem that his difficulties are 'unrealistic' because they all admit of some kind of solution. *But only if he is empowered to act within the space available to him.* Why, for example, shouldn't he wear a mask (as he is supposed to) at work if he is worried about bronchial trouble? Because his much 'tougher' workmates ridicule him if he does. Why doesn't he get another job, then? He has tried, but there aren't any. If he's worried about the state of the world, why doesn't he become socially and politically active? Because he is barely literate and doesn't know where to start; he has not learned the highly complex conceptual competence which comes as second nature to those, for

example, who have received a middle-class education. His hori-
zons are all but inescapably limited by the comics he reads, ITV
news and the *Sun* newspaper. The tragedy is that he is a gentle,
intelligent, loving and thoughtful man whose very sensitivity, in
contrast to the hardened survivors who surround him, makes
him feel aberrant and even unhinged (which of course, in relation to his context, he is). He likes his West Indian and Asian
workmates, but still thinks they ought to go 'home' because
'they are taking the jobs of real people'; this is the best judgement he can make not because he is a 'racist' but because he has
been denied the conceptual and informational equipment
which makes any more sophisticated view possible. (If this
seems incredible, remember how difficult it must have been to
learn things which seem so easy to you now; or imagine, for
example, suddenly being required to perform some complex
task which is somebody else's child's play – glass blowing,
perhaps, or speaking Finnish. 'All very well,' you may say, 'but
at least he could look at Channel Four instead of ITV.' But
from his point of view, 'people like me' don't do things like
that: they no more read unusual books or watch unusual television programmes than the average professional person attends
court functions or rides to hounds, and for precisely the same
reason.) Why, again, does he not wash the vegetables in his
garden to accommodate what is after all a perfectly legitimate
concern? Because authority has instructed him that there is no
need to, and he therefore experiences his own doubt as irrational (those at the base of our power hierarchy are trained to
trust unquestioningly in authority).

At the bottom of the heap there is not a great deal of room
for manoeuvre, and whatever autonomy one has is likely to be
strictly limited to the most immediate personal concerns. Those
sufferers from diabetes, for example, who knowingly risk severe
future injury to their health by eating and drinking too much of
the wrong things, do so largely because the pleasures and possibilities of their lives are limited to eating and drinking: their

conduct in these respects, though immediately 'motivated' by such restricted satisfactions, is in fact held in place by a network of interlocking interests quite out of their sight, and is far from irrational in terms of their personal circumstances.

It is no doubt easier to see how one can be the victim of the hierarchy of power than the victimiser, and yet both roles are played out unconsciously by the vast majority of us. People further up the hierarchy, having more room for manoeuvre, more access to information and ideas, etc., are perhaps likely to be more plausibly convinced of their personal autonomy, but here again their conduct will be powerfully shaped by the interests bearing upon it from above, and in the process will interlock in a coercive way with that of those in a weaker position.

In the barest possible outline, then, one may be able to glimpse in these far from polished reflections the potential for a psychology of interest which psychology itself has not even started to make *explicit*, but in which it has been extensively *complicit*. Indeed, the growth of psychology as a 'scientific' discipline is itself instructive of the way interests interlock to bring about particular forms of socio-economic organisation *as well as* to shape the direction taken by supposedly disinterested academic and intellectual bodies. Though, arguably, European, and in particular German academic psychology towards the latter half of the nineteenth century was overshadowed by the relatively abstract concerns of philosophy, it received an altogether more practical impetus when it was imported into the USA. As K. Danziger argues, rather than having to justify themselves to their more academically respectable colleagues in faculties of philosophy:

. . . psychologists had to justify themselves before a very different tribunal. Control of university appointments, research funds, and professional opportunities was vested in the hands of either businessmen and their appointees, or politicians who represented their interests. If psychology was to emerge as a viable independent discipline, it would have to be in a form acceptable to these social forces. The inclinations of those on whose decisions the fate of American psychology depended were clear. They were men in positions of genuine social power who were anxious to use their positions to control the actions of others. They were interested in techniques of social control and in tangible performance. Their image of man was hardly that of the contemplative philosopher: a huge system of secondary and professional education had to be built practically from scratch; the human fallout from wide-scale migration and urbanisation had to be dealt with; man had to be made to adapt to a rapidly rationalised industrial system; products had to be sold. In view of the weakness of alternative sources of professional expertise, psychologists might become acceptable if they could reasonably promise to develop the technical competence needed to deal appropriately with these problems.*

Bearing in mind the researches of Foucault, one would probably be unwise to take the difference between European and North American psychology as one of kind rather than merely as one of degree. However that may be, it does seem that present-day Anglo-American psychology cannot by any stretch of the imagination accurately be cast in the role of disinterested scientific pursuit, nor its practical branches be understood as merely the therapeutic application of insights derived from the laboratory.

As I hope I have already made clear, I do not wish to say that there is no scientific truth in psychology and even less do I want to suggest that there is no good to be derived from psychotherapy. But if we are to extract what is true and good from psychology and psychotherapy, it is essential that as far as we can we disentangle the strands of truth and goodness from

*K. Danziger, 'The social origins of modern psychology'. In R. Buss (ed.) *Psychology in Social Context*, Irvington Publishers Inc., 1979.

those of magic and interest. In particular, it is of vital importance to expose the extent to which psychology has been used to mystify an understanding of the reasons for our conduct, and therapy to stifle our often anguished protests at the injustices of our world, all in the interest of the smooth running of a society which threatens to destroy us.

CHAPTER FOUR

Faults and Reasons

Who is to blame? Whose fault is it? That is the question which seems these days to leap to the mind of anyone who tries to understand the causes of unhappiness. It is, for example, conspicuously the question which obsesses all those – particularly journalists, 'media people' and politicians – who have some part to play in the public analysis of misfortune or unrest. Most inquiries into politically significant disturbances or catastrophes seem to come to rest once the blame for them has been established, and indeed the haste to identify a blameworthy person or group is often positively indecent. 'Activists', 'extremists', 'criminal elements' – these are the familiar targets of blame whose identification somehow satisfies, or perhaps rather preempts, our need to understand the causes of disturbance in our society. The search for a person or people to blame is equally remorseless in the case of less obviously politically loaded misfortunes. A child is battered to death: do we blame the parents, or do we blame the social workers, health visitors, doctors who had contact with the family? An aeroplane crashes: do we blame the pilot, the manufacturers, the maintenance engineers, the air traffic controllers? We do not, it seems, rest happy until we have located the cause of the disaster *inside* a person or group of people.

The case is no different with our individual conduct and experience. Whose fault is my unhappiness? Is it mine, is it yours, my spouse's, mother's, employer's?

And yet we have not always been so obsessed with blame. Explanations for why people do things, or react in the way that they do to what has been done, seem to conform (within limits) to fashion. Not long ago, for example, the fashion was to refer for explanations of human distress to concepts of illness, i.e. to impersonal, 'dysfunctional' mechanisms within people. Just recently, the fashion has become more to look for some kind of (largely unelaborated) moral failing. In psychotherapy, it used to be an advance for patients to accept a measure of responsibility for their actions, since this allowed them to get a subjective grip on their circumstances rather than seeing their 'inadequacy' as the result of some kind of mechanical deficiency. Now, however, it seems a positive disadvantage for patients to see themselves as responsible for their actions, since they appear not to be able to make a conceptual differentiation between responsibility and blame. What formerly was a route to at least a measure of subjective effectiveness has now become a terminus in guilty despair.

The reason for these movements of fashion in explanation lies in the fact that individual psychology cannot be understood outside the context of a social world. Times change, and with them our individual conception of ourselves. It would be absurd to suppose that any one of us can escape the influence of our social, political, economic and cultural environment, and hence any attempt to construct an *absolute* psychology appealing to unchanging fundamental principles must be a mistake. But, as I tried to show in the previous chapter, our psychology may not be designed so much to reflect the 'truth' of our situation as to shape our ideas about ourselves, and in this it has not been so inconsistent: it does indeed seem clear that, though fashion may change in the explanations we seek for what we do, they have consistently and increasingly over the last few centuries been focused on the *individual*. Whether 'fault' is mechanical or moral, it is seen as inside individual people, and it is precisely the 'psycho–' disciplines, with their internal probing, measuring, normalising techniques, which make the plausibility of individual fault seem almost unassailable.

To depart from the norm in virtually any direction is, practically by definition, to become conspicuously deviant, and conspicuousness is attended for most of us by a kind of rush of anxious shame. It is this emotion – the panicky dread of being 'different' – which signals our departure from, and so pushes us back into conformity with, the internalised values of a society which turns us into standardised objects. Completely accustomed to a bureaucracy of power which measures, assesses, evaluates, dockets and labels us from birth to death, we have now, through the transformation of outside blame into inside shame, become our own disciplinarians. In precisely this way, people who have been damaged by the callousness and injustice of our social organisation become not angry but anxious, and see their predicament as a function of their own inadequacy. The most perfect form of social control is that which is accepted by those it oppresses as necessary and inevitable. The progression from punishment to discipline traced so brilliantly by Foucault finds its completion in our time in the imposition of *self*-discipline – a conformity, that is, which is self-imposed, and which we experience as (for the most part inarticulate) shame.

If, however, we are to elaborate an accurate understanding of our condition, we must come to recognise the barbaric fallacy involved in the individualisation of fault. The current fashion for blame (which, after all, so obviously does not *explain* anything) seems to me to reveal more clearly the fallacy of individualisation than did the (also by no means defunct!) fashion for mechanistic, 'illness' explanations, since the latter were able to draw 'credibility' from the fundamentally technological nature of modern cultural concerns. Both, however, serve the same purpose: they assist the repression of interest. For as long as we seek the explanation for pain, despair and catastrophe *inside* people, we shall fail to observe that they are in fact the result of our construction of a society serving the functions of power and interest as they operate coercively and manipulatively *between* people. If we are to preserve from ourselves and disguise from others the spectacle of the damage and injury done by our ruthless pursuit of our own interest (in the form of 'happiness') we must create unquestioning allegiance to the view that our misfortunes stem from personal failings, whether mechanical or moral: the casualties of our system can 'only have themselves to blame'.

The transparent irrationality of equating blame with explanation does, however, make it hard to understand the extent to which people seem ready not to inquire into the reasons for events or circumstances beyond a mere imputation of blame for their occurrence. Though neither have a great deal to recommend them, in an apparent 'progression' from scientism (mechanistic explanation) to moralism (moral faultfinding) we seem if anything to be in retreat from rationality, since moralism offers no form of explanation at all. And yet, perhaps, the degree of popularity seeming recently to be enjoyed by the 'New Right', by fundamentalist religions, and by moralistic tracts masquerading as psychiatry,* may reflect an undercurrent recognition that our troubles are indeed *of our own making*, and in this sense such popularity may appear to be not entirely undeserved. At the same time, as long as any such implicit acknowledgment of our moral responsibility for ourselves is set within an individualising psychology, it is not only utterly misleading, but adds cruelty to error. To see people's despair as arising from internal mechanical fault is simply incorrect, though convenient and even humane; to see it as arising from *personal* moral failing is both wrong and cruel even if it does gain a degree of plausibility through a relatively healthy reaction against the radical *impersonality* of mechanistic explanations. The persuasiveness, such as it is, of Wood's heartless book may in fact derive from an intelligent, if fairly obvious, analysis of the rank improbability of many of the more scientistic approaches to 'neurosis', but it shares with them a

*See for example the insightlessly uncompassionate view of psychological distress taken by G. Wood in his *The Myth of Neurosis*.

view that the cures as well as causes of distress lie *inside* the person.

Even psychoanalysis – perhaps one of the most honest and, at least potentially, genuinely scientific attempts to elaborate a human psychology – fails to get far beyond the notion of individual responsibility, despite recognising that people act for reasons of which they are not conscious. Implicit in the psychoanalytic understanding of the reasons for our conduct is the view that they are rooted, beyond the reach of awareness, in our personal history, but that, through the consciousness-raising procedures of analytic therapy itself, their effects may be put within the influence of our will.* One could not possibly say that this kind of view is entirely wrong, but at the same time it leaves too much out of account not to be harmfully misleading. In locating the causes of distress in individual experience, and in implying that the amelioration of distress is a task for the individual will, psychoanalysis places itself squarely with the other 'psycho-' disciplines in fostering the interests of power; it obscures the fact that what damages us above all are the injuries we cause ourselves and each other as we struggle in the net of inducements and constraints thrown over us by our interest-saturated social organisation.

It is indeed the case, as any psychotherapist well knows and as I have already had occasion to point out more than once, that people do not know why they conduct themselves as they do. Partly (as I argued at greater length in *Illusion & Reality*) this is because so much of what we do falls outside the sphere of words. The fact that we possess language gives us the mistaken idea that we can describe everything, including the reasons for our day-to-day activity, in its terms. But, of course, a great deal of what we do is unconscious in the sense that we cannot put it into a verbal form. Beyond this, however, is the fact that the

*Some analysts, however, have struggled hard to take account of the difficulties involved in this view – see in particular R. Schafer, *A New Language for Psychoanalysis*, Yale University Press, 1976.

reasons for much of what we do are not even *in principle* available to our consciousness, and it is *this* fact which our beliefs about our reasons for our conduct, and our official psychologies, are above all designed to repress: we come to feel personally to blame for social injustices which are in fact perpetrated far beyond the reach of our awareness.

Our society is constructed as a hierarchy of exploitation based on power. Its satisfactory functioning *depends upon* those lower in the hierarchy not being able to gain sight of the way their conduct is shaped by the interests of those higher in the hierarchy. At every level in this society conduct is shaped by the manipulation of interest in the relations *between* people. Society, in this way, organises itself around an unequal distribution of power through the 'sliding together' of interlocking interests. Since responsibility for this state of affairs is itself distributed, no doubt unevenly, throughout society (in the sense that we all contribute to it), and since there is no *necessary* correlation of interestedness with awareness, the blueprint for social organisation is not to be found in any person's head, nor in the heads of any group of people (though it may well be true that it is likely to be more available for articulation to those high in the hierarchy). The explanation of our conduct is thus not to be sought in a psychological analysis of individuals, but in a socio-economic, historical analysis of relations between people, and of the ways these have shaped the world we have to live in. Even in the case where an oppressor is perfectly aware of the principles whereby his or her oppression is maintained, and of what are its fruits in terms of personal gain, and even if he or she actively furthers the oppression, it would still be misleading to seek an *explanation* for it *inside* the oppressor. This is presumably why, whatever its morality, assassination is of doubtful practical value as a solution in cases of tyranny.

The imputation of blame, and also of self-blame in the form of guilt, usually arises in circumstances where a wider social view is for some reason blinkered. Where, as it so frequently is, it is in the interests of the unequal distribution of power within society to cloud this wider view, blame and guilt are likely to be actively fostered, whether directly (e.g. in the form of political vilification) or indirectly (e.g. in institutional forms of individualising 'treatment').

It is often hard to see how these processes – of blame and guilt – operate within one's own experience. One tends to be caught up totally in blaming or feeling guilty, and it is frequently difficult to see how any other reaction could be more appropriate. Occasionally, however, perhaps even in the most trivial of situations, the blinkers slip a little, and one does indeed catch a glimpse of the wider view. I have not found it easy to think of examples, but perhaps the two following will do.

It has usually been part of my car-driving experience that in congested traffic conditions a certain, fairly high, percentage of drivers can be relied upon to make way for one to enter or leave a dense stream of traffic which otherwise, without their courtesy, would block one's progress for a long time. Usually, that is, someone will pause to make a gap for you to get into the stream or else to allow you to turn through or out of a stream in order, for instance, to enter a side-street. There is, however, one particular right turn I have to make on my way to work which involves turning across heavy traffic on the main road to enter a side road. The on-coming traffic through which I have to turn moves very slowly and haltingly, and all the car, bus and lorry drivers have a perfect view of my car patiently signalling its wish. It would cost none of these drivers any inconvenience or loss of time to pause to let me through, since they would be able immediately to catch up with the vehicles in front of them. And yet, absolutely consistently and day after day, they will crawl past nose-to-tail, stopping almost provocatively across the mouth of the side road, seeming nearly intentionally to block my getting into it. Drivers causing me this frustration will have been able easily to see for themselves that I have been waiting much longer than necessary to make this simple manoeuvre. Before I realised the inexorability of this phenomenon I used to fume with rage at the selfishness and lack of consideration of the on-coming drivers; every time someone eased to a halt across my bows I would mime sarcastic gratitude or perhaps even mouth a reproof. But it soon became clear that blame was not appropriate – it could not be the case that *all* these people were so brutally inconsiderate; there must be a *reason* for them to behave the way they did.

It was not until I happened to find myself in the same situation as the drivers who had so consistently frustrated me that I discovered what the reasons were. I found that their arrival at my usual turning-point is preceded by about half a mile of solid congestion, which may easily take fifteen to twenty minutes to negotiate. Though a car or two may be waiting to turn right across this agonisingly slow stream, their wait seems a relatively short one, and the roundabout ahead, which is the cause of the congestion, is tantalisingly close. When in *this* situation, the troubles of one or two would-be right turners seem as nothing when compared with *ours*!

We have, in other words, reasons for what we do, and they lie outside us. The 'selfishness' of a driver cannot be invoked as an explanatory concept out of the context of a situation in which he or she is to be found.

A woman I know whose job it is to be responsible for children in care, and who is as conscientious and concerned as anyone in this position could be, once described how she came to terms, in part at least, with her tendency to feel guilty over 'not caring enough' for her charges. She had had to go to a school open evening to discuss with the head teacher the almost total lack of progress of a twelve-year-old girl in her care. As she was waiting her turn she listened to a mother in front of her talking about the apparently very much more successful performance of her daughter. What struck my friend was the strength of this mother's *anxious concern*: clearly, she felt worried about her daughter in a way which was simply not possible for someone whose interest in a child was merely professional. She saw, in other words, that there were *reasons for* the relative indifference to 'her' children's school performance about which she had often felt guilty. Her guilt had consisted in a feeling that there was something lacking *inside her* which made it impossible to care properly for her charges, but as the result of this experience she was somewhat comforted by the realisation that such feelings depend upon the *relation between* self and world. One cannot create in oneself certain forms of feeling just because they are thought desirable; the relation between mother and child is inescapably different from that between child care officer and child, not only (and perhaps not most) because of the emotional bonds involved, but also because of the way being-a-parent is given shape by the social world in terms of the expectations, obligations, etc., it entails.

The structures of the world are experienced by us as *feelings*, and not as a series of intellectual, articulate appreciations. A parent *feels* the expectations and obligations of parenthood, and for most parents it would be both impossible and unnecessary for them to be able to 'unpack' these feelings into a verbal catalogue of their constituent parts. But we all, when placed in the appropriate situation, do experience the feelings, and because they are experienced personally, inside our own bodies, it is all too easy to form the mistaken impression that we as individuals are in some way totally responsible for them – i.e. that we are 'to blame' for them. To return for a moment to my example, because 'the system' renders her acquaintance with 'her' children inevitably intermittent and temporary, the child care officer cannot be expected to feel caring about them in the same way as a parent whose connection with and commitment to her child is expected to be life long. The extent to which we 'care' is shaped by such issues as these, and not by some capacity within us for which we are somehow individually responsible. 'Caring' is not some kind of internal faculty, possession, emotional gift, or 'skill' – it is a complex phenomenon which stretches out beyond the individual who experiences it as a feeling into a network of external significations.

Over and over again we are seduced by the intimate internality of our experience into believing that the source of that experience is also to be found inside us, or that we can alter the nature of the experience by tinkering with our 'inner' workings. The fact that this is so easy to believe is quickly seized upon by the structures of interest as a way of mercilessly exploiting the world while leaving individuals preoccupied with personal guilt over the damage done: that huge proportion of humanity, for example, which must *inevitably* suffer privation if the powerful minority are to achieve 'happiness', may quite easily be led to feel that its miseries are caused not by the necessary consequences of social injustice, but by the personal failings of its members.

My unhappiness seems to stem from inside myself because that is where I *feel* it. Does it not therefore seem reasonable to suggest that it will best be alleviated through working on the internal feelings? This is a fundamental assumption of Western culture and yet it is as sensible as looking for (and trying to change) the details of a picture in the camera that took it. We are so conditioned to accept this 'therapeutic assumption' (that unhappiness, or 'dysfunction', is to be 'cured' within the individuals who experience it) that to question it may earn one relegation to the lunatic fringe. Those who have, as for example Ivan Illich,★ questioned the effectiveness as well as the rationality of a high technology medicine which attempts to 'cure' the world's ravages on our bodies merely by patching up the bodies themselves, have barely managed to obtain a hearing because it seems so 'obvious' that illness and disease are individual matters. (It is, at the same time, quite common for people to feel personal guilt or shame over being victims of disease.)

★I. Illich, *Limits to Medicine*, Penguin Books, 1977.

Once again (and all the time) one must bear in mind that as well as being highly *plausible* (because of the way we experience our ills), the 'therapeutic assumption' is highly *convenient* because it allows us to plunder the world and exploit each other without having to be accountable for the damage we do in the process. Just as our 'memory of bliss' renders us vulnerable to the sales pitch of a society which depends for its continued viability on selling us 'happiness', so our bodily experience of pain and disease makes them only too intelligible as *individual* 'problems'; in both cases bodily experience combines with interest to mystify our understanding.*

In the case of psychological distress, the therapeutic assumption applies if anything even more powerfully than in the case of physical disease. This may in part be because *feelings* of distress or unhappiness are not seen as necessarily *bodily* things at all. Our mechanistic culture at least gives us a certain respect for the 'reality' of 'physical' entities like diseases, which we would on the whole not expect to be able to influence merely through the exercise of will or wishfulness, but when it comes to feelings, these seem to many so insubstantial as to be potentially

*It is interesting in this respect to note the reception given by the British government to the report of the Working Party on Inequalities in Health set up, also by government, in 1977. The report showed that mortality rates for almost any category of disease or accident are much higher among the less advantaged members of society, and suggested that health inequalities on this scale cannot be explained 'except by invoking material deprivation as a key concept'. This of course implies that merely treating the damage after it has been done (the therapeutic assumption) fails to touch the root causes of ill health and injury, which are more accurately identified as consequences of socio-economic exploitation. The report subsequently appeared in book form (P. Townsend and N. Davidson, eds., *Inequalities in Health*, Penguin Books, 1982), the editors noting that: 'The report was submitted to the Secretary of State in April 1980, but instead of being properly printed and published by the DHSS or HM Stationery Office, it was arranged for only 260 duplicated copies of the typescript to be publicly made available in the week of the August Bank Holiday in that year. Major organisations within the NHS, including health authorities, did not receive copies.' Such are the ways of repression!

much more amenable to quite easily conceived operations of will power or self-control ('pull yourself together!'), or failing that, wise counsel and sympathetic therapy from the experts.

In fact, however, not only are we bodies, but we are bodies within a world. Our feelings, whether of joy or sorrow, ecstasy or pain, our most seemingly abstract intellectual and spiritual appreciations and accomplishments, our most finely tuned social sensibilities, all depend to be experienced at all on our bodily location within a particular spatio-temporal context (i.e. a situation and a history). I do not mean to say that our feelings are 'nothing but' physical events, that, for example, Beethoven's Fifth Symphony could in principle (or even best) be understood as a series of demonstrable events in his brain. This kind of crude mechanistic thinking has for too long obscured our understanding of the nature of human experience and achievement, and in fact relies on dislocating the human body from the world in which it is situated, precisely in order once again to emphasise individuality rather than relatedness. But it is equally absurd to disregard our embodiedness, to-'psychologise' our experience so that it becomes dislocated and disembodied – a play of imagery upon which, it seems, we can operate with the procedures of magic and fantasy to make of ourselves anything we wish.

We experience the world through our bodily engagement with it, and our conduct is for the most part the rational product of the physical structures of our bodies on the one hand and the social structures and exigencies of the world on the other. We can, it is true, *pretend* that the world is not as it is, and that our experience of it, especially when painful, is other than what we feel, and it may be (which was my theme in *Illusion & Reality*) that such pretence may become the norm, but in fact we cannot *escape* our suffering. However much we mystify our understanding and deceive ourselves about the meaning of our experience, there is in the last analysis absolutely no way in which we can avoid the consequences of being bodies within a world, and of knowing (even if we cannot say) what it is like to be such. It is this fundamental knowledge, the irreducible knowledge of the embodied subject, which affords us membership of a human community; however hard we may struggle to differentiate ourselves from our fellows, to render ourselves invulnerable to the terrible threats that human society creates, we can never really obliterate a knowledge of the truth of our situation, since it is given to us all in exactly the same way. However ingeniously we may play with words, seek to create objectivities on the one hand or relativities and perspectives on the other, we all know what it is like to feel cold, just as we bleed if you prick us. The 'truth', such as it is, of our situation lies, then, not in the discovery of some absolute reality beyond ourselves, nor in the constructions of our infinite ability to dream alternative worlds, but in the experience of the inescapable relation between our bodies and the context which envelops them.

Having for some years now watched, as attentively as I am able, people (including myself) struggling to feel and act differently from how they do feel and act, I am convinced that feeling and acting are far from being matters of will,★ but are, as it were, held in place by the situation in which people find themselves – unless, that is, the person is in some way impelled to act contrary to reason. This is not to say that people's conduct is *determined* by their environment, but rather that they conduct themselves the way they do for good reasons. Determinism fails when applied to human conduct not so much because it is wrong as because it is logically inappropriate when applied to conscious beings: there is no conceivable situation in which human beings could have full knowledge of their circumstances and yet still be completely determined by them, and for this reason determinism becomes of no further relevance to psychology. On the other hand, this does not mean that we are free to do what we like or to feel what we want or

★See in this respect L. H. Farber's wise little book, *Lying, Despair, Jealousy, Envy, Sex, Suicide, Drugs, and the Good Life*, Basic Books, 1976.

think we ought to feel. We act and feel *rationally* according to our circumstances, and indeed our interests. To say that we act rationally is not to say that we act necessarily correctly or sensibly, but simply that we have reasons for what we do which follow from our experience of the world and our bodily relation to it.

The 'New Right' provides a good example of the kind of moralism which makes use of the implausibility of mechanist determinism to instil in its victims a sense of guilt (self-blame) for their predicament, for it seems that if we are not *determined* by our environment to 'behave' the way we do, we must be *held responsible* for our 'freely' chosen responses to our world. But how 'free' people are to choose depends upon the range of choices open to them. My experience of people in psychological distress is that the combination of their history and their personal circumstances leaves them little reasonable alternative but to be distressed, just as if you let a naked man loose in the middle of the countryside in January he will be liable to feel cold, however 'free' he may in theory be to seek the equatorial sun or to imagine himself wrapped in a blanket before a blazing fire. In this way, the New Right uses banalised versions of eternal verities ('the freedom of the human spirit', etc.) to disguise a concerted and brutal attack precisely on what freedom people have by undermining the very grounds upon which they can rationally exercise it. To erode people's financial security, to limit their access to ideas and education, to impoverish their environments, swamp their consciousness with gutter propaganda and stupefy it with televisual soporifics, to constrain their protest through abuse of the law and its enforcement, and *then* to tell them to stand on their own two feet quite clearly constitutes cruel and cynical mystification. *Of course*, all things being equal, a person can be said to 'choose' those courses of action which he or she actually takes, but if the grounds upon which those choices are made are grossly skewed or distorted, he or she can scarcely be *blamed* for the direction taken. If apples cost five pence a pound and oranges five pounds, my choice of the former is neither forced by any mysterious process of determinism nor attributable to any particular moral quality I may possess – it is, even if highly predictable, merely rational.

Those people who, through their experience or expression of pain or confusion, fall into the arms of the 'helping professions', perhaps becoming psychiatrically diagnosed as psychotic or neurotic or 'inadequate personalities', have in my experience almost all arrived at their predicament through an entirely comprehensible, rational and (of course with hindsight) predictable process. If you run over a pea with a steam roller you don't blame the pea for what happens to it, nor, sensibly, do you treat its injuries as some kind of shortcoming inherent in its internal structure, whether inherited or acquired. Similarly, if you place the (literally) unimaginably sensitive organisms which human babies are in the kind of social and environmental machinery which we seem to be bent on 'perfecting', it can be of no real surprise that so many of them end up, as adults, as lost, bemused, miserable and crazy as they do. The only surprise, perhaps, is that so many pass as 'normal'.

The understanding which psychotherapists reach of the difficulties and unhappiness of their patients is unlikely to reveal any kind of absolute psychological 'laws', or any *necessarily* fundamental psychological 'problems'; what we find will depend as much upon the times we live in as upon any basic 'facts' about 'human nature'. It might well be, for example, that a psychological consultant to a closed and egalitarian order of peace-loving and scholarly monks would find himself focused upon issues of a quite different order from those facing the contemporary secular therapist – perhaps, for example, in that situation questions concerning the operation of the will would become paramount. In our situation, however, what can no longer be ignored, it seems to me, is the extent to which people are inevitably and in fact quite transparently damaged by the kinds of life which they cannot but be expected to 'choose' to lead. None of us, rationally, can escape the pursuit of happiness, nor the meshes of the net of interests through which we pursue it. What damages us are not our individual faults or shortcomings, but the instruments through which we wreak our inhumanity upon each other. We use our 'official' conceptualisations of the 'causes' of 'behaviour' to blind ourselves to – to repress – our involvement in a process of mutual exploitation and injury which serves the interests of a hierarchy of power.

In many respects the 'therapeutic assumption' constitutes an attempt to replace values of justice and equality (which make social demands upon us and place limits upon the extent to which we may indulge ourselves as individuals) with a reassurance that whatever harm the pursuit of happiness and self-interest may inflict can easily be put right. Furthermore, so deep within us is the therapeutic assumption established that even when a case for greater social justice and mutual care and compassion is conceded, we are still apt to say: 'That's all very well in the long term, but in the short term there are still all these inadequate and unhappy people who, damaged by the system though they may be, must still have something *done* about them.' In other words: 'Though therapy may not be the ultimate answer, we still need therapy.' We find it virtually impossible to *abandon* the idea of therapy, to contemplate *seriously* the possibility that in fact therapy may *really not work*. It is not just that such a possibility is seen as empirically unlikely: to voice it is liable to be taken by many as a kind of offence, if not against decency, then against fundamentally sane, rational discourse. And yet I think it may be true.

Even in my own reflections about patients I have known very intimately, I find it difficult to acknowledge that the circumstances which seem to attend real improvements in their 'condition' are the kind of thing which really *ought* to count as 'cure' – i.e. changes in the structure of their world such as job improvements, better housing, alterations in their personal relations (this, however, with provisos to be inferred from the discussion in Chapter Six). I still, in other words, find it hard to shake off a conviction that there ought to be some kind of 'pure' therapeutic change which stems directly and solely from the processes of therapy itself. I feel guilty that I cannot make magic.

But, like everyone else, my patients feel and act the way they do because they are bodies in a world, and only in so far as 'therapy' can affect *that* relation can it be of any help. On the whole, it is of much less help than almost any of us can bear to think. That is not necessarily quite such a bad thing as it sounds, for if therapy were as effective as we would like it to be – if the relation of the body with the world were so easily manipulated human life would quickly be rendered almost entirely trivial. To gain a deeper understanding of these issues we need, I think, to examine the processes of 'change'.

CHAPTER FIVE

Change: The Limits of Therapy

Psychotherapists have always had the greatest difficulty in demonstrating that their activities actually lead to anything remotely resembling a 'cure' of the 'conditions' presented by the patients who consult them. The focus of this book is not psychotherapy, and it is not my intention to try to deal exhaustively with the question of the usefulness or otherwise of the therapeutic enterprise as a whole; rather, I want to use the experience of therapy and therapists to examine the processes whereby people change. For nowhere do people try harder to change than in psychotherapy, and few people can have put more effort into trying to get other people to change than have psychotherapists.

There can, surely, be very few people who do not at some time in their lives want to change either the way they feel (because they feel distressed or unhappy) or the way they act (because alternative courses of action would be practically or morally preferable). But the possibility of change is not just important as a way of making life more pleasant, it seems also that flexible modification of characteristic forms of conduct will be necessary if people are to bring to bear an influence on the world. If we are to understand, and perhaps even give some deliberate direction to the way the social world evolves, we shall need to gain some kind of articulate idea of the ways in which people may change and how these may be facilitated. I do not believe that the kind of people who consult psychotherapists are particularly unusual, nor that the kinds of 'problems' they have are any different from anyone else's. Differences between the kinds of emotional pain and distress people feel, and whether or not they experience them through 'symptoms', are matters of degree rather than of kind. For these reasons, what one learns from the observation of people trying to change through psychotherapy almost certainly has, I believe, more general relevance. I suspect also that it is in the various ideas about change which psychotherapists have developed that the most 'sophisticated' psychological concepts concerning the processes of change in our culture are to be found. As will become apparent, this, I think, is not saying very much about the levels of sophistication psychologists have achieved in this respect.

There is a truly huge literature bearing upon research into the outcome of psychotherapy. For obvious reasons, it is very much in the interests of therapists to show that their procedures 'work', and most satisfactory of all would be if they could be shown to work straightforwardly as 'cures' in the way that we commonly conceive of cure in the field of physical medicine. However, as I have indicated, despite their best efforts psychologists and psychotherapists have been able to demonstrate no such simple achievement. Carrying out research in this field is by no means easy, and the complexities of research methodology are often cited as the main reason why results have not been encouraging, but few of those familiar with the literature could in good faith deny that therapeutic approaches have failed to live up to the hope once invested in them as 'cures'. Interestingly, this has not led to a lessening of therapeutic activity, nor, I think, to a lowering of expectations of therapy on the part of patients. Most therapists now agree that the 'does it work' question is far too oversimplified to allow of a sensible answer, and have become preoccupied instead with research into the *processes* of psychotherapy rather than its outcome, in the hope that a more intricate understanding of the kinds of events which take place in the 'therapeutic relationship' will lead to the formulation of more considered and sophisticated questions about change.

It is not my purpose here simply to attack or condemn psychotherapy as a means of offering help to people, but rather to indicate that the *kind* of help it offers cannot accurately be seen as one constituting a technology of change. I have no doubt at all that psychotherapy has a valid role to play within our society, but if we are to gain a clear idea of what is its value and what should be its place, and if, more importantly for present purposes, we are to understand better the processes whereby people actually do change, we need to absorb a little more honestly the lessons taught by the experience of psychotherapy, and question much more rigorously the grounds upon which we hold so tenaciously to the 'therapeutic assumption'. Most therapists, I suspect, have been rather traumatised by the research literature: the lack of hard evidence that any form of therapy really 'does any good' in the way that it is supposed to is something to set the seeds of panic sprouting in those who can see no obvious alternative way of making a living. Hence, the attempt by and large has been to explain this kind of evidence away rather than take it seriously and reflect on its significance. To do precisely this, however – to take it seriously – might lead to a considerable advance in our psychological understanding, and would not necessarily invalidate therapeutic activity itself, since therapy may have other uses than trying to change the way people are.

My own experience certainly accords with the findings of the research literature. What is striking, and at times even surprising, is precisely the extent to which patients do not change. This is not to say that people – whether 'patients' or not – do not change at all, but that, as I have already suggested, they do not change in the way and for the reasons that one might, on the basis of the best informed psychological 'knowledge', expect them to. This, I think, is because, in relation to change, the assumptions of both practical psychotherapy and the theoretical psychology it is based upon are almost entirely misleading, and entrenched in our thinking so deeply that we cannot make use of our actual experience of therapy in order to revise them. We insist that people must change in the ways we expect them to, rather than learning and intellectually elaborating the ways in which they actually do change. We are caught up in a psychological mythology which is designed to support our dreams of how we would like to be (and the structures of interest which maintain them) rather than developing a psychological science which takes serious account of what it finds. The practical upshot of our error is to persist in the construction of an ineffective and ultimately damaging psychological technology, rather than taking account in our moral conduct toward one another of the relative permanence of the damage we can inflict, and trying to avoid it.

There are, I think, three main strands to be identified in the accounts theorists of psychotherapy have put forward of the basic factors involved in change. These suggest that psychotherapeutic change may be brought about through the operation of (a) insight, (b) learning, and (c) love. The first two of these strands rest in essence on technological values, the third (far less widely represented) on a 'humanistic' view of the curative powers of relationship. In the actual practice (as opposed to the theoretical creed) of almost any kind of psychotherapy, one is likely to find all three of these strands at work, though in different proportions. The belief that they should 'work' in the sense of bringing about change owes much to the tradition of magic from which, as I suggested in Chapter Three, they may be traced.

The value of insight as a vehicle of change purely in itself is certainly less readily accepted by most thoughtful psychotherapists than it used to be, and yet many still work very hard to try to get their patients to achieve it, and I know from my own experience how difficult it is to overcome the frustration one feels when people at last come to see why they act and feel the way they do, and yet *still* persist in carrying on as before. There is a natural inclination, embedded as we are in a technological culture, for us to assume that we only need to know what the trouble is to be able to put it right – the greatest challenge appears to lie in the making of an accurate diagnosis. Patients, certainly, are frequently convinced that if only they can once discover what 'it' is which is troubling them it will be a simple matter to take the appropriate steps to recovery. Most of us in everyday life also probably subscribe to a tacit belief that a causal understanding of any particular emotional or 'relationship problem' leads more or less automatically to a prescription for effective adjustment.

Some of the early literature on psychoanalysis testifies to an enthusiastic confidence in the power of insight simply to evaporate so-called neurotic 'symptoms' – once the patient accepted that, say, her functional paralysis was related to an infantile wish to sleep with her father, it would simply disappear. Whether or not such spectacular cures were then achieved, they are certainly hard to come by now, and most therapists today recognise that knowledge of the history of a 'problem' is not of itself sufficient to make it go away. Hence the importance of learning. Even if you know very well why you act and react in the way that you do, you still, in order to change, have to *learn* to act differently.

I have no doubt that learning is indeed the single most fundamentally important factor in the kind of self-initiated change which psychotherapy seeks to achieve, and yet, because of their need to justify their activity in terms of a *technical* rhetoric (which in turn contains a still compelling appeal to magic) therapists have handled the concept of learning very badly. For the most part, they have cast the processes of learning in almost entirely mechanistic categories, and have thus reinterpreted them in terms of training or conditioning. In this way, it is expected that 'faulty responses' may, through an appropriate course of training designed, naturally, by therapists who are experts in the relevant 'laws', be replaced by more 'adaptive' ones. There are many varieties of mechanist vocabulary in which this fundamental idea is expressed, and it would be unnecessarily tedious for me to attempt to outline them here, but they all add up to more or less the same thing. At the present time, the most widespread version of human beings as 'learning machines', and one which has penetrated deep into popular culture, is that which characterises people as bundles of 'skills' whose acquisition is, for the most part, a matter of obtaining the necessary training from the appropriate experts.

Virtually any competence or ability which can be named, including those which involve our dealings with others, comes to be broken down into some more or less plausible combination of 'skills'. Thus we have 'interpersonal skills' and 'social skills' along with 'language skills' and 'footballing skills'. There is, of course, something immensely reassuring about a 'skills' model of human activity: for those needing to acquire some, it becomes merely a matter of getting the right input from a relevant training source, and for those whose job it is to purvey knowledge the whole matter of teaching and learning becomes a relatively simple one of 'skills transmission'. In this way training, or learning, becomes conceived of as in principle no more complicated than popping a program into a computer. Programs may be popped in or out, erased or replaced, according to whatever skills you or your trainers may consider it desirable for you to have at any particular time.

Despite the fact that there is a very deliberate and extremely heavy investment within 'official' psychology in the people-as-computers model of psychological functioning, it seems to me that the propensity of ordinary people to consider themselves as programmable vehicles of skills has developed alongside rather than as the result of any campaign on the experts' part to popularise such a view. Quite why this should be so is unclear, but it is striking how readily, and with what an unselfconsciously smug satisfaction, people talk about the skills they 'have' or intend to 'polish up', etc. Suddenly, and quite without noticing it, we appear to have entered a world in which people can talk without absurdity of, for instance, going on a course to 'acquire management skills', and having been on it, can in all seriousness and in the correct anticipation of being 'credible', list their mere attendance at the course on their CVs as *evidence* of their acquisition of the skills in question. There is here, it seems, an interlocking of the interests of trainers and learners, in a society where there is in fact not enough of importance to train or learn, such that both subscribe, symbiotically as it were, to an illusion. In an economy which depends upon the highly artificial production and consumption of worthless tokens of 'happiness' (and in particular upon the 'management' of such production and consumption), it is precisely because there is to be found no real appreciation of skill at anything that we are able to convince each other that we are the proud possessors of such a variety of 'skills'. Because our society has drifted so far from preserving and encouraging in its members activities of any real meaning or value, we collude in a kind of collective fantasy of achievement and ability.

In psychotherapy likewise, though not perhaps always quite so crassly, the assumption is that 'learning to be different', though not necessarily easy, involves an erasure or replacement of experience, as though, again, experience were acquired in the manner of tape-recording. In this way, therapists, and indeed their patients, may expect that through facing up to 'problems' or practising new 'responses' to old 'stimuli', patients' 'maladaptive behaviour' and the experience which maintamed it will be wiped out. This mechanistic approach to learning, though certainly it is not without some therapeutic value, is much too simplistic, and in my view grossly underestimates the enormous *difficulty* of change. The difficulty is, of course, that we are not computers, and our conduct is not the result of any kind of erasable programming. This is a point to which I shall return shortly.

Implicit in some currently quite influential varieties of psychotherapy (so-called 'cognitive' therapies) is a kind of combination of 'insight' and 'learning' assumptions which results in the view that psychological or emotional distress is best dealt with by learning to take an alternative view of things. This really amounts to nothing more than a variant on the maxim 'look on the bright side', and since I have dealt with its inadequacies at some length in *Illusion & Reality* I shall not go into greater detail now. Here again, however, what seems to be suggested is that people's distress is generated from a program somehow buried inside their heads, that what matters is the way they see things rather than the way things are.

The failure of attempts based on the operation of insight and learning to change 'behaviour' and alleviate distress in any consistently demonstrable way, despite the often plausible claims made and the plethora of techniques spawned by the various therapeutic schools, has led some therapists to pass beyond a purely technical view of change to consider the significance of the personal relationship between patient and therapist.

There is little doubt, I think, that the personal influence of therapist on patient, and indeed of patient on therapist, is a highly potent factor in nearly all forms of psychotherapy, whether theoretically acknowledged or not. There could be no more superfluous statement of the obvious than that, in all kinds of relationship and in all kinds of spheres, people are profoundly affected by other people. Psychotherapy is no exception, and there has always been a significant minority of psychotherapists who have insisted on making the personal relationship between therapist and patient central to an understanding of therapeutic help.* There can be very few psychotherapists who have failed to notice the importance patients attach to their opinion of them and the extent to which people may blossom under and

*Valuable accounts of this kind have more recently been given by Peter Lomas, *The Case for a Personal Psychotherapy*, Oxford University Press, 1981, and R. F. Hobson, *Forms of Feeling. The Heart of Psychotherapy*, Tavistock Publictions, 1985. See also my *Psychotherapy: A Personal Approach*.

draw courage from the 'positive regard', as Carl Rogers called it, of the therapist. Even Freud (who is not usually credited with obvious 'humanistic' tendencies), in his study of the 'rat man' betrays an awareness of the effect on his patient of an expression of warmth: 'In this connection I said a word or two upon the good opinion I had formed of him, and this gave him visible pleasure'.*

Some writers on psychotherapy† have overcome professional reticence sufficiently to be able to suggest that it is essentially the power of love that lies behind therapeutic potency, but while I would certainly not want to quarrel with the view that patients are indeed moved by therapists' affection and concern, and that their self-confidence may be greatly boosted and their resolve to tackle their difficulties strengthened, the degree to which ultimately they do move is still often disappointing. I must say again that I do not by this mean to belittle the value of therapeutic love, but only to suggest what should be the limits of the claim it makes. I have no wish to deny that in some sense or other – perhaps in many senses – psychotherapy may be 'good for' people, but I do wish to question how far it *changes* them, and further, I wish strongly to cast doubt on any assumption that it 'cures' them.

It is a very frequent experience that patients who have felt quite seriously disturbed for months or even years may feel an enormous sense of relief and improvement following their first consultation with a sensitive and attentive psychotherapist. For a few days their troubles seem to fall away as if by magic. But this state, sadly, does not last for long: the initial relief at finding a sympathetic ear, the surge of joy at feeling less alone, quickly recede as the world closes in again and the features of it which were causing the distress in the first place reassert their claims. Of course, in one's battles with the world, it helps to find an

*S. Freud, 'Notes upon a case of obsessional neurosis'. Pelican Freud Library, vol. 9.

†See for example I. D. Suttie, op. cit.

intelligent, experienced, wise and loving ally, and those adequately provided with such (especially early in their lives) will never need a psychotherapist. But allies of this calibre are, in the present-day world, in desperately short supply, and if you need one badly enough the chances are you will have to pay for one.

For all the technical mystique psychotherapists have managed to erect around themselves, for all the reverential awe in which they have, sometimes rather sentimentally, managed to intone their rhetoric of love, for all, even, the draining and dedicated effort they put into what is often a very demanding job, they are still but weakly allies. Unlike (in ideal circumstances) family or friends, therapists play an only temporary role in the lives of almost all their patients, and their commitment to help is strictly limited in terms of their actual involvement in patients' lives (were this not so, the job would become demanding beyond endurance). To talk of love in these circumstances is to edge close to hypocrisy, and indeed I strongly suspect that the efficacy of therapeutic love is strictly proportional to the real commitment of therapists to their patients. Though in almost all ways the comparison is far from fair, it is nevertheless not totally irrelevant in this respect to point to the worlds of difference there are between the late Mother Teresa of Calcutta and the average Hampstead psychoanalyst (and the supposed technical expertise of the latter in no way matches in therapeutic potency the commitment of the former).

Therapeutic love may, I think, most accurately be seen as a convenient, and infinitely less effective, substitute for the real thing. Therapists are liable quite happily to talk of 'corrective emotional relationships', of patients reliving, and somehow exorcising the traumata of their infancy under their therapists' soothing tutelage, and though such talk is, I am sure, uttered with complete sincerity and in the best of faith, I think the time has come for us to acknowledge that there is really not a shred of convincing evidence to support it, and nor would one expect there to be. On the question of 'cure', not all psychotherapists are as confident as I may have seemed to suggest. Roy Schafer, for instance, comes very close to the position I am adopting here:

> . . . while the past may be partially re-experienced, reviewed, and altered through reinterpretation, it cannot be replaced: a truly cold mother, a savage or seductive father, a dead sibling, the consequences of a predominant repressed fantasy, years of stunted growth and emotional withdrawal, and so forth, cannot be wiped out by analysis, even though their hampering and painful effects may be greatly mitigated, and the analysand freed to make another, partly different and more successful try at adaptation. The analysand whose analysis has been benignly influential retains apprehensions, vulnerability, and characteristic inclinations toward certain infantile, self-crippling solutions, however reduced these may be in influence and however counterbalanced by strength-ened adaptiveness.★

But nestling innocently even in this far from over-optimistic text is the view that patients may be 'freed' from a past which is (magically) alterable through reinterpretation, and once again we see the therapeutic assumption refusing in the end to relax its grip.

For while therapy may be or achieve all kinds of things – it may be comforting, encouraging, inspiring, healing of hurt – one thing it cannot do is free people from their past, because people are not computers with programs which can simply be removed and replaced.

Not only are people extremely resistant to the kind of change which we see as the hoped-for result of therapeutic 'adaptation', but it is highly undesirable that they should be anything else.

★*A New Language for Psychoanalysis*, op. cit.

Only if one unquestioningly accepts an individualistic view that all that matters is the personal happiness people manage to achieve in a particular lifetime can one feel anything but nervous about the prospect of a really effective technology of change. It is, after all, far from obvious that we yet know what form of society is truly good for us, and if there is to be a sufficient range of conduct and experience within humanity to ensure a future which makes possible the evolution of a *variety* of (at present unknowable) social developments, it is important that *particular* lines of experience and conduct are pursued doggedly, not only throughout individuals' lives, but from one generation to the next. If we really were as easily alterable as many therapeutic systems (as well as other more sinister techniques of change) would have us believe, there can be little doubt that a politically dominant power group would quickly establish those norms of 'personality' and 'behaviour' which best served its interests.

This, of course, is exactly what politically dominant power groups already try to do (and not without a degree of success) but they do it by standardising the environment, not people. In this respect, the modern state which attempts to control people through a standardisation of their environment, shows a more sophisticated understanding of 'what makes people tick' than do professional therapists who focus their attentions on what is inside people's heads. In this way, a standardised, uniform 'psychology' is likely to be established much more easily by controlling what goes into people's heads than by trying to alter it once it has got there. Television is a much more powerful means of ensuring uniformity of belief than was the Inquisition, and the mentality which invented factory farming is not slow to appreciate the regularity and predictability to be achieved by standardising experiential as well as nutritional diet. Used to it though one is, it is still quite an eerie experience to walk round any residential suburb after dark and to note the extent to which people are imbibing exactly the same impressions and information from the glowing screens; one only has to check the evening's programme to know what people will be talking about the next morning.

To try to alter people's experience after they have acquired it is a bit like trying to control the weight of battery chickens by surgery – in fact the latter would be by far the easier task. The fact is that people are organisms and their experience is acquired organically, and so deeply and inextricably bound up is it with the very structures of the body that erasure of the experience would entail destruction of the organism. We cannot, like magnetic tape, be wiped clean of our history, which is, on the contrary, acquired as are the growth rings of a tree. Our history, the knowledge we have built up of the world, is our physical, organic structure. Body and mind are not just inseparable, they are one and the same.

It is certainly an expectation of our therapeutic culture that somehow our painful experience can be eradicated, or at least that the misery we feel in the present can somehow be wiped away to leave us with a 'clean slate' on which to start to chalk up a new and more promising future. Only an entirely unreflective ideology of mechanism allows us to think in this way and to shut our eyes to the obvious fact that our present feelings and perceptions have a history which is, as it were, deeply and ineradicably inscribed upon our bodies. In clinging on to a therapeutic illusion, we exempt those aspects of our conduct and experience we would like magically to change from rules of common sense which we would think it close to madness not to apply in other, related areas. Our ability to construct a social world at all depends on our being able correctly to anticipate a high degree of regularity and predictability in the character and conduct of other people. It is in many ways important that leopards should not be able to change their spots, and it is certainly our experience that they do not. Nor do any of us expect to be able to change as the result of any kind of 'therapeutic' intervention the way we speak, or move, or argue, think, interpret, react, and we pursue our aims, enact our abilities and competences, speak languages and ride bicycles without expecting ever to be 'cured' of doing so. It is not, of course, that there is no possibility of our being able to learn new and different ways of doing things, but in learning of this kind we anticipate the *difficulty* involved in a way which is less characteristic of our therapeutic aspirations, and we also know that what we learn does not expunge (again, in the manner of magnetic tape) what was there before.

Over and over again the rooted, organic nature of our experience has been misinterpreted as indicative of some form of malfunction or maladjustment. If people do not operate in a *mechanically* adaptable way in relation to some particular set of circumstances defined (usually by a professional group) as ideal, they are seen as somehow resistant or faulty, for example as demonstrating 'transference neurosis', 'inappropriate conditioning', etc. However, a person is not formed by what goes on physically or psychologically inside his or her own skin, but from a highly permeable relation with a context – the world in which we are situated flows into us and we into it in a way which makes us inseparable from it, and which is indelibly recorded in our history. This is the basis of the importance to human beings of familiarity; we make sense of and struggle with and grow from our roots in whatever world we happen to be, and to have been, located. You will not want to exchange your Belfast back street for a desert island paradise not because you are crazy or stupid, but because your experience is inseparable from the one and irrelevant to the other. We can only deal with what we know. If you suspect that all men are bullying tyrants as your father was, this is not so much a mistake you are making as a particular, and quite valid, form of knowledge you are not merely unwilling, but, as it were, organically unable to abandon. Our bodies make sure that we do not forget the lessons of our past. I do not want to say that people are incapable of developing or modifying experience as they go through life, but that such development or modification must fit in with and grow out of what has gone before – it must be organic. People *grow* from one position to the next, they cannot be *switched*. Our experience is hard won, built into our living tissue, and it should be respected rather than measured disparagingly against a set of professional norms of 'adjustment' or 'mental health'.

Unhappily for those who place their hopes in therapy, the lessons of our exposure to pain, deprivation, injustice and misfortune, are registered as indelibly on our bodies as are those of love, security and nurturance, and indeed as are those practical acquisitions (like learning a mother tongue or being able to swim) which we tend to take for granted. There is no difference in terms of the quality of the knowledge itself between what an insecure and anxious person *knows* about the world in terms of its brutality and unpredictability, and what a secure and confident person knows about its potentialities for affection and achievement. There is no reason at all why one should consider the one person's experience and expectations 'pathological' and the other's 'adjusted', except of course that a confusion of social with *quasi*-medical values makes it much easier to ignore the harm we do each other and to establish a uniform view that any casualties which may occur in what purports to be a fundamentally benign society are solely the result of individual 'dysfunction', inappropriate 'projection', and so on.

It is, of course, against the interests of a hierarchy of power which depends on exploitation for people to recognise that the distress or despair they feel stems from their bodily relatedness to a noxious world, since any such recognition, should it occur on a wide enough scale, would quickly lead to demands for social change. In view of this one must note again that, paradoxically, the fact that people are so resistant to therapeutic change has a positive value: even if a kind of uniformity and docility can be imposed through the unification of experience (as through television) the actual suffering caused by the injustices and inequalities of our society cannot easily be concealed under a blanket of therapy. People cannot but register what happens to them, and they cannot but spend their lives following out its significance. In some respects, then, we are less easily turned into battery chickens than one might fear. I do not, of course, wish to suggest that suffering is a good thing, only that perhaps it is good that mystification of the reasons for it may still meet with considerable resistance.

However, though therapy does not 'work' in the way that we would like it to, it is still difficult to cast doubt upon its efficacy without appearing to be cruel. To say that a person's distress arises, at least in so far as it is historically rooted, out of ineradicable experience seems to be close to condemning him or her to a lifetime of unhappiness; after all, our society runs on the expectation that, in principle at least, happiness is attainable for all. In fact, however, it is my experience that more often than not people meet the 'truth' of their predicament with relief, and that what is most painful to deal with is not the difficulty – even tragedy – of our situation, but the tantalising but empty promise of its betterment or 'cure'. I have often been, and I am sure shall continue to be, amazed at the fortitude and resilience of people who discover that what they thought was a curable illness is in fact the outcome of an unalterable history and (usually) a highly inimical set of circumstances which may be desperately hard if not impossible to influence. Most people are *glad* to be rid of the mystification which prevented them from understanding and getting to grips with, often, appallingly difficult features of their past and present, and enormously relieved if they find someone who will share with them an unflinching view of cruelties and injustices whose marks they will always bear.

The errors of our mechanised and wishful view of ourselves are very often more damaging than the injuries they are designed to conceal. It is on the face of it paradoxical that a culture which so much stresses individuality for the purposes of promoting 'happiness' and instilling blame, should at the same time, through the imposition of uniformity and the standardisation of 'normality', make it so difficult for people to accept and allow for the uniqueness of their experience. For example, because, in a standardised society, we not unreasonably take our own experience as the standard for all, we tend to have a tacit expectation that we should be instantly 'understandable' by others. If, then, you do not 'understand' me, it must be because of some unusual obtuseness or quirk of personality on your part. We have very little tolerance for the differences there are between us, the differences which, presumably, stem from the organic relation of each of us with varying sets of circumstances. Many people, indeed, live their lives in a kind of perpetually terrified comparison with a non-existent norm. Thus people may spend a lifetime trying to achieve an objective standard (as human being) which in fact does not exist at all, and in so doing by-pass, discount or try to invalidate their own subjective experience. But subjective experience is inescapably rendered by one's embodiment in a world, and the attempt to replace it with some form of normative, 'objective' ideal is likely to result in either a kind of mad artificiality or else torments of confusion and despair.

If therapy cannot cure our distress it can, in some cases at least, clear our confusion, and once this has been achieved it may be possible for some people to engage with the world, or to change their situation within it, in a way which leads to its impinging upon them less painfully. For a small proportion of articulate and socio-economically advantaged people, it may even be that psychotherapy has value as an insight-giving procedure enabling them to see and act upon idiosyncrasies of their history or mistakes of interpretation about the significance of factors in their past or present circumstances. But therapeutic benefit of this kind arises only because such people have *available* to them (not *inside* them) the freedom to do something about their lives. If this is so it is, I think, of very little general relevance, if only because people in difficulties of this kind are very likely eventually to work them out and put them right for themselves.

For the vast majority of people who are driven to despair (whether they know it or not) by the nature of our society, the means of rectification of their predicament are usually beyond their own resources. One should not because of this underestimate the value psychotherapy might have as a means of clarifying their situation and offering comfort in their contemplation of it, but nor should one overestimate its ability to change them. As far as change is possible, it is likely to be achieved only with great difficulty. We have been misled by our metaphor of mechanical change to ignore almost totally the difficulties inherent in organic change and to overlook the extent to which its possibilities are limited by both the environment and the bodily history in which we are organically rooted. Perhaps we can, with painful effort, learn to do differently some things which we learned to do unproductively or self-destructively, but we would be foolish to overlook the influence of the world around us.

We would do better to see ourselves as plants rather than as machines, and we might benefit from applying to our own lives some very elementary rules of horticulture. Any kind of treatment for plants which consisted solely of attempting alterations to their internal structure would be unlikely to recommend itself to gardeners. Plants grow best in well-understood and carefully prepared conditions − of sun or shade, damp or dryness, heat or cold, in this or that kind of soil. A plant which grows poorly or mis-shapenly may well be improved through careful attention to its environment, provision of light or water, but it will still bear the scars of an inauspicious beginning. I do not want to overwork the analogy, but it does seem strange to me that we should often lavish so much more attention on our gardens than on our fellow beings and our progeny. Nobody expects their cauliflowers to grow by magic.

The alternative to reliance on a technology of change is the cultivation of a society which takes care of its members. If we cannot cure the damage we have done we can try to mitigate its effects on future generations, and to achieve this we have to recognise the importance of the conditions in which we live and the way we conduct ourselves towards each other.

CHAPTER SIX

'Relationships'

By far the greater part of the misery which is experienced by people in the modern world is unquestionably inflicted through human agency. It is the things we do to each other which are the immediate causes of our distress. Superficially, therefore, it might seem as though one need look no further than our 'relationships' one with another to identify, and in principle also to rectify, the origins of our unhappiness.

At no time in previous history, certainly, have 'relationships' so directly been a focus of concern and discussion as in our own time. Entire industries have grown up around our ability, or lack of ability, to attract or be pleasing to others and to enjoy what they have to offer us. Not the least important section of this market is that exploited by the therapy industry: 'interpersonal relationships' are acknowledged as the core concern of a hundred different 'schools' of therapy and counselling, and not surprisingly so, for anxious rumination about one's personal adequacy in relation to others, dread of rejection by them and frustration at lack of satisfaction in 'relationships' seem to lie at the very centre of much of our acute personal unhappiness. For most of us our 'relationships' – or at least our fantasies of how they might or ought to be – seem to constitute the very meaning of our existence: life would appear to have no point at all were it not for the promise it holds of satisfying personal relationships.

However, far from exposing or providing an understanding of the nature of our predicament, this pervasive, almost obsessive concern with 'relationships' seems to me actually itself to form a large part of what ails us. Indeed, our desperation to enjoy 'good relationships' lies behind a great deal of the damage we do each other, and constitutes much more a reflection than a critique of social values stemming from the commercialised pursuit of happiness.

The commercial process turns abstractions like 'happiness' into saleable commodities. In exactly this way, abstract relations between people have been turned into 'relationships' which are treated as the end-product of a process in which people themselves form the raw material. Thus people have become secondary to the relationships of which, interchangeably and expendably, they form a part: what matters is the 'quality of the relationship', not the characteristics or conduct, or even ultimately the welfare, of the people who form its terms.

The language we use testifies to this state of affairs quite clearly. 'My relationship is breaking up'; 'I think she's looking for a new relationship'; 'they've got a really good relationship.' The following extract from an advertisement for one company's 'double cassette twin-pack courses' puts the issue at its most vulgarly basic:

MAKE AN IMPRESSION!

This course deals with all aspects of self-presentation, whether in the workplace or in social or family life. The idea of 'self-marketing' is a major theme and situations in which the skills have an important role include:

- starting and maintaining relationships

- interview training

- self-presentation in groups

- developing closer relationships

- building better interactions at work

- handling rejection effectively

- establishing arenas for 'self-marketing'

- making and clarifying agreements with others.

This, then, is the 'arena' where people ('selves') have become caught up in a commercialised and competitive jockeying for position, in which the adequacy of 'self-presentation' will determine how satisfactory 'relationships' are, and in which the terrors of rejection may be 'handled effectively' through development of the appropriate 'skills'.

As the virtually inexhaustible supply of raw material for saleable satisfactions in the form of 'relationships', people become almost less than commodities, and this no doubt accounts for the intense and obsessive anxiety which they experience over their relations with others. Usually from bitter experience, most people know how easily dispensed with they are as those 'significant others' with whom they come into contact during their lives seek *through* them the satisfaction of their needs. At the centre of our anxiety, then, is to be found the terror that we shall simply *disappear* if we are not wanted, needed, or 'loved' by someone. Our very sense of identity and existence depends upon the gaze of someone else falling upon us – and it is noticeably with identity and existence that twentieth-century people, as well as much of their literature, art, psychology and philosophy, have been particularly preoccupied. We are objects, and as such have to be *noticed* in order to achieve full 'objectivity'. Objects exist only for others; only subjects can exist independently of the regard of 'the Other'. And, of course, we use others in precisely the way we fear they may use us – we treat them not as ends in themselves, but as means to more or less satisfactory 'relationships'. As far as you do not satisfy some aspect of my needs, you do not exist for me. In other words, if one is nobody's object one is, quite literally, nothing. The value of people thus becomes entirely utilitarian –

if they are no use to anyone, they are simply expendable. It is no longer human lives which are important, but the quality of the relationships and satisfactions to which they contribute.

Our acceptance of the expendability of people who fail to contribute to our personal happiness is perfectly obvious if one examines the content of our fantasy. In the media of popular entertainment, for example 'successful' television drama, characters are kept in existence only so long as they contribute to the sexual or material satisfaction of the protagonists. In the glossier American television series, moreover, these vehicles of gratification are completely interchangeable, conforming to a standard mould of youth and 'beauty' which, even though it makes them hard to tell apart, becomes the heartbreakingly unattainable ideal of those more normally fashioned viewers who dread being exposed as substandard. And one should not be led by the tastelessness of such fantasies as these into believing that they bear no relation to the values we really hold dear – indeed, their very popularity betrays the coarse directness of their celebration of what we have come to be interested in.

Up until very recently there seemed to be little conscious awareness among people I saw as patients (whom, again, I single out only because I know them best, not because I see them as different from the rest of us) that the injuries they occasioned and incurred in the course of their pursuit of happiness were anything other than the necessary result of failures in 'relationship'. People longed for relationships they fancied they had never had, or pined for lost relationships they feared they would never have again. They fretted and seethed over frustrating relationships they could no longer abide, they struggled with the panicky loss of identity consequent on scarcely having any relationships at all, or they tried desperately to piece themselves together after emerging from years of being the victim of punitive or destructive relationships. In nearly all cases these seemed to be 'relationship problems' arising more or less directly out of human nature itself, and the 'answer' to them seemed to lie in 'finding a good (or better) relationship'. All that was needed, so it seemed, was love.

Now there are, I think, signs of a change taking place: no longer do patients see 'the problem' quite so much as one of being on the wrong side of a split between 'good' and 'bad' relationships, but rather they begin to articulate a sense that there is something not right with the very concept of relationship itself. This feeling tends to be expressed in one of two ways: either in complaints that our relations with each other are *generally* bad and that the world has become a place of brutality and indifference from which there appears to be no haven, or in a conviction that the game of 'relating' has become no longer worth the candle, that *any* kind of relationship, good, bad or indifferent, somehow imposes an intolerable strain. I sometimes get the feeling that where not long ago people longed to be loved, they now long to be left in peace.

Whether or not this is so, and I certainly do not wish to make a major issue of it, it would not be a particularly surprising or unpredictable result of our 'commodification' of relationships, for anything one tries in this way to elevate into being the point of our lives is bound in the end to turn to dust and ashes. Just as one is bound to generate despair by trying to turn the 'epiphenomenon' of happiness into a concretely attainable commodity, so attempting to make abstract relations between people into 'marketable' sources of satisfaction is certain in the end to lead to a situation in which people are in fact treated with heartless unconcern or are experienced as objects of frustration.

Our mistake has been not to see – or to forget – that relations become established between people not as ends in themselves but in the course of doing something else. Over and over again we try to turn actions into entities, conduct into commodity, abstract into concrete, quality into quantity. This, of course, not out of wilfulness or stupidity, but because we are immersed in a society which depends for its continued functioning on the manufacture of satisfactions and the manipulation of interests.

The state of the consumer's nervous system becomes the most potent 'variable' in the selling process: if there are pleasant sensations attached to any form of activity, including activities which we pursue together (i.e. relatedly), they must be isolated, commodified and brought into the market-place. We no longer see people as there to do things with or for, but as the interchangeable terms of relationships which may be more or less satisfying. Love itself ceases to have a *function* in the moral sphere of human conduct but becomes a kind of gratification of need to be sought or even extorted from people as a good rather than striven after as a form of commitment *for the sake of* something beyond personal satisfaction.

The fate of our 'relationships' provides another example of what happens when human beings are deprived of a function in the world – when, that is, the possibilities open to people to act on their environment are, so to speak, drained out of their embodied existence and re-presented to them as mechanised commodities for their consumption. Those things which we could do together are done for us and sold back to us in the form of entertainment, spectacle or consumer goods. Our communal activities, those things which we could do in relation with each other, thus become empty, collapsed in on themselves, literally without meaning. Our relatedness is overcome by a kind of paralysing self-consciousness because it can no longer point beyond itself to any kind of purpose.

The most satisfying relationships are again probably those of which the participants are almost entirely unaware. Even though opportunities for activity giving rise to relationship of this kind have become pitifully rare, most of us have probably had the experience of doing things with someone – working, perhaps, or playing – in which the complementary abilities and contributions of the participants achieved a result which neither could possibly have managed alone, and which led, almost certainly retrospectively, to an awareness of warmth and appreciation which never needed to be mentioned. It would seem completely artificial for friends, or lovers, or spouses, suddenly to stop dead in the course of their mutual activity to comment on the quality of their relationship, and yet, more and more, this is exactly what is happening. Partly because there seems to be so little of value to do and partly because we have become objects of gratification for each other, we spend more and more time talking and thinking about our 'relationships' rather than doing anything with them. It may help in thinking about this state of affairs to consider one at a time some of those spheres of relationship which have been rendered particularly problematic by our social organisation.

FRIENDSHIP

With one or two notable exceptions – for example the American psychiatrist H. S. Sullivan – friendship is a form of relationship little discussed in the 'clinical literature' of psychology and psychiatry, though loneliness and isolation play a very prominent role in the kinds of emotional distress which drive people to seek help from the 'experts'. The ideal 'therapeutic' solution to such loneliness is often seen as the formation of a long-term sexual bond, and when most people talk of their need to establish 'a relationship' what they usually mean is an exclusive liaison with someone of the opposite sex. In this way, and with consequences I shall come to consider shortly, heterosexual pair-relationships carry a very heavy *therapeutic* load in our society: warmth, safety, fulfilment and 'understanding' are the hoped-for results of shutting yourself cosily away with your lover.

Outside this kind of exclusive, sexually based therapeutic intimacy (as it turns out, itself largely fantasy) the development of friendly relations with others appears to be problematic, particularly in the adult population. The reason for this, it seems to me, again cannot be put down to the internal characteristics of individuals, but to a social organisation which renders adult life, for most people, both competitive and aimless. We compete in 'the market' for satisfactions and empty tokens of achievement which in practice dictate that our activity has no aim beyond its own temporary satiation. It is thus impossible for the vast majority of people to find anything to do together in which they can collaborate wholeheartedly, unreflectively and constructively. Those activities around which friendships may be formed tend of necessity to be contrived leisure-time pursuits, failing which friendships must be manufactured self-consciously as ends in themselves. Apart from this, relations between people are characterised by a kind of watchful hostility as they compete with each other in the struggle to gain recognition of an artificially constructed pseudo-identity. In a world organised exclusively around commercial and material interests, the focus of concern for the individual becomes the *self* and the gratification which may follow from ministration to its appearance ('presentation of self') and its needs (the ideal of the quiescent nervous system). It is only when people are able to focus beyond themselves as objects on to a goal or aim in pursuance of which they may *lose* themselves, that they may join in collaborative, as opposed to competitive, activity with others. It is probably for this reason that the most rewarding friendships made tend to be at times of one's life, for example childhood, adolescence or (particularly perhaps for some women) young parenthood, when one finds oneself thrown together with other people in activity which is at least not completely dominated by the ethics of the market-place.

I wonder if men have particular difficulty in making friends. My experience with male patients leads me to suspect that the much-maligned characteristics of masculine insensitivity and emotional unresponsiveness are much more the consequence of spiritually mutilating economic values than of any inherently macho personality features of men themselves, or indeed of any real advantage in power or status to be gained by toughness. In fact we have all – men and women – been driven by ruthless economic competition, and by the unavoidable demands which have been placed upon us to cherish our selves, to retreat into the last embattled refuge of tenderness, i.e. sex, where undefended intimacies may, if but briefly, be exchanged. In other times and places men seem to have been no more reticent than women in expressing their (non-sexual) love for others, and my patients (and indeed nearly all the men I have got to know intimately) experience the necessity to be stereotypically male as an imposition rather than an advantage. But the hierarchy of power is held in place by occult violence, not by love, and its values must be reproduced in the individuals who are shaped to maintain it; men are its victims no less than women.

Because there is relatively so little scope for the unself-conscious generation of friendship through cooperative absorption in constructive activity, our need for friendship has often to be met artificially. For friendship, which might once have been a, so to speak, inevitable accident of social relations, an unreflected-upon bonus of communal life, has now indeed become a *need*. If the point of life is the celebration of self, one cannot do without others with whom to celebrate; if others are not there to confirm my identity, to reflect my image, I just disappear. As friends we are, then, mirrors to each other, taking turns to reflect our images back at each other, entering, for the sake of our emotional survival, a kind of cowardly pact not to break the rules by saying what we really see. Like schoolboys in a boxing match who secretly agree not to hurt each other, we nervously acquiesce in a mutual lowering of defences on condition only that we shall not criticise. This kind of fake mutuality is quite explicitly advocated in some half-baked North American forms of 'therapy', and results in some quite extraordinarily false types of 'relationship' in which the hollow exchange of reciprocal 'strokes' is quite likely to end in a burst of bitter recrimination when one of the participants can no longer stand the dishonesty and begins to tell the truth.

Increasingly, the precarious fragility of our 'self-images' and the pervasive treachery of our competitive social existence means that intimacy becomes altogether too dangerous, and as with so many other aspects of life, it slowly becomes the business of professionals to manufacture a marketable substitute for it. More and more the hazardous birth of undefended intimacy between people is seen as needing to be attended by professional midwives of some description, and people are taught the ritual 'skills' which are supposed to ensure safe and 'meaningful' relationship. In an increasingly wide range of settings – from evening classes to church congregations – lonely people are propelled into a mutually self-deceiving 'togetherness' by means of superficial 'techniques' and games (e.g. 'ice-breakers') which are claimed by their professional inventors to be the answer to our 'alienation'. Instant intimacy becomes something you can buy from your local encounter group centre.

When people have nothing other than themselves to talk about, conversations become parallel monologues in which the participants take turns to recite their likes and dislikes, complain or make confessions which (because of the 'no criticism' pact) are guaranteed a blandly tolerant hearing. Groups or congregations of people who are aware of their own or others' isolation become for want of any real activity artificially (semi-professionally) constructed round a collaborative contemplation of self, with the result that the group soon finds itself enmired in utterly futile discussions of how its members 'relate to' each other – as though 'relating' were a special and specific kind of activity which people can do.

There is something very sad and touching about our frustrated need for companionship. Though it is not a fashionable view, and is one rejected by most of those whose opinions I respect (as well as espoused by some whose opinions I do not), I do have a sneaking feeling that, given half a chance, most people would treat their fellows reasonably decently. The almost desperate love which people lavish on their dogs, for example, leads one to wonder how basic to human *nature* human cruelty is. Might it not rather be that the kinds of threat to which we respond so violently and brutally are built into our society more than into our selves? If the sheer scale of our inhumanity towards each other to which both our history and our current conduct and experience testify is to be taken as an indication of the depth of some kind of original sin or ineradicable natural trait, we might as well consign our species to an atomic oblivion forthwith. It does appear to me, though, that many of those who have been lovingly cared for care lovingly for others, and that many of those who cause pain and injury to others do so out of a kind of anguished blindness born of circumstances which they could not escape rather than of any kind of ill will or avoidable impulse. Unquestionably there is the most appalling violence built into the structure of our society (its hierarchical inequality could be maintained no other way), but the more intimately I get to know those (i.e. all of us) who are the agents of that violence, the less easy I find it to identify things *within them* to blame.

Without doubt, many of the people I have worked with who have been badly damaged through their relations with others have been or are being equally damaging to others, but from the unthreatened – and hence I think more clear-sighted – position of psychotherapist, that has not made them any harder to understand or like. For example, one watches people struggle in vain not to make their children insecure, or listens to a young couple recount with uncomprehending hopelessness how their baby died through their neglect, and all one can feel is a kind of helpless sympathy. The reasons for the violence we do each other are all too clear, but do not reside in the individual agent. This insight – common, I think, to many of those who work in the 'helping professions' even if they do not always make it explicit – is one which renders particularly repugnant the righteous indignation of those who pontificate about the state of public morality, and utterly disgusting the 'media's' baying for the punishment of people whose wretchedness leads to tragedy.

Given a safe enough environment, then, it seems to me that most people are glad of an opportunity to love their fellows. The travesty of friendship which one sees in our rituals of fake intimacy, the timid confidences which are barely heard by partners absorbed in the formulation of what they intend to confide in their turn, indicate an altruism stunted and frustrated by a society which dislocates people from a world of constructive action and turns them against each other in bitter competition. If we do not truly 'open up' to each other, 'be sensitive', 'show our feelings' in the way that the therapy industry encourages us to do, it is because we have good reasons not to – we live in a social world which really is dangerous. To try to solve the 'problem' by, again, manipulating the surface phenomena of individual behaviour (i.e. simulating behavioural effects rather than tackling socio-economic causes), is to foster just the kind of faking and artificiality with which we are so familiar from the world of 'marketing' and to ignore the abuses of power which underlie our rational fear and suspicion of each other.

On the evidence to date, it would stretch credulity beyond all reasonable limits to suggest that human beings, or human society, were truly perfectible in any absolute sense, and I do not want to lay claim to a vision of a Utopian world in which sweetness and light will reign supreme and undisturbed. One need not lapse into 'biologisms' concerning human 'nature' or 'instincts' to observe the hair-trigger nervousness and violence with which people and societies react to threat,* and the quite appalling terror and oppression which they will resort to in establishing and protecting their interests. But however inevitable much of this may be there is still enormous room for improvement, and such improvement can only sensibly be

*Interesting treatments of the question of violence and destructiveness are to be found in, for example, E. Fromm, *The Anatomy of Human Destructiveness*, Penguin Books, 1977, and F. Wertham, *A Sign for Cain. An Exploration of Human Violence*, Hale, 1966. It is inevitable that such books raise questions rather than provide answers, but these at least raise interesting questions.

looked for in the social, moral and political spheres. Individual consciousness and relations between individuals reflect rather than cause the power structure within society. In situations where threat is absent or minimised (there can be very few of these – the nearest I can think of are some of the artificially constructed 'therapeutic communities' which were created in the sixties for the treatment of 'mental illness'*) or where people are united in opposition to a *common* threat (as in war), people do seem to be able to conduct themselves towards each other with concern, interest and affection.

Concern, interest and affection are becoming precisely those characteristics of relationship which have to be either faked or bartered. We have an awareness of each other's neediness, but the latter is so great that we have to make special arrangements for its (very partial) fulfilment, which is either bought from professionals, carefully shared out in parallel conversations in which turns are taken at self-revelation, or merely simulated in ritual but empty gestures of intimacy (e.g. the technology of the 'encounter' group).

SEX

It has become almost impossible to think clearly or constructively about sex, since sexual satisfaction is the pivot around which our commercial culture turns, the sacred central axiom of a dogma of gratification which will not allow itself to be questioned or criticised. To suggest, for instance, that sex should be *for* anything other than itself, or to speculate that there could be *any* grounds for control of or abstinence from sexual indulgence (even, for example, in order to avoid a risk of fatal disease) is to invite immediate dismissal from the community of rational beings, even to occasion worried concern for the state of one's mental health. The isolation of sex from procreation

*See D. Kennard, *An Introduction to Therapeutic Communities*, Routledge & Kegan Paul, 1983.

and the refinement and promulgation of sexual pleasures of every form and variety, the 'liberation' of women by the pill and the widespread acceptance and endorsement of forms of sexuality once considered 'perverse', all these are seen as the triumphs of an age which has freed us from sexual prudery, repression and hypocrisy, and given us permission to pursue our pleasures, to explore and exploit each other's orifices without a shred of shame.

Let me hasten to reassure the reader at this point that I am not about to advocate a 'return' to no doubt mythical standards of a past sexual propriety, to suggest that we abandon contraception, impose unnecessary abstinence upon ourselves or make homo-sexuality illegal. What we do need to do, however, is to restore to sexuality a meaning, to re-embed it in our personal lives and relations such that it regains significances beyond itself.

In his book *The History of Sexuality*,★ Michel Foucault suggests that the nineteenth century, far from being an era of sexual repression, was one when sex in fact became the focus of attention, discussion and scientific investigation as never before. And indeed it does seem to be the case that in the course of the past hundred years or so, and with a rapid acceleration in very recent decades, sexuality has been torn out of any kind of context to be presented before us as the absolute raw material of gratification; sex becomes as inherently meaningless but as essentially important to personal survival and satisfaction as money, and, like money, it is attached to both people and things – commodities – to lend them a certain kind of value.

Dislodged from the spatial context of the embodied relations of men and women, as well as from the temporal context of our personal histories, sex is installed as the irreducible absolute at the centre of a commercialised religion of satisfaction, and to ask questions about its meaning and its value is to commit a kind of blasphemy. Where once sex may have been surrounded by a

★Published by Penguin Books in 1981. The title is somewhat misleading in the light of the original French, *La Volonté de Savoir*.

moralism of prudish disapproval, it is now hedged about with, if anything, an even more thornily impenetrable if quite different moralism, i.e. one which permits no challenge to the creed that everyone shall be permitted to enjoy themselves in any way they choose – 'whatever turns you on'.

The main reason for sexual pleasure's having come to occupy this central and unassailable position as a kind of cultural imperative is, I suspect, because of its extraordinary efficacy in selling things. Whether or not Freud was right to make 'libido' the foundation of human psychology, there seems little doubt that sexual energy has become the basic fuel of the commercial interests which structure our society. We are sold 'happiness' and 'satisfaction' by an appeal to their crudest and most basic 'fulfilment', and it seems as though organisations and institutions at virtually every level of society conspire progressively to loosen us from any restraint we may feel in giving the fullest rein to sexual indulgence. Industry, advertising, education, health, therapy and counselling combine to give us the green light to pursue gratification to the utmost, to douse in any way we dream up the nervous itch of our desires.

Sex is a marvellous medium for commodity sales in a market which demands infinite expansion and the endless obsolescence of fashion, for no sooner has the nervous system achieved a blissful sexual peace than the engine starts once more to hum, and before you know where you are the cycle starts all over again. There is, it is true, an overall element of satiation in this process which necessitates a continuous escalation in the stimulation of desire, so that appeals to the 'joy of sex' need, step by step, to be made ever coarser and more direct. (Where once the camera dwelt shyly on knees, it now stares straight into the crutch.) But presumably there is still considerable mileage left in sex.

I do not wish to say that we have become a society of sex maniacs, or to expostulate indignantly about our 'shame', but only to suggest that what we take to be liberation may be in fact enslavement. For the pursuit of sexual gratification seems to be doing very little for 'relationships', and couples seem to become increasingly split and isolated from one another as each partner concentrates anxiously on his technique, worries obsessively about her attractiveness, and assesses self-consciously the scale of his or her satisfaction. Indeed, it seems to have become for many people a source of irritation that they have to depend on someone else to meet their sexual needs, and when not actually in bed, men and women tend to eye each other with hostility and contempt, secretly promising themselves an exchange of partner as soon as a more satisfactory 'relationship' appears, reluctantly and frustratedly settling for what they have got when it no longer seems that it is going to. As with 'relationship' itself, sex has become the commodity of which people are the inter-changeable vehicles, anonymous purveyors of reassurance or an ego-boost, a momentary respite from sexual restlessness. We use each other to satisfy needs so personal as to be almost autistic, and sex becomes a kind of suspicious bartering of incompatible self-indulgences rather than the unifying joy which sexual rhetoric proclaims. This situation is epitomised in the 'sex therapy' industry, which advocates a technicised exchange of gratifications whose 'demandingness' may be carefully graded and controlled.

Although I have no doubt that it would be going much too far to suggest that sexual love has become entirely an outdated romantic notion, it does seem to me that, though people may expect and long for 'deeply fulfilling' sexual relationships, what for the most part they actually find are uncomfortably combative liaisons of the kind I have outlined above. The reason for this, once again, is to be sought not inside individuals, but may be traced to the nature of our society. As well as being split off by commercial interests from any relational meaning (sex no longer arises from a relation to a *particular person*, but, like 'consumer durables', is a product to which the agents of production are irrelevant), sexuality is located in a social context in which men and women confront each other in a spirit of competition. In a brave and brilliant book* which I imagine must, despite its artistry, have lost him a good deal of support among 'conventional' feminists and other critics of contemporary society, Ivan Illich has suggested that an economy which engineers competition for goods and resources perceived as scarce, encourages men and women to conduct themselves as beings of essentially the *same kind*, apart from an accidental difference in sex, who must compete uniformly for the goods and services on offer. In this way we become what Illich calls 'sexed neuters', stripped of any kind of complementary gender, and distinguishable from each other only by the 'bulge in the blue jeans'. As more and more of the traditional fields of 'gendered' work and activity are thrown into the modern unisex economy – for example as men begin to concern themselves with the arts of baby care – so the battle-ground of hostile competition between men and women is widened. 'Invidious comparison now replaces awe as the reaction to otherness.'

In almost everything one hears or reads, those 'sexual partners' who are not simply burying their emotions in some kind of wishful mythology seem to be asking themselves where they went wrong, or hurrying from the bloody wreckage of the last 'relationship' to peer hopefully round the corner to see if the next one looks more promising. But we are caught up in processes beyond our selves and our individual strengths and weaknesses. Once again, it has to be pointed out that we cannot escape (unless completely artificially) the ground we stand on and the air we breathe: relations between men and women have been cast into confusion by forces beyond their control, and consequently the experience and meaning of sex – apart from its com-modity value – has also been thrown into question.

*I. Illich, *Gender*, Marion Boyars, 1983.

It seems unlikely that the solution to this predicament can lie in some artificial form of retrogression to a time when men and women accepted (however unjustly) roles in society which were gendered and complementary. Rather, we are confronted with a situation in which the nineteenth-century psychological myth of the primacy of sex is peeling away to reveal a 'more primary' issue of power, and how that issue will be resolved only time will tell.

Sex, if ever it was, is no longer a matter for repression, but questions concerning power and interest are, and our, as it were, cultural assertion of the absolute value of sexual pleasure makes it surprisingly difficult to inquire into the history and phenomenology of power which seem to lurk behind and within the difficulties people experience and the injuries they inflict on each other in their sexual encounters. There is an enormous contrast between the images of sexual satisfaction in which our culture trades and the actual experience of the people who are subjected to them, but attempts to *explicate* sexual experience (rather than to tend it or stoke it 'therapeutically') are quite often met with refusal or even anger. But, I suspect, if one is to gain any understanding of the painful strife which so often these days infuses both hetero- and homosexual relations, one will have to be prepared to trace them back into the power relations which society imposes on its members. In this way, the sexual experience and proclivities of individuals cannot be fully understood without investigating their personal history, particularly in terms of the permutations of relations between mothers and fathers and sons and daughters, since it is through these relations that the wider social influences make themselves felt. Inevitably, *we* are the agents of our society's exploitation, and the most potent source of learning in the ways of relationship (for good or for ill) is the family. The purpose of trying to trace, for example, the significance of (among other things) individuals' sexual conduct back into their personal histories is not, as will be evident from the previous chapter, to seek to change it, but rather to develop the beginnings of an understanding of how we come to shape our children in ways of relationship which they cannot escape.

MARRIAGE

For the psychologist (or anyone else) interested in the kinds of 'relationship' which seem so to preoccupy us, marriage provides the magnifying glass through which they may be most closely studied, for it is in the (relatively) long-term contract of marriage that our mythical expectations as well as our actual experience of 'relationship' are most clearly exposed.

More than any other form of relationship, marriage carries our hopes for a warm, fulfilling, safe, confiding, mentally and physically satisfying bond with another person. Yet in practice marriage causes more bitterness, resentment, disappointment and inarticulate pain than all our other 'relationships' put together. For countless people, what is confidently embarked upon as an exclusive mutual alliance against an indifferent or hostile world, a search for a haven of warmth in a cold and competitive society, turns out to be a journey into a totally unexpected, private and unanalysable hell – one seeming, furthermore, to constitute an entirely personal and exceptional misery which, if it is not ended in a burst of hatred and recrimination, can only be endured with dumb incomprehension.

I do not wish either to decry or to discredit the institution of marriage, and I have no doubt that for many people (though, if they are honest, I suspect not unequivocally) it does provide a refuge of warmth and support without which they would find emotional survival extremely difficult. However, I do not believe that this can be the best or most creative function of marriage: if our world is so beastly that we need to escape from it into the comparative safety of an isolated pact with one other person, we need to indict the world rather than extol marriage. It is in any case almost impossible to gain a clear view of marriage through the haze of wishful fantasy which surrounds it and which, as ever, is endlessly and relentlessly fuelled by commercial interests. In modern marriage, we have been overtaken by a phenomenon of relationship of which we have no sober or reflective understanding, but only the wildest and most unrealistic expectations. To be able to spend forty or more years living happily, or merely reasonably comfortably, with a single partner – even, or perhaps especially, if bonded initially by intense sexual desire – is one of the most testing demands people can place upon themselves, and it is thus small wonder that attitudes generated by the experience of marriage tend to split between cynical dismissal and self-deluding sentimentality. Neither of these extremes seems appropriate to me: precisely because marriage is so central to our social structure, and yet so demanding and so much a source of pain and bewilderment, it seems to me that our stance towards it should be one of honesty and respect. We need to gain an accurate and honest appreciation of the emotional demands of marriage and to develop a sober assessment of what marriage may be *for* if it is not to be simply *for itself* in the sense of constituting the ultimate in gratifying and fulfilling 'relationships'. Above all, I think, we need to illuminate the men and women who stand at either term of the marriage 'relationship', i.e. to 'de-commodify' the relationship and to discover the people who are so easily sacrificed in its pursuit and who suffer so bitterly as the result. Respect for the extraordinary difficulty entailed by marriage may lead to respect for the partners who enter into it. If it is not to disintegrate in reciprocal hatred or become submerged in a deadening sentimental banality, marriage cannot be expected to be an end in itself, a pact of mutual self-indulgence, but must be recognised as a kind of commitment partners make to each other *for* something beyond the commitment itself and the 'happiness' it is (falsely) expected to generate. It may of course turn out to be the case that in the modern world there is nothing much other than itself which marriage can be for. In which case, we may safely expect its gradual demise as an institution.

Up until comparatively very recent times marriage was linked much more clearly to economic necessity and the social power structure than to the search for blissful 'relationship'. As Lawrence Stone points out,★ the 'companionate marriage' was largely a creation of the eighteenth century, by which time many of the socio-economic, contractual reasons for marriage had diminished, leaving an increasingly individualistic and plea-sure-seeking middle and upper class in pursuit of forms of happiness for which the still officially indissoluble bond of marriage offered to provide a ready receptacle. Furthermore, it is only even more recently that marriage can be almost relied upon to last a lifetime (hence, Stone argues, our need for divorce to perform the task more frequently performed before by death). From serving hard-headed and practical interests, then, marriage came to serve as a kind of private personal indul-gence, the satisfaction of needs for emotional comfort and companionship.

The romanticising of love and marriage in this way had dangers which were not lost on observers of the time. Stone quotes Oliver Goldsmith's warning concerning the 'mystifica-tion' of marriage:

> How delusive, how destructive, are those pictures of consummate bliss. They teach the youthful mind to sigh after beauty and happiness which never existed, to despise that little good which fortune has mixed up in our cup, by expecting more than she ever gave.

However, Stone's work also suggests that changes in the social structure in which marriage is embedded, giving rise as they did to the 'companionate marriage', led concomitantly to generally

★L. Stone, *The Family, Sex and Marriage in England 1500–1800*, Penguin Books, 1979.

more gentle and affectionate relations within families and to a greater interest than hitherto in questions of education and child welfare, so perhaps it would be ungracious to dismiss too quickly as mere self-indulgence any indication of social movement towards a climate of opinion which begins to take seriously the well-being of others. Perhaps, again, this was one of those points in history where, in another context, enlightened and altruistic thought (for example like that of Rousseau) might have led to a sustained improvement in social conditions generally. However, nothing demonstrates more clearly than the career of our attitude to marriage the pervasiveness of the corruption of interest. For, as with sex, the comforts and consolations of 'companionate' marriage have been commercially isolated and magnified, infused with our greedy fantasies and served up to us as a 'package' at once so attractive and so illusory that we can scarcely any longer bring to bear upon it any form of coherent criticism.★ Whatever else may be the case, it certainly seems that the 'affective individualism' of which Stone writes has arrived in our own time at a point where any possibility of our being meaningfully related to a social world outside ourselves has become, as it were, imploded into an intensely focused 'relationship' which is expected to be not only 'companionate', but even therapeutic, not only sexually fulfilling, but self-sufficiently and completely emotionally gratifying. If we continue on this course, there is, saving death itself, only one more stop on the way to our destination, and that is

★A characteristically honest (if almost brutally sour!) antidote to the kind of false sentimentality concerning marriage which is so evident in popular literature is provided by Leo Tolstoy in an observation in his diary for 30 August 1894: 'Novels end with the hero and heroine getting married. They should begin with that and end with them getting unmarried, i.e. becoming free. Otherwise to describe people's lives in such a way as to break off the description with marriage is just the same as describing a person's journey and breaking off the description at the point where the traveller falls into the hands of robbers.' (*Tolstoy's Diaries*, Vol. 1, edited by R. F. Christian, Athlone Press, 1985.)

complete individual self-sufficiency; the ultimate in security is being able to do without *anyone*.

There is virtually nothing in, on the one hand, the welter of sentimentality, mythology and wishful thinking, and on the other the angry disillusion surrounding marriage, by which we may begin to make sense of our experience of married life. Over and over again people run up against completely unexpected obstacles to their continued marital happiness from which they recoil hurt and bewildered, believing themselves in an entirely individual predicament which must be put down to someone's 'fault' – either their partner's or their own. The irony is that this is in fact the almost inevitable fate of all those 'embodied subjects' who find themselves located in this particular world.

There are three particularly frequent constellations of marital difficulty which may be taken as examples of what I mean. They correspond roughly to what may be expected (when troubles do arise) in the early, middle and later stages of marriage, and might be termed accordingly the phases of disillusion, re-illusion and resignation.

The disillusion of early marriage is, despite its near-universality, experienced by those it affects usually silently and very privately, as a particularly unfortunate and personal failing. As the absorption in each other wears away and the exigencies of the world outside 'the relationship' begin to reassert themselves, each partner reads in the conduct of the other a personal betrayal, or in their own disappointment a shameful failure of commitment. The husband (to take the still typical case) finds his wife's lack of understanding for the call on his attention of his work commitments, and her demand for continual demonstration of his interest in and affection towards her, irksome and unfair – can't she *see* how much he thinks of her? Can't she tell that the work he does is for her (and perhaps for their young children)? Can't she see that he needs to relax when he gets home, not to talk about a day he wants to forget, nor to hear the trivial details of hers? These feelings his wife interprets as a treacherous decrease of the loving involvement he had shown. He no longer seems to care, and all she experiences is the enervating isolation of a life incarcerated with small children, few friends and a family she rarely sees. Her husband is uncommunicative, elsewhere, absorbed in a world of power and money (even if only at the very bottom of its hierarchy) which seems to mean more to him than she. They no longer talk to each other as they did. He gets more out of talking to the people who share his working world, she makes a confidante of one or two young mothers she knows. She feels his sexual interest in her as invasive and insincere, mere lust. He is hurt and bewildered by her lessened sexual interest in him. Each feels that 'the marriage' threatens to be a failure; it is not what it was, and has not turned out either as they expected or as it should. Perhaps they were, after all, not right for each other.

And so to the phase of re-illusion, in which the partners cast around to rediscover what they feel they have lost. For the wife, busy with tending to the needs of children, this may mean little more than daydreaming, fantasising the appearance of a kind and attentive, gentle man who will love her for herself alone. As long as she is dependent on her husband for her keep, she can afford to show him little of these feelings, but if she becomes more financially independent as the children get older, she may begin to allow her contempt and resentment to show rather more boldly; perhaps also she will turn the children into partners in an alliance against the unfeeling and insensitive male, the father/husband whose still too powerful figure begins to throw a shadow almost of dread over the household. Re-illusion is perhaps particularly the province of the male. The husband, sexually rejected, hurt and perhaps excluded (though perhaps none of these, but rather just pining for the lost adulation of a woman) finds himself embroiled in a 'relationship' with another woman – the disillusioned wife of a friend, possibly, or a younger unattached woman at work. The springtime of his life miraculously reappears – it is possible to be loved! And so, confident in the belief perhaps that he now knows enough from his experience of life *really* to make 'the relationship' work, off he goes with his new-found love to start the cycle all over again, leaving at home a woman too old, too tired, too encumbered with children and far too angry to be very likely to take a similar course.

Resignation comes when you look up after fifteen or so years of child-rearing to find yourself sharing a lonely life with a hostile stranger. Darby and Joan bickering and sniping at each other with practised weariness. Far from finding their lives a cosy therapeutic oneness, they tolerate each other's presence filled with a kind of seething irritation in which their all-too-familiar mannerisms, even the rustle of their clothes or the sound of their breathing, are enough to trigger in the other a barely suppressed wave of frustrated rage. For simply sharing a home and a family does not automatically lead to unity of soul and body – indeed many people could probably more easily share their declining years with a workmate of long standing than with a spouse. Partners' concerns and interests diverge over time more often than they converge, and the second half of life – particularly perhaps for women who have invested a great deal in now fully fledged children – can plunge people into a sense of isolation and despairing futility at once inescapable and totally unexpected. Professional guidance and 'the media' as well as popular literature and entertainment all emphasise the positive value of 'relationships' and proffer a technology for making them 'work'. For this reason it is often with stunned bewilderment that people come face to face with their predicament. *Nothing* prepares us for the difficulties of marriage in a world which imposes on people the way, in what roles and arenas, they shall live their lives. The end is resignation, the discovery that, after all, you have been cheated of happiness, and can only wait for death in a state of armed truce with your 'one and only'. But your disappointment will be of no concern to society as a whole, as by now you have lost your economic significance. The advertisement, like all advertisements, turns out in the end to be a lie, but no one will mind, since you will have spent as much on the product as you can be expected to.

To look at the way we treat the elderly with a gaze as far as possible unclouded by custom and practice – as if newly arrived from some other planet where they order things better – is to be overcome with horror. These are not people sustained by years of therapeutic relationship, but rather people no longer serving the purposes that never were their own – no longer serving any purpose at all.

I should probably emphasise once more at this point that what I want to draw attention to are the constraints placed upon our lives by the structure of the society in which we live and the mythology which has become established in its service. I have known enough people who, sometimes in the face of almost unimaginable adversity, live their lives with the greatest concern for and commitment to those they share it with, not lightly to devalue their undertaking. My intention is not cynically to disparage the loving concern many people still, against all the odds, manage to show to others, including their spouses, but rather to attack the values of a society which makes preparation for and understanding of 'relationship' so difficult and successful 'relatedness' so rare.

We need in fact to dismantle the mystifying rhetoric of 'relationship' which, in order to sell us a whole range of illusory satisfactions and to maintain us in isolated, inactive and uncomplaining battery units, promises us total gratification in blissful union with our loved one, and to construct instead a realistic appreciation of what a commitment to other people must entail. It seems obvious, for example, that to found the happiness of one's life on another *person* is to lay upon him or her a strain which the human spirit is just too weak to bear, and for two people who are historically and organically different from each other to be expected to provide a *mutually* supportive programme of more or less therapeutic 'understanding' and emotional tolerance, not to mention sexual indulgence, is stretching the bounds of possibility beyond all reasonable limit. As far as this is our expectation of marriage it is bound to be disappointed. The task of couples who wish both to stay married and to maintain some kind of contact with reality must be to learn to accept in the self and permit (and tolerate) in the other an inevitable degree of isolation and 'difference'. There must be, as it were, permissible areas of non-understanding, recognition of untouchable and impenetrable uniqueness, preparedness to enter some experiences entirely alone and unaided by emotional support, not because such support is being wilfully withheld (and might be available in a 'better' relationship) but because its supply is illusory. This calls for a tolerance of pain, and an understanding of its nature, which few of us these days are able to command. Each partner needs to see in the other a man or woman with needs, weaknesses, fears and idiosyncrasies parallel to (though far from identical with) his or her own, not the more or less adequate purveyor, or indeed recipient, of satisfactions – 'love' and 'understanding' – which are the stuff of commodified relationship.

If, of course, marriage is an end in itself, a bid for emotional security in an otherwise hostile world, the kind of tolerance of difference I am advocating would amount to an entirely unacceptable renunciation of bliss. But precisely because of the impossible demands marriage-for-itself places on its partners, I do not believe that it can survive as such. It is easy enough to see what marriage has been *for* in the past (economic advantage or security, the forging of familial alliances, etc.), but less easy to see what form it may take in the future. If, however, we come to acknowledge that 'relationships' of all kinds can arise meaningfully only from being for something other than themselves, there is no reason why marriage should not continue as an institution 'for' something. Even now, it may legitimately enough be seen as for the rearing of children.

PARENTS AND CHILDREN

The way in which the human body is constructed makes it certain that power will arise as a central issue in human life, and the way in which human society is organised will determine how power is to be distributed, used or abused. Inevitably, some people are stronger than others – men (on the whole) than women, adults (always) than infants. It is for this basic and obvious reason that at the very root of the inequality of our power-infused social hierarchy are to be found violence and the threat of violence (terror). Nowhere is the issue of power more salient than in the relations between parents and children, and nowhere are its roots in violence and terror more frequently, and sadly, exposed.

I find it a matter of some considerable surprise that psychologists, and especially those clinically involved in the study and 'treatment' of families, have not thought about and addressed more centrally the issue of power. It has not, certainly, been totally absent from the thinking of some psychologists, especially those interested in people's social relations more than merely in their internal psychic workings – one thinks, for example, of Alfred Adler and those influenced by him – but on the whole the issue of power has been overshadowed by, one might say hidden behind, that of sex, and there seems little doubt that Freud's influence in this has been enormous. It is tempting to think that concern with the 'repression' of sexuality which Freud and his colleagues worked so assiduously to lift served, however unintendedly, as a screen for a much deeper and more pervasive repression – that of power, its inequalities and injustices. For if, as Foucault argues, sexuality was far from being the taboo subject (and practice) of Victorian society which we have been led to believe, it was precisely in this period of European history and colonial domination (not to mention familial relations) that the oppressive use of power reached unprecedented heights of organisation and sophistication. It is, again, surprising that, despite the resistance Freud felt he encountered (and resented so bitterly) towards his theories, his ideas on sexuality were in fact accepted almost eagerly and adopted into twentieth-century culture with great rapidity, when even now one might expect them to stretch the credulity of an averagely critical mind beyond the normal bounds of reason. And yet at the same time, the quite obvious importance of disparities in power between adults and children was largely ignored, and indeed it still is ignored by most of us today. The basest of human motives lie not in our sexual affiliations, but in our violence towards one another, and it is above all these motives which we repress most effectively.

In the orthodox view of the 'Oedipus complex', for example, the power struggle between son and father is treated in psychoanalytic thinking as secondary to a sexual struggle for the mother/wife. I must confess that I have always had difficulty in being able to take seriously the psychoanalytic view of sexuality in infancy and childhood, not least because I have never been struck, as psychoanalysts clearly seem to be, by a particularly significant sexual component even to the most honest and undefended accounts people give of their childhood experience, nor have I observed any particularly potent or impressive sexual activities or impulses in pre-pubertal children (which is not to say that such children are innocent of all sexual feeling or conduct, nor that they may not imitate sexually mature activity). I have, of course, come across very powerful and often very destructive sexual components in the relations of adults *towards* children, not infrequently their own, but this is of course quite another matter. Competition between parents for the alliance of their children is very often observable and frequently not without elements of sexual seductiveness. In this way a renaming of the 'Oedipus complex' as the 'Jocasta complex' (after Oedipus's mother) would make a kind of psychological sense more often supported by actual clinical experience: mothers who seduce their sons (and none the less powerfully for being only metaphorically) in order to isolate and in a sense castrate their husbands are a far from rare phenomenon (and certainly have a part to play in the genesis of male homosexuality) – but here again the essential theme, the key to the understanding of the 'dynamics', is one of *power*. Though, of course, a small child can play on the weaknesses of its parents and so exploit their differences, its power in such situations is merely passive or negative; its resources of positive power are, in relation to those of its parents, negligible.

Sons struggle against paternal domination; fathers crush, tyrannise or patronise daughters; mothers manoeuvre fairly or foully against male oppression, monopolise their sons' affection or competitively drain their daughters of female competence in exactly the way that a father can use his power never to allow his son to surpass him in anything. The 'pathology' of family relations knows many permutations and variations, but most centre on the misuse, abuse and fear of power. One can very often detect, even on quite casual acquaintance, how people have learned to deal with their earliest experiences of the power of others. In the way, for example, that they characteristically try to assert their own interests – charmingly, perhaps, or cajolingly, defiantly, fearfully, obliquely, seductively, angrily, sullenly, insistently, etc., etc. – one can almost see the shadow of a parent falling over them.

We have not developed very much in the way of an ethics of child-rearing in our culture, and the very idea that we should give much thought to what might be good for our children seems, in modern times at least, to have struck us as at all significant only since the eighteenth century.* We have yet to

*L. Stone, op. cit. See also Phillipe Ariès, *Centuries of Childhood*, Jonathan Cape, 1962.

meditate seriously on the *overwhelming* disparity of power between adults and children (though, of course, we do not hesitate to make remorseless use of it) and where we do get a glimpse of the ravages the powerful (adults) wreak on the powerless (children) our first – and so far only – thought seems to be to 'disband' the family and seek other ways of organising the basic units of society. However, nothing will eradicate the disparity of power between adults and children, and we might, rather than trying to get rid of it, attempt to find ways of using it for good rather than ill.

Once again we have at present no concepts even to begin to think about this undertaking other than those of a semi-articulated authoritarian moralism or various forms of laissez-faire. This, I think, is because of the extent of the repression of power in the wider society. Because we do not comment about or reflect upon injustice and inequality to any really serious degree, because we are all to some extent involved in turning blind eyes to the free play of violence and exploitation in the pursuit of interest, we can only watch helplessly as these forms of relation reproduce themselves within our families.

It is not that parents harbour any evil intent towards their children, and it is the cruellest of errors to suppose that they do by, for example, dragging the concept of blame into a consideration of who causes whom psychological injury or distress. It is rather that, in a culture in which we have no articulate conception of the loving use of power (and if we ever had one in the past we have lost it), we are thrown together in contexts – as for example families – in which our relations are going inevitably to be shaped by the social forms of the wider environment.

I do not think it any exaggeration to say that we are approaching a state of affairs in which we simply do not know how to relate to one another except coercively and exploit-ingly, and the effects of this are going to be particularly severe in cases where – as between children and adults – there are gross disparities in power. My reasons for feeling this are based on no mere abstract consideration of social speculation or political theory, but on the endlessly and dishearteningly repeated experience of witnessing the deformation and ineradicable emotional scarring of people who were once children by parents whose only conscious wish was to love them.

At a relatively coarse level of analysis, there are several almost standard ways – familiar, I would suggest, in most people's experience – in which the fundamentally baleful nature of our society is reflected in the manner in which parental power comes to be exerted over children. Without running into further volumes, I can do no more here than sketch some of them rather as caricatures.

At the bottom of the pyramid, the very base of the social hierarchy, many people are just too drained and oppressed, too robbed of ability or initiative to feel that they can or want to do anything for their children but simply to keep them quiet. In this kind of situation children are likely to be indulged, neglected, bullied or mistreated, handed over to 'experts' in the welfare services, and generally left to find their way through the system as best they can. Nobody will have the resources of time, money or personal concern to observe their talents or nurture their interests and abilities, though they may encounter a degree of formal (but, because overstretched, highly undependable) support from official agencies. To avoid becoming nothing more than fodder for a depressed labour market or marginally useful for the consumption of mass-produced junk, the child in this position needs an almost miraculously lucky encounter with someone (most often an unusually strong and capable grandparent or aunt or uncle) who will through his or her affection, wisdom and energy, open up for it a world of possibility and a realisation of its own potentialities which would otherwise be missed. The only consolation to occupancy of this level of society, and it is indeed the smallest of mercies, is that tired neglect, though it generates the most dreadful waste, often avoids the malign distortion of growth which leads to such emotional pain in people who have been subjected to more positive abuses of power.

It is virtually impossible to occupy a precariously insecure position in the power hierarchy without the anxiety and hostility such a position occasions being reflected in family relations. People who, as it were, find themselves perched on a ledge a little way up the social pyramid – far enough to want desperately to hang on to the small advantage gained but not far enough to be unaware of the unattractiveness of rock bottom – live particularly threatened lives, and it can be little surprise if they hedge their children round with all kinds of exhortations and prohibitions, keen for them to climb higher and anxious lest they drag the family back down to what they see as social ignominy. Here is to be found the much-maligned 'petty bourgeoisie', renowned for its mean-spirited narrow-mindedness, envy and authoritarian moralism. But the values of generosity and liberalism make little sense to anyone having to cling to this perch, where the threat of economic power is probably felt at its most acute and life becomes an unrelenting pursuit of an always just-unattainable security, a panicky clinging to advantages gained and an angry contempt both for people who have silver spoons in their mouths and for those who have fallen back into torpid resignation. The reality here is of economic survival and obedient subservience to power, and other values, other ways of perceiving the world, become mere self-indulgence. Rigid conformity to narrowly ideal standards and denial and repression of emotions, perceptions and values which do not meet them, resentful respect for authority and uncritical acceptance of established social institutions breed an atmosphere in which children are likely to find it hard to develop a firm sense of subjectivity, but will be moulded to occupancy of stereotyped social and sexual roles and will experience considerable anxiety and guilt when they find themselves departing from them. Self-deception and hypocrisy, emotional deprivation and defensiveness follow naturally from this kind of situation, which, not surprisingly, is one of the most psychologically mutilating in which one can find oneself.

It is in this stratum, and those close to it, that the course of development most typical of our society is perhaps most obviously to be found – the transformation of a lively and promising human infant, through a period of indoctrination, disillusion and rebellion, into an emotionally constricted, competitively hostile adult saturated in the values of commodity consumption, desperately conforming, anxiously pursuing an ever-receding 'happiness', bereft of any ability to criticise the society in which he or she is located, pathetically eager to enjoy those of its 'fruits' (consumer durables) which are within reach. This is the great, inertially stable backbone of our society, the guardian of its values and the target of its mass media, working tirelessly in the interests of others and blindly against its own, forced by the crushing vice of economic power into reproducing itself reliably and endlessly in its children.

At the upper level of this stratum, and extending into the managerial and professional strata, one finds family relations set in a rather less rigid context in which a degree of economic security allows room for, on the one hand, genuinely realisable ambition, and on the other economically riskable (though strictly one-dimensional*) criticism of the *status quo*. Here, for example, managers may manage their children, organising their experience (e.g. controlling what television programmes may be watched) and to a lesser extent their social and educational environment in accordance with aims seen as desirable and attainable. The relatively greater degree of power available at this level makes in general for a rather more relaxed and less moralistic hedonism, but the culture is still likely to be highly

*I mean this in the sense developed by Herbert Marcuse in *One-Dimensional Man*, Beacon Press, 1964, i.e. that criticism of the social and conceptual *status quo* is possible only in the forms and language prescribed by the self-same *status quo*, and hence never challenges its fundamental values.

materialistic in one form or another and the emphasis in child-rearing will probably be on the gaining of increased status, so that children will often experience strong pressure to achieve and 'succeed'. In the absence of crude economic threat (e.g. relative security of parental job tenure and provision of pensions, etc.), the atmosphere is more often likely to be one of alienation rather than anxiety: the pursuit of comfort and satis-faction, the possibility of actually obtaining recurrent quies-cence of the nervous system, may lead to a kind of flaccidity in values, an incipient sense of purposelessness and a desperation to realise purpose in 'relationships', which result in fact in chaotic, manipulative and dishonest relations between parents. Children in this type of situation may be or feel emotionally distanced from their families, and their parents, intent on pursuing their own gratification, may simply buy their offspring's upbringing from educationalists and 'experts' of one sort or another. Particularly in the families of middle-class intellectuals and acad-emics children may be permitted or actually encouraged a kind of rebellion against conventional norms as long as they 'achieve' intellectually. In adolescents from this kind of background one can often encounter an intelligent criticism of their parents' apparently dishonest involvement in materialist values and lack of emotional commitment to anything very much, but idealism seems to give way all too soon to a learned indifference to people, a sort of profound disaffection which in the end simply reproduces a drifting indulgence in commodified relationships and embarkation on one of society's more comfortable voca-tional bandwagons, propelled more by fashion than commit-ment.

It is only perhaps towards the apex of the social hierarchy that one any longer comes across the most direct application of economic power within the family itself, i.e. the parental control of children through the straightforward manipulation of money-power. It is no doubt a blessing that for the vast majority of us institutions such as male primogeniture no longer exist to poison family relations, but even so it seems to me that we vastly underestimate the psychological consequences of inheritable wealth for those who stand in line actually to inherit it. This does not of course constitute a widespread social problem, but it does throw into relief the way that power may be socially exerted and reflected in individuals' personal lives and relations. I cannot claim that my knowledge of people in this position is extensive, but it has struck me as interesting how often those I have come across – i.e. people who have wealthy parents and who profit or stand to profit by the relationship – seem simply to have failed to grow up. For such people as this, however advanced in years themselves, the parental shadow seems to fall heavily over them, in such a way that emotionally and socially they remain perpetual adolescents – angrily dependent, sulkily rebellious, rather unstable and changeable in their personal relations, apparently vocationally paralysed, i.e. dilettantish and unable to strike out for themselves in any independent direction. However firm our intentions, very few of us manage to be disinterested, and it is extremely difficult for even the most affectionate parent not to wield at least unconscious power over a son or daughter who stands to gain financially from the relationship. It is not the habit of psychologists to inquire closely into the financial background and circumstances of those whose 'behaviour' and 'attitudes' they are trying to understand. On the whole, I suspect, to do so would be far more enlightening than to pursue, for example, the much more common inquiries into sexual history.

Whatever the level of the socio-economic circumstances in which a given family finds itself – and I should stress that the above reflections constitute only the broadest and most impressionistic of sketches – none can escape the prevailing cultural climate, which rains equally on the just and the unjust, the advantaged and the disadvantaged. The setting in which emotionally deprived and economically oppressed men and women compete with each other for equal shares of satisfaction, the intrusion into personal relations of inequalities in economic power and its veiled abuse, the pursuit and inevitable frustration of the desire for 'understanding', all these lead almost necessarily to a state of affairs in which children's experience and perceptions are marshalled or distorted to satisfy parental ambitions or emotional alignments, to 'validate' familial mythology or to deny uncomfortable truths. If in this process the adults' power is not ruthlessly if unconsciously used to transmit forms of 'socialisation' which are built, ultimately, on exploitation and violence, it is likely simply to be withdrawn as an available resource, in which case children merely grow up like weeds as their parents fend off any demand which intrudes on their search for personal satisfaction. This in fact does seem to be the ultimate destination of our individualistic pursuit of happiness – simple indifference to the fate of the next generation. It seems more and more to be the case that parents are coming to experience their children as a threat to their emotional peace and independence, as yet more competition for scarce satisfactions, so that adult power comes to serve the struggle for personal 'happiness' more than cultivation of a future for our progeny. This becomes the business of a professional stratum of educational and therapeutic 'experts'.

What seems increasingly to be characteristic of our 'relationships' as a whole is a lack of charity, an absence of the forbearance and respect in the face of 'otherness' which are necessary to an acceptance of each other as fully human. The perception of each other as vehicles of commodified satisfaction which market values impose feeds fantasied expectations, the inevitable frustration of which can only result in desperate neediness and anger. Human beings denied the possibility of acting *creatively* out into the world *for* something become in the end reduced to acting out dreams *destructively* in a way which pays no regard to the embodied actuality of their fellows. This tendency is clearly to be read in the often horrifyingly detached or fantastic sexual and aggressive preoccupations of modern literature and cinema, etc. ('enjoyment' of which necessitates a kind of defensive steeling of the sensibilities if one is not to emerge at least temporarily scarred) but is no less easily identified in the sense very many 'ordinary' people have these days of a pervasive *cruelty* in the world.

Frustration and neediness compounded by recognition of failure to meet the needs of others create a despair and *unintentional* cruelty (i;e. a form of cruelty carrying with it no sense of personal 'ownership') which are reflected as surely in our intimate relations as they are, for example, in the wider world of national and international affairs. The profoundly sinister, largely unseen but enormously complex apparatus of nuclear warfare, the South African policeman almost frenziedly whipping a peaceful demonstrator, and the father who regards with stony hatred the despair of a daughter he cannot love are not separate phenomena, but together speak to the way in which we have become caught up in issues of power and competition beyond our immediate comprehension or control. Any improvement in this state of affairs will depend on a great deal more than our merely 'working on our relationships'.

CHAPTER SEVEN

Growing Up and Taking Care

Understanding, as I have tried to show, does not equal cure. For the individual starting out on psychotherapy it often seems as if all that is needed for the relief of his or her nameless distress would be a clear sight of what the reasons for it are. But even though the gaining of such a clear sight may be a lengthy, painful and testing procedure, its difficulties are as nothing compared with those which arise once the mist disperses and the person can see quite clearly the nature of his or her predicament. For the predicament is where one *is*, and though one may be able to envisage in perfect detail where one would *like* to be, the greatest difficulties are encountered in knowing how to get there. There are, of course, some advantages in knowing where you are, and for many patients this is an improvement on the confusion and discomfort of their original condition, and indeed one which often they have to settle for, if only because their history or their situation precludes their being able to act on their world in such a way as significantly to change it. But even for those who do have some prospect of being able to influence their situation through their own conduct, the way is never less than daunting and always demands great effort and courage.

Precisely the same kind of constellation of difficulties, though on a vastly greater scale, faces the analysis, such as it is, presented in this book. Whatever clarity may have been gained through having broken free of the conceptual restraints placed on our understanding of human distress by the disciplinary structures, greedy individualism and meshed interests of a hierarchy of power, we are still no nearer to knowing how to change our lives or to escape the influences we may now see as damaging us. However, perhaps it is a little easier to catch a glimpse of how, if only we could change them, our lives *ought* to look: the ends may be fairly clear even if the means are as obscure as ever. In this chapter, then, I shall undertake the relatively uncomplicated task of suggesting what indications for less destructive and deluded ways of living seem to me to follow from the foregoing analysis. In the next, and final, chapter I shall discuss, without hoping to resolve, some of the difficulties and dilemmas involved in trying actually to bring into existence forms of social conduct which are, I think, easily enough identified as desirable.

For no particular reason other than convenience of organisation, I shall divide into two broad strands this discussion of how, perhaps, our lives should be if we wish to escape the ravages of the pursuit of happiness. The first strand deals with our personal expectations of life and entails the necessity for growing up. The second deals with our relations with others and the world we live in, and entails the necessity for taking care. It is with some embarrassment that I find myself treading this territory, which is not customarily regarded as the legitimate habitat of 'scientific' psychologists, and I am afraid that what I write may sound too much like preaching. I do not, however, regard myself as in a different boat from anyone else, and though I certainly feel a degree of diffidence about this undertaking I make no apology for it: its justification will, I hope, be argued in the next chapter.

GROWING UP

The blissful security of infancy – the inevitable if for some pitifully short foundation of our experience – is, as has been noted, not to be recaptured. In circumstances rather saner than those pertaining in the 'civilised' world at the beginning of the twenty-first century, it is likely to be the natural course of a person's life that it should, once delivered from the womb, turn progressively outwards towards the world. The process of growing up corresponds to the cultivation of a 'public' life in which the person is enabled, as well perhaps as obliged, to make a contribution to the social world before coming to the end of his or her brief sojourn in it. This is not to say that 'private' life – the internal world of feelings and 'relationships' – is unimportant or to be despised, but rather that it is of little interest to anyone other than the individual in question and those with whom he or she comes into intimate contact.

It is in the public sphere that one may have a more or less formal *function* through which one contributes to the world, and it is in the private sphere that one may tend to the concerns of the self. The 'pursuit of happiness' is properly a private matter, the *instrumental* use of one's body in a social context properly a public matter. We are, in ways and for reasons which may become a little clearer in the course of this discussion, chronically confused between the public and private spheres.

The possibility of public life confers a kind of dignity, a social as opposed to a purely personal value, even at the lowliest level. The doorman, for example, in his commissionaire's uniform, may for many be little more than a slightly comical symbol of petty authority, but the 'publicness' of his role at least permits him to wear an expression of pride which will almost certainly be absent from the face he watches in the bathroom mirror as he stands in his pyjamas cleaning his teeth. He contrasts strongly in this 'publicness' with the young girl who walks past him. His body, his privacy, is hidden behind his function, nobody's business but his own; her body is packaged and displayed as seductively as it can be made – she is imprisoned in a kind of cocoon of private sexuality which is at the same time constructed to be looked at. On the one hand her appearance issues the strongest invitation to desire, on the other she meets nobody's gaze, her eyes unseeing, her expression contemplating some secret inner space. Her determined avoidance of the gaze her objectified sexuality invites seems to acknowledge the inappropriateness of publicising an essentially private concern. In any case, she is given no function but to be her body, a pure object; she has been turned inside-out.

The economic structures we inhabit rob most of us of any function extended out into public space, so that our existence becomes imploded into an impacted preoccupation with our selves and our needs; they *exploit* private impulse at the same time as *appropriating* public function.

But privacy is to be respected, not exploited. As far as there can be a 'point' to our lives, it must, surely, reside within the public sphere; to focus the point of living on the personal and perhaps idiosyncratic experiences of individuals and their particular satisfactions and gratifications is to give the private a degree of importance and centrality far beyond anything morally or rationally warrantable. Indeed, the emphasis on private satisfaction in our commercial culture is so inflated as to obscure the sphere of public living altogether. The promise of bliss holds us within an endless infancy, or at least makes it impossible for us to progress beyond a greedy adolescence, and in assuring us that this is the point of life, it in fact cruelly robs our lives of meaning. It is not merely that our longing for a blissful past beyond the reach of memory is nurtured and exploited, but it is also the case that in many ways the sphere of public living has contracted to a point where most people cannot enter it even if they want to. It may be true that in most 'developed' societies the world no longer imposes upon people a harsh necessity for growing up (our children are not forced to drop their toys so that they may lay their hands to the plough, indeed our adult lives are at least as engrossed with toys – mostly made in Japan – as is our childhood), but it is also true that if we wish to put away childish things we actually cannot find anything serious to do. In other words, growing up in our situation has ceased to be a natural process. To observe that growing up is no longer a

natural process is, however, not to imply that it is not a necessary one if we are to escape the dlslntegratlon and despair consequent upon meaninglessness. We have, quite literally, bought
the idea that the point of life is the pursuit of happiness, and so
we have become, as it were, collapsed in on a life of private
contemplation of how we feel. Private individualism of this
kind leads to public (social) disintegration. It is far from the case
that *really* life's 'problems' have been solved to the point where
we can now just sit back and enjoy ourselves – even the most
casual glance at the state of our own society, let alone of the rest
of the world, reveals that this fantasy of the 1960s no longer
holds any plausibility at all. Furthermore, if ever that distant day
should be reached when human society *does* seem to have
solved all its problems, human beings will have to think of
something better to do than just enjoy themselves having fun
and therapy, for it does not take much imagination to see how
deadening and futile such a life would be.

The greatest violence that is done to people in our society is
to rob them of a public life. As people are persuaded by an
unremitting barrage of commercial propaganda that their
happiness lies in the indulgence and satisfaction of their private
needs and impulses, they are simultaneously stripped of the
possibility for developing and using talents, resources and
interests which they can place at the disposal of others and enact
for the public good. This is a large part of the reason for the
despair which lies behind our satiation. Once again one is
reminded of battery chickens, whose only difference from us
lies, presumably, in their lack of a consciousness. Since it knows
no other, the battery chicken (if only it could talk to itself)
would no doubt believe that it existed in the best of all possible
worlds, and would see the point of its existence as being fed
regularly and nourishingly, kept in comfortable – if
overcrowded – circumstances of even light and heat, and
medicated to keep it free of disease and maintain its proper rate
of growth. What the chicken would not see, of course, is that

there is indeed an altogether darker and less bland purpose behind its pampered life of easy passivity, and even on the day of its sudden and terrifying end it would not realise what its life had been for. Our case is not so different, for our lives also have a purpose beyond that (the pursuit of happiness) which we can immediately see, and though it is one to which, if we are lucky, our private life is not sacrificed, it is certainly one which claims our public lives. It is however, for most of us, not a purpose of our own choosing nor one to which we would consider it right to subscribe, and for most of us also its nature is located at a point in the hierarchy of interest which we cannot even see. In order to develop our *own* purposes we need to break the unnatural barriers to our own maturity: if we do not grow up in response to the pressures of the world, we shall have to learn how to do so for ourselves.

The infrequency with which one comes across people who have achieved maturity is perhaps an indication of how difficult, in the modern world, it is to do so. Even from the perspective of purely private experience, to *grow* older, rather than simply to become advanced in years, is to leave an almost-memory of certain safety and blissful peace and to penetrate further and further into the uncertain and unknowable, to relinquish passivity for activity, to unwind oneself from wishful dreaming and in the process discover pains and sorrows which no mythology can eradicate. In order to embark upon any such risky journey, one needs a social world and a culture which at least make an effort to map the way as far as possible and to provide support at the most dangerous and distressing junctures. In fact, of course, that is precisely what is missing – at every hesitant step we are called back by seductive promises of security and ease and encouraged to regard any sign of departure from the standard aim of happy consumption as close to madnesss. Life does indeed tend to force the inevitable experiences of increasing age on those of us who live long enough, but our culture withholds from us (has repressed or failed to develop) both the conceptual equipment and the compassion we would need to make sense of what happens to us and perhaps to put it to some use in our public lives. Almost every milestone we pass – adolescent sexuality, marriage, parenthood, the departure of children, the demands of old age, death, to name but the most basic and obvious – is mystified by the apparatus of interest so that at any point we are likely to be stunned into guilty silence as we discover that our actual experience fails to match the social norms it pays to believe in, and at the first opportunity we are likely to fall back on comforting but illusory formulations which seem to relieve us of the necessity for progressing further into a threatening unknown.

This kind of process illustrates the meaning of the psychoanalytic term 'fixation'. We settle for that point of our development beyond which we dare not advance, and we elaborate a life out of the *safe* knowledge thus far gained. Sometimes the point settled for may not be very far along the chronological path at all – perhaps merely a matter of months. Unless as a society we provide people, as far as we are able, with both the understanding and the encouragement to risk and pass beyond the difficult and painful experiences which are bound to present themselves at intervals throughout their lives, we can scarcely be surprised when they settle for what they know best and baulk at entering areas of experience which lie, so to speak, outside their field of expertise. We tend to traumatise our children early: rather than trying all we can to use our adult knowledge and power to stand in their position and to make sense *for* them of *their* experience, to make space in which they can act from their own perspective, we tend to impose upon them a cold objective gaze which monitors their every departure from our norms and enables us to force them back into the ways of *our* choosing. In this way, the child becomes terrified of its own 'interiority': it discovers that most of what it experiences and feels and thinks is not permissible, and so, as soon as it can, it opts for any state of 'objectivity' in which it seems to be moderately successful and reasonably comfortable, and beyond that state it does not pass.

Partly, this is because the exploitation of privacy for both commercial and disciplinary purposes, the spilling out of what is inside us into the field of view of others who need to sell us things as well as keep us under control, leads us vastly to over-estimate and over-extend the significance of our private lives and the way we feel inside ourselves. It is not that such feelings are unimportant – indeed, as I have indicated, they deserve the greatest respect and care – but rather that their importance does not extend so far as to account for or give meaning to our function as social beings. Once centred on how you *feel*, however, it becomes very difficult to concentrate unselfconsciously on what you want to *do*, especially when what you feel seems to bear no relation to how you have been led to expect you *ought* to feel.

Most of us, I suspect, spend our lives elaborating a way of objective being discovered relatively early in life, rather than moving through a progression of subjective experience. The changing nature of one's embodied position in the world (given as much as anything by the alteration in one's circumstances) and the accretion of one's history which are necessarily consequent on becoming older, provide one with an endlessly unrolling sequence of experience which demands a capacity for continuously learning anew. For most of us, as already suggested, this is experienced rather as a series of incomprehensible blows to a (probably tacit) philosophy of life which we accepted early on as finished and immutable or else took over uncritically from the 'official' mythology of our time. Life is not seen as something 'open-ended' and new and requiring learning, but rather as a relatively fluid period of childhood followed by a relatively stable period of adulthood,* both calling for nothing more taxing than the acquisition of already

---

*An alternative to this conventional view is, however, put by Phillida Salmon in her *Living in Time*, Dent, 1985.

clearly defined 'skills'. It is because of this sharp discrepancy between the official mythology and what people actually experience of life and death and love and work that it is common for them to feel traumatised and to 'fixate' on what they know best. It is not difficult to think of examples – most of us know people who, whatever the situation they find themselves in, rather than *experiencing* it, work out within it their practised form of objectivity. The young man, for instance, who is always beautiful and clever no matter what is being asked of or enacted around him: his specialism in life is to be beautiful and clever, and his eyes are cast modestly down when he feels the eyes of others noting his beauty, and his aphoristic speech turns every occasion into an appreciation of his wit and intelligence. This kind of self-conscious objectivity is the curse of a society which penetrates private life with a public gaze, which maintains discipline and furthers interest by censoring our experience and so making it impossible for us to act out into public space without worrying too much how we look or feel. The result is that we become paralysed, unable to *function*. With a longing backward glance at a safer past we turn ourselves into pillars of salt.

In order to grow up, we have perhaps above all to learn renunciation rather than longing. All promises that we may return again to the blissful ease of infancy are false. Though we may entirely legitimately mourn its passing, and no doubt enjoy those beautiful if brief times when (as in falling in love) something like it seems to reappear, it is not wise to pine for the paradise which, because we cannot quite remember it, seems like a hope for the future. Wishful dreaming merely renders one vulnerable to commercial promises of its coming true and sucks one into a life in pursuit of the illusory. This is the entirely private life of personal satisfaction, which even if we could achieve 'fulfilment' would be totally devoid of meaning. The renunciation of bliss constitutes not some kind of self-imposed penance or unnecessary asceticism, but rather a sober recognition that a life lived in the public domain (i.e. one in which thought, feeling and action are turned outward to the world) is one which necessarily involves difficulty, uncertainty, isolation and a measure of pain.

What is needed is a degree of stoicism. What so often we anticipate as unbearable we might better come to see as inevitable, and possibly even not all that bad. (The aim here of course is not to submit stoically to the authority or values of an immutable hierarchy of power, but to liberate oneself from the mythology through which it furthers its interests and maintains its discipline.) There is, certainly, not such virtue in emotional pain that one need seek it out, but there is an inevitability about it which makes repression of any familiarity with it counterproductive: no life spent running away from the inevitable can be particularly worth while. There *are* risks inherent both in forming attachments to others and in trying to make whatever contribution one can to tne public good, but a knowledge of risk and a readiness to experience loss, rejection or failure actually make them easier to bear when they do occur than does the single-minded pursuit of gratification.

There is, of course, nothing the matter with the enjoyment of private pleasure or happiness (nor with eccentric personal suffering) but, being private, they need to be covered by a decent reticence. It is characteristic of modern marketing strategy to drag values and feelings out of the private domain and to harness their power as 'motivators' to saleable commodities. In this way the domain of public life – the sphere of conduct in which we act outwardly to and with each other *for* something beyond our private satisfaction – has become inverted into a kind of public privacy, i.e. emptied of public significance and filled instead with objectified personal feelings and needs. Our privacy and interiority have been invaded, raped, and dragged out for public scrutiny in a way which only seems without shame because we are *all* involved. The barriers by means of which a personal interiority used to be defended, and which thus permitted the living of a private life, have one by one been broken down, and our legitimate concern with ourselves and our feelings has been exposed to an objective gaze and made public property. One thinks, for example, of the erosion of the right to the dignity of a surname through the generalised use of first names by which was once conferred a gift of intimacy. The touching and gazing and exteriorising of thoughts and feelings which are the stock-in-trade of the therapy industries are little more than techniques for making us less resistant to the demands and blandishments of the market as well as more uniformly vulnerable and obedient to the discipline of social norms. All this, it seems, amounts to another form of one-dimensionality: in becoming fused into a single realm of publicly private commodification, our lives have lost both a decent and enjoyable (or sufferable) privacy as well as the possibility for altruistic action in a public domain.

It is not, then, that our private lives are unimportant or of no consequence, nor that the pleasures and pains they contain should be a matter of indifference to us, but that they are indeed a private concern. We need to *take back* our private lives, to retrieve them from the intrusive interests both of the market and of social discipline (norms) so that we can live them, in privacy, as diversely, eccentrically, and if the occasion demands as unhappily as we like. It is indeed a particular privilege of the grown-up to live a private life however he or she likes. (It is, furthermore, the business of the psychotherapist, if asked, as far as possible to help people to do precisely that, and not to try to push them into conformity with some standardised conception of 'mental health'. Rather than being, as they unwittingly too often are, representatives of a form of social discipline, psychotherapists could better become the reticent and unheroic assistants of people whose private struggles are nobody's business but their own and that of those in whom they choose to confide. In this way psychotherapists should occupy a status position more similar to that of those old-fashioned physicians who in order to test their patients' urine had to taste it than to that of magicians or social engineers; there is, in other words, not a great deal of glamour or mystery in examining the difficulties and distress we encounter in our private lives.)

While an individual's happiness or despair may indeed reside in his or her private life, the *point* of living has more relevance to the public sphere. Indeed, the very possibility of being able to contribute to the society in which one lives may well redeem or give meaning to a life lived otherwise in misery. Even were our exclusive interest in people's private lives compassionate rather than commercial, we should still, by draining off the possibility for public conduct, render them meaningless. Suffering is not to be desired for itself, but better suffering with the possibility of redemption than a purely private bliss.

It is almost impossible to envisage what sort of society it would be which permitted or encouraged all its members to turn their lives towards some public function. Our own society, certainly, is diametrically opposed to this: it syphons off the possibility of 'other-directed' (altruistic) conduct in order to commodify its products and sell them back to people as consumers. But if there is any 'point' to living, it must surely lie in what we can do; our embodied organisms are surely *for* something other than their own satisfaction. Only if we live in the perpetual 'now' of the advertiser's euphoric world could we really believe that a life which is not permitted to develop and apply its talents for the benefit of all is not, no matter how great its private satisfaction, a life wasted. It is the instrumentality of the body which renders it indispensable to the evolution of a social world, not its capacity for enjoyment, nor even, I would suggest, its inclination towards spiritual 'fulfilment'.

It is indeed the very uni-dimensionality of our materialistic philosophy which leads us to think it essential that we should know what the 'point' of living is in any case. We tend to assume, for example, that unless we can identify a 'point', life becomes point*less* or absurd. But there is no compelling reason to believe that, for there to be a point, we should know what it is. It is, after all, likely to take many more thousands of centuries before we have got as far as learning how decently to live together, without worrying about what the point of it all might be. The very most we can hope to do is make what contribution we can in the vanishingly brief time available to us. In view of the heartless waste of talent, the systematic destruction of intelligence and the commercialised emptying-out of mentality which, in particular, characterise our treatment of the young, it seems to me that to aim at maximising the possibility of our contributing, through our embodied instrumentality, to a future none of us can foretell, is far from an unworthy or uninspiring goal.

For it is certainly not that there is nothing for us to do. A world which is built on injustice, inequality and violence, in which the relative comfort and 'happiness' of a few is founded on the exploitation and degradation of the vast majority, leaves plenty of room for improvement, and we certainly need not yet despair that human life is rendered meaningless through its very affluence and technological success (in this respect it is interesting again to remember that all those epochs of our history which have been characterised by self-confident assertions of comfort and sufficiency in fact seem to have derived their security from a basis in some form of slavery). Far from there being 'nothing to do' the domain of public life is in fact empty behind the illusion of activity created by the pervasive concern with what is in truth private indulgence (the moral bankruptcy of Western politics may perhaps be seen as testimony to this state of affairs: politicians become the cautious representatives or 'front' men and women for the interests of managerial, marketing and military power, and public policy is sacrificed to and for private interest).

It is a frequent complaint of 'patients' growing out of their longing for the bliss of infancy that their struggle to influence the circumstances of their lives 'doesn't have any effect'. This, again, seems to rest on the failure of a mature appreciation of scale: somehow, it seems, we have come to accept the values of instancy (instant availability and instant success) to the point where we lose sight of the smallness and relative insignificance of the individual. We have bought the belief that if one cannot change the world it is not worth trying, and so we become morally and politically paralysed. Part of the process of growing up entails the recognition that 'trying' is something to be done whether or not it has any degree of observable success. We have to reckon with the wastefulness of human society, to accept what is a fact as a fact: not only is it in most cases impossible to tell whether one's efforts in a given direction are or have been of any avail, but one must be prepared for the near certainty that they will have no *measurable* effect at all. Societies evolve through the agency of their members, but with a profoundly disheartening degree of redundancy – for every contribution that 'succeeds' there will be countless contributions which, at the very least, appear to go unnoticed. This state of affairs is an occasion for neither complacency nor despair, but sober recognition of it will at least militate against a belief in magic which can in the end only weaken our purchase upon our predicament.

Both the future of the species and the meaning of the individual's life cannot but be attended by great uncertainty. Despite the confident promise of the 'experts' to reveal and train us in the 'skills' required, there are no guarantees concerning the course of our lives, if only because that depends as much upon the context in which they occur as on the personal aims we have. The conduct of a life cannot be reduced to a technical performance of achievement or acquisition, but opens out into a range of possibilities which can only be acted *into* with faith. Faith is thus not a wishy-washy substitute for technical certainty, a form taken by lack of knowledge, but rather a necessary attitude or stance without which life cannot be lived except as private self-indulgence. Faith, moreover, does not have to be faith *in* anything more than possibilities which one cannot see, meanings not yet revealed, values whose worth one will never have a chance to measure.

TAKING CARE

It is not easy to think of the privileges and obligations of growing up in any terms other than those relating to an economics of consumption, the values of which are essentially passive and mechanically automatic. Thus progressive maturity becomes a question of the widening availability of certain commodities or pleasures (initiation into smoking, drinking, sex and 'adult' entertainment, availability of credit facilities, mortgages, etc.) and responsibility in observing certain legal and fiscal rules (e.g. in relation to taxation, military obligations, etc.). Since our ethics are those of the marketplace and our view of knowledge and learning mechanistic and 'objective', we tend not to regard the transmission of our culture as a central task of all those 'embodied organisms' who go to make up our society, but rather as something which can safely be, and probably should be, left to professional experts of one kind or another. The rest of us can then get on with the serious business of making enough money to enjoy ourselves.

If, however, one takes seriously the argument put forward earlier in this book that indeed we *are* embodied organisms, that we are formed in the context of a history and a current set of circumstances whose effects are likely to be ineradicable, and that the society we build is the creation of human agency rather than the result of some kind of inexorable, natural objectivity, then it begins to become evident that one of the greatest responsibilities of maturity resides in the fact that we ourselves are the custodians and transmitters of our culture. What is known about the world of human society, and what therefore forms the basis of its further evolution (or indeed dissolution), is passed on to later generations *through* us: our culture is transmitted and developed through its assimilation and elaboration in the embodied practice of people. We cannot, then, merely pursue happiness while leaving the stewardship of the social world to nameless experts without risking a fundamental rupture in our cultural evolution and the complete loss of any sense of meaning to our lives.

It is, for example, easy to see how human knowledge and craft can be wiped out in two or three decades if it does not travel *through people* from one generation to the next. Even though the invention of printing 'de-skilled' large sections of the population by removing from them the necessity for the 'organic' transmission of knowledge, at least that knowledge is to some extent recoverable (if only with great effort) from books. In the case of mechanised knowledge, however, not only do we risk losing sight of the origins of our knowledge altogether (human knowledge literally *disappears into* the computer program in such a way that it is not recoverable without the aid of complex machines the destruction or non-comprehension of which would necessitate the re-invention of the knowledge) but we also render people functionless, and it is above all this which creates despair. It seems to me to follow from this that it is an essential part of human, and particularly of adult, existence to pay respect to our own nature as organisms and the organic nature of our culture by taking care both of each other and of those structures and institutions of the man-made social and cultural world which we wish to preserve and develop. This means taking care *of* people as ends in themselves and taking care *that* the best possible conditions are created for the performance of their functions (i.e. that we value people's instrumentality above their economic worth as consumers).

Attention to the conditions which make possible a public life would do much to alleviate what so many of us experience as purely private pain. The manipulation of people as units of consumption and re-recordable registers of fashion (in cultural as well as material life) places them in an endless, self-indulging present which has no past (in the sense of organic tradition) and no future (in the sense of evolving purpose). Rather than trying to 'normalise' the infinite range of differences between people and to 'pathologise' the extraordinary tenacity with which they live out their experience, we should be attending to those very conditions which make culture historically transmissible and the future open to forms of social evolution which cannot now even be guessed at. We should, in other words, seek to nurture, not reduce, the diversity and tenacity with which cultural forms are embodied in people. For older generations to attempt to shape younger ones to predetermined ends and ideas concerning the 'good life' amounts no matter how good their intentions to a form of spiritual murder, since by this means the young are deprived of the one function (to open up a future) which may give life a sense of meaning. But most of our effort seems to be put into repressing or destroying those very factors which make it possible to develop one's gifts to the full and to become unselfconsciously absorbed in public activity.

As already suggested, mechanistic ways of thinking about human experience and learning threaten to lead to a cata-strophic loss of social as well as practical and intellectual ability in both range and depth. Precisely because of the organic nature of human experience one cannot quickly replace what has been lost to human mentality, although, by neglecting to pay atten-tion to the importance of history and embodiment, one can very quickly wipe out human culture. Ivan Illich★ writes of having seen children of ten in New York slums who 'could not speak a word, although the television was blaring, sometimes two televisions in the same welfare apartment'. Novels such as *Last Exit to Brooklyn* should have alerted us years ago to the likely fate of a society which ignores 'organic' values. Despair and brutality are the entirely natural recourse of people who llave been dislocated from the flow of human culture and deprived of the possibility of putting their bodies to good use. It

★'Vernacular values', in Satish Kumar (ed.), *The Schumacher Lectures*, Abacus, 1982.

is scarcely surprising that both our 'entertainment' and our 'news' media should be almost obsessively concerned with rape and murder, since these are the rational end-points of any disintegrated society which is concerned more or less solely with removing the obstacles to getting what you want. Very pertinently does R. D. Laing write that all of us are born as Stone Age babies (though even Stone Age babies were born into a culture which was transmitted through embodied human beings).

One does not have to search our own inner cities very far before coming across indications of what an uncultivated Stone Age baby may become in this 'technologically advanced' society. Four boys, for example, idle down a back street in the city centre, truanting from school one week-day morning. Every few yards they stop, for no apparent purpose, looking around them with a kind of menacing casualness, aimless and yet embodying some kind of want. One of them gobs every twenty seconds or so with a contemptuous accuracy, exercising listless pride in a negative art. Their faces have an expression of sardonic brutality, a youthful energy but empty of purpose and unlit by intelligence; their eyes are watchful, but veiled, unfocused and dead. They seem sadly at home in this quiet, unpeopled street with its few tradesmen's shops, service entrances to the backs of stores, empty Coca-Cola tins and refuse blown from black polythene sacks; there are no demands here that they cannot meet. The overwhelming impression is that these are wasted people, bodies in which no function dwells. They seem to exist outside of any developed culture, unanimated by any refined tradition, and there is about them a heavily threatening air – one senses that they do not know how to do anything but respond to their own most basic, private impulses, that they could not negotiate social rituals which have become to them mysteries bristling with the risk of ridicule; one senses that they could only take.

A number of social phenomena – for example the strange

mixture of therapy and programming, the gradual fusion of teaching with social work, the transformation of 'parenting skills' into a professional training 'package' to be delivered by experts – suggest that we have become extremely confused over the means as well as the ends of taking care of those for whom we are responsible. The ineradicability of human experience coupled with the ample evidence we have of its so frequently distressing nature should make us much more concerned about what we want to teach our children and why, and far less sanguine about being able to control or alter the 'input' in any way we happen to feel like. Confidence in technology makes us scornful of tradition, and it may no doubt be true that senti-mental attachment to tradition for its own sake can have a dead-ening effect on cultural evolution. However, recognition that a culture can be stably transmitted only through the painstaking induction of 'Stone Age babies' into a *history* is something that should make us revise our too unthinking trust in 'techniques' of training and therapy. What actually happens to people is of the most fundamental importance, and the nature of the world in which they are located will have far more significance for their experience than will the latest fashions in educational 'technique'.

At the very simplest level, our faith in and dependence upon 'experts' leads many people (both parents and teachers) to over-look the importance of *doing things with* children, of passing on to them what we know through living, embodied contact, just as it was passed on to us. Nobody entirely in his or her right mind would expect someone to learn to play the violin purely from audio-visual displays, and yet there is no difference in principle between the ways in which this and more simple kinds of knowledge are learned. Even where there is anything to be learned beyond the means of mere private gratification, because our own functional activities have become so minutely specialised, managerially fractured, pressured by time, and often simply meaningless, children tend not to be admitted into a participatory involvement in the lives of those adults to whom they are closest. Children occupy a separate world, or rather a separate market in which they consume commodities designed specifically for them (e.g. 'toys') rather than starting to practise functions mastery of which would admit them in due course to an adult world. This has the result that knowledge and ability die out with the bodies of an older generation by which they have been organically acquired, while the bodies of the younger generation are for the most part empty of instrumental function. Even when a talented boy or girl teaches him- or herself something (say, for example, playing the guitar) by virtue of persistent curiosity and observation, the result, even if greatly admired and commercially successful, often betrays a kind of untutored rawness, an uncultivated creative potentiality which, however, would need the knowledge and tradition of a culture were it to be fully realised. The rhetoric of our marketing society betrays well enough an awareness of this kind of loss – in prattling of 'excellence', for example, it somehow hopes to compensate for its systematic destruction. We end up with a culture in which each generation discovers for itself anew forms of unrefined knowledge the 'excellence' of which is never honed beyond the span of an individual life: yet another form of 'built-in obsolescence'.

If we need to pay much closer attention to the *way* people learn, we may well need to be far less controlling than we are about *what* they learn. Only a society interested in establishing a disciplined conformity will try to legislate for exactly what experience a person ought to have, and I do not wish to suggest that we need to construct any *particular* kind of world for our children. The very openness of the future means that the wider and more exuberant the diversity of their knowledge, interests and talents, the better. What *is* important to remember is that whatever world people do find themselves in, they learn its lessons well, and we do therefore need to consider very carefully what we want our own contribution to it to be. We have in fact not developed anything like an articulate understanding of what the *forms* of 'taking care' might be. We are much more tempted, in accordance with the values of technology, to develop ideas about the *content* we consider desirable for programmes of instruction, etc., and in that very process have substituted a mythology of training for a philosophy of learning.

There is, of course, an enormous amount of inarticulate knowledge about teaching and learning embodied in all kinds of people who have care of others at all levels of society, whether informally or formally, privately or institutionally, but when such people do try to articulate their knowledge they usually do so in the prescribed technological manner with which we are so familiar, and while this does not necessarily invalidate their actual conduct, it certainly does not facilitate it. I know many people – parents as well as professional 'carers' – who in fact develop and cultivate with the greatest sensitivity and intelligence a world in which their charges can grow, who teach and transmit an embodied mentality and a cultural ethics of the highest complexity, without having the slightest *articulate* idea of what they are doing. If asked, they are as likely as not to fall back on the crassest banalities drawn from current 'skills' or 'relationship' jargon. Not the least penalty of our mechanistic, ahistorical, individualising and objectifying culture is that it deprives us of a language in which we can elaborate what we know (and by means of which also, of course – and hence the deprivation – we could begin conceptually to dismantle the ideology which underpins our way of life).

Loving cultivation of a child's interests and abilities, painstaking construction of a world in which he or she may practise them, respect for the embodied experience through which traditional knowledge is communicated – all those ways in which care is *actually* taken form no part of our official systems of training and treatment. This is of course not to suggest that they could or should be formalised into a system of technical expertise, in which they would swiftly be appropriated by 'professionals', but rather to suggest that we should value and where possible facilitate their very informality. It would help in this to recognise our formal systems of 'care' for what they are (i.e. institutions built around a disciplinary interest) and to try to develop a language by means of which we could talk to each other in terms which are, precisely, subjective and informal (i.e. as nearly as possible uncorrupted by power).

One cannot, of course, say how this might be achieved. One thing, certainly, would be to withdraw from the 'experts' the right tacitly accorded them to have the final (and indeed often the only) say in how things should be done. Because we have come to see knowledge and learning as purely technical matters we have not only become blind to the manner of their transmission, but indifferent to the structures in which they are organically embedded. Traditions associated with human intercourse of all kinds, whether in work, 'gendered' activity, religious ritual and so on, are likely to be seen as unintelligible or absurd merely because there issues from them no digitally unambiguous 'read-out' of their meaning. The wisdom built into the apprenticeship model of learning (and not only, of course, in the manual trades), the knowledge of social and familial roles and conduct transmitted through direct participation in them, the understanding that ability is acquired only through the taking of pains (and is then not quickly forgotten) – all these ways of coming to know have become atrophied or lost because they have to be passed on through a process of embodied activity rather than articulated in verbal instructions, and since we overvalue the latter we cease to practise the former.

Our preference for professionally specifiable, highly symbolised and mechanizable 'knowledge' is simply a mistake, and one which empties out an impoverished culture into machines while rendering us blind to what we do learn from the world. Children know television advertising jingles and the detailed personal histories of popular singers and guitar players; they learn informally from the culture which engages their interest, but because we *define* learning in terms of the highly oversimplified 'modules' of school curricula, we barely even notice what is indelibly finding its way into the structure of their bodies. We no longer initiate them into the social processes of a communal life not only because these are in any case sadly deprived of meaning, but also because we assume that when necessary they will be able to get all they need to know from audio-visual displays put on by the experts.

It may be the case that no society has yet been very good at articulating and understanding the processes whereby it evolves, and hence at preserving those traditional forms within which its members' conduct may carry its culture forward. Part of the reason for the rejection and abandonment of traditional modes of cultural transmission may be that the, so to speak, embodied rituals through which they were enacted tended to be accompanied by a justificatory rhetoric which lost authority through its very implausibility. The ethics of Christian society, for example, are unquestionably weakened for most people when associated with an insistence on a belief in miracles, immaculate conception, resurrection, etc., which can no longer command credence. But as long as the culture was embodied in the traditional practices of its members the rhetoric never really mattered. A problem with modern society is that *we really do believe* in our techno-scientific rhetoric to the point where we have almost ceased to pay attention to anything but words and images, and our actual embodied existence has slid out of sight to become the prey of repressed interest and hence the unidentified source of our distress.

We need to recover our knowledge of the world and of the conditions of human experience and learning in terms of an informal language which strives after truth rather than authority, compassion rather than power, care rather than control (a language, in fact, which reflects what Ivan Illich calls 'vernacular' rather than market values). No society, as far as I am aware, has yet tried in any concerted or protracted way to develop such an 'ideology', though there have of course always been scattered individuals who have argued for it; perhaps all this shows is that there are little grounds for optimism about the future.

Knowledge of the essential conditions for the development of an embodied existence capable of contributing to public life is automatically repressed by the *dis*embodied technical language of training and therapy, which on the contrary moulds people to disciplinary norms and shapes them as the means to commercially determined ends. The modern conception of an ideally adjusted social being, technically programmed for maximum success and happiness, sets up an entirely fictional standard which everyone fails more or less painfully to meet. The practical effect of this is to engender in people a guilty awareness of their own shortcomings in relation to the norms even while they insist that those with whom they 'have relationships' should themselves strive harder to reach them. We have, in short, a pervasive sense that we are not as we should be. If, however, we could begin to see ourselves and each other as embodiments of ineradicable experience and, because of this, as bearers of a multifarious knowledge of the world which has contributions to make to a future we cannot predict, we might then learn to 'relate to' each other more as what we are rather than as what we think we ought to be, and to treat each other as ends rather than as means.

When reading, for example (but perhaps also especially), the works of Dickens, one gets a feeling of entering a strangely unfamiliar world in which others exist as distinct entities with a value inseparable from their individuality, as living forces to be attended to and learned from because of rather than in spite of their 'otherness'. There is something in the brilliance of Dickens's caricatures which draws *sympathetic* attention to the way a person is made in relation to a context rather than a standard; though he disapproves of and frequently punishes his villains, there is nevertheless behind their villainy the sense of a history which cannot be wished away, and those characters he approves of are appreciated because of their very quirkiness. This feels more like a forgotten than a fictional world, but in any case points to a way of seeing and treating people which has become almost foreign to us. Our instinct is to approve of those people who most completely meet our standards for the gratification of our needs, and we do not on the whole see it as the task of 'relationship' literally to *learn* to live with the idiosyncrasies of the other. And yet, if it really is the case that we are each of us inescapably the unique embodiment of a particular history, the 'Dickensian' approach to 'otherness' is by far the more appropriate, if also more demanding.

Because, inevitably, there will be areas of your experience which do not overlap with mine, things you know about, as part as your emotional embodiment, of which I have no inkling, and because similarly my experience is shaped by events of which you have no knowledge or understanding, we must both take care not to confuse each other with our dreams of who we are and ought to be. Perverted by the blandishments of a commercial culture which markets people, we expect to be able to transform ourselves within relationships in such a way as to meet each other's needs, and if we cannot we assume that it must be because of a lack, if not of willingness, at least of 'interpersonal skills' or sexual 'technique', and so on. If the person does not come up to the demands of 'the relationship' he or she must either be trained to 'shape up' or exchanged for someone more malleable. You must fit my dreams, and I yours.

But it is part of the process of growing up to realise that some dreams are just dreams and will not be fulfilled, and it is part of a process whereby we might take care of each other to learn to accord to each other a reality which can be neither changed nor penetrated – the aim of 'relationship' cannot therefore be 'understanding'. My guess is that people who vow that their 'long-term relationship' shall be for better or for worse do so more as an expression of an exalted passion in the present than out of a sober commitment to a future in which the balance between better and worse may really be judged as no better than even. If we expect our 'relationships' to be matters of more or less unalloyed satisfaction we are certain to discover that they will be for worse rather than for better, but if we could learn to appreciate and protect each other's difference without having to 'understand' it, to tolerate and perhaps even be ready to explore a degree of isolation, we might then be able to avoid inflicting upon each other some of the pain we currently take as justified in our pursuit of happiness.

In renouncing the standards we set for each other we would allow ourselves to emerge before each other as embodied presences each containing a core of private 'interiority' which we would feel no compulsion to reveal even if we could. Rather than being the transparent vehicles of 'relationship', trembling with anxiety before the discipline of the norm and pierced by the gaze of a market searching for deficits to be made good, we might become people whose privacy, beyond the point at which it could be shared in a privileged intimacy, would be appreciated, protected or cherished, not emptied out into an arena where it becomes the focus of competition or frustrated rage.

On the 19 June 1896, Tolstoy* noted what seemed to him a 'very important' thought: 'What is beauty? Beauty is what we love. *I don't love him because he's beautiful, but he's beautiful because I love him.*' In other words, it is in the commitment to the other (for example in coming to know the other's difference) that the value of 'relationship' lies, not in the acquisition through the relationship of commodity-characteristics which the other possesses somehow objectively.

Only very partially can we repair after the event the damage we so easily inflict upon each other in the pursuit of happiness. It is for this reason above all that we need to establish now

Tolstoy's Diaries, Vol. 2, op. cit.

procedures of care-taking which will bear fruit only in a future we shall not see. Our most reliable guide in the formulation of our conduct in this respect is not the longing for an unattainable bliss but rather the private knowledge of pain. For though the knowledge is private, the pain is not merely personal, but arises from an embodiment in the world which is our common fate. It is not only you who are the victim of the other's indifference, contempt or spite, but the other is the victim of yours: you are other for others exactly as much as they are other for you. This is a fact which is necessarily overlooked in the struggle for resources which the pursuit of happiness entails; the inevitable individualism of the latter reduces universality to, at most, a grudging reciprocity, and transforms the public world into a projection of private dreams in which others become sacrificed to the needs of an insatiable 'self' or its various extensions (family, tribe, nation, 'the free world', etc.). It is the sensations of our bodies which give us knowledge of the world we share: as close as we can ever get to it, reality is revealed most undeni-ably in the experience of pain. One might almost say that reality is rooted in pain, and over and over again it is the pure sensation of pain which calls us back from disembodied reverie to habita-tion of a common world. And it is only in the knowledge that your embodiedness exposes you to the same risks as mine that we may make common cause to share the world. Lust for power and fantasies of invulnerability, trust in the magic of technical cure, lead us only into dreams of destruction.

The only way significantly to reduce the virtually universal distress and damage which our way of life causes is to construct social institutions which take account of the 'organic embodiedness' of our experience, the way we learn, etc., and to replace the 'pursuit of happiness' with an ethical awareness capable of making room for generosity, love, justice, equality and truth (i.e. values which – it cannot be overstressed – are *necessarily* sacrificed in a way of life which depends on competition and the creation of illusion). There will no doubt always be a place for therapy (i.e. for kindness, encouragement and comfort), but it is surely too much to expect a professionalised, and hence interest-saturated, therapy industry somehow to replace or take over the function of an ethics of human conduct.

However, although the statement of what needs to be done is so obvious as to be almost embarrassingly trite, one is still no nearer being able to see how to do it. The difficulties, certainly, seem insuperable, and it is virtually impossible for us even to imagine how we could find the courage to renounce our current ways of doing things, if only because we are all equally restrained by the enticing safety of familiarity from venturing into forms of conduct of which we have no practised under-standing. Not that a reorientation of our lives, just supposing that we could make it, would necessarily be all gloom and self-sacrifice. The renunciation of a commodified gratification which is in any case illusory and the readiness to inhabit a degree of private isolation which is in any case inevitable may not be asking as much as it at first sight appears. Just as 'patients' who do screw up their courage to launch themselves into situa-tions previously imagined as impossibly terrifying often find the reality positively liberating, so escape from the discipline of the norm, if only we could effect it, might prove to be a joyous relief. But this cannot be a 'boot-strap' operation to be achieved through exhortation or will power. Our conduct and our way of life are held in place by that world to which they are a rational response (in the sense elaborated in Chapter Four), and we are the embodied products of a history from which there is no escape.

The present – our current predicament – is, I suspect, irre-deemable to an extent far beyond anything our self-deceiving therapeutic optimism has permitted us to see, and indeed there seems to be little sign that we are going to employ anything more substantial than 'public relations' and the machinery of illusion to appear to counter a continued squandering of human (not to mention other) resources. The damage we have done, and the damage we do now, will be felt for generations. If the future is to be rescued, it will not be through magic or wishful thinking, but through the creation of a social structure which encourages us to take care of each other.

CHAPTER EIGHT

Morality and Moralism

It is hard to conceive of a society in which all its members actually treat each other well. Presumably there has never been one. There have been, and are, societies in which a (usually religious) ethical code prescribes how people ought to treat each other even though they fail lamentably to live up to it. It is becoming increasingly apparent that contemporary Western society has no such ethical code. The empty shell of a system of Christian ethics, having for many centuries been laid siege to by the interests of power, has at last been taken over by the values of the market: Christianity becomes simply another way of getting things, achieving 'fulfilment' or a kind of exclusive 'salvation'. Most of us, therefore, live in a society in which there is no formal moral authority, no ethically based, publicly institutionalised code of conduct to which people subscribe in common. This is not to say, of course, that people do not still behave decently towards one another, but the grounds of this decency are hidden away tacitly and informally (and vulnerably) in their private lives. The maxims of public life centre around competition, cost–effectiveness and the 'creation of wealth'. Ours, in short, is no longer an ethical community.

There are many perfectly understandable reasons for this state of affairs, but I suspect that the most important are those of which 'ordinary people' are least aware. For many people moral attitudes and prescriptions have too often been associated either with no longer credible religious magic or with hypocritical abuse of authority for them to be able to submit to rules which so often turn out to be in somebody else's interest. The gradual fusion since mediaeval times of religious ethics with powerful commercial interests has more recently accelerated to culminate in the supplantation of the former by the latter, has rendered moral understanding increasingly obscure, and has bred an entirely justifiable distrust of what has come to be seen as moralism. However, by far the most important reason for the disappearance of what one might call a 'public ethical code' is that its continuation would place unacceptable restraints on commercial exploitation. However brutal the mediaeval feudal lords may have been, and however corrupt the Church, at least, officially, they were not supposed to be. We have now reached a stage when the precepts of exploitation and self-interest are being slid into the place of moral values which can scarcely any longer be remembered.

The very idea of 'morality' – again understandably – is likely to arouse in people a range of unfavourable reactions. Apart from those who feel confident that they know what 'moral standards' are and are only too ready to say who ought to be made to conform to them, most people are quite likely to feel embarrassed, suspicious or contemptuous if asked explicitly to define what moral conduct in the public sphere might be. Morality has in this way come to be associated with sentimentality, hypocrisy, or 'unscientificness'.

However, unless morality is rescued from its obscurity – what is even almost a state of ignominy – and reinstated at the centre of our public life, it is hard to see how we can begin to construct a society worth living in. There are some ways, obviously, in which this will not happen. For example, morality as the revelation of a magical religious authority is surely something no longer likely to command widespread acceptance (far more likely, perhaps, is a resurgence of moral consciousness as the result of some kind of global catastrophe). Rather than having ethical standards imposed upon us through either magic or the law, it may be that we have reached a stage where, if we are to survive socially, we shall have in some way willingly to adopt an ethics of public life as our own. To employ an analogy which I have no doubt is dubious from many points of view, it is as if, having overthrown parental authority (religious morality) and 'enjoyed' a prolonged and irresponsible adolescence (the pursuit of happiness) we must now take upon ourselves the cares and responsibilities of adulthood and create out of our own ethical awareness and conduct a world in which human society can continue to evolve. Whether we can actually do this must seem doubtful if only because it is impossible to see what changes in our circumstances will force such a course upon us. It can certainly do no harm, however, to try to clarify what might be meant by 'moral' conduct.

It is important at the outset to distinguish 'morality' from 'moralism'. The form in which the majority of us these days are most likely to encounter overt discussion or prescription of 'moral values' is perhaps as pronouncements by one individual or group concerning what other individuals or groups ought to do or how they ought to conduct themselves. Thus, it seems to me, it is characteristic of moralistic injunctions that they are one-sided, and most frequently they are delivered by the stronger or more privileged as admonishments to the weaker or less privileged concerning how they should behave. Moralism is thus usually designed to protect the interests or 'image' of the relatively more powerful in their efforts to maintain others in their position of relatively less power. The idea, for example, that those who are well off in our society owe their fortune to some kind of *moral* superiority is taken as an entitlement for them to lecture the less fortunate in the ways of prudence and thrift, when they might better consider the purely logical dependence of wealth upon poverty and the social issues raised thereby.

Moralism is typically exemplified in the imputations of blame through which, as was argued in Chapter Four, the inequalities and injustices of our society are 'explained' as the moral failings of individuals. It is characteristic of moralism to attempt to cast morality in an explanatory form, either as causes of distress or failure or as motives which may be appealed to in exhortations to bear with adversity. But, of course, moral precepts are not things or forces which can be appealed to as operating somehow mechanically inside people, but rather are formulated as guides to public conduct. People, clearly, may conduct themselves morally or immorally, but they do not do things *because of* morality or immorality.

Moralism 'privatises' morality. 'Moral responsibility', writes the archpriest of monetarism,* 'is an individual matter, not a social matter.' This, of course, leaves one conveniently placed to chide individuals who have succumbed to misfortune for their lack of moral fibre while allowing public conduct to be determined by the dictates of 'the market'. The 'invisible hand' of the market relieves one of the disagreeable necessity for deciding whether one's public activity is right or wrong, since its guidance is regarded as somehow infallible. Moral values thus become prescriptions identifiable by powerful people whose public conduct is seen itself as somehow above moral judgment, and applied to private individuals usually in the form of explanations concerning the personal failings that have led to their lack of success. The apparatus of interest, by transforming morality into moralism, turns it to its own advantage: the undoubted force of moral precept is deflected from its valid function of guiding public conduct and reshaped as a mystifying 'explanation' (as individual fault) of evils which are in fact the consequence of an immoral abuse of power.

One of the most striking and interesting things about the concept of morality itself is precisely its force. However disguised its operation or mystified its application, morality will simply not go away. Despite a widespread dissatisfaction people seem to feel with having to base their conduct on anything so vague and uncertain as moral judgment, and despite also the

*M. Friedman, *Free to Choose*, Penguin Books, 1980.

success of technological approaches which are based on a science supposedly 'value free', we can still, it seems, not dispense with words like 'right' and 'good' and 'ought'. It is no doubt easy to confuse technical with moral prescription: there are many areas in which accurate knowledge of how to do something has replaced the necessity for argument over which approach might be 'right' or 'wrong'. But to conclude from this that technical 'know-how' reduces the need for moral judgment is based on an obvious confusion between 'right' and 'wrong' in their moral sense and their use in the sense of 'effective' and 'ineffective'. The passion to be free of moral uncertainty results over and over again in attempts to find infallible guidelines which will remove from us the necessity for thinking about whether or not we *ought* to do something. Despite conclusive philosophical arguments that one can never replace an 'ought' with an 'is' – i.e. never decide what it would be right to do merely through a knowledge of the 'facts' – the search for some kind of infallible technical rule shows no sign of abating. The current craze, of course, is to supplant moral values by economic ones.

The result of this and other such attempts is always the same: the force of what is essentially moral judgement becomes attached to what purports to be a merely technical or dispassionately 'scientific' judgement, so that the latter comes to be asserted with a strangely puzzling ferocity. Michael Polanyi★ called this process 'moral inversion'. In the case of apologists for the operations of 'the market' this kind of moral ferocity is unmistakable, and Adam Smith's 'invisible hand' becomes tacitly invested with positively awesome authority, while opponents of the system are attacked with all the vituperative fervour of religious bigotry.

Moral judgement and moral values cannot be avoided, but only inverted. The attempt to remove questions of ethical value

★M. Polanyi, *Personal Knowledge*, Routledge & Kegan Paul, 1958.

from the public arena leaves a vacuum which is immediately filled by fiercely moralistic systems of prescription and control which assert a claim to absolute sovereignty even as they protest their 'freedom' from values.

That something is cheap, for example, or 'cost-effective' involves nothing more exciting than its monetary value, and certainly confers upon it no *moral* worth. But if we attempt to remove from the sphere in which costs are counted the *moral* judgement of whether or not we *should* count them, we leave a vacuum which is immediately filled by the inverted moral passion inhabiting, for example, the epithet 'effective' which seemed so innocently linked with 'cost'. Invertedly moral expressions have a secret power which to some extent accounts for their ferocity: we bury in the expression 'cost-effective' an assertion of moral superiority which is at the same time disclaimed and therefore cannot be submitted to ethical discussion. In fact, in supposedly making a purely 'scientific' economic judgement, we assert an invertedly moral judgement which, simply because it is out of sight, makes it almost impossible for us to ask whether something is right just because it is cost-effective. All forms of discourse or rhetoric which purport to be 'value free' and yet which attempt to give direction to our lives are riddled with moralistic maxims disguised as matters of fact.

Human beings cannot escape moral judgement and ethical precept if only because they alone determine the ends of their own conduct. We are the subjects, not the objects of our world, and nothing (except, perhaps, the unexpected revelation of itself by a Supreme Being) could relieve us of the necessity for deciding what we do. Once power has become distributed unevenly within a society, however, it is in the interests of those with more, to hide from those who have less both the universality of the application of moral standards and the inevitability of moral action as the way of making the future. The inversion of moral values, and the discrediting of ethical conduct as somehow 'unscientific' both have the merit, from a viewpoint towards the top of the power hierarchy, of furthering the idea that our social order is based upon natural rather than man-made laws: inequality, injustice and exploitation thus become the natural order of things rather than issues which could or should be open to moral questioning and debate.

The airing in public of issues having a high moral content, except at carefully prescribed times and places, comes to be associated with disreputability or bad taste. The discussion of 'politics or religion', for example, is almost proverbially seen as something bordering on the indecent if performed outside those arenas specially constructed to contain it. The 'privatisation' of ethical considerations not only removes them from the public sphere in which they may challenge established forms of exploitation, but also renders them more amenable to manipulation. Mystification in this respect is quickly achieved: it is hard for us now to see why men of good will in the eighteenth century were outraged by the idea of the secret ballot as a way of voting on matters of political importance. However, a little reflection suggests easily enough how secrecy in this respect, while purporting to allow people's political will to operate in unmolested privacy, actually makes it more possible to manipulate their conduct through underhand appeals to their interest. The slightly furtive atmosphere of the voting booth is thus by no means an entirely accidental phenomenon, but reflects the extent to which public courage and candour in discussing and contributing to policies which determine the nature of our communal life have been transformed into an officially sanctioned reticence about what we stand for and why. We discharge our public duty, or such remnants of it as are left, in silence and secrecy in a solitary act of political consummation once every four or five years.

The attachment of shame to public passion in matters of moral debate is but another way of maintaining discipline without the use of force at the same time as permitting the networks of interest to proliferate unchallenged. At the time when Kant wrote his *Critique of Practical Reason* it was still possible to regard the airing of ethical questions in public as one of the noblest activities in which people could engage, and he leaves us in no doubt either as to the error of confusing moral principles with considerations of interest. Since this was close to the time when the 'pursuit of happiness' was being written into the American Declaration of Independence and the British Utilitarians were busily trying to construct a calculus of happiness with which to solve the problem of moral uncertainty, Kant presumably had a clear sight of what was afoot. In formulating his 'categorical imperative' ('So act that the maxim of your will could always hold at the same time as a principle establishing universal law') Kant is at pains to show that, since one person's happiness is not necessarily linked with that of others, happiness cannot rationally be pursued without transgressing the fundamental moral rule that you should do as you would be done by. Though his language is a little awkward on modern ears, his contempt for the pursuit of happiness is plain:

Now, if I say that my will is subject to a practical law, I cannot put forward my inclination ([e.g.] my avarice) as fit to be a determining ground of a universal practical law. It is so far from being worthy of universal legislation that in the form of a universal law it must destroy itself.

It is therefore astonishing how intelligent men have thought of proclaiming as a universal practical law the desire for happiness, and therewith to make this desire the determining ground of the will merely because this desire is universal. Though elsewhere natural laws make everything harmonious, if one here attributed the universality of law to this maxim, there would be the extreme opposite of harmony, the most arrant conflict, and the complete annihilation of the maxim itself and its purpose. For the wills of all do not have one and the same object, but each person has his own (his own welfare), which, to be sure, can accidentally agree with the purposes of others who are pursuing their own, though this agreement is far from sufficing for a law because the occasional exceptions which one is permitted to make are endless and cannot be definitely comprehended in a universal rule.

It is moving now to encounter in his text Kant's uncomplicated faith in reason and his commitment to a social community in which it seemed axiomatic that others should be valued as the self. But while he puts to shame those professional apologists for the maricet economy some of whom pass for moral and political philosophers these days, we have nevertheless become so saturated in and hardened to the values and rhetoric of interest that it is almost impossible to share with Kant the inarticulate premises of his argument – he takes for granted a moral sentiment in the reader which today has all but disappeared from view.

Its disappearance from view does however not entail a diminution of its force – as I have tried to show, inverted moral passion becomes attached to statements of 'scientific fact' or to moralistic exhortations to others to conform to standards which are taken as indisputably valid, and comes to be used as a kind of, literally, secret weapon with which to bludgeon doubters. But it *is* always possible to ask of 'indisputable' standards, and indeed of any prescription masquerading as fact, whether it is good or right and whether we ought to obey it. These are questions we cannot escape because it is inconceivable that any authority other than our own will ever be established to guide our conduct, and even the fact that our moral decisions could in theory be shown by an (again inconceivable) objective observer to be determined by our history and experience does not relieve us from the necessity of making them. It is an absolutely inescapable necessity of human existence that we assign value to our conduct.

For this reason, the ways in which society is ordered must always be open to ethical questioning, and all attempts (guided by interest) to associate the social order with some kind of impersonal necessity or authority are bound to be mystifications aimed at obscuring from people their freedom to challenge the *status quo* on moral grounds. While the pursuit of private happiness has become the obsession of our age, the possibility of 'public happiness' – the opportunity to engage publicly in the discussion, determination and implementation of value – has become eroded to the point of disappearance, and an apparatus for involvement in public affairs is excluded and prevented by an apparatus of discipline. Ethical instruction and discussion has become a purely private and informal matter unsupported by any institution of public life, and indeed for most people does not take place at all in any organised way. Even the churches, though of course always deriving ethical guidance from an essentially magical authority, have now more or less entirely abandoned moral teaching in favour of a euphoric commodification of magico-religious and deeply irrational 'goods' supposed to protect 'Christians' from the brutalities of this world and provide them with spiritual satisfactions barely distinguishable from the gratifications we are led to expect from the purchase of consumer durables.

The inescapable facts of existence – the exigencies of being embodied in time and space – mean that there is no possibility that the process whereby we assign value to conduct will disappear (and indeed without an at least tacit sense of right and wrong one could not act at all), but our articulation of this process and our development and institutionalisation of an explicit understanding of it may well do so. If our interests, particularly in the shape of greed, exploitation and mindless damage, are not to run riot completely unchecked, we are going rapidly to have to recollect and recover our ability to submit them to ethical criticism and to repudiate any sense of intellectual disreputability or even shame which may, through the structures of interest, come to be attached to our endeavour. This task is appallingly difficult, since it will have to be done without the help of God, indeed without the help of any objective authority at all, and in the face of the concerted opposition of all those who, knowingly or unknowingly, stand to gain from the inequalities of our hierarchy of power (not to mention those who *think* they gain from what they believe to be the best of all possible worlds).

Because much of our conduct is inevitably enacted towards an open and evolving world, there is no possibility that we can settle upon a kind of permanently enshrined code of ethics, and the content of our moral prescriptions need be no more stable than our judgment of truth (the degree of accuracy of 'factual' statements changes constantly over time even though at any one point we are, not unreasonably, quite ready to say what 'the truth' of a given question is). This suggests that, for example, Kant's attempt to identify the *form* of moral precepts is much better founded than attempts to decide, in any absolute sense, upon their content. But there are in any case some chracteristics of ethical conduct which do not seem reasonably disputable, and one is the likelihood that observance of moral principle will often operate against individual interest. Treating others as one would wish to be treated oneself means that on occasion, indeed perhaps frequently, one will have for the sake of others to forego pleasures or advantages which would otherwise be quite easily obtained. Unless one defines 'interest' so widely as to make self-indulgence synonymous with altruism, then, what is in one's interest is often likely to conflict with what is right, and in fact one might almost say that such conflict is a *mark* of moral conduct.

It seems altogether likely that human societies are unable to organise themselves without a degree of inequality, and that, therefore, disparities in power are inevitable. The ideal of a just and equal society in which care is taken that every member of it shall be able to develop his or her potentialities to the full, and in which, for example, largely illusory processes of therapy are rendered unnecessary through the ministrations of love, represents an achievement so distant as to be indescribable in any coherent formulation. But this does not mean that we should attempt to make a virtue of necessity, or even take advantage of our plight, by arguing that we should morally endorse forms of social organisation which we can see no way of changing. It is precisely the function of an ethics to combat and contain forms of conduct envisaged as ineradicable. Were sin easily banished, merely a technical imperfection on the face of the social world, there would be no need for morality.

What is so disturbing, if also so inevitable, about the structure of interest, is that it equates moral value with an assertion of its own aims. Such an equation is already apparent in embryo in the formulations of 'enlightened self-interest' of the Utilitarian philosophers of the eighteenth century, though they would no doubt have been horrified to see where their arguments would lead. Today, the 'freedom to choose' on the basis of an accepted and unquestioned inequality already built into the social structure, the valuation of appearances and 'public relations' above respect for embodied actuality, and the translation of exploitation into appeals to the virtuousness of 'giving people what they want', suggest an almost total submergence of morality in interest.

Most of the evils of our society, and certainly by far the greater part of the so-called 'pathological' emotional distress experienced by its members, are more or less directly attributable to the unequal distribution of forms of (usually economic) power which are abused and corrupting. Up until very recently even those maximally benefiting from the abuse of power and maximally corrupted by it would at least have paid lip-service to the view that such abuse was wrong, and, even if hypocritically, would have been able to make a conceptual distinction between morality and interest. The time is now fast arriving when to make such distinctions is seen simply as 'wet', and before long it may become almost impossible for 'ordinary people' to make it at all; already it has become virtually impossible for many people to see beyond a blinkered interest-stratum in the power hierarchy, and even in my personal experience I have come across many situations in which people are unable to conceive that economic considerations – for example questions of 'efficiency and effectiveness' in the running of the British National Health Service – do not coincide exactly with moral questions of right and wrong.

And yet, if one is to be able to understand the processes whereby people become unable to realise their potentialities in public living, to learn how to make a bodily contribution to the social world, to treat each other with kindness and forbearance as ends rather than means, and to become, as it were, the organic custodians of an unknowable future, the ability ethically to criticise the social structures in which we live is one which will have actively to be presened. Not, of course, that the ability to make moral judgements will of itself change the world, but it is certainly a prerequisite to the kind of moral and political action by which the actual structures and institutions of society may be altered. The ills we suffer are not consequent upon our personal inadequacies or moralistically attributed faults: they are the inevitable result of publicly endorsed and communally practised forms of indifference, greed and exploitation, and require a moral reformation of our public, not our private ways of life. Instead of abusing power, we need to use whatever power we have to increase the power of others, to take care rather than treat, to enlighten rather than mystify, to love rather than exploit, and, in general, to think seriously about what are the obligations as opposed to the advantages of power. Ideally, the foremost obligation on power is to 'deconstruct' itself.

All this, no doubt, is hopelessly idealistic, and it is salutary to remember that, even were they possible, changes of heart would have little impact on the real world unless accompanied by highly organised and concerted action. However, an impotent recognition of moral failure is in my view preferable to a misguided trust in technical solutions which simply serve to justify further abuses. It is in any case difficult to be optimistic about the future: perhaps the only way the social world evolves is by lurching forward through revolution and catastrophe.

It is difficult enough – indeed bordering on the impossible – for individuals to mend their ways following therapeutic insight; how societies do it (unless, indeed, through the shedding of blood or the making of catastrophic mistakes) is infinitely more difficult to see. But unless our society *does* mend its ways we may expect no improvement to occur in our private lives, no greater satisfaction in 'relationships'; there will be no 'breakthroughs' in scientific or psychological understanding to patch up our unhappiness and allow us to carry on as before.

In trying to think about the future, it may be instructive to consider for a moment a more or less random selection of the views of some of those whose thought has contributed to these pages. All of them are people who were deeply critical of the economic and political structures in which they found themselves, in some cases making just about the blackest possible diagnosis of the social ills of their time, and yet all of them also orientate themselves to the future with optimism.

Particularly poignant is the view expressed by William Godwin, the Utilitarian political philosopher whose *Enquiry Concerning Political Justice*, published in 1793, is taken by many as one of the principle intellectual foundations upon which to build opposition to governmental power and its abuse:

Wealth was at one period almost the single object of pursuit that presented itself to the gross and uncultivated mind. Various objects will hereafter divide men's attention, the love of liberty, the love of equality, the pursuits of art and the desire of knowledge. These objects will not, as now, be confined to a few, but will gradually be laid open to all. The love of liberty obviously leads to a sentiment of union, and a disposition to sympathise in the concerns of others. The general diffusion of truth will be productive of general improvement; and men will daily approximate towards those views according to which every object will be appreciated at its true value. Add to which, that the improvement of which we speak is public, and not individual. The progress is the progress of all. Each man will find his sentiments of justice and rectitude echoed by the sentiments of his neighbours. Apostasy will be made eminently improbable, because the apostate will incur, not only his own censure, but the censure of every beholder.

A century later, Leo Tolstoy, who spent the second half of his life close to despair over the state of society but whose world-wide influence and fame as a moral thinker is now largely forgotten, wrote the following:

'One trembles before the present horrible condition of human life: taxes, clergy, great landed properties, prisons, guillotines, cannon, dynamite, millionaires and beggars. In reality all these horrors are the result of our own acts. Not only can they disappear, but they must disappear, in conformity with the new conscience of humanity. Christ said that He had conquered the world; and in fact He has conquered it. Dreadful as it may be, the evil no longer really exists because it is disappearing from the consciences of men.

'Today humanity is passing through a transitory phase. Everything is ready for passing from one state of the human condition to another; it needs only a slight push to set it off and it can take place at any minute.

'The social conscience of humanity already condemns the former way of life and is ready to adopt the new. The whole world feels it, and is convinced of it. But inertia and fear of the unknown retards the application in practice of what has for a long time been realised in theory. In such cases it sometimes needs only one word to make the force called public opinion change the whole order of things at once, and do it without struggle or vlolence.

'The freeing of men from servitude, from ignorance, can not be obtained by revolution, syndicates, peace congresses, etc., but simply by the conscience of each one of us forbidding us to participate in violence and asking us in amazement: Why are you doing that?

'It is enough for us to emerge from the hypnosis that hides our true mission from us, for us to ask with dread and indignation how any one can insist upon our committing such horrible crimes. And this awakening can take place at any instant.'

This is what I wrote fifteen years ago, and I repeat today with conviction that this awakening is about to take place.

Certainly I shall not be there to take part in it, I, an old man, more than eighty years of age; but I know with the same certainty as I see spring follow winter and night day, that this hour has already come in the life of Christian humanity.*

In 1921 R. H. Tawney's *The Acquisitive Society* was published. In its final paragraph Tawney states its principal conclusions and predicts the disappearance from society of purely economic preoccupations with a confidence beginning to sound rather familiar:

The burden of our civilisation is not merely, as many suppose, that the product of industry is ill-distributed, or its conduct tyrannical, or its operation interrupted by embittered disagreements. It is that industry itself has come to hold a position of exclusive predominance among human interests, which no single interest, and least of all the provision of

*L. Tolstoy, *The Law of Love and the Law of Violence*, Anthony Blond, 1970.

the material means of existence, is fit to occupy. Like a hypochondriac who is so absorbed in the processes of his own digestion that he goes to his grave before he has begun to live, industrialised communities neglect the very objects for which it is worth while to acquire riches in their feverish preoccupation with the means by which riches can be acquired.

That obsession by economic issues is as local and transitory as it is repulsive and disturbing. To future generations it will appear as pitiable as the obsession of the seventeenth century by religious quarrels appears today; indeed, it is less rational, since the object with which it is concerned is less important. And it is a poison which inflames every wound and turns every trivial scratch into a malignant ulcer. Society will not solve the particular problems of industry which afflict it until that poison is expelled, and it has learned to see industry itself in the right perspective. If it is to do that, it must rearrange its scale of values. It must regard economic interests as one element in life, not as the whole of life. It must persuade its members to renounce the opportunity of gains which accrue without any corresponding service, because the struggle for them keeps the whole community in a fever. It must so organise its industry that the instrumental character of economic activity is emphasised by its subordination to the social purpose for which it is carried on.

Many of those writing in more recent times, particularly perhaps in the US, tend to combine the bleakest views of the past and present with an optimistic trust in youth to put matters right. Paul Goodman, for example, saw in the attitudes of the 'beat generation' and the 'angry young men' of the 1950s hope that the tide might be turning:

I think that the existential reality of Beat, Angry, and Delinquent behaviour is indicated by the fact that other, earnest, young fellows who are not themselves disaffected and who are not phony, are eager to hear about them, and respect them. One cannot visit a university without being asked a hundred questions about them.

Finally, some of these groups are achieving a simpler fraternity, animality, and sexuality than we have had, at least in America, in a long, long time.

This valuable program is in direct contrast to the mores of what we have in this book been calling 'the organised system', its role playing, its competitiveness, its canned culture, its public relations, and its avoidance of risk and self-exposure. That system and its mores are death to the spirit, and any rebellious group will naturally raise a contrasting banner.

Now the organised system is very powerful and in its full tide of success, apparently sweeping everything before it in science, education, community planning, labor, the arts, not to speak of business and politics where it is indigenous. Let me say that we of the previous generation who have been sickened and enraged to see earnest and honest effort and humane culture swamped by this muck, are heartened by the crazy young allies, and we think that perhaps the future may make more sense than we dared hope.★

Only a few years later Lewis Mumford's almost savagely revealing analysis of the evils wrought on society by the impersonal violence of a technology of power is unexpectedly and almost incongruously muted by views such as the following:

The yearning for a primitive counter-culture, defying the rigidly organised and depersonalised forms of Western civilisation, began to float into the Western mind in the original expressions of Romanticism among the intellectual classes.

★*Growing Up Absurd*, op. cit.

That desire to return to a more primeval state took a folksy if less articulate form, in the elemental rhythms of jazz, more than half a century ago. What made this idea suddenly erupt again, with almost volcanic power, into Western society was its incarnation in the Beatles. It was not just the sudden success of the Beatles' musical records that indicated that a profound change was taking place in the minds of the young: it was their new personality, as expressed in their long, neomediaeval haircut, their unabashed sentimentality, their nonchalant posture, and their dreamlike spontaneity that opened up for the post-nuclear generation the possibility of an immediate escape from mega-technic society. In the Beatles all their repressions, and all their resentments of repression were released: by hairdo, costume, ritual, and song, all changes depending upon purely personal choice, the new counter-ideas that bound the younger generation together were at once clarified and magnified. Impulses that were still too dumbly felt for words, spread like wildfire through incarnation and imitation.*

What strikes a chill in the contemporary reader's heart about such passages as these (which fell easily to hand – I did not have to comb libraries to unearth them) is that their future has now come, and perhaps even gone, with none of the expected improvement. What possibilities Godwin saw in an understanding of the nature of 'happiness', his faith in the good will of those with the power to reason, have been mercilessly betrayed in the pursuit of interest. Tolstoy's intimation of a revival of Christian ethics would surely have been sadly extinguished by now. Tawney's was no doubt a longer view, but even in this case one wonders whether he would have been so sanguine could he have witnessed the speed with which the more caring society for which he worked so hard is currently

*L. Mumford, *The Pentagon of Power*, Secker and Warburg, 1971.

being dismantled. And we have now had the chance to observe for ourselves the growing up of the beats, the angry young men and the Beatles: all securely locked within the deadly serious world of the market, privately preoccupied with success or survival, some dead and some assassinated.

So how to account for such optimism on the part of people whose gaze on their contemporary scene was so penetrating, so honest and so unflinching? Perhaps in part they were the victims of the mistaken belief that cure must follow an accurate diagnosis, perhaps they were misled by their passionate hope or by overgeneralising their own good will. Perhaps, again, it is impossible for humane men and women, however black the portents, to envisage the future with anything but at least a degree of optimism.

It is not at all difficult, certainly, to bring out the ostrich in those unable to contemplate without pain the ways we conduct ourselves towards each other. We can drop out into 'counter-cultures'; we can become 'born again' into the magical belief systems of fundamentalist religions. Perhaps, even, we really can create through science and technology a dream-world shaped entirely by our wishes and in which we could live our lives encapsulated in fantastic gratification. But in the end, I believe, none of these 'solutions' represents anything other than extremes of wishful thinking, a kind of communal madness from which embodied truth would one day drag us back to a devasted reality.

The development of 'counter-cultures' relying on some form of magical or ideological escape from the larger social world, simply evades the difficulties of getting to grips with the structures which cause us such distress. An entirely justified and understandable disgust with the abuse of scientific knowledge and technological power leads to the wishful positing of alternatives which side-step experience and challenge rationality. While welcoming and endorsing much of the theory and practice of what he calls the 'party of Narcissus' – i.e. of those aligning themselves with feminism, environmentalism and the peace movement, etc. – Christopher Lasch takes a line very similar to that argued in this book:

> It is the deterioration of public life, together with the privatiza- tion and trivialization of moral ideas, that prevents a collaborative assault on the environmental and military difficulties confronting modern nations. But the party of Narcissus does not understand the source of these difficulties: the confusion of practice with technique. It shares this con- fusion and thus repudiates all forms of purposeful action in favor of playful, artistic pursuits, which it misunderstands, moreover, as activities without structure or purpose. When it insists on the pathology of purposefulness, it merely reverses industrial ideology. Where the prevailing ideology swallows up practice into a cult of technique, the 'counterculture' indiscriminately rejects both and advocates a renunciation of will and purpose as the only escape from Promethean technology. Disparaging human inventiveness, which it associates only with destructive industrial technologies, it defines the overriding imperative of the present age as a return to nature. It ignores the more important need to restore the intermediate world of practical activity, which binds man to nature in the capacity of a loving caretaker and cultivator, not in a symbiotic union that simply denies the reality of man's separation from nature.★

In the last few paragraphs of his sweeping and deeply impres- sive three-volume historical analysis of the economic structures of the modern world, Fernand Braudel perhaps comes closer than anyone to giving us a glimpse of what we are up against:

> Jean-Paul Sartre may have dreamed of a society from which inequality would have disappeared, where one man would

★*The Minimal Self*, op. cit.

not exploit another. But no society in the world has yet given up tradition and the use of privilege. If this is ever to be achieved, all the social hierarchies will have to be overthrown, not merely those of money or state power, not only social privilege but the uneven weight of the past and of culture. The experience of the socialist countries proves that the disappearance of a single hierarchy – the economic hierarchy – raises scores of new problems and is not enough on its own to establish equality, liberty or even plenty. A clear-sighted revolution, if such a thing is even possible – and if it were, would the paralysing weight of circumstances allow it to remain so for long? – would find it very difficult to demolish what should be demolished, while retaining what should be retained: freedom for ordinary people, cultural independence, a market economy with no loaded dice, and a little fraternity. It is a very tall order – especially since whenever capitalism is challenged, it is invariably during a period of economic difficulty, whereas far-reaching structural reform, which would inevitably be difficult and traumatic, requires a context of abundance or even superabundance. And the present population explosion is likely to do little or nothing to encourage the more equitable distribution of surpluses.*

The conclusion to Braudel's gargantuan intellectual undertaking, though stated undramatically enough, strikes, especially in the light of others' optimism, an unusually sombre note:

If people set about looking for them, seriously and honestly, economic solutions could be found which would extend the area of the market and would put at its disposal the economic advantages so far kept to itself by one dominant group in society. But the problem does not essentially lie there; it is

*F. Braudel, *Civilization and Capitalism 15th–18th Century*, 3 vols., Fontana, 1985.

social in nature. Just as a country at the centre of a world-economy can hardly be expected to give up its privileges at international level, how can one hope that the dominant groups who combine capital and state power, and who are assured of international support, will agree to play the game and hand over to someone else?

Can one then really not *hope* that people will act against their own immediate interests? Either the question as posed by Braudel is a rhetorical statement of despair, or it demands an answer.

Hope is a very private matter, and what grounds for hope I may find in my own experience are therefore likely to be of little use to anyone else. However, perhaps there are some observations which may be found sustaining. One – the most important – is that people uncorrupted by power and unblinded by interest (and therefore most often to be found at the very base of the social hierarchy) are in my experience perfectly able and often eager to act lovingly and altruistically when permitted (which is rare) the space to do so. It seems to me, again, that reflection able to break free from injunctions to the pursuit of happiness quite quickly suggests that the only life worth living is one which points beyond itself. And from the perspective of history the past is short and the future long; we have yet to try living by an ethics which is based neither on God nor on slavery.

From the point of view of public life, however, there are altogether cooler and more rational reasons for conducting ourselves *as if* hope for the future were justified. Not the least of these is that, even though we may be sure that they will involve us in the greatest difficulty, we cannot possibly foretell what our endeavours may lead to.

It may indeed be impossible from our present position to envisage a society in which the hierarchies of which Braudel writes could be dismantled, but though the weight of the evidence which he reviews is almost crushingly dismaying, the span of history is still extremely short. What lends a note almost of fatuity to some of the more optimistic prognostications quoted above is the *immediacy* of the improvement they envisage. Having correctly identified the grave shortcomings of a society which pursues instant happiness, they then themselves propose an instant remedy for them. The absence of an instant remedy, however, the impossibility of the 'cure' we all – as I have argued, misguidedly – so readily seek also for our personal distress, is not a reason for resigned acceptance of the inevitability of exploitation and greed and the harm they do. What we need, rather, is to develop the very seriousness and honesty which Braudel acknowledges as possible, to foster a patient 'care-fulness' designed to last over generations, and to recognise that greed and exploitation, even if they cannot be wiped out within any imaginable span of time, must be opposed. It is precisely the possibilities for the development of any such opposition which have become so drastically eroded in recent times by interests which have the power to collapse the kind of moral space in which they *can* develop.

The privatisation and inversion of the moral impulse of 'ordinary people' impose upon them a moralism which asserts that not only are their difficulties and distress their 'own fault', but that the remedy also is somehow up to them as private individuals. Moral responsibility, which should be *socially recognised* as an integral part of an individual's public duty, thus becomes a kind of private burden, and the onus for changing the world falls with a punitive heaviness on each one of us as something we have to wrestle with on our own. Now there is of course a perfectly acceptable sense in which 'things will only change' through the separate contributions of individual embodied subjects, but in saying this it is easy to overlook the fact that a person cannot act at all unless he or she has the space in which to do so.

There are very many people, worried and concerned about

the state of the world and of society, whose moral integrity and fortitude lead them to accept with resignation that 'you can only do what you can'. In this, they are rather like those 'patients' not infrequently encountered in psychotherapy who accept that 'there's only me who can do anything about it' and who struggle bravely against an often inimical world. But though there is certainly truth in this attitude as far as it goes, it overlooks a dimension absolutely essential to the effectiveness of action, i.e. the public dimension which combines with private intention or impulse to open up a moral space.

In order to change things for the better – in order, that is, to be able to *act* morally – the individual must have the moral *space* in which to do so. This is not something which people can create for themselves as private individuals, but something which is socially created and maintained through the proper use of concerted (political) power. A politics which perverts and abuses power in order to operate a network of vested interests collapses the space in which people can conduct themselves instrumentally to exercise a public function, and it does this mainly by focusing attention on purely private needs and treating 'politically motivated' conduct as somehow suspect or reprehensible. If, however, we are to come to see that we are inflicting incurable but avoidable damage on each other rather than merely suffering personally unavoidable but curable 'breakdown', if, that is, we are to move from an ideology of therapy to a culture of care, we shall have to force open around ourselves a moral space which gives us room for concerted action, and this can only be done through the re-insertion into that space of a 'public dimension'. We shall have, to put it another way, to re-establish an ethical politics in the place of an apparatus of power for the manipulation of interest. It is important to remember, furthermore, that we need to do this not to change our *selves* nor to try magically to put right injuries irrevocably inflicted, but to set up a framework in which future injuries may perhaps be avoided.

It is simply too much to expect people to take on the moral burden of their own suffering, however much therapy we may offer them. Much of what people take to be their own private misery is generated within the social structure in which everyone is located, and is therefore, in every sense, a matter for the greatest public concern.

Index

Other titles available from Robinson Publishing

The Nature of Unhappiness David Smail   **£10.99** ❑
Why personal distress is not your own fault. This book contains *The Origins of Unhappiness* and *How to Survive Without Psychotherapy*.

The Limits of Interpretation Peter Lomas   **£7.99** ❑
In this ground-breaking book, Peter Lomas discusses the importance of the relationship between patient and therapist, and puts forward the merits of a more open, honest, and personal engagement.

Zen Therapy David Brazier   **£7.99** ❑
A Buddhist approach to psychotherapy by a practising psychotherapist and Zen Buddhist.

Perfect Mothers Susan Van Scoyoc   **£7.99** ❑
Not only is there pressure to be a good mother, there is also pressure to be the perfect carer, perfect spouse, perfect all-rounder. In striving to be perfect you sacrifice everything – yet in the end you do your family no favours

Robinson books are available from all good bookshops or can be ordered direct from the Publisher. Just tick the title you want and fill in the form below.

TBS Direct
Colchester Road, Frating Green, Colchester, Essex CO7 7DW
Tel: +44(0) 1206 255777   Fax: +44(0) 1206 255914
Email: sales@tbs-ltd.co.uk

UK/B.F.P.O. customers please allow £1.00 for p&p for the first book, plus 50p for the second, plus 30p for each additional book up to a maximum charge of £3.00.

Overseas customers (inc. Ireland) please allow £2.00 for the first book, plus £1.00 for the second, plus 50p for each additional book.

Please send me the titles ticked above:

NAME (Block letters) ....

ADDRESS ....

....

POSTCODE ....

I enclose a cheque/PO (payable to TBS Direct) for ....

I wish to pay by Switch / Credit card

Number..

Card Expiry Date..

Switch Issue Number..